Fully Human

Fully Human

Personhood, Citizenship, and Rights

LINDSEY N. KINGSTON

OXFORD
UNIVERSITY PRESS

Oxford University Press is a department of the University of Oxford. It furthers
the University's objective of excellence in research, scholarship, and education
by publishing worldwide. Oxford is a registered trade mark of Oxford University
Press in the UK and certain other countries.

Published in the United States of America by Oxford University Press
198 Madison Avenue, New York, NY 10016, United States of America.

© Oxford University Press 2019

First issued as an Oxford University Press paperback, 2022

CIP data is on file at the Library of Congress
ISBN 978–0–19–091826–2 (hardback)
ISBN 978–0–19–767484–0 (paperback)

9 8 7 6 5 4 3 2 1

Paperback printed by Marquis, Canada

CONTENTS

PREFACE

The word "statelessness" had not yet entered my vocabulary when I first arrived in Thailand during the spring of 2005 as an eager (and somewhat naïve) graduate student. I had come to conduct research on human trafficking and I was under the false impression that everyone had legal nationality *somewhere*. At first I caught glimpses of the problem from Bangkok—murmurs of "hill tribe" women on *Soi Cowboy* in the red light district, offhand remarks about "illegal" Indigenous groups that sent children south to work in resort towns such as Pattaya and Phuket. It wasn't until I headed north to the border town of Mae Sai, where I was scheduled to intern with a local nongovernmental organization (NGO) dedicated to rescuing Akha hill tribe children from the sex industry,[1] that the term "stateless" began to have meaning for me. It was in Mae Sai and the surrounding countryside where I witnessed the human costs resulting from lack of legal nationality: children who could not attend public schools, adults who could not secure legal employment, families who could not register major events such as births and deaths, and even abandoned children who could not be adopted because they lacked birth certificates to prove their identities. From those situations of statelessness resulted the crushing poverty that convinced parents, either knowingly or through trickery, to submit their young sons and daughters into lives of forced prostitution. At the most fundamental level, these stateless people were denied rights of *place* (including the right to live within a territory without threat of arrest, deportation, or police harassment) and the rights of *purpose* (such

---

[1] The organization was the Development and Education Programme for Daughters and Communities (DEPDC). For more information, see https://depdcblog.wordpress.com/.

as the ability to attain an education, work legally, and found a family that is recognized under the law). These individuals, in short, were denied the barest necessities for enjoying a life of human dignity.

Given the incredible human rights impacts of statelessness, I was surprised and disheartened to learn, on my arrival back in the United States, that this issue had not received meaningful attention from the international community. Not only had I never heard of this problem despite my graduate studies in the human rights field, but it seemed that very few rights specialists had heard of it, either. David Feingold, director of UNESCO's Highland Citizenship and Birth Registration Project in Thailand, had warned me that statelessness simply wasn't something that the international community was yet concerned about.[2] My own subsequent searches for information—hunts for library books and journal articles, online searches, calls to refugee law centers and immigration NGOs in the United States—yielded few results and seemed to confirm the inattention Feingold had described with annoyance. At the time of its completion in May of 2006, my limited and surely flawed master's thesis was arguably the most comprehensive discussion of Thai statelessness available in English anywhere. A few years later, my doctoral dissertation explored the concept of "issue emergence" and analyzed why the problem of statelessness had not emerged onto the international human rights agenda despite its severe human rights consequences. Indeed, interviews with twenty-one decision makers at leading human rights and humanitarian nongovernmental organizations confirmed that this complex issue was truly a "forgotten" crisis, despite international laws guaranteeing the human right to a nationality (Kingston 2013). Only very recently has statelessness begun to attract mainstream media and NGO attention—and that attention is often in relation to other human rights concerns, such as human trafficking or child soldiering. Perhaps the issue's best chance for forward movement is through the advocacy of the United Nations High Commissioner for Refugees (UNHCR). In November 2014, the UNHCR launched a ten-year "I Belong" campaign to eliminate statelessness globally; their focus is on achieving a "critical mass" of states party to the statelessness conventions and eliminating barriers to legal nationality for children and minorities (United Nations High Commissioner for Refugees 2014b).

Much like the UNHCR campaign, my early work on statelessness centered on its causes and consequences—and relied on legal solutions to

---

[2] David Feingold, United Nations Educational, Scientific and Cultural Organization (UNESCO), interview by author, Bangkok, Thailand, June 7, 2005.

enforce human rights norms and protect nationality rights. Yet once the oft-ignored problem of statelessness was on my radar screen, I found myself noticing citizenship gaps and ensuing complexities in ways I would have otherwise missed. By the time the UNHCR announced its "I Belong" campaign, my concerns about statelessness had expanded into a broader questioning of political membership, personhood, and universal norms. In an age of so-called universal human rights, why does legal nationality to a state matter so much for basic rights protection? How does the international community actually recognize someone as being worthy of rights—and how are hierarchies of belonging created? Realistically, does a birth certificate or passport really prove any sort of meaningful relationship to a government? These questions led me to assert that while current advocacy work against statelessness is vital and well-intentioned, its legalistic focus on citizenship provision tends to ignore important, subtle realities about the nature of marginalization and rights abuses. While I argue that legal nationality is "an essential prerequisite for the mere possibility of enjoying a variety of basic human rights," I also believe that a narrow emphasis on citizenship acquisition is misguided; "legal status is only one step in a long journey toward full rights protection" (Kingston 2017b, 17). Indeed, statelessness provides a stark example of how basic human rights are threatened whenever a person's relationship to the state is weakened or destroyed. Statelessness is a first indicator—a "canary in the coal mine," if you will—that ought to alert us to serious, dangerous gaps in our current approaches to human rights protection.

I began writing this book in the midst of the Syrian refugee crisis and unprecedented levels of unaccompanied child migration. These are two issues, among many, that illustrate what life looks like when your relationship to a state breaks down and basic rights to place and purpose are violated. In my countries of legal nationality—the United States and Italy—virulent politicians argued, in no uncertain terms, that some lives simply mattered more than others. US presidential candidate Donald Trump was gaining popularity with promises to ban Muslims from entering the country and to build a massive wall to thwart undocumented migration across the country's southern border with Mexico. In Italy, rising anti-refugee and anti-immigrant sentiments focused on the zero-sum equation of Italian economic prosperity versus human rights protection. (The irony of a dual national being fascinated by citizenship is not lost on me. Indeed, the ability to hold two passports and invoke the protection of two powerful state governments makes me, in our current world system, one of those people near the top of the human rights hierarchy. I write this with discomfort while fully acknowledging my position of privilege, which I inherited rather than earned for myself.) My motivation for writing this book was not simply to expose protection gaps but to seek out better ways of recognizing rights holders. In a system built on state sovereignty and legal nationality, my aim was to reassess our ideas of political membership and universal rights—and to contribute to the ongoing process of breaking down the hierarchies that perpetuate human suffering.

I am indebted to an extraordinary support system of colleagues, mentors, students, and loved ones who made this book possible. I have been guided by amazing faculty members at American University and Syracuse University, who taught me that some theoretical questions have very practical, deeply important consequences. Special thanks to Julie Mertus, Lucinda Joy Peach, Vernon Greene, Hans Peter Schmitz, and John Burdick—as well as Mary T. Olszewski, the heart of the social science program during my time at Syracuse. I will be forever grateful to Elizabeth F. Cohen for her guidance and friendship; I aspire to teach my students with the same empathy, care, and wisdom that she has shown me. I am thankful for my dedicated colleagues for their ceaseless human rights research and advocacy—with particular thanks to Brad Blitz, Maureen Lynch, Greg Constantine, Kathryn Stam, and Laura van Waas. I am also lucky to have loved ones near and far who have supported me throughout this endeavor and countless others. Much gratitude to my wonderful parents Jonetta and Keith, my brother Ryan, my lifelong friend/ sister Kimberly Zebrowski Venuk, my office bestie Amanda Rosen, my sabbatical writing partner Danielle MacCartney, my Maxwell School and Webster University crews—and members of my incredible "urban family," scattered around the globe but always there when I need them. You have all given me a sense of place and purpose; I hope that I can, in some small way, do the same for others.

Fully Human

PART I | Constructing Political Membership and Worthiness

| Introduction

THE PREAMBLE TO THE United Nations' 1948 Universal Declaration of Human Rights (UDHR) asserts that "recognition of the inherent dignity and of the equal and inalienable rights of all members of the human family is the foundation of freedom, justice and peace in the world" (United Nations General Assembly 1948). It lays the foundation for modern rights based on personhood—not political membership, religious affiliation, ethnic identity, or any of the other categories that humans have historically separated themselves into. Although the UDHR hardly ignores the important role of the state in international politics, it affirms the principle that all people are worthy of rights by virtue of simply being human—of being "born free and equal in dignity and rights" regardless of their relationship with a government (United Nations General Assembly 1948, Article 1). The modern human rights regime is therefore grounded in the ideals of equality, universality, and inalienability. If the "human family" mentioned in the UDHR trumps national identity, then (in theory) the power of rights is vast; its norms cut across borders and unite humanity with shared values based on inherent dignity and worth.

Yet one hardly needs to be a human rights scholar to know that some people easily claim their so-called universal rights while others are denied their equal status as rights bearers, worthy of the most fundamental protections. Almost daily, current events cast a shadow over these normative aspirations. News clippings fill my bulletin boards and accumulate in piles on my desk, a collection of reminders that the enjoyment of basic rights remains intricately connected to state recognition. Skim a 2016 article about French president François Hollande withdrawing a controversial proposal to strip French citizenship from dual nationals convicted of terrorism, for instance, which highlights a growing tension between civil liberties and national security initiatives. Critics of the proposal argued that the plan would create two classes of citizens, recalling France's dark history of government collaboration during World War II that rendered hundreds of Jews stateless (Nossiter 2016a). Look closely at the photographs of ramshackle boats on the Mediterranean, adrift and overflowing with desperate people from war-torn and impoverished countries whose fate is often dependent on their national origins.[1] Their lack of political status is rendered visible not only by official barriers to their freedom of movement; their value as human beings is regularly disrespected by those they relied upon for safe passage, as well. One example comes from May 2016, when members of an Italian rescue operation easily identified sixteen human smugglers by the life jackets they wore. In the midst of their panic at sea, smugglers had secured life jackets for themselves but not for their passengers. "Their lives, in other words, had more value than those of the unfortunate people who had shelled out good money to face this long and risky journey," observed journalist Matteo Guidelli (2016, para. 2).[2] And consider a front-page story about how Native American students continue to struggle in high school and university, despite US president Barack Obama's very public goal of boosting American Indian graduation rates (Field 2016). Although most Indigenous peoples are able to claim legal nationality within a state—with some notable examples of groups rejecting that legal status—they are often unable to access the same rights and protections as non-native citizens. At the same time, their national identities often extend beyond (or are completely separate from) the state and the government duty-bearer of their fundamental rights.[3]

---

[1] Sadly, examples abound: The United Nations' Palestinian refugee agency (the United Nations Relief and Works Agency for Palestine Refugees in the Near East, or UNRWA) reported that more than 110,000 Syrian-born Palestinians had fled Syria since the start of the country's civil war, with another 450,000 internally displaced—marking a second wave of displacement for these "twice refugees." Children of Palestinian fathers or grandfathers are considered Palestinian nationals by the Syrian government, regardless of the mother's citizenship, and are provided with Syrian travel documents in lieu of a passport. These complexities have created confusion for Syrian Palestinian asylum-seekers in European states such as Germany, where applications are often delayed at the local level despite equal rights to asylum under international law (Bolongaro 2016). Similarly, many Syrian refugees born in Lebanon are left stateless because both Lebanon and Syria have restrictive nationality laws that often prevent women from passing their citizenship on to their children (Sengupta 2016; United Nations High Commissioner for Refugees 2016a).

[2] This quote was translated into English by the author. In its original Italian, the sentence reads: "La loro vita, in parole povere, aveva più valore di quella dei disgraziati che avevano sborsato fior di quattrini per affrontare questo viaggio lungo e rischioso."

[3] It is noteworthy that movements to protect Indigenous rights frequently utilize terms such as "nation" and "sovereignty," thereby using language that many scholars traditionally reserve for discussing states. In his account of the "rise of modern Indian nations," for instance, Charles Wilkinson (2005) writes of the "modern tribal sovereignty movement" and equates it with fights for the abolition of slavery, suffrage for women, and civil rights for African Americans (xiv).

What ties these stories together—despite vast differences in geography and issue specifics—is that they cannot be understood if we accept, at face value, the UDHR's idealistic beliefs about universality and the existence of a "human family" uncoupled from legal nationality. That is, these issues arise because *hierarchies of personhood*—inequalities that render some people more "worthy" than others for protections and political membership—have been created and perpetuated around the world. Despite human rights norms to the contrary, the rights and dignity of some people are more valued and respected than those of others; in a sense, some individuals are accepted as more "fully human" than others. Legal nationality and one's relationship to a nation-state often serve to determine who "counts" and who does not. Certainly there is a difference between human rights violations and the pessimistic view that basic rights simply don't exist, but this disconnect hints at deep flaws in the international system. "These millions of people are not enjoying the goods to which they have inherent moral birthrights," explains Johannes Morsink (2009). "They live in poorly functioning Westphalian states or they have fallen between the cracks in that system," which represents an "enormous and scary underbelly to this cosmopolitan vision of one unified ethical world" (205). Indeed, Hannah Arendt (1973) acknowledged that despite the universality of rights, man had "hardly appeared as a completely emancipated, completely isolated being who carried his dignity with himself without reference to some larger encompassing order" (291). Since the beginning, proclamations of rights involved a paradox between inalienability and the value of political membership. "The whole question of human rights," wrote Arendt, "was quickly and inextricably blended with the question of national emancipation; only the emancipated sovereignty of the people, of one's own people, seemed to be able to insure them" (291).

These hierarchies of personhood threaten the *rights to place and purpose* that make a life of human dignity possible. Rights to "place" center on geographical location as well as political space; one's place may be as intricately tied to a piece of land as to the person's conception of homeland or belonging. Relatedly, rights to "purpose" revolve around the basic rights and protections necessary to put a life of dignity within reach. The things that define us as individuals and bring us joy and fulfillment vary widely, but they might include education, employment, expression, religion, and family. The combination of rights to place and rights to purpose offers us, at a most fundamental level, the bare necessities required for living a life of human dignity—the theoretical framework of our modern human rights regime. These ideals are at the heart of universal human rights, but in reality we must acknowledge that some people have an easier time than others in protecting these rights. In a world system where the cover of someone's passport positions that passport holder within the power structure of our international community—or where minority identity makes another person's citizenship less valid than the status of their majority counterparts—we must consider how the universality of rights is threatened by the ordering of human lives.

In response to these challenges, this book advances the notion of *functioning citizenship* for filling dire human rights protection gaps. I argue that functioning citizenship "requires an active and mutually-beneficial relationship between the state and the individual" and signifies membership in a political community (Kingston 2014, 127). Yet at the same time, an inclusive understanding of functioning citizenship also acknowledges that political membership cannot always be limited by the borders of the state or proven with an identity card. Indeed, this concept requires us to reformulate how we recognize rights-bearers and how we facilitate the processes of rights claims-making and protection. In today's international system, citizenship is limited by the norms of state sovereignty and has been traditionally used to recognize a person as fully human, or worthy of rights protection—yet this robust form of membership is limited or missing entirely for vulnerable populations around the world. To understand the true scope of this problem, this discussion requires a more critical understanding of the role of legal nationality within the international system, as well as an exploration of how citizenship confines and sometimes obstructs the enjoyment of rights. Rather than focusing solely on the provision of legal status, we must understand citizenship as a relationship between the state and the individual that is not always healthy or fully functional.

Individuals who lack functioning citizenship—including the stateless, the forcibly displaced, irregular migrants, and marginalized minorities such as Indigenous and nomadic groups, as well as people of color in countries such as the United States—require new ways of enjoying political membership and claiming basic rights. This calls for creating spaces that expand our traditional conceptions of citizenship and acknowledging political categories of noncitizens and multi-citizens. Functioning citizenship necessitates resistance to hierarchies of personhood that value some lives above others. It demands that the rights to place and purpose of all human beings are respected and actively supported. This is no small or easy task, but it is necessary for the survival of—or perhaps the true recognition of—our human family.

Human Dignity, Place, and Purpose

The rights to place and purpose center on the concept of human dignity, which is the cornerstone of modern human rights. The UDHR relies on the recognition of "inherent dignity" to pursue not only universal rights but also the aims of freedom, justice, and world peace (United Nations General Assembly 1948).[4] These assertions are tied to a key cluster of normative ideas: "that each and every human being has inherent *dignity*; that it is this *inherent* dignity that grounds (or accounts for) the possession of human rights; that these are *inalienable* rights; and that, because all humans have dignity, they hold these rights *equally*" (Brownsword 2014). According to this rationale, human dignity is "the foundation on which the superstructure of human rights is built" (Brownsword 2014). At a general level, human dignity is invoked across a diverse array of legal systems in support of two interrelated ideas: "an ontological claim that all human beings have an equal and intrinsic moral worth," and "a normative principle that all human beings are entitled to have this status of equal worth respected by others and also have a duty to respect it in all others" (Carozza 2013, 616). Some critics worry that the term "dignity" may be used so widely that it becomes "vulnerable to charges of inconsistency and even incoherence, and even to ideological manipulation" (Carozza 2013, 619). In his defense of the concept of human dignity, however, George Kateb (2011) relies on the basic assumption "that the dignity of every individual is equal to that of every other; which is to say that every human being has a status *equal* to that of all others. The idea of individual dignity thus applies to persons in relation to one another, and moves ideally in a progression from an individual's self-conception to a claim that other persons have no less than equal status" (5–6). From this perspective, one cannot insist on human dignity on a limited basis; "I also see that what I insist on, which is universal in nature, I cannot claim just for myself or my group, but must claim for all human beings. Each person must claim for all, and all for each" (Kateb 2011, 6).

Even before the adoption of the UDHR in 1948, human dignity already held social and constitutional value—and today the norm continues to influence our understandings of duties and rights. According to its

---

[4] The term "dignity" appears in consequent human rights law, including Article 13 of the International Covenant on Economic, Social and Cultural Rights (education for the "full development of the human personality and sense of its dignity") and Article 10 of the International Covenant on Civil and Political Rights (referring to the need to treat all persons with humanity and "respect for the inherent dignity of the human person").

modern meaning,[5] "human dignity" has three aspects: as a social value, a constitutional value, and a constitutional right. Human dignity is a social value that has held a place among society's values throughout history, as expressed in religious and philosophical texts, in literature, and in poetry around the world. As state constitutions were developed primarily during the second half of the twentieth century, the value of human dignity was expressed, explicitly or implicitly, within their language and structure. From that foundation came constitutional rights in many states, where governments recognized the basic right to human dignity as part of their constitutions (Barak 2015, 12–13). Later, these gave rise to the universal and global interpretation that forms the heart of human rights. One of the latest codifications of human dignity comes from the Charter of Fundamental Rights of the European Union, which enshrines the concept under its Title I. It explicitly lists what are "arguably the core components of human dignity in the EU [European Union]"—including the principle of inviolability and the duty to respect and protect, the rights to life and respect for physical and mental integrity, the prohibition of torture and inhuman/degrading treatment or punishment, and the prohibition of slavery, forced labor, and human trafficking, as well as two explicit mentions of dignity in Articles 25 and 31 (European Union 2012; see also Dupré 2013, 114). For rights advocates, the privileging of status-holders for the protection of human dignity runs counter to modern norms of universality and human community.

The ideal of human dignity feels like a faraway goal when one is confronted by the reality of global human rights abuses, however. The familiar image of a refugee camp with its seemingly endless rows of tents and dirt pathways, for instance, is frequently associated with what Giorgio Agamben (1998) called "bare life"—a space outside the norms and expectations of political society, where the exception (such as violence and various human rights violations) becomes the routine and human dignity is eroded. The camp is a place where one's rights to place and purpose are suspended; long, uncertain days in this liminal zone provide few opportunities to engage in purposeful activity, including the sorts of meaningful work and study that so many people consider central to their sense

---

[5] Theorists of dignity must navigate between two different conceptions: the traditional idea of dignity, following the Roman *dignitas*, which is a "status attached to a specific role or rank in a system of nobility and hierarchical office" (much like we might conceptualize legal citizens in modern nation-states), or the egalitarian ideal of human dignity that is "understood as invested in every person from the highest to the lowest" (following universal norms central to human rights) (Waldron 2013, 327).

of identity and worth. As displaced persons pour across borders and seek refuge in humanitarian camps, many are surprised by the grim situations they encounter even under the protection of governments and aid organizations. "I have visited refugee camps on three continents," writes journalist Ian Birrell (2016). "At best they tend to be soul-destroying—places that keep people alive but stop them from living. . . . But they can also be grim centres of incarceration, designed to herd traumatised people into places that make it easier to control them, either for host governments or aid agencies trying to help" (para. 5). He recalls a woman he met near the Syria-Turkey border, who preferred returning to war-torn Syria rather than continuing to live confined to a refugee camp without work, electricity, or anything to fill her days (Birrell 2016, para. 2). Indeed, such reports are common from journalists and aid workers in the field. In her chronicle of being a humanitarian aid worker, Jessica Alexander (2013) criticizes short-term responses to long-term suffering, such as ongoing human rights abuses in Haiti. She asks: "How long could an emergency response last before it became routine? When did living in the aftermath of a disaster turn into simply living?" (350). She asserts that humanitarian aid has become a professionalized field where emergency fundraising works "exactly like a business except in one critical way": recipients of aid and charity funds "weren't paying for what they received, their requests and opinions were rarely taken into account" (364).

These stark realities help explain why the image of the refugee camp resonates so strongly within the public imagination as a scene of human suffering and bare life. Indeed, the refugee camp often exemplifies the liminal zones where basic rights to place and purpose are severely restricted or missing entirely. These rights are central to the protection of human dignity—a basic starting point for modern visions of morality that "can act as a guide for our behavior" by requiring us to "behave in ways that 'honor' or 'respect' humanity in our person" (Rosen 2012, 153). Rights to place represent basic entitlements to home, both in the sense of geographic location as well as in the sense of belonging. In a refugee camp, the right to place is denied first and foremost by the simple fact that individuals have been forcibly displaced from their homes. During that process, however, rights to place are further violated by the destruction of community ties—and, in some cases, by denationalization and other rights abuses that strip individuals of their ability to return home. Relatedly, the right to purpose encapsulates a collection of rights provisions aimed at providing the opportunities necessary to pursue one's goals and actualize the right to self-determination. At the most basic level, the right to purpose centers on the belief that people must have control over their own destinies; the self-determination to pursue their goals and at least a basic level of opportunity so that the achievement of those goals is a possibility. In transitory camps, the right to purpose is violated by lack of resources (such as inadequate schools, teaching staff, and work opportunities) and by the continued threat of physical violence. Even in more established camps, those challenges continue—and in many cases, the liminal zone of camp life continues for years, even generations. While the refugee camp is certainly not the only place that the rights to place and purpose are violated, as this book will explore in detail, it is certainly a clear and poignant illustration of how these rights abuses represent an affront to human dignity.

A life of dignity requires not only the bare necessities to sustain human life and survival, such as food and water, but also includes opportunities for action, expression, and belonging that make life worth living. If we recognize "life" in relation to the world and as the "time interval between life and death" limited by a beginning and an ending, Arendt (1958) argues that we cannot limit ourselves to the "motor of biological life" alone. Instead, "the chief characteristic of this specifically human life, whose appearance and disappearance constitute worldly events, is that it is itself always full of events which ultimately can be told as a story, establish a biography" (97). For Arendt, (1958), that human biography includes events related to labor (corresponding to the biological process, which ensures survival of the individual and the species), work (related to production, which "bestow[s] a measure of permanence and durability upon the futility of mortal life and the fleeting character of human time"), and action within political life (which creates "the condition for remembrance, that is, for history") (8–9). Drawing from Arendt's work, Ayten Gündoğdu (2015) contends that action and speech—particularly in the context of asylum seekers, refugees, and undocumented migrants who are confined long term in camps and detention centers—although often denied are crucial components necessary for "the ongoing constitution of political subjects, political community, and humanity" (153).

Even though the modern human rights regime does not specifically use the terms "rights to place and purpose," the foundations for these bundles of rights were laid out by the UDHR and reinforced by international human rights law. Like all of these fundamental protections, they were intended to be equal, universal, and inalienable. For instance, the rights to place within the UDHR consist of freedom from arbitrary detention or exile (Article 9), freedom of movement and residence within state borders (Article 13.1), the rights to leave any country and the right to return to their own (Article 13.2), the right to seek and enjoy asylum (Article 14), and the right to a nationality—including protections against arbitrary deprivation and the right to change one's nationality (Article 15). The rights to purpose may include marriage and family rights (Article 16), the right to property (Article 17), freedom of "thought, conscience and religion" (Article 18), freedom of opinion and expression (Article 19), freedom of assembly and association (Article 20), rights to political participation and public service (Article 21), entitlements to the "economic, social and cultural rights indispensable for [one's] dignity and the free development of [one's] personality" (Article 22), employment rights (Article 23), rights to rest and leisure (Article 24), educational rights (Article 26), and rights to culture and community (Articles 27 and 29) (United Nations General Assembly 1948). These ideals were further outlined in the 1966 Covenants (the International Covenant on Civil and Political Rights [ICCPR] and the International Covenant on Economic, Social, and Cultural Rights [ICESCR]), as well as human rights instruments outlining special protections for vulnerable groups. For instance, Articles 18 and 19 of the Convention on the Rights of Persons with Disabilities emphasizes the rights of place and purpose by asserting that one's disabilities cannot be used to deny nationality, freedom of movement, or inclusion within their community (United Nations Human Rights n.d.).

Yet despite these normative and legal underpinnings, the modern human rights regime does not adequately acknowledge the intricate relationship that binds the rights of place and purpose together, or recognize the protection gaps that threaten these ideals. From the start, human rights are deemed "interdependent and indivisible" because all human rights are essential for the respect of human dignity; any pattern of rights abuse constitutes an intolerable deprivation (Donnelly 2013, 23). However, place and purpose are more tightly connected than this general assertion suggests. In this case, rights to place are necessary for the protection of rights to purpose; the second social good cannot be fully achieved without attaining the first. Unfortunately, modern human rights frequently take the rights to place for granted by relying on state governments to protect the rights to purpose. By positing states as the duty-bearers of human rights, the international system assumes that every person is claimed and respected by a government—which is clearly not the case. While human rights center on the concept of human dignity and assert that all people have equal rights by virtue of being human, in reality we tend to equate "human" with "citizen"; we equate personhood with membership in a state community. This is all well and good if the international system is fully functioning and all people are represented, equally and fairly, by a state government. But this is not a perfect world and this reality has not yet been achieved. As such, we must problematize our understandings of citizenship and political community to uncover the protection gaps that these central concepts help to create.

The (Current) Limitations of Citizenship

The value and meaning of citizenship has changed dramatically since its earliest origins in classical antiquity, but modern political debates tend to focus on its emotional and practical values. Indeed, Chapter 1 outlines how three contradictory approaches to citizenship view it as a right, identity, and even as a commodity. Within the popular imagination, citizenship holds emotional meaning because it is often equated with identity and community. Those who fall outside the confines of state citizenship, or perhaps exist at its margins, represent the "other"—foreign, suspect, different. From this perspective, it should come as no surprise that dual citizenship and multiculturalist policies are met with suspicion; if citizenship is the ultimate marker of identity, there is little space for alternate nationalities—legal or otherwise. The "place" in this construct is the homeland, with specific state borders that are controlled by immigration policies and national security mechanisms. The "purpose" relates to narratives about national pride, unity, and patriotism; in many cases, with little space or respect for diversity within the polity. On the practical level, citizenship brings useful goods such as state-issued documentation and passports, various social services, and diplomatic protections. For those who subscribe to the staunch emotional value of citizenship, these practical goods represent a reward for one's loyalty to the state above all other forms of identity. The concept of citizenship is much more complicated than this quick emotionality/practicality construction suggests, but rarely is this term problematized or unpacked in popular discourse. Indeed, therein lies a major problem as we attempt to protect the human rights of noncitizens and marginalized groups.

The standard Western (or civic) model of the nation assumes that a national identity is possible, yet the formulation of citizenship-as-identity uncovers differences between the state (with political boundaries and a system of government) and the nation (an identity group that may or may not have a state of its own). The Western model of national identity involves some sense of political community, with common institutions and a code of rights and duties for all members. This model also suggests a definite social space, with a bounded territory in which members identify and feel they belong. Non-Western (or ethnic) conceptions of nation include components such as genealogy and ties of descent, languages, customs, and traditions (Smith 1991, 9–12). Considering common assumptions from both models, Anthony Smith (1991) defines a nation as "a named human population sharing an historic territory, common myths and historical memories, a mass, public culture, a common economy and common legal rights and duties for all members" (14). Benedict Anderson (2006) views the nation as "an imagined political community—and imagined as both inherently limited and sovereign" (6). In international relations and international law, however, scholars deal in terms of the "state" or the "nation-state" (the latter assuming that the state represents a unified nation); the state is a country, marked with borders and a system of governance, yet there is no guarantee that the people living within those borders will identify as a unified polity. Indeed, there is no real guarantee that those same people will be legal citizens at all, or that nationals will enjoy equal protections afforded by the state. How governments navigate the murky waters between emotional identity and legal, practical belonging is often contentious—and frequently it is central to human rights challenges. In the struggle to define the national identity of a state, minority populations are often marginalized or ignored entirely. Those who do not fit within the tidy category of "good citizen" (which is determined by the majority population, usually created in their own likeness) are often denied legal or social status within the state, with little political space for nations that do not align with the nation-state. Sadly, these tensions have marked political discussions about citizenship and belonging with devastating consequences not only for human rights protection and the recognition of dignity, but also for peace and stability within and across state borders.

In the United States, American nationality "must contend with its contradictory character"; it harbors a civic creed that emphasizes human equality, yet it "has also contained religious and racial ideologies that have defined the United States in exclusionary ways" (Gerstle 2015, 33). Religious nationalism privileging Protestantism, for instance, led to anti-Catholic fury against Irish immigrants in the mid-1800s—including the rise of America's first mass nativist movement, the Know-Nothings, who sparked vigilante attacks against Irish neighborhoods as well as Catholic schools and churches. Protestant religious nativism was also used to justify territorial expansion (and the repression of Native Americans), nineteenth-century wars against Catholic countries such as Mexico and

Spain (in Cuba), and the preservation of "Anglo-Saxon ascendancy—in the presidency, Congress, judiciary, military, foreign service, universities, corporations, and in the immigration stream itself" in response to non-Protestant waves of migration (Gerstle 2015, 39). Relatedly, racial nationalism conceived of the United States as a "home for white people" and was used to justify the enslavement of African Americans, as well as the subsequent discrimination against free people of color, including Jim Crow laws and discriminatory practices against people of Chinese and Japanese origin (Gerstle 2015, 39). In an 1866 debate about birthright citizenship, US senator Garrett Davis of Kentucky argued: "The fundamental, original, and universal principle upon which our system of government rests is that it was founded by and for white men; and that to preserve and administer it now and forever is the right and mission of the white man." Furthermore, "when a negro or Chinaman is attempted to be obtruded into it, the sufficient cause to repel him is that he is a negro or Chinaman" (quoted in Gerstle 2015, 39).

Fully 150 years later, similar racial nativism returned with a vengeance during (and following) the 2016 US presidential election. The ascendancy of Donald Trump as the Republican nominee was marked by rising racist sentiments within American society, including renewed recruitment and organizing activities by White supremacist groups against Black Americans, Muslims, Jews, and Mexican Americans. Trump was criticized for sharing racist memes on Twitter, refusing to disavow former Ku Klux Klan leader David Duke, and seemingly condoning attacks against Black protestors at his political rallies. Political correspondent Jamelle Bouie (2016) argued that Trump's popularity (which he calls "nativist demagoguery") was a backlash against the popularity of President Barack Obama, in which White voters hoped to restore the racial status quo. "Obama didn't herald a post-racial America as much as he did a racialized one, where many whites were hyperaware of their racial status" and fearful of losing their "pre-eminent status" writes Bouie (2016). Such emotionally charged issues continued to mark public opinions of Obama and his family, with conservatives often lamenting the need to be "politically correct" and to avoid discussing issues that could cause discomfort or division within US society. After noting that she awoke every day in a house built by slaves during her speech at the 2016 Democratic National Convention, for instance, First Lady Michelle Obama was accused by conservative critics of spreading lies about American history and engaging in race baiting. Fox News commentator Bill O'Reilly acknowledged that slave labor helped build the White House but assured his program viewers that those slaves were "well fed and had decent lodgings provided by the government"—drawing swift criticism online from those who accused him of downplaying the atrocities of slavery and perhaps even justifying its use in certain circumstances (Victor 2016).

In Western Europe, debates about immigration often frame newcomers as threats to social cohesion and identity; culture is frequently portrayed as a "closed, timeless, and conflict-free whole," with different cultures seen as "irreconcilable" and of possible danger to the original, core citizenry (Slootman and Duyvendak 2015, 147). In the Netherlands, for instance, the rise of right-wing populist politicians coincides with growing nativist fears of Islam—and this "culturalization" and "emotionalization" of Dutch citizenship is not necessarily anything new. Marieke Slootman and Jan Willem Duyvendak (2015) contend that the Netherlands has been misconstrued as a multicultural paradise in the past; in fact, its tolerant but monoculturalist policies have simply developed into tolerant monoculturalism (148). As an example, Slootman and Duyvendak (2015) cite the Dutch program that allowed "guest workers" from countries such as Turkey and Morocco to maintain their identities while living and working in the Netherlands. Rather than celebrating cultural differences and pluralism in the 1970s, this stance was really meant to facilitate immigrants' eventual return to their countries of origin. By the 1980s, the ideal of group empowerment (temporarily) emerged, but "only as a vehicle for improving immigrants' socioeconomic status"—not with the goal of promoting multiculturalism (Slootman and Duyvendak 2015, 149). Despite the prevalence of progressive ideals related to social issues such as gay rights and women's empowerment, the Dutch majority population defines cultural difference as a growing problem. In fact, culture is regularly presented as a root cause of social problems among minority groups—blamed as causing public nuisances and high crime rates—and government policies increasingly insist that immigrants adjust to Dutch culture, norms, and values with little attention to respect for multiculturalism (Slootman and Duyvendak 2015, 150–151).

In the United Kingdom, discussions about the place of Muslims in British nationhood has led to a deep questioning of British culture and identity—including a sort of British civic national identity that involves not only allegiance to the state but also "intuitive, emotional, symbolic allegiances to a historic nation" even when the idea of a nation is contested and complex (Meer et al. 2015, 170). Political debates in this regard tend to be contradictory; politicians often accept as reality that Muslim values are now part of British society, but they also frequently question whether a person can truly integrate into British society while remaining true to the Islamic faith. Some politicians contend that Muslims simply do not "feel British," although survey data since the 1990s suggest the opposite (Meer et al. 2015, 182). In the period immediately following the 2016 "Brexit" vote, in which citizens of the United Kingdom decided to leave the European Union, more than 500 racist incidents were compiled in a national database using several social media sites. Journalist Adam Lusher (2016) reported in the *Independent* that "blatant hate" had beset post-Brexit Britain in only a few weeks since the referendum vote. "The hatred that has divided British society in the past month features 'F*** off to Poland' letters in Tunbridge Wells, wealthy London diners refusing to be served by foreign waiters, dog excrement shoved through letter boxes in Rugby, and racist abuse from children as young as ten," he writes (para. 1–2). Similar concerns and debates occur in states such as Germany, where discussions about migration and the compatibility of Islam with democracy and gender equality are inextricably linked to the non-integration, failed integration, or disintegration of minority groups (Faist and Ulbricht 2015, 189).

It is tempting to dismiss this political discourse as blatant, simple racism—and certainly racism has a powerful role to play in current debates about political membership—but these tensions also highlight key weaknesses in universal rights norms as well as confusion about the very concept of citizenship. Despite fundamental rights related to place and purpose, discrimination against minority groups (noncitizens and citizens alike) means that some individuals are more able to protect and enjoy those entitlements. The enduring persistence of citizenship-as-identity has cast a shadow over legal immigration and asylum-seeking processes throughout the West, while people who are stateless or who identify with a nation and/or group outside of (or in addition to) the nation-state are viewed with suspicion. Many of these narratives rely on false assumptions; for example, the idea that any state ever had a single, unified "nation" that can be viewed as somehow under attack by immigrants and refugees is a fiction that is usually easily disproven with a cursory glance backward in history. (A popular image of Apache warriors, including the famed Geronimo, has made the rounds on social media and illustrates this point nicely. The image features four Native American men, each holding a rifle, and the caption: "Homeland Security—Fighting Terrorism Since 1492." Clearly the narrative of the United States being a White, Christian homeland fails to account for the Indigenous peoples who lived there prior to European conquest.) Yet these political debates have become so impassioned that the

Economist featured a cover story in July 2016 entitled "The New Political Divide," arguing that the main political divide in the United States and Europe was no longer left versus right but rather between open and closed borders. Concerns about national identity, competition for resources, and security mean that the stakes for granting citizenship are perceived as being higher than ever before. And, as minority groups gain louder political voices within the citizenry—as exhibited by the rise of the Black Lives Matter movement in the United States, for instance—people will continue to push for the full enjoyment of citizenship rights and even a redefinition of what it means to be a citizen in the first place.

(Non) Functioning Citizenship

To conceptualize functioning citizenship, it is necessary to identify the positive aspects of legal citizenship while also recognizing its limitations and potential negative consequences. Traditional views of citizenship tend to see its central function as making members of a political community equal, which is accomplished by creating a "single, unitary political identity" (Cohen 2009, 3). At a broader level, citizenship signifies inclusion within a bounded group that enjoys a range of fundamental rights. T. H. Marshall (1965), for instance, begins his foundational work with the premise that there is a basic human equality associated with full political membership, or of citizenship. He asserts that citizenship cannot be fully attained until every citizen enjoys a full array of rights, including essential civil, political, and social rights. The state has a duty to uphold the rights of its citizens from this perspective; the ideal of citizenship requires equal membership in a rights-protective community. As such, legal nationality is increasingly viewed as a tool for promoting human dignity. Following the work of Immanuel Kant, Jeremy Waldron (2013) assumes that citizenship "is a certain sort of dignity" and constitutes a "status-term," similar to human dignity itself (333). Although he does not argue that human dignity and the dignity of citizenship are the same, he contends that "when citizenship is taken to be an important status that, in one state or another, should be available to everyone, then what it amounts to may be a good guide to the way in which human dignity can be realized in a world of separate states" (333). Waldron further notes that "the remarkable thing about citizenship as a dignity—something it shares in common with human dignity—is that it is a status that is cherished as special notwithstanding the fact that it is widely spread among the members of a community" (333). This view has shaped modern understandings of nationality and belonging, yet the ideal of fully functioning citizenship is rarely achieved. Indeed, current discussions of political membership often ignore the reality that various peoples have been marginalized—and left out of our conceptions of personhood—for far longer than current debates about migration or terrorism have been occurring. Sometimes they are stateless people, but they also include groups such as nomadic and Indigenous peoples.

Rather than accepting the concept of citizenship at its idealistic face value, we must critically assess its meaning and value in the modern world system. Elizabeth F. Cohen (2009) argues that citizenship itself is a gradient category that has never been a unitary or binary concept. Indeed, "all manner of exceptions to rules of inclusion abound" (4). She writes that norm-driven definitions of citizenship often don't reflect reality and that many individuals fit on a spectrum somewhere between full and noncitizenship; they are what she has termed "semi-citizens," and she notes that "extrapolating what citizenship is from a notion of what citizenship ought to be has the tendency to produce misleading and sometimes troublesome conclusions" (18–19). Using the political membership of migrants, children, and the disabled as examples, she illustrates situations of semi-citizenship—when individuals may hold legal nationality but cannot access their full range of rights for a variety of reasons. This is closely related to Iris Marion Young's (1990) concept of "differentiated citizenship," which highlights injustices within the structure of state society and shows that not all of those considered full citizens are treated as such. If we keep Marshall's premise that citizenship requires full equality in mind, this spectrum of belonging (or semi-citizenship) quickly raises questions about our understanding of legal nationality and its consequences for the universality of rights. Ronnie Lipschutz (2004) contends that political participation in the institutionalized, public sphere is not enough for full membership. Instead, a more robust form of belonging is required to move beyond a thin set of rights. He argues that we must not only consider the notion of meaningful political participation but must also think critically about how to achieve that participation and make it matter (50). He writes that "only by belonging—which goes beyond a membership card—to those movements that provide the tools to critically and constantly analyze and reflect on the political are we able, I believe, to fulfill the promise inherent in a richer notion of citizenship" (49).

I argue that the concept of functioning citizenship, which moves beyond mere legal status, is a possibility for strengthening human rights norms and building this richer notion of political membership. Functioning citizenship requires a relationship between the state and the individual that is active and mutually beneficial but that also signifies membership in a broader, inclusive political community. In this relationship, citizens support their government in various ways while the state provides them with protections and services. In our current system, this relationship is often *assumed*—with the critical error being that legal citizens are often denied this healthy relationship with their state government and a plethora of others lack even the thinnest of legal status. Even when these gaps are acknowledged, solutions tend to center on traditional conceptions of citizenship that posit legal nationality as a practical solution. Advocacy related to statelessness focuses on providing legal nationality—defined narrowly as "a legal bond between a state and an individual" (United Nations High Commissioner for Refugees 1954)—for instance, and discussions of forced displacement continue to center on resettlement quotas and (by extension) the ability to naturalize elsewhere. Importantly, an emphasis on functioning citizenship does not equate citizenship with the trappings of belonging (such as government-issued identification and passports) but rather requires states to provide those benefits *as well as* recognize the human dignity and personhood of all individuals, which aligns with modern human rights norms. At the same time, full rights protection requires the opening of political space for those who may not fit traditional conceptions of the citizenry but who are entitled to the same human rights as members of the social majority. This not only requires states to live up to their expectations as duty-bearers of human rights; it also requires us to rethink how we approach citizenship (and noncitizenship) and the protection mechanisms built into the international system.

Accomplishing the provision of functioning citizenship is no easy task, since it requires majority populations to share power with minorities and it weakens the principle of state sovereignty. It is an unabashedly idealist call to break down the hierarchies of personhood that make widespread human suffering and rights abuses possible. Yet it also opens up political spaces for marginalized groups that would otherwise not fit within the current system; that disconnect, as it exists today, leads to practical concerns such as regional and global instabilities, poverty, rising crime rates, higher incidences of domestic violence and drug use, and (in limited cases) recruitment into terrorist organizations. Reflecting on human rights in Europe after World War I, Arendt (1973) wrote that "once [the displaced] had left their homeland they remained homeless, once they had left their state they became stateless; once they had been deprived of their human rights they were rightless, the scum of the earth" (267). Today, that same quote can be used to describe Syrian refugees and desperate migrants attempting to cross the Mediterranean—two groups who are routinely discussed in political debates as potential criminals and terrorists. Gündoğdu (2015) notes that legal personhood is an "artifact and not an inherent essence"; therefore, it can be "unmade or undermined" in certain cases, including the situation of statelessness (92). Possibilities for "qualifying and evading personhood are nowhere more visible than in the cases of asylum and immigration" due to the principle of territorial sovereignty and the organization of the international system, according to Gündoğdu (2015), meaning that "rightlessness" is a critical concept for understanding how the legal personhood of migrants can be undermined (92–93). More broadly, the global poor and marginalized minority groups continue to struggle for basic resources and for political voice in a system that, despite universal protections, routinely fails to acknowledge the rights of those who are different or economically vulnerable. If the international community abides by human rights norms, "there ought not to be debates about a 'right' to basic needs such as food and shelter; these needs should be available without condition" (Lipschutz 2004, 48).

In the face of globalized crises and political debates, the reality is that categories of membership are linked to one's ability to access functioning citizenship and ensuing rights to place and purpose. Legal nationality is not particularly useful for human rights protection, for instance, if a state is too weak to ensure human security. There are failed states—states that have lost control of their territories, legitimate authority, and the ability to provide basic services such as access to clean water and basic education. People connected with these entities might hold legal nationality but they cannot rely on the state as their duty-bearer of human rights. Such weak and failed states face a "sovereignty gap"; the sovereignty they are afforded by the international community does not accurately reflect an ability to provide the rights and protections afforded by citizenship (Ghani and Lockhart 2009, 3). In response to such political crises, along with various economic push factors, many individuals undertake "illegal" or undocumented migration and often expose themselves to situations of de facto statelessness that severely limit their ability to access basic human rights. They are located in zones of semi-citizenship, in sites "more akin to a spatially rescaled conception of the state than to clear-cut distinctions between two sides of a territorial border" (McNevin 2011, 3). I argue that these individuals, unable to access functioning citizenship at home, "seek out opportunity and security elsewhere—only to take on the burden of *de facto* statelessness in countries where they are often unable to access rights protections due to their fear of incarceration, deportation, and perhaps even physical abuse as a result of their undocumented migration status" (Kingston 2014, 131).

Categories of membership are created and perpetuated, in part, by definitional inaccuracies and limitations in our vocabulary when it comes to discussing belonging. Although the international community tends to frame global issues in terms of universal human rights, in reality we have created hierarchies of personhood that privilege some while marginalizing others. Indeed, the system has different, unequal processes for determining who counts as a person worthy of basic human rights—and those differences are reflected in the language we use to talk about vulnerable populations. Often these terms and categories are porous, and their shifting nature helps states shirk their responsibilities for protecting human rights. For example, consider the juxtaposition of "refugee" and "migrant" within current political debates. Although human movement around the world is often motivated by the requisite "well-founded fear of being persecuted" (Office of the United Nations High Commissioner for Human Rights 1951, Article 1.A.2), many of these vulnerable individuals are labeled "illegal" migrants and denied refugee protection. "The non-recognition of refugees and those asking for help produces, at the end of the day, people whose every right is 'rejected'; they stubbornly ask for a right to life, and find no state in which this minimal human right is extended to them," writes Michel Agier (2011, 15). He uses the term "undesirables" to describe rights-bearers who cannot access basic protections, noting that the inability to access the "citizen relationship" leads to the act of movement being deemed "illegal"; the search for one's right to life is a criminal act in the face of this "amputated relationship" between an individual and a state (15). Similarly, differentiations between de jure and de facto statelessness emphasize the value of legal status while at the same time acknowledging that citizens may face the same rights abuses as noncitizens in the absence of functioning citizenship. In recent years, the international community has increasingly expanded its view of de facto statelessness to include "persons who do not enjoy the rights attached to their nationality; persons who are unable to establish their nationality, or who are of undetermined nationality; [and] persons who, in the context of State succession, are attributed the nationality of a State other than that of the State of their habitual residence" (Massey 2010, 32).

Scholarship is further complicated by a limited vocabulary that makes it difficult to adequately discuss notions of membership and status. Katherine Tonkiss (2017) writes that the terms "nationality" and "citizenship" are often used interchangeably despite vital differences between these concepts. In her work on statelessness, she seeks to problematize this interchangeability and advocates a post-national approach to understanding belonging and rights. (It's notable to mention that I use the terms "citizenship" and "legal nationality" to connote state-sanctioned, recognized legal status. Yet I also recognize that not all nations constitute nation-states—as is the case with identity groups that lack their own nation-states, such as the Kurds—and that legal status alone does not constitute full membership in a given society or guarantee the full enjoyment of fundamental human rights.) Similarly, the term "noncitizen" is a "surprisingly elusive term" that cannot be adequately defined simply as the absence of citizenship; "such a definition fails to capture the complexities of practices and constructions of noncitizenship, many of which challenge traditional understandings of what it means to be included within a political community or society" (Tonkiss and Bloom 2016, 837). Tonkiss and Tendayi Bloom (2016) argue that noncitizenship is "a membership category in its own right" (and one that is not always connected to human migration); before scholars can determine how to extend justice and rights protection to noncitizens, we first need a "full, robust and accurate conceptualization of noncitizenship" (840).

At the moment, however, legal nationality remains an essential prerequisite for human rights protection—and that reliance on state-sponsored membership and recognition is the Achilles heel of modern human rights. While the UDHR guarantees the "right to a nationality," such nationality can offer rights only if it is attached to a state that can confer legal rights domestically and protect rights internationally. "Hence a *right to a nationality* makes sense only as a *right to citizenship* in some nation or another" (Gregg 2016, 25). Benjamin Gregg problematizes the role of the nation-state in the protection of human rights. He writes that a state's status in the current world system does not depend on the recognition of rights. Rather, such recognition is "an act of gratuitous generosity" that by definition is "uncertain, unpredictable, without guarantee—all the more for those who need it most," including marginalized minorities, refugees, and the stateless (26). He proposes the concept of the "human rights state" for overcoming the rights challenges inherent to state sovereignty. This concept would "transfer the basis of human rights from national, territorial belonging to human action and political performance," thereby changing the way we conceptualize citizenship (45). The human rights state offers deterritorialized rights that are "worn" by participants in what Gregg calls a "backpack"; from this perspective, rights are political, and their content and validity are social constructed (42). It will take these sorts of reconfigurations and reassessments to move forward with filling glaring protection gaps for individuals around the world who lack functioning citizenship.

Hierarchies of Personhood

To truly protect people's rights to place and purpose, we need to take issue with the ways in which the international community recognizes people as worthy of rights. That not only requires us to challenge binary comparisons between citizens and noncitizens, but also to acknowledge hierarchies of personhood in our own societies. This book seeks to problematize how we recognize people as deserving—as fully human and entitled to dignity— and to posit the ideal of functioning citizenship as a way to remedying structural weaknesses in the modern human rights regime. To begin, Chapter 1 ("The Changing Value and Meaning of Citizenship") outlines how citizenship has evolved within political thought, with particular attention to how debates have intensified in relation to the protection of modern human rights. With the creation of the United Nations and the adoption of rights norms, the international community made assumptions about identity and membership that effectively limited the inclusiveness of so-called universal rights. By privileging state sovereignty and legal nationality, the human rights regime created protection gaps for noncitizens and people at the margins. Exacerbating these shortcomings are the forces of globalization, including growing concerns about terrorism and global migration. The rise of nonstate actors, from terror networks to nongovernmental organizations (NGOs), also complicates traditional conceptions of membership. Scholars continue to debate whether globalization has eroded the importance of state citizenship and the nation-state or whether it has in fact strengthened the state's role in the world system. I argue that citizenship continues to have persistent power and appeal, and that this complex concept is often conversely viewed as a right, an identity, and a commodity.

If we consider citizenship to exist along a spectrum of belonging, then statelessness represents the starkest example of life without political membership. Statelessness is recognized not only as a violation of the "right to a nationality" but also as a root cause of additional rights abuses and threats to human security. Yet I argue in Chapter 2 ("Statelessness and Elusive Political Membership") that while legal nationality is an essential prerequisite for the mere possibility of enjoying a variety of basic human rights, the international community's narrow emphasis on citizenship acquisition is misguided. Legal status is only one step in a long journey toward full rights protection; statelessness is both a *cause* of marginalization and a *symptom* of it. That is, most stateless populations lack legal nationality because they are part of a marginalized group that faces systematic discrimination and oppression from the beginning. Their circumstances are made worse by statelessness, but legal status alone cannot guarantee full rights protection. Rather than relying on the acquisition of legal nationality alone to ensure access to human rights, human rights advocates must acknowledge the deeply rooted complexities of statelessness and seek out solutions guaranteeing functioning citizenship rather than simple legal status.

Part II, "Newcomers and Noncitizens," expands the scope of this discussion to consider the realities of the forcibly displaced (including asylum-seekers, refugees, and internally displaced persons) in Chapter 3 ("Forced Displacement and Broken Ties"), as well as irregular migrants in Chapter 4 ("Irregular Human Movement and the Creation of Liminal Spaces"). Although most displaced persons are legal nationals of a state, they lack functioning citizenship with their governments; in fact, their governments are often responsible for the human rights abuses and conflict that prompted their displacement to begin with. While some protections under international law are meant to fill the gaps created by these broken ties, in reality displaced persons suffer widespread human rights abuses in the absence of a reliable state duty-bearer. Anti-Syrian refugee sentiments in Europe, refugee detention in Australia, and the stubborn refusal to acknowledge many "illegal immigrants" as asylum-seekers in North America are just a few examples of how the forcibly displaced face severe challenges to their basic human rights in the absence of functioning citizenship. The inadequacies of refugee rights, including the false assumption that displacement is anything less than normal in our current system, leads to glaring denials of the rights to place and purpose.

Similarly, various forms of illicit human movement leave many individuals without functioning citizenship, often because they are outside their country of legal nationality and cannot claim rights for fear of arrest, deportation, or some other form of retribution. These categories of migration include irregular migration—which is often called "illegal" or "undocumented" migration, and has encompassed a recent increase in unaccompanied child migrants—as well as those who, often as part of this process, cross borders via human smuggling or trafficking. Here we see definitional lines blurring; there are debates about who counts as a migrant versus a refugee, at what point smuggling becomes trafficking, and so forth. In some cases, lack of functioning citizenship is what necessitates migration in the first place; consider marginalized stateless groups and citizens of corrupt, oppressive governments. Yet these forms of illicit movement also create liminal spaces where migrants and trafficking victims exist outside the law, beyond the reach of functioning citizenship and dangerously vulnerable to rights abuse.

Part III, "Marginalized Nations and Minorities," explores challenges to functioning citizenship among minority groups such as nomadic peoples, Indigenous nations, and "second-class" American citizens. Chapter 5 ("Nomadic Peoples and Alternate Conceptions of Place") considers the serious threats nomadic peoples face to their cultural survival and livelihood, under pressure from sedentary majority populations. Nomadic groups have long experienced suspicion and discrimination—as illustrated by the ongoing marginalization of European Roma and Travellers, the Maasai of Tanzania and Kenya, and the Bedouin of the Middle East and North Africa (MENA) region—and modern human rights tend to frame basic rights, including freedom of movement and property rights, through a lens that privileges settlement. Indeed, nomadic peoples are often viewed with suspicion and excluded from the citizenry because they move "too much" and do not conform to majority views related to settlement, land use, and community membership. This bias leaves nomadic peoples without functioning citizenship in state governments that fail to understand their basic needs and perspectives. Resulting rights abuses center not only on rights to land and natural resources but also on cultural and political expression.

Chapter 6 ("Indigenous Nations and Tribal Sovereignty") focuses on the Indigenous rights movement, which has embraced the idea of self-determination for Indigenous people, framing their demands for economic, political, and cultural survival. Indeed, calls for tribal sovereignty problematize the international community's central focus on state governments for legitimizing human rights claimants. For communities such as the Onondaga Nation of Central New York state, state membership comes second to the ties that bind one to an Indigenous nation. (Indeed, the Onondaga Nation maintains a legally distinct territory just outside of Syracuse, New York, and some members have rejected US citizenship in favor of tribe-issued passports and other documentation.) While this chapter explores the historical trajectory leading to modern Indigenous rights concerns—which include, I argue, an ongoing process of cultural genocide—it focuses on how Indigenous nations and tribal sovereignty challenge the reliance on state citizenship for recognizing personhood and claiming human rights. Calls for Indigenous sovereignty offer alternative pathways for conceptualizing identification, legal status, and political membership.

Chapter 7 ("Second-Class Citizens in the 'Land of the Free'") shifts the discussion to focus specifically on the case study of the United States, where "second-class" citizens are often unable to access fully functioning citizenship and enjoy their rights to place and purpose. Drawing from the work of Margaret Somers (2008), this chapter argues that the "contractualization of citizenship" and "colorblind" politics often lead to situations of "internal statelessness" in one of the world's wealthiest, most powerful states. Issues of police brutality and inequality before the law, for instance—which are central to the rise of the Black Lives Matter movement—stem from pervasive systems of unequal citizenship and structural violence against racial minorities, many of whom occupy lower socioeconomic strata than their White counterparts in American cities such as Detroit, Flint, and Saint Louis. Human rights challenges such as forced eviction, lack of clean drinking water and affordable healthcare, and widespread racial inequalities highlight the denial to many people of their full rights to place and purpose despite their status as American citizens.

The book turns to solution-seeking in Part IV, "Creating Inclusive Forms of Membership." Chapter 8 ("Conveying the Problem[s] and Representing Personhood") explores the international community's responses to these hierarchies of personhood by considering how violated rights to place and purpose are communicated and interpreted. Drawing on concepts such as issue emergence, visual narratives, and framing, this chapter assesses the representation of human rights concerns such as statelessness, forced displacement, and Indigenous rights. This assessment is useful for better understanding the ways in which vulnerabilities to human rights abuse are constructed and translated for media consumption, fundraising initiatives, and public advocacy campaigns. An important example comes from the UNHCR, which is largely responsible for framing the issue of statelessness with its "iBelong" Campaign to End Statelessness. At the same time, this analysis also highlights the vastly different responses that are given to the problems stemming from lack of functioning citizenship depending on political circumstances—including how these responses align with the hierarchies of personhood that operate at local, state, and international levels. Ultimately, this chapter argues that we must reevaluate the ways that we *see* problems related to lack of functioning citizenship, which includes facilitating the empowerment and representation of vulnerable communities.

Guided by the limitations of traditional citizenship, Chapter 9 ("Actualizing the Ideal of Functioning Citizenship") seeks to move the ideal of functioning citizenship from theory to practice. After we reevaluate how we see the problem, we must then adjust our responses accordingly. This chapter first offers "practical" recommendations for filling protection gaps and alleviating some immediate causes of human suffering. These recommendations include legal, bureaucratic, and policy responses to hierarchies of personhood. While these steps are useful starting points, they are not (and will never be) enough. Instead, actualizing the ideal of functioning citizenship further requires expanding our notion of citizenship to include political space for those who cannot be neatly categorized as "citizens" or "noncitizens." By acknowledging the limitations of our current system—and recognizing the existence of hierarchies of personhood—we can begin the difficult work of broadening political membership and delinking worthiness from legal status and state recognition.

CHAPTER 1 | The Changing Value and Meaning of Citizenship

THE VALUE AND MEANING of citizenship has been debated, reinterpreted, and reinvented by political thinkers for centuries, yet attention to this concept has intensified in recent years—particularly in relation to the protection of human rights. Derek Heater (1999) argues that present interest in the study of citizenship is different because "it is virtually global in its extent" (1). Beginning in the 1980s and 1990s, a confluence of events and concerns renewed interest in the complex issue of citizenship. These developments included the dominance of the New Right in the United States and the United Kingdom, which questioned the validity of "social citizenship" that viewed welfare state benefits as a right; accelerated human migrations and growing awareness of multicultural differences within states; the related development of multicultural consciousness that loosened or fragmented previous notions of the nation-state; the need to construct rights-protective constitutions in previously autocratic regimes; the realization that citizenship remains a meaningless idea for people around the world who are deprived of basic protections; and questions about the validity of the state with growing recognition of regional and even global membership (Heater 1999, 2–3). Discussions of citizenship have been further complicated by the rise of nonstate actors—from nongovernmental organizations (NGOs) to transnational terror networks. These developments have raised profound questions about state sovereignty and duty, political membership, and the real meaning of citizenship itself.

Earliest conceptions of citizenship come from the civic republican model, which has its origins in classical antiquity—most notably from the ancient states of Sparta, Athens, and Rome—and stresses the importance of duty. Thinkers such as Aristotle argued that citizens were expected to be publicly active and educated, displaying goodness and virtue in order to be good citizens and moral human beings (Heater 1999, 45–46); similarly, Cicero believed that men must use their skills for virtuous actions and be involved in public work. Centuries later, Niccolò Machiavelli contended that a good citizen must lead an active life, whether as a civilian or in the military, and was joined by other Renaissance thinkers in reviving the classic conception of citizenship as duty (Heater 1999, 47 and 49). In the eighteenth century, philosophers such as Jean-Jacques Rousseau looked toward civil republicanism to formulate the social contract between individuals and the state. Rousseau's concept of the General Will stressed that the sovereign people make judgments that benefit the entire community and agree to abide by those outcomes, living obediently as subjects of the state (Heater 1999, 50). To achieve these goals, the civic republican perspective emphasizes the need for community built on social friendship and harmony; society must be an organic community of the state and its citizens, not a collection of separate and self-interested people (Heater 1999, 55). A model citizen therefore exhibits selfless civic duty and civic virtue, or "martial patriotic devotion" (Heater 1999, 60). The purpose of citizenship, according to the civic republican tradition, is "to connect the individual and the state in a symbiotic relationship so that a just and stable republican polity can be created and sustained and the individual citizen can enjoy freedom. Thus, the individual can be truly free only in a republic; a republic can exist only through the support of its citizens" (Heater 1999, 53).

Despite the longevity of civic republican thought, the liberal tradition of citizenship—and its emphasis on rights—has been dominant for the past two centuries. Compared to civic republicanism, liberal citizenship demands less of the individual. "It involves a loosely committed relationship to the state, a relationship held in place . . . by a set of civic rights, honored by the state, which otherwise interferes as little as possible in the citizen's life" (Heater 1999, 4). Contemporary understandings of liberal citizenship are often aligned with the work of T. H. Marshall (1950), whose seminal essay *Citizenship and Social Class* emphasizes the equality of citizenship. He outlines the evolution of citizenship in the combination of civil rights (individual liberties, such as freedom of speech), political rights (ensuring representation and participation in government), and social rights (protecting one's standard of living, such as the rights to an education or healthcare) (10–14). Marshall's rights-based, closed system of social welfare—termed "social citizenship"—focused on social rights that were ensured to citizens of the state rather than extended universally to all human beings. Recent interpretations of this model have called for pluralistic approaches to law, expanding social citizenship by decoupling it from legal status to ensure rights provisions for citizens and noncitizens alike (Revi 2014, 452, 461–462). This perspective has influenced operational conceptualizations of the term "citizenship" in modern politics; a 2005 European Policy Centre report, for instance, noted that "protection and empowerment are inherent to the notion of citizenship" and lack of citizenship created conditions for human insecurity (Sokoloff and Lewis 2005, 4). The report, which focused on the problem of statelessness at a time when the issue was still largely ignored by the international community, found that "the right to citizenship appears fundamental to ensuring the conditions of human security as most human rights derive from and depend upon it" (Sokoloff and Lewis 2005, 3).

From this view, citizenship is an instrument of empowerment—not merely a set of passive rights—and it represents the essential link between an individual and a state government. Yet as this chapter illustrates, the ideals of liberal citizenship are frequently not realized or equally enjoyed. Modern conceptions of human rights that arose after World War II made assumptions about legal nationality and political membership that inherently limited the scope of "universal" rights, forcing individuals to rely on government duty-bearers for fundamental protections. Despite idealistic language about universality and inalienability, human rights rely on state citizenship and help draw clear distinctions between citizens and noncitizens, locals and foreigners, majorities and minorities. The forces of globalization further complicate this discussion, calling the meaning and value of state citizenship into question as states grapple with global issues such as terrorism, mass migration, and the rise of various nonstate actors. While the concept of citizenship endures, understandings of its significance vary widely and often contradict each other; citizenship is framed as a right, an identity, and a commodity. Understanding these diverse perspectives is necessary to fully comprehend the pitfalls and possibilities of citizenship—always in pursuit of the more just, rights-protective ideal of fully functioning citizenship.

State Citizenship in an Age of Universal Rights

Historical accounts of international politics following World War II largely focus on the building of norms and institutions, such as the adoption of universal human rights and the creation of the United Nations, and stress the embrace of a global political community. Yet these developments made assumptions about identity and membership that effectively built challenges directly into the international system and placed limitations on its inclusiveness. Attempts to build a global community and guarantee universal rights were laid on foundations that created hierarchies of belonging, privileged state power, and diminished capacities for upholding norms. The postwar order, including the newly formed United Nations (UN) and the basic rights outlined in the Universal Declaration of Human Rights (UDHR), assumed legal nationality and presumed that each national group needed its own state. This left little space for individuals who did not fit neatly into citizenship categories after the dissolution of multi-ethnic empires, including a variety of migrants and stateless individuals. Existing mechanisms such as repatriation assumed that everyone had a homeland to return to, while naturalization and asylum—historically reserved only for exceptional cases—could not cope with postwar waves of irregular migration, including the pressures of mass statelessness. Ayten Gündoğdu (2015) argues that the international community thus dogmatically applied existing rules "without heeding the unprecedented challenges posed by this crisis" (30), and also that these realities quickly led to skepticism about the true universality of newly declared human rights (31).

Writing after World War II, Hannah Arendt (1966) viewed the plights of minorities and stateless persons as evidence of fundamental flaws in the new international human rights regime. She was skeptical about the idealism underpinning the newly adopted UDHR as well attempts by the then-defunct League of Nations to protect minority rights. The League's Minority Treaties, which conferred basic rights on minority populations living within states, were unable to stop the Holocaust—and she doubted they could have prevented the forced assimilation of minorities in newly formed states after World War II (Arendt 1966, 270–272). She argued that the arrival of stateless refugees ended any illusions about the Minority Treaties, noting that only "the emancipated sovereignty of the people, of one's own people, seemed to be able to insure [the protection of human rights]" (291). Minorities and stateless persons were therefore convinced "that loss of national rights was identical with loss of human rights, that the former inevitably entailed the latter" (292). While the United Nations' UDHR espoused universal ideals based on humanity rather than state citizenship, Arendt famously equated legal nationality with one's "right to have rights" in the midst of a state-centered international system that relied heavily on the protection of sovereignty. This contrasted with Marshall's account of citizenship as a product of rights acquisition; Arendt instead viewed citizenship as a prerequisite for acquiring other rights (Macklin 2007, 337). She wrote:

> We become aware of the existence of a right to have rights (and that means to live in a framework where one is judged by one's actions and opinions) and a right to belong to some kind of organized community, only when millions of people emerged who had lost and could not regain these rights because of the new global political situation. The trouble is that this calamity arose not from any lack of civilization, backwardness, or mere tyranny, but, on the contrary, that it could not be repaired, because there was no longer any "uncivilized" spot on earth, because whether we like it or not we have really started to live in One World. Only with a completely organized humanity could the loss of home and political status become identical with expulsion from humanity altogether. (Arendt 1966, 297)

The concept of state sovereignty played a pivotal role in the formation of the United Nations, yet scholars debate the intended role of nation-states in the promotion of human rights. Article 2(1) of the UN Charter stipulates that the organization is based on "the principle of sovereign equality of all its Members," and its purposes and principles include upholding the norms of nonintervention and self-determination (United Nations 1945). During that postwar period, the UN Human Rights Commission was busy drafting the UDHR, extending references to human rights found within the Charter (see Morsink 1999) while simultaneously placing limitations on state sovereignty by outlining individual rights—and by extension, placing limitations and obligations on governments. Human rights scholars such as Jack Donnelly (2013) contend that states are the primary duty-bearers of human rights, and that international law is meant to overcome initial presumptions of sovereignty. He writes that international human rights law "is the record of restrictions on sovereignty accepted by states" (Donnelly 2013, 26). The UDHR thus presents a paradox; it "speaks the language of universally valid propositions when it proclaims human rights as if they were always already universally valid," but it presupposes the nation-state as the venue for human rights practice (Gregg 2016, 44). This requires a state-based legal system with the government as the enforcer, as well as state-based institutions of political participation and economic institutions (44). Yet while the UDHR's Preamble references states as members of the United Nations, cosmopolitan scholars are less concerned with the role of states for asserting universal values. Johannes

Morsink (2009) argues that the UDHR's "resounding" silence on the role of the modern nation-states supports the position that personhood, rather than attachment to a particular state, should mark an individual as worthy of rights (149). This approach relies less heavily on states as the duty-bearers of rights and puts greater emphasis on the role of the international community (meaning the human family rather than a society of states) for rights protection.

This ambiguity may exist, in part, because in 1948 the UDHR wasn't adequately equipped to handle the forthcoming challenges of multicultural societies and a globalized world system. The omission of a special minority rights article within the UDHR, for instance, hints at the underlying assumption that the nation and the state are one and the same, with one's identity intricately linked to one's relationship to a state. Rather than outlining special rights for the protection of minority cultures, Article 27(1) of the UDHR stipulates, "Everyone has the right freely to participate in *the* cultural life of the community" (United Nations General Assembly 1948). Pluralistic wording that outlined the right to participate in "the cultural life of *his or her* community" could have opened the possibility that citizenship and the cultural life of a community are not one and the same; instead, Article 27 "seems to assume that 'the community' one participates in and with which one identifies culturally is the dominant one of the nation state. There is no hint here of multiculturalism or pluralism" (Morsink 1999, 269).

Indeed, traditional views posit citizenship as fundamentally a status of belonging to a particular group; of reflecting the ideals of a given state and perpetuating its identity. A modern state is not simply a territorial organization; rather, it is "a membership organization, an association of citizens" (Brubaker 1992, 21). Rogers Brubaker (1992) writes that "the state claims to be the state of, and for, a particular, bounded citizenry; it claims legitimacy by claiming to express the will and further the interests of that citizenry" (21). Furthermore, "this bounded citizenry is usually conceived as a nation—as something more cohesive than a mere aggregate of persons who happen legally to belong to the state" (21). Citizens are socially bonded based on common values and symbols, sharing a national identity that is largely internally inclusive (Smith 1991, 16–17). Although multiculturalists such as Kymlicka (1995) have called attention to the exclusions of minorities within states, traditional models of formal citizenship serve to create a baseline measure of belonging against which foreigners may be compared. As Brubaker (1992) notes, "There is a conceptually clear, legally consequential, and ideologically charged distinction between citizens and foreigners" (21).

For displaced persons in Europe following the World Wars, increasing state surveillance and reliance on passports to facilitate freedom of movement meant that lack of documentation created glaring challenges to the "right to have rights" outlined by Arendt. For the stateless especially—who had been denationalized by their governments or whose countries had simply ceased to exist—the inability to document their relationship to a state made it incredibly difficult to protect their rights to place and purpose. The birth of the modern passport system in the twentieth century marked shifts in the ways people moved across borders and identified themselves. World War I reversed a trend toward the relaxation of passport requirements, renewing a state preoccupation with controlling movements and viewing foreigners with suspicion (Torpey 2001, 257). John Torpey (2000) argues that the relationship between citizenship and modern documentation impacts a person's life and prospects in ways related to mobility, identity, and lack of state protection. First, he asserts that states have usurped the "monopoly of the legitimate means of movement" from rival claimants such as churches and private enterprises over the last few centuries, and that a focus on borders and citizenship has made people dependent on states for legitimacy (Torpey 2000, 1–2). Ultimately, nationality and its resulting documents have become essential prerequisites for travel worldwide (162, 166). Second, documentation forces people to rely on a state-sponsored identity for their placement within world affairs, and this requirement poses serious threats to those who lack formal citizenship. Torpey and Jane Caplan write: "Establishing the identity of individual people—as workers, taxpayers, conscripts, travelers, criminal suspects—is increasingly recognized as fundamental to the multiple operations of the state" (Caplan and Torpey 2001, 1). Furthermore, the creation of what James Scott (1998) calls "legible people" (65), or people who are open to the scrutiny of officialdom, has become a "hallmark of modern statehood" (Caplan and Torpey 2001, 1). A critical aspect of this process has been people's increasing dependence on states for the possession of individual identity; citizens can escape from this dependence only with difficulty, and it may significantly shape their access to various spaces (Torpey 2000, 4). Third, Torpey illustrates the "othering" of noncitizens when they lack documentation, a condition that denies them protection by state powers and leaves them vulnerable to abuses. A passport "vouchsafes the issuing state's guarantee of aid and succor to its bearer while in the jurisdiction of other states" (160). He notes, "Possession of a passport thus constitutes *ipso facto* evidence of a legitimate claim on the resources and services of the embassies or consulates of the issuing state—not to mention, in extreme cases, on its military power" (160).

Indeed, the international community has been struggling with issues of documentation for a century. During the interwar period, certificates of identity (commonly referred to as "Nansen passports") were issued by the League of Nations to allow stateless refugees to travel internationally. Later termed "travel documents" in 1938, these passports represented the international community's first attempt to provide documentation that was not legitimized by any one state (United Nations High Commissioner for Refugees 1984). Following World War II and the creation of the United Nations, provisions were made for refugee documentation under the 1951 Convention Relating to the Status of Refugees (Refugee Convention) in Articles 27 and 28 (United Nations High Commissioner for Refugees 1951). In 1977, the Executive Committee of the UN High Commissioner for Refugees (UNHCR) recommended that refugees should be informed of their status and issued documentation certifying their refugee status as one of the basic procedures in the asylum process. Today, it is general practice for states with established refugee determination procedures to provide some form of documentation attesting to a person's identity and refugee status, such as a refugee certificate or identity card. These documents frequently serve as evidence that an individual has the right to reside and work in a country. In states that are not parties to the Refugee Convention, however, it is rarely possible for a person to obtain refugee identity documentation (United Nations High Commissioner for Refugees 1984). While stateless individuals fleeing a well-founded fear of persecution can sometimes qualify for refugee documentation under the Refugee Convention, most stateless persons are blocked from a variety of rights protections and everyday necessities. Without legal nationality and its resulting identity documentation, a person cannot accomplish simple tasks such as opening a bank account, boarding a flight, or enrolling in a university (United Nations High Commissioner for Refugees n.d.b.).

While postwar discussions of legal nationality were often tied to freedom of movement, borders were not always limited to boundaries between states; the processes of categorization and exclusion inherent to border crossings may appear *within* the state as well as at its limits. Various forms of identity within states may serve as foundations for defining boundaries and hierarchies of belonging within societies, or to differentiate between friends and enemies in times of conflict. The Soviet regime, for example, inaugurated a formalized system for classifying identity groups in the early 1930s, thereby ascribing social, occupational, and ethnic-national identities for all who received internal passports (and indirectly identifying those who were not issued passports). This same system became linked to the larger project of Soviet socialism, which included policies of systemic mass repression, mass deportation, and the wholesale moving of populations to reconstruct geographic, social, and ethnic boundaries of the country (Shearer 2004, 838). In places like Northern Thailand, the Cold War changed the value of citizenship for minority groups that had once lived largely outside the intervention of state bureaucracy. The Thai state aligned with the US anticommunist political stance and "sought to strengthen the defense of its border with arms and by reassuring itself of the loyalty of its resident population" (Hanks and Hanks 2001, 157). The communist threat fulfilled preexisting fears of outsiders living within northern borders, creating a highly militarized state that often targeted groups that had little or nothing to do with communism itself (Gillogly 2004, 120–121). The political forces set into motion by the Cold War, and later perpetuated by the US-led "War on Drugs" in the 1980s, established hill tribes as enemies of the state. They continue to be routinely classified as undocumented immigrants and denied Thai citizenship, leaving many members of these ethnic minority groups stateless and vulnerable to human rights abuse.

These complexities highlight tensions at the intersection of human rights ideals and the practical goods of state citizenship, challenging the rights to place and purpose well after the adoption of the UDHR. Human rights are meant to be inclusive, based on universal personhood rather than connection to a particular state or other identity group. In some respects—theoretically, at least—citizenship should no longer be necessary for accessing basic entitlements and protections. Article 1 of the 1948 UDHR clearly states: "All human beings are born free and equal in dignity and rights." Indeed, human rights require three interlocking qualities: they must be *natural* (inherent to all human beings), *equal* (the same for everyone), and *universal* (applicable everywhere) (Hunt 2008, 20). The cosmopolitanism of human rights views the world as "one unified ethical community," traversing state borders to emphasize the moral rights that each individual has as a member of humanity (Morsink 2009, 148). "The individual human beings—who are the primary addressees and the subjects about whom the Declaration was being made—are not isolated, mutually disinterested, and possessive human beings," argues Morsink

(2009). "They are members of the family of humankind" (151). Yet legal nationality itself is exclusive, "having as its aim the proscription of certain rights, and serving as de facto gate keeper to the enjoyment of other derivative rights" (Weissbrodt and Divine 2016, 870), and persistent human rights violations among those lacking functioning citizenship highlight weaknesses in the system.

In some cases, the universality of rights conflicts with issues of state sovereignty—including national identity, economy, and security. Noncitizens in the United States are prohibited from voting in federal elections, for instance, and have been blocked from doing so ever since the country experienced a rise in anti-immigrant sentiment in the early twentieth century. Undocumented migrants and many refugees are denied legal employment around the world, even though various economic studies have shown that these workers bring positive financial benefits to host countries.[1] Passports and other forms of government-issued documentation are often denied to (or revoked from) groups and individuals who are regarded as threats to the state.[2] Freedom of movement is also limited by hierarchies of personhood that privilege some passport holders over others, making it difficult for certain nationalities to secure the visas necessary for international travel.[3] Laura van Waas (2011) writes that "while

---

[1] Data suggest that immigrant and refugee workers help, not hurt, economies. In 2007 (as the governors of New Mexico and Arizona were declaring a "state of emergency" over illegal immigration in 2007 and US President George W. Bush approved the construction of a $1.2 billion, 700 mile fence along the US-Mexico border), Gordon Hanson (2007) assessed the economic impacts of immigration and concluded that stemming illegal migration would likely have a negative impact on the American economy and result in a net drain on economic growth. Shortly thereafter, the White House (2007) issued a report by its Council of Economic Advisers noting that US citizens benefit financially from immigration, on average, and that immigrant workers tend to complement the workforce by raising productivity and overall income. More recently, research suggests that panic over Syrian refugees harming European economies is unfounded. In countries such as Lebanon and Turkey, where most Syrians did not have formal work permits in 2015, informal refugee workers had positive economic impacts—including generating jobs, increasing overall wages, and contributing to state economies (Calì and Sekkarie 2015).

[2] For instance, anti-apartheid activist-citizens were regularly refused passports by the South African government, blocking them from engaging in activism internationally (Associated Press 1986). Two decades later, the Chinese government revokes passports of Tibetan activists to control their movement and intensify regional control (International Campaign for Tibet 2015). The government similarly detained and barred Chinese citizen and artist-activist Ai Weiwei from traveling internationally in 2011, finally returning his passport in July 2015 (Phillips 2015).

[3] The financial firm Arton Capital recently ranked the world's most powerful passports based on the global mobility they provide, measured by the ability to visit foreign countries without a visa. Arton, which specializes in helping wealthy individuals obtain multiple citizenships, ranked the United States and the United Kingdom as the top most powerful passports in 2015, followed closely by France, South Korea, and Germany. Perhaps not surprisingly, the bottom-ranked countries included developing countries where human rights violations are often prevalent, including South Sudan, the Palestinian Territories, and Burma (Passport Index n.d.). Similarly,

the majority of human rights are, indeed, guaranteed to everyone regardless of, nationality . . . there are, in fact, still a number of citizens' rights dressed up as human rights" (26). The right to participate in government, freedom of movement, and economic rights are all formulated "in such a way as to call into question the inclusiveness of the term 'human rights,'" suggesting that one's relationship to a state is often vital for at least some basic protections (van Waas 2011, 26).

For many noncitizens, lack of adequate identity documentation is an obstruction to freedom of movement, both across international borders and frequently within states themselves. Many states have enacted compulsory identity card laws that require individuals to carry documentation on their persons, with the threat of fines or imprisonment for those who do not register for an ID and/or who are unable to present documentation upon demand by local authorities.[4] Even in countries that do not require citizens to carry ID, lack of documentation creates often insurmountable barriers to everyday essentials such as opening a bank account, renting an apartment, securing legal employment, and registering for public education. "Those who have never been deprived of official papers may find it hard to imagine the powerlessness which results; powerlessness that can and does lead people to take up arms," writes Bronwen Manby (2009). "Even in the poorest countries, a passport or identity card does not just provide the right to travel, but forms the basis of the right to almost everything else." Yet passport-holders from the global North—who can easily access identity documentation and who enjoy relative ease of international travel—may be tempted to argue that borders are becoming increasingly porous and inconsequential. Travelers in Europe, for instance, may move

---

Henley & Partners ranks countries in its annual Visa Restrictions Index by how many countries can be visited without applying for a visa. In 2016, Germany ranked first—its passport holders can travel to 177 countries out of a possible 218—followed by Sweden in second place and several European states (Finland, Italy, Spain, and the United Kingdom) in third (Smith 2016; Henley & Partners 2016).

[4] Some states do not require people to actually carry identity cards, but they do require that anyone must present identity documentation when requested by relevant authorities; in practice, individuals must carry ID on their person at all times to comply with these regulations. In the Netherlands, for instance, police officers and ticket inspectors on public transport can request to see documentation in cases of traffic management, the maintenance of public order, or the investigation of criminal offenses. Those who fail to comply with the requirement to identify themselves are subject to a fine of €60 (or €30 for persons aged fourteen and fifteen) and risk being taken to a police station to establish their identity (Government of the Netherlands n.d.). Similar rules apply in Spain, where El Documento Nacional de Identidad (DNI) has been in use for more than fifty years—although recent developments include the collection of electronic and biometric data—and it is an essential document when dealing with both public and private agencies (Comisión Técnica de Apoyo a la Implantación del DNI Electrónico 2014).

between countries party to the Schengen agreement without slowing for border controls or visa inspections. This sort of mobility is reserved for a privileged few, whose state-issued documentation reflects membership in a powerful political community. These global elite enjoy a form of "mobility citizenship" that includes the right to be mobile (that is, to cross borders legally) and the right to stay (Mau 2010, 340). Human movement across borders is still the domain of state sovereignty, with governments still firmly controlling "legitimate means of movement" (Torpey 2000, 1–2) via the issuance of passports and visas, the strict enforcement of migration and naturalization policies, and border control measures that prioritize the norms of national security rather than universal rights. The distinction between members and foreigners is formally institutionalized in state-issued documents, such as passports and visas. Such documentation constitutes a verifiable identity and a claim of recognition while one is outside one's home borders. With passport in hand, citizens show their claim as members of a political community—and worthy of entrance, safe passage, diplomatic protection, and eventually the right of return (Staples 2012, 100).

Formal membership is used as a key to unlock vital resources, but this social good is not evenly distributed. Ayelet Shachar (2009) argues that the current system of birthright citizenship, which confers legal nationality based on place of birth or ancestry, constitutes a "birthright lottery" that privileges some while excluding others. By relying on "the accident of birth" to determine one's political status, the international community perpetuates cycles of inequality within developing countries and traps the poor by "the lottery of their birth" (4). "Access to affluent polities in our unequal world is still reserved primarily to those born in a particular territory or to a particular ancestry while at the same time shutting out everyone else born on the wrong side of the border of security and prosperity," writes Shachar (x). Legal nationality also plays an important role in resource allocation within developed states, and it takes on new importance (and is more hotly contested) when it signifies a stake in the distribution of wealth. In the United Arab Emirates (UAE) and neighboring states, for instance, identity was traditionally determined by tribe or locality and few people saw the value of registering or obtaining a passport when the administrative structures that distinguish between natives and foreigners were constructed. Others were nomadic and traveled too often to register, or simply weren't called into a government office to do so. Yet as the UAE became a powerful state, those without official documentation were excluded from accessing government services in the oil-rich society

(Abrahamian 2015, 52–53).[5] As a key to resources, legal nationality therefore creates hierarchies within states and across the globe. Various essential resources—including necessities for attaining an adequate standard of living, such as food, shelter, medical care, and social services—are posited as universal rights but are distributed unequally in practice.

Globalization and the Role of the State

Shortcomings related to state citizenship in an age of human rights are exacerbated by forces of globalization, starkly calling into question the true value and meaning of state citizenship as ideals clash with growing concerns such as terrorism and mass migration. "There is an inherent friction in the relationship between international human rights law and citizenship," write David Weissbrodt and Michael Divine (2016, 870). Alison Brysk (2002) contends that globalized migration flows and open markets create new human rights threats that duty-bearing states are not fully equipped to handle. The resulting "citizenship gap" represents "a lack of political mechanisms to ensure individual membership, power holders' accountability, and respect for human rights in a globalizing world system" (246). It is vital to investigate the sources of these "cracks" and "gaps," and the intersection between political membership and rights protection provides a key starting point. While current events strengthen the role of the state in certain regards, the growing importance of nonstate actors raises the issue of whether the state alone can be regarded as the duty-bearer of human rights. As the global human rights landscape shifts—to include a growing list of actors who both contribute to violations and provide vital resources for protecting basic entitlements—the role of the state becomes increasingly complicated and tenuous.

Scholarly debates about citizenship may seem ironic in the face of current political developments that seem to privilege strong governments over the ideals of universal rights or an inclusive international community. Widespread concerns about global migration, terrorism, and growing

---

[5] Similar exclusions have occurred within Indigenous nations, which sometimes have special minority rights and access to resources within a larger state. In the US state of California, thousands of Indigenous persons have been disenrolled from native tribes—and stripped of their rights to collect a share of gambling profits from tribal casinos. California Indian casinos earned nearly $7 billion in 2010, and the financial impact of losing membership in a tribe may include the loss of housing allowances, college scholarships, access to tribal schools, and monthly profit shares of up to $15,000. Although rivalries and group politics often trigger disenrollment, critics contend that lucrative casino gambling has driven recent actions (Dao 2011).

multiculturalism continue to inform matters of state jurisdiction, such as nationality laws and governance, and have taken on new resonance in recent years. National security concerns following the terrorist attacks of September 11, 2011, in the United States "revived the security role and territoriality of the sovereign state in dramatic form," at least within the United States and among its allies (Falk 2004, 181). The use of denationalization has been advocated in the United States and the United Kingdom to deter and punish acts of terrorism by state citizens, despite objections that such practices can lead to statelessness (thus ignoring international human rights law), violate liberal principles of equal respect, and serve as an arbitrary and illegitimate exercise of state power (Gibney 2013, 651–652). Security-centered worries have been heightened by mass migration created by the civil war in Syria, which forced millions to flee across borders into countries of the Middle East and Europe. Displaced Muslims have received a mixed welcome in Western European countries, including Germany—where Chancellor Angela Merkel announced an open-door refugee policy and then saw her approval ratings plummet, particularly after dozens of women asserted that they were sexually assaulted by Syrian men outside of Cologne's train station on New Year's Eve in 2015 (Donahue 2016). In France, existing anti-refugee and anti-immigrant sentiments were enflamed by terrorist attacks by Islamic fundamentalists—including 2015 attacks in Paris that targeted the satirical journal *Charlie Hebdo* and, less than a year later, that killed at least 130 civilians in the Bataclan concert hall and its surrounding neighborhoods. From this perspective, the state still matters and so does formal citizenship; legal nationality distinguishes between friends and strangers and provides protections against perceived enemies.

Yet at the same time we see the rise of nonstate actors, which certainly complicates traditional formulations that equated citizenship with membership—particularly in relation to groups that sometimes behave (at least in part) in ways that have been historically ascribed to states. At the most basic level, a state is generally assumed to meet four fundamental conditions: (1) it must have a territorial base; (2) a stable population must live within its borders; (3) it has a government to which its population owes allegiance; and (4) it is recognized diplomatically by other states. These criteria are not absolute and they are subject to various interpretations. The Palestinian Authority is sometimes viewed as a "quasi-state," for instance, after attaining some measure of territorial control of the West Bank and Gaza and later being granted nonvoting observer status in the United Nations General Assembly in 2012 (Mingst and Arreguín-Toft 2014, 132).

The Kurds, the world's largest ethnic group without a state to call their own, have been working toward the goal of creating a "Greater Kurdistan" and are gaining territory in Syria and Iraq. Some experts say that these gains could shape the contours of a de facto Kurdish state if existing countries splinter apart (Soguel 2015). Although regarded as a terrorist organization by countries such as the United States, the Islamic State (also known as ISIS, ISIL, and Daesh) has held vast territory and built its capacity to govern, albeit using tools of terror and extreme violence. The Islamic State provided relative stability for many civilians accustomed to corrupt governments and ongoing conflict; among other things, the group issued identification cards for residents and enacted conservation guidelines for preserving fishing stocks (Arango 2015). Traditional definitions of "state" and "citizenship" thus may not resonate with people whose allegiances and identities are not reflected by formal borders, or whose most effective human rights protections come from dubious sources.

The increasing political importance of nongovernmental organizations (NGOs) and other transnational nonstate actors also complicates conceptions of membership and the state as legal duty-bearer of rights. In many parts of the world, NGOs are tasked with providing services and protecting basic rights that should, under international human rights law, be the responsibilities of states. Médecins Sans Frontières (MSF, or Doctors Without Borders) is often the sole provider of medical services in conflict areas, attempting to protect health rights for civilians isolated by war and ignored by governments. In conflicts such as Syria's civil war, MSF endured challenges and suffered losses normally associated with the circumstances of military doctors—including airstrikes that destroyed MSF hospitals and harmed medical providers (Médecins Sans Frontières 2016). In the Mediterranean and elsewhere, the Migrant Offshore Aid Station (MOAS) has used private ships since 2014 to rescue migrants from drowning at sea. These lifesaving efforts have saved thousands of people (Migrant Offshore Aid Station n.d.) and fill a glaring protection gap left by ineffective state responses in the region. In these examples and countless others, vulnerable populations are increasingly relying on NGOs to protect their rights and provide essential services, despite the legal imperative placed on states for doing so. Relatedly, broader networks and coalitions are building transnational membership bases to hold governments accountable and pressure them to fulfill their obligations. Engin Isin (2012) calls these groups "citizens without frontiers" and includes among them WikiLeaks, Anonymous, the Occupy movement, the Pirate Party (a European political party founded in Sweden), and the international network "No One Is Illegal." These are all examples, according to Isin, of "those who traverse frontiers citizens, blurring, if not obliterating, the boundaries between migrants and citizens" (6). This conversation calls into question the narratives of sovereignty and connectivity (12); a growing "traversal citizenship" recognizes the right to act across or against frontiers (149). "The question about citizenship is not about whether sovereignty is waning or waxing," writes Isin. "It is that the narrative of the nation-state-people-territory has become contested to the point where it is losing its credibility" (32).

In the face of these globalized challenges, scholars vary widely in their interpretations of the value and meaning of legal nationality. In response to the increasing acceptance of universal human rights norms and the growing impacts of nonstate actors, discussions frequently turn toward the erosion of state citizenship and the decline of the nation-state. James Rosenau (1990), for instance, writes that fundamental changes in the world system, or "turbulence," is relocating the authority of states outward toward trans-national collectivities and inward to subnational actors. Many scholars contend that human rights frameworks have shifted the basis of entitlement from legal nationality to universal personhood, providing noncitizens with a vocabulary for claiming rights and privileges that were once normally assigned only to citizens. According to this logic, even undocumented migrants "can stand before the courts as equal persons and demand rights such as access to public education—a development that is taken as proof of the blurring distinctions between citizens and aliens" (Gündoğdu 2015, 9–10). Yasemin Nuhoğlu Soysal (1994) advocates "postnational" citizen-ship that confers upon every person "the right and duty of participation in the authority structures and public life of a polity, regardless of their his-torical or cultural ties to that community" (3). Often these approaches do not predict the end of the state altogether but rather argue that a broader conception of citizenship is necessary for understanding membership in a globalized world. The legal aspect of citizenship may remain firmly rooted in state governments—and many people may identify primarily with their immediate political communities—but the concept of global citizenship is becoming less elusive as human communities shift, spread, and interact (Schattle 2008, 137, 159). Rather than understanding citizenship merely as a fixed, legal relationship between individuals and states, citizenship can also be understood as a signaling activity in politics and society; "a series of habits, dispositions, and practices in which individuals situate themselves in all kinds of communities and immerse themselves in public narratives, as well as public debate and often public controversy and struggle" (Schattle 2012, 13–14). From this perspective, legal nationality is only one piece of what it means to be a citizen within larger human communities—and individuals may have obligations, as "good" citizens, that go beyond traditional duties to the state.[6]

Other scholars acknowledge that globalization has indeed changed the nature of membership, expanding membership in some ways while also reinforcing some roles of the state—thereby making the concept of global citizenship a complex, and perhaps unlikely, outcome. Rainer Bauböck (1994) uses the term "transnational" because it expands citizenship beyond the traditional, national frame but doesn't go so far as to constitute global political membership (20). He writes that there is a clash between the normative principles of democracy and current forms of exclusion, such as blocking many immigrants from legal nationality and permanent residency status. This has led to the emergence of interstate citizenship (for instance, in the European Union) and the evolution of human rights law, albeit with weak enforcement mechanisms (20–21). Conversely, Étienne Balibar (2011) argues that agreements such as the Schengen Convention in Europe are not building transnational citizenships at all, but rather are *anti-citizenship* by extending the jurisdictions of security forces and coordinating efforts to violate basic rights, including the rights to asylum and nationality. These transnational mechanisms of exclusion extend borders and create new, invisible boundaries within broader societies (78). Christian Joppke (2010) similarly notes that "the diagnosis of postnational membership" leaves out the "role, if not the revenge" of the state; only formal citizenship status entitles a person to a full range of rights, and noncitizens never reach the "position of comfort allotted to them by postnationalists" (84). Alexander Diener and Joshua Hagen (2010) acknowledge that processes of transnationalism and transmigration have changed the roles of borders, but they caution against accepting the notion that state sovereignty, national economies, and human identities have been de-territorialized. Arguing that all borders and territories are social constructions, they believe that the development of supranational institutions such as the EU and the North American Free Trade Agreement require scholars to reconceptualize the ever-changing function

---

[6] Trevor Stack (2012) offers an example with his research on the meaning of citizenship in two regions of Mexico, where he discovered that respondents understood citizenship in terms of rights (such as participation in politics and accessing an array of social rights) but also according to what he termed "civil sociality." In contrast to rights-based notions of citizenship, many of Stack's interviews focused on obligations that arise from living in society; such citizenship is grounded in sociality and the ideal of trying to live, as a good citizen, in a civil way that benefited a given society—a community, yet not necessarily a state.

and meaning of borders—but to keep in mind that "a borderless world is not an imminent possibility" (4). Indeed, Gündoğdu (2015) notes that globalized reconfigurations of sovereignty, citizenship, and rights have not solved pervasive problems for migrants; the distinction between citizen and alien "has proved to be quite resilient" and migrants "are still more likely to be subject to numerous forms of violence and abuse" while facing various types of discrimination and being excluded from protective legal mechanisms by which to claim their rights (10). In her related work on statelessness and political membership, Kelly Staples (2012) argues that human rights discourse is "limited by its need to hold on to the fiction that the importance of citizenship (or membership) has been eroded" and contends that "the reliance of the idea of human rights on this assumption inevitably constrains its ability to constructively theorize the value of membership" (7).

Contradictory Notions of Citizenship

Despite the challenges of globalization, the concept of citizenship continues to have persistent power and appeal. Around the world, people who possess citizenship devote enormous amounts of energy to exclude others from attaining the same legal status, while ample evidence suggests that citizenship afford privileges that noncitizens cannot access. Sheila Croucher (2004) notes that "citizenship's apparent demise as a central or salient form of belonging exists alongside equally persuasive examples of its invigoration or reinvigoration. And, ironically, citizenship's invigoration is often a reaction or response to many of the same aspects of globalization that are deemed responsible for its demise" (61). Interestingly, conceptions of the value and meaning of citizenship vary greatly—and often contradict each other. Citizenship is framed as a universal human right—and a necessary tool for protecting other rights—by members of the global rights regime, including the UNHCR and various NGOs. Yet citizenship is frequently equated with national identity, narrowing the space for multiculturalism and actions to provide universal access to legal status and documentation. At the same time, an increasing number of the world's financial elite are obtaining multiple citizenships, taking advantage of "passports for sale" schemes to increase their access to resources and mobility. Citizenship as a commodity, which privileges citizenship as a resource rather than a right or a national identity, highlights the impact of neoliberalism on current approaches to citizenship. Taken together, these three contradictory approaches to citizenship highlight the complexity of this issue and ensuing debates about its value and meaning.

Citizenship as a Right

The "right to a nationality" was established by Article 15(1) of the UDHR and has been reinforced by numerous sources of international human rights law since 1948,[7] yet the deprivation of citizenship has only recently entered global consciousness as a widespread human rights concern. Despite evidence that statelessness led to other human rights violations in cases around the world, the issue largely remained a forgotten human rights crisis (Kingston 2013). That situation began to change rapidly when the UNHCR launched its ten-year "I Belong" campaign to eliminate statelessness globally in November 2014. Their focus is on achieving a "critical mass" of states party to the statelessness conventions and eliminating barriers to legal nationality for children and minorities (United Nations High Commissioner for Refugees 2014b). Like the other actors currently working on this issue, the UNHCR's main strategies for combating statelessness tend to be primarily focused on gaining (or re-gaining) legal status for those who do not currently have citizenship to any state (see United Nations High Commissioner for Refugees 2014a).

While it can be argued that the current legalistic focus on citizenship provision ignores subtle yet key realities about marginalization and rights abuse (an issue we return to in Chapter 2), this work has nevertheless achieved important goals related to the "right to a nationality" in a relatively short amount of time. In the first year of the UNHCR campaign, for instance, four countries acceded to the 1961 Convention on the Reduction of Statelessness—including Italy, which became the sixty-fifth state in the world (and the nineteenth in the twenty-eight-member European Union) to accede to the legally binding convention (United Nations High Commissioner for Refugees n.d.c.). In West Africa, the Member States

---

[7] Article 15(2) of the UDHR further stipulates that no one shall be "arbitrarily deprived of his nationality" (United Nations General Assembly 1948). Article 24(3) of the 1966 International Covenant on Civil and Political Rights contends that "every child has the right to acquire a nationality" (United Nations High Commissioner for Human Rights 1966a). The 1954 Convention Relating to the Status of Stateless Persons and the 1961 Convention on the Reduction of Statelessness are key legal instruments for protecting stateless people around the world and reducing lack of legal nationality (see United Nations High Commissioner for Refugees 1954 and 1961). Issues related to statelessness, such as access to birth registration and nondiscrimination in nationality laws, are addressed in the Convention on the Elimination of all Forms of Discrimination against Women (UN Women 1979) and the Convention on the Rights of the Child (United Nations High Commissioner for Human Rights 1989).

of the Economic Community of West African States (ECOWAS) adopted the Abidjan Declaration on the eradication of statelessness in February 2015. Since then, thousands of birth certificates have been reportedly distributed to populations at risk of statelessness in the disputed area of Kourou Koualou, which is claimed by both Burkina Faso and Benin, and to children of Mauritanian parents in the southern region of Kai in Mali. Countries such as Guinea, Burkina Faso, Liberia, and Togo have announced revisions to their nationality laws, while Senegal is working to elaborate on protections against childhood statelessness (United Nations High Commissioner for Refugees 2016b). In November 2015, Members of Parliament (MPs) from thirty-nine countries gathered in South Africa to collaborate on a plan for eliminating statelessness; their final outcome document advocated seven concrete steps, including reviewing nationality laws and linking the issue to plans for achieving the United Nations' Sustainable Development Goals (Boroto 2015).

These achievements represent heartening progress toward the full protection of the right to citizenship, yet challenges remain—particularly in instances in which the state interests and identities are threatened by the provision of legal nationality. Indeed, approaching citizenship from a human rights perspective directly challenges traditional approaches, which posit the granting of legal nationality as a sovereign right of the state. Concerns about national security and identity—heightened by the risks of terrorism and waves of migration noted previously—give pause to many governments on the issue of citizenship as a universal human right. If citizenship becomes more accepted as a human right in itself rather than a matter of state interest, Peter Spiro (2004) contends that "international discipline of state citizenship practices will become more exacting and universalist" (88)—but with a range of consequences in regard to identity and belonging. The protection of nationality rights and the acceptance of plural nationality, for instance, would protect the "right to a nationality" outlined in international law but could diminish "state-based solidarities" in the long term, weakening the ties of territorially defined communities (101). Dual citizenship, once considered "obnoxious to international order," is now perceived "in part as a matter of individual autonomy and identity" (88). Naturalization and birth citizenship, once under the jurisdiction of state governments, are now matters (in some respects, at least) for international law. Standards for the elimination and prevention of statelessness, for instance, place constraints on citizenship practice and state sovereignty. These baselines "will constrain a state's core capacity to define its citizenry" (88).

Citizenship as Identity

Citizenship is frequently equated with shared national identity, laying the foundation for intense political debates about globalized threats to cohesive identities in the face of mass migration. Worries about the loss of cultural hegemony underpin anti-migrant sentiment in Europe and North America, for instance, although these fears tend to manifest in different ways. In Western Europe, fears often center on cultural fragmentation and stress challenges to integration—particularly in relation to Muslim newcomers, who are viewed with increasing suspicion in the wake of terrorist attacks and the rise of ISIS. In the United Kingdom, politicians and journalists frequently debate whether Muslims can "feel British"—that is, share common civic values with the majority population and exhibit a wider knowledge of (and self-identification with) British culture, history, institutional heritage, and approved kinds of political activities and engagement (Meer et al. 2015, 170). Similarly in the Netherlands, the building of mosques and the use of religious symbols such as the headscarf have led to nativist debates about the potential harmful impacts of Muslim minorities. This "closed, static conception of culture" leads Marieke Slootman and Jan Willem Duyvendak (2015) to argue that the "culturalization and emotionalization of citizenship has taken place," making citizenship less about rights and duties and more about "norms and values of a culturally defined community" in this case (147–148). In North America, national identity is often linked to multiculturalism and the value of diversity,[8] yet frequent debates still focus on issues of language, race, and legal status. Anti-immigrant sentiments aimed at Mexicans and Mexican Americans in the United States, for instance, often contend that a lack of American identification (which alleges lack of commitment and loyalty to the United States) will hurt national stability and prosperity.[9] The widespread acceptance of these

---

[8] Irene Bloemraad (2015) notes that recent survey data show that Americans and Canadians tend to view multiculturalism positively, linking diversity to national identity despite nativist strains within political debates. To explain transatlantic differences in contemporary national identity, Bloemraad challenges simplistic readings of history—which contend that the United States and Canada are natural bastions of multiculturalism because of their long history of immigration—and argues that three key causal processes ensued. First, national identity change was initiated by native-born minorities before the onset of large-scale non-White migration. Second, generous citizenship policy (through birth or naturalization) and a relatively open political system, combined with political engagement by migrants, opened political space for ethnic minorities. Third, civil rights and diversity gains were formally institutionalized through law, policy, and social systems such as public education and state bureaucracies (60–61).

[9] Drawing on results from a large-scale telephone survey in 2004, Deborah Schildkraut (2015) argues that "fears of widespread rejection of American identity are overblown and that adopting a non-American identity is often inconsequential" (84). Rather, trust in American political

beliefs was exhibited by US presidential candidate Donald Trump, who regularly disparaged Mexican immigrants on the campaign trail in 2016, calling for mass deportations and the building of an extensive border wall between the United States and Mexico. He famously insisted that the Mexican government would "happily" pay for the construction, prompting former Mexican President Vicente Fox to declare: "I am not going to pay for that f*cking wall" (Krauze 2016) and inspiring widespread international criticism from many individuals, including the head of the Roman Catholic Church, Pope Francis. On both sides of the Atlantic, competition for resources also factors into nativist fears; citizens worry that their access to jobs, housing, and other opportunities will be reduced by the presence of migrants and their children (see Foner and Simon 2015).

While political debates frequently center on national identities, the formulation of citizenship-as-identity is wrought with difficulties. As noted in the Introduction, Anthony Smith (1991) defines a nation as "a named human population sharing an historic territory, common myths and historical memories, a mass, public culture, a common economy and common legal rights and duties for all members" (14). However, the legitimacy of such long-standing identities is increasingly called into question. Isin (2002) cautions one to be skeptical toward "harmonious and continuous narratives provided by citizens, noting that national identities are often defined by contrasting the "virtuous" against a foreign other (3). Group affiliation is a tactical resource for survival and power accumulation, and Isin notes that the creation of identity groups requires "specific practical work" (27) as well as relationships to others that value certain attributes while devaluing others (30). Ernest Gellner (1983) argues that globalized forces of industrialization led to many of the ethnic-national traditions that were later central to the establishment of modern states. From this modernist perspective, nationalist identities in recent centuries have been imaginary constructions rather than organic sources of identity. Benedict Anderson (2006) famously revised such modernist theses, arguing that almost all forms of community are imagined in some way. He wrote that national identities are created or produced—they are often *imagined* from the very beginning. Anderson contended that nationalism is rooted not in "self-consciously-held political ideologies," but rather with the large cultural systems that preceded it, such as religious communities (12). In his

---

institutions and obligations to national community depend greatly on "how people feel they or their group is treated"; identity attachments are far less important than perceptions of discrimination for building trust and obligation to one's new "home" country (85).

attempt to interpret the concept of "nationalism," Anderson wrote that it was vital to understand how nations came into historical being, how they changed over time, and why today they command "such profound emotional legitimacy" (4). From this perspective, the nation is not a natural unit or an organic community but rather an identification that has been culturally influenced and created by historical forces over time—subject to change and reinterpretation, like all social constructions.

Understandings of the nation and national identity are also problematized by the fact that nations do not always represent states; indeed, many states recognized within the current international system are multicultural states comprising various nations—with only one system of formal state citizenship. In multicultural states, discussions of citizenship have shifted "from a focus on political practice based on shared civic rights and responsibilities to an insistence on the protection of cultural differences," particularly as new waves of migrants challenge hegemonic majority cultures (Ong 2004, 53). In the past, theorists such as Rosseau sought to assure recognition by converting human equality into identity (via citizenship), but multiculturalist scholars such as Amy Gutmann (1994) contend that this formulation simply doesn't work. She writes that citizenship cannot constitute a comprehensive identity because first, "people are unique, self-creating, and creative individuals," and second, "people are also 'culture-bearing,' and the cultures they bear differ depending on their past and present identifications" (6–7). Indeed, Charles Taylor (1994) notes that a focus on human dignity and individual identity, made possible in part by global human rights norms, have made the modern preoccupation with identity and recognition inevitable (26–30). He contends that "due recognition is not just a courtesy we owe people," but rather it is "a vital human need" (26). From this perspective, nonrecognition or misrecognition—including attempts to encapsulate all perspectives under the broad notion of citizenship-as-identity—can inflict harm and constitute a form of oppression. Will Kymlicka (1995) similarly argues that common citizenship strategies disadvantage minority groups, since the stance that state citizens constitute a single political community assumes that the state takes precedence over smaller nations located within its borders. He contends that imposing common citizenship will increase conflicts in multinational states, creating unchecked vulnerabilities for minorities when it comes to economic and political decisions of the majority (183–184). Kymlicka (1995) notes that it is impossible to eliminate nations or minority identities; "If anything, attempts to subordinate these separate identities to a common identity have backfired, since they are perceived by minorities as threats to their very existence, and so have resulted in even greater indifference or resentment" (185).

Citizenship as a Commodity

Neoliberalism is often approached as an economic doctrine that limits state power, but market ideology can also be framed as a new relationship with governments that allows some governing activities to be reframed as nonpolitical problems in need of technical, market-driven solutions (Ong 2006, 3). Aihwa Ong (2006) writes that the elements commonly associated with citizenship—rights, entitlements, territoriality, and nation—"are becoming disarticulated and rearticulated with forces set in motion by market forces" (6). Mobile individuals who possess human capital or expertise are highly valued in the global economy and can exercise "citizenship-like claims" in locations around the world, claiming entitlements and benefits outside the state of their legal nationality (7). Yet citizens who don't have such competences or potential are devalued and subject to exclusion (7). Elizabeth F. Cohen (2015, 2018) illustrates this dynamic in her work on "immigrant time," which analyzes the inequalities of US naturalization policies. For much of US history, continuous time-in-residence plus good moral character and civic knowledge eventually equaled the attainment of citizenship. Yet for increasing numbers of noncitizens, this equation no longer applies; those who lack human capital and expertise, as outlined by Ong (2006), find that their time-in-residence is assessed as politically valueless. These individuals include those registered with deferred departure, guest workers, people with temporary protected status (TPS), and undocumented workers (Cohen 2015, 2018). "Because time and work and other variables are proxies for demonstrating people's capacities for citizenship, the denial of citizenship expresses the belief that these individuals are *incapable* of citizenship," Cohen (2015) writes (349). She further notes that suggesting certain groups are less capable of citizenship conjures "the kind of arguments that were once used to claim that women and racial minorities were incapable of consent, patriotism, or other means of entering the *demos*" (Cohen 2015, 350).

Citizenship is increasingly being viewed as a commodity that provides resources and opportunities—and that can, in many cases, be purchased from state governments by members of the global financial elite. A second (or third) citizenship may provide a range of benefits, from tax incentives to ease of international travel to paths around trade restrictions. Christian Kalin of Henley & Partners, the largest firm specializing in "turning citizenship into a commodity," notes that multiple citizenships provide security to his clients: "It's a question of mobility and also security," Kalin says. "If you're from a country that's politically unstable, where you're not sure what the future holds, you want to have an alternative" (quoted in Clenfield 2015). Individuals can purchase citizenship to the Caribbean state of St. Kitts and Nevis by investing $250,000 USD without having ever set foot on the island; the price tag buys new citizens visa-free travel to 132 countries, limited disclosure of financial information, and no taxes on income or capital gains. Similar citizenship-by-investment plans have been laid out in states such as Cyprus, Grenada, Antigua, and Malta—among others (Clenfield 2015). Critics contend that such plans create loopholes to assist terrorist activity, fraud, and tax evasion (Clenfield 2015) as well as diminish the value of citizenship as a marker of identity and belonging. In the European Union, member states criticized Malta for "cheapening" the value of EU citizenship by effectively selling Maltese citizenship for an investment of 1.15 million euros (with lower rates for extended family members). The Maltese government bowed to pressure by requiring a one-year residency period for naturalization while at the same time it considered raising naturalization caps to issue more passports to new citizens (BBC News 2014). In Kuwait, the issuance of "economic citizenship" to the country of Comoros (without the right to vote or even live permanently in the state) has even been advanced as a "solution" to stateless individuals among the *bidoon* minority (Abrahamian 2015, 47). While the process of citizenship-by-investment is markedly different from the ways in which migrants illegally obtain documentation, it is nonetheless related; for the right price, it is possible to purchase "documentary citizenship" in countries with weak bureaucracies, such as India and Malaysia (Sadiq 2009). The purchase of false documents does not constitute the acquisition of citizenship itself, but the need for black market passports and identity documents highlights how at least the semblance of citizenship is treated as a commodity—sometimes to protect basic human rights, and sometimes to access far less basic opportunities.

Although evidence shows that citizenship is sometimes viewed instrumentally as a means of attaining other ends, recent studies suggest that citizenship has "several layers of meaning," including resources, rights, identity, and emotional connections (Fein and Straughn 2014, 700). A qualitative study of stateless Russian-speakers in Estonia found that when offered a citizenship choice between Russia and Estonia, individuals had varying motivations and ways of viewing citizenship itself. Some respondents cited the practicalities of Estonian citizenship, such as the right to ongoing residence, the ability to secure a loan, and access to employment opportunities; others made choices based, at least in part, on "matters of the heart" such as emotional connections to territory, ethnicity, or culture (Fein and Straughn 2014, 700–701). Deliberations about citizenship choice were also affected by norms of justice and propriety, reciprocal obligations, and mutual respect "that transcend citizenship's legalistic dimensions and exceed the bounds of utilitarian rationality" (Fein and Straughn 2014, 700). Similarly, a study of formerly stateless resettled refugees living in the US state of New York found that the attainment of US citizenship was valuable because it meant access to resources and protections—including the enjoyment of physical security, diplomatic protection while traveling overseas, and adequate access to food and medicine—but also because it created a path to a state-sponsored identity and political community (Kingston and Stam 2017). Israeli citizens who acquired dual nationality reported that their second citizenship was detached from identity, yet it became a powerful symbol of freedom. The second citizenship was used "as a means for negotiation and agency, not due to its legal entitlements or its binding status as an identity precursor, but because it was imagined to embody other life possibilities, thus allowing for an active negotiation of belonging" (Leuchter 2014, 787). Noa Leuchter argues that this case study shows that while people still understand citizenship in relation to national identity, such forms of dual citizenship make loyalty "a matter of choice, not of chance" (787) and highlight how various dimensions of citizenship can be entangled in both theory and in praxis (788).

These diverse perspectives on the value and meaning of citizenship help us begin to understand the challenges inherent in any discussion of legal nationality and human rights protection. A passport—something that seems so simple and straightforward—has the ability to invoke the strongest of emotions about belonging and community, as well as to represent immense power, wealth, and privilege. From a human rights perspective, the political membership tied up in the ideal of citizenship ought to belong to all human beings; the right to a nationality is meant to guarantee a right to place and, by extension, rights to purpose. Yet we have seen how citizenship is not an equally distributed social good, and that noncitizens and various vulnerable groups suffer protection gaps that threaten their human dignity. Simply put, legal nationality is not enough to be recognized as fully human. If we acknowledge that citizenship exists on a spectrum, then we must fully understand the hierarchies of personhood this creates. Let us begin in Chapter 2 with the most extreme deprivation of status, the most troubling and stark example of life without functioning citizenship: statelessness.

PART II | Newcomers and Noncitizens

CHAPTER 2 | Statelessness and Elusive Political Membership

REFLECTING ON THE STATE of Europe, political theorist Hannah Arendt (1966) wrote that "the days before and the days after the first World War are separated not like the end of an old and the beginning of a new period, but like the day before and the day after an explosion," except "the quiet of sorrow which settles down after a catastrophe" had never come to pass (267). Indeed, the World Wars ushered in a new era of mass displacement and statelessness previously unknown to Europe or beyond. By the end of World War II, millions of displaced persons emerged from their work camps, factories, mines, makeshift shelters, and prisons to find a "landscape of chaos" where "hundreds of thousands were effectively abandoned to look after themselves" (Lowe 2012, 69 and 29). For those seeking protections from the international community in the face of fascism and Nazism, the essential feature of refugeehood was persecution rather than the absence of legal nationality. Yet most European refugees at the time were assumed to be stateless and few challenged the "automatic portrayal of refugees as legal anomalies" (Cohen 2012, 85). Statelessness was thus equated with a loss of fundamental rights yet relegated to a lesser role as a legal category, failing to confer minority protection or rights to self-determination. Instead, the aim was to alleviate statelessness by providing legal nationality, assuming that citizenship was the "natural guardian of human rights" (Cohen 2012, 88). In the era of postwar liberal internationalism, statelessness was viewed as "repairable through reinstatement into a community of rights, the sovereign nation-state kept in check by international guarantees" (Cohen 2012, 88).

Generations later, the condition of statelessness—lack of legal nationality to any country—continues to trap millions of people around the world, ranging from displaced persons fleeing persecution to individuals who simply want to securely remain "home" in the communities where they were born. Just as photographs of exhausted and seemingly hopeless faces of stateless refugees stare back at us from our history books, we see similar expressions of frustration and despair on the countenances of stateless people alive today. "No one can imagine what it is like to be stateless," a stateless man told documentary photographer Greg Constantine in 2011. "I fly through this life with nowhere to land." Images captured by Constantine show the human faces of denied rights; children unable to attend school, parents unable to work legally, families denied healthcare and police protections against violence (see Constantine n.d.; Constantine 2015). For many stateless people, attempts to move beyond the catastrophes of denationalization or denied nationality claims have been stalled by a human rights regime that assumes one's relationship to a government. Indeed, the international community's emphasis on state duty-bearers for rights protection inadvertently provides a tool to marginalize minority groups and punish dissenters. Within the hierarchy of personhood, the stateless represent the starkest instance of denied human worth; they are claimed by no government, often lacking the legal entitlement to exist in a territory or be part of a community. Denied recognition and rights protection, they are often caught in a state of limbo that prevents them from accessing the rights to place and purpose necessary for fully achieving a life of dignity.

Yet despite these challenges, many stateless people continue to fight against the hierarchies of personhood that render them legally invisible and exclude them from mainstream political participation. The stateless claim political agency in various ways despite government efforts to silence their voices and separate them from the citizenry. They strategize ways around immigration rules and through residency loopholes; they establish advocacy networks to help spread their messages to the broader international community; they engage in activism despite persistent threats of state-sanctioned violence. These acts of political agency (and rebellion) show us that governments don't hold the keys to all political power and expression. Instead, membership in a political community can stem from shared conceptions of personhood and human dignity—with or without legal nationality. Even as rights to place and purpose are challenged by the very governments tasked with protecting them, stateless people continue to push for their fundamental human rights and, ultimately, for functioning citizenship. Political membership in these circumstances is indeed an elusive goal, but stateless people forcefully remind us that legal status should not—indeed cannot—be confused with worthiness as human beings.

Statelessness and the "Right to a Nationality"

Modern discussions of statelessness are often linked to the work of Arendt (1966), who famously argued that the stateless were denied the "right to have rights." Stripped of her German citizenship and forced to flee the Nazi regime, she lived as a stateless person for more than a decade before becoming a naturalized US citizen. She argued that the "stubborn" and "far-reaching" mass phenomenon of statelessness was tied to political events since the end of World War I and continued to add new categories to those "who lived outside the pale of the law" (277). Statelessness in Europe was created by the dissolution of states, by the denationalization of citizens, and sometimes from the actions of individuals who took refuge in statelessness to avoid being deported to foreign "homelands." Arendt (1966) criticized idealists and their dreams of inalienable human rights, which she claimed "are enjoyed only by citizens of the most prosperous and civilized countries," versus the "rightless" who were unable to access such protections (279). Despite guarantees of "inalienable" Rights of Man, conceptualized as being independent from governments, Arendt (1966) wrote that "it turned out that the moment human beings lacked their own government and had to fall back upon their minimum rights, no authority was left to protect them and no institution was willing to guarantee them" (292). Those rights "proved to be unenforceable," even when inscribed in state constitutions, "whenever people appeared who were no longer citizens of any sovereign state"—leading Arendt (1966) to lament attempts to frame a new bill of rights (in reference to the 1948 Universal Declaration of Human Rights, or UDHR) as something separate from the rights of state citizens (293). The key problem, according to Arendt (1966), was that stateless people lacked the protections and recognition provided by functioning citizenship. She argued:

> The calamity of the rightless is not that they are deprived of life, liberty, and the pursuit of happiness, or of equality before the law and freedom of opinion—formulas which were designed to solve problems *within* given communities—but that they no longer belong to any community whatsoever. Their plight is not that they are not equal before the law, but that no

law exists for them; not that they are oppressed but that nobody wants even to oppress them. Only in the last stage of a rather lengthy process is their right to live threatened; only if they remain perfectly "superfluous," if nobody can be found to "claim" them, may their lives be in danger. Even the Nazis started their extermination of Jews by first depriving them of all legal status (the status of second-class citizenship) and cutting them off from the world of the living by herding them into ghettos and concentration camps; and before they set the gas chambers in motion they had carefully tested the ground and found out to their satisfaction that no country would claim these people. The point is that a condition of complete rightlessness was created before the right to live was challenged. (295–296)

Giorgio Agamben (1998) further considers the condition of rightlessness by conceptualizing the juxtaposition of "inclusive exclusion" through the life of *homo sacer* (sacred man). *Homo sacer* represents a form of "bare life" that "may be killed and yet not sacrificed" (8). Agamben argues that Western politics centers on the categorical pairings of bare life/political existence, exclusion/inclusion; within *homo sacer*'s "state of exception," bare life is no longer an object of political power, but rather it is a subject of it. "At once excluding bare life from and capturing it within the political order, the state of exception actually constituted, in its very separateness, the hidden foundation on which the entire political system rested," he writes (9). Indeed, "life is sacred only insofar as it is taken into the sovereign exception" (85); despite the fundamental right to life, Agamben contends that "the production of bare life is the originary activity of sovereignty" (83). From this perspective, the ideals of human rights can be "shattered by the dominance of the politics of fact and situation" as determined by the sovereign state (Lechte and Newman 2013, 4). For instance, particular situations have driven the application or suspension of law, such as waiving protections if security is perceived as being under threat. The state of emergency serves as a state of exception in which ideals are suspended in response to current political events. Here "power works by the threat or application of violence and the use of force in the state of exception"; for Agamben, human rights effectively cannot survive because they "have been contaminated by the logic of fact and situation, so that the human has become the factual biological entity without any transcendence" (Lechte and Newman 2013, 4).

From these perspectives, it is perhaps no surprise that statelessness serves as a root cause of further human rights abuse and creates serious obstacles to claiming the basic rights central to a life of dignity, place, and purpose. Although legal nationality does not guarantee the full pro-tection of human rights, its provision is often viewed as an essential pre-requisite for the mere possibility of its achievement. The Institute on Statelessness and Inclusion (2014) notes that the "harsh reality for many stateless persons is a story of lack of opportunity, lack of protection, and lack of participation" (29). These limitations affect all areas of life, in-cluding receiving an education, accessing healthcare, working legally, buying or inheriting property, signing contracts, obtaining official paper-work (such as birth certificates, driving licenses, marriage certificates, and even death certificates), opening bank accounts and accessing credit, claiming social security and pensions, obtaining a passport and traveling freely—and the list continues (29–30). Clearly there are cases in which citizens struggle to enjoy the full range of these rights, but research on formerly stateless populations confirms that the acquisition of legal na-tionality leads to significant human rights gains. A comparative global study on the benefits of citizenship highlights the positive impacts that formerly stateless individuals experience when states provide legal nation-ality to some minority populations; findings from Slovenia, Sri Lanka, Mauritania, and Kenya show how resulting identity documentation is es-sential for accessing public services, reducing the risk of police brutality and deportation, and participating in the political life of one's community (Lynch and Blitz 2011). A 2014 qualitative study of formerly stateless resettled refugees in the United States further shows that the acquisition of legal nationality and status are key for accessing resources, enjoying polit-ical membership and identity, and protecting physical security (Kingston and Stam 2017).

For stateless children—including infants who are denied registration and legal nationality at birth—countries are "letting them down, right from the start" by denying them the essential resources for claiming rights to place and purpose. Legal nationality serves as children's "legal bond that formalizes their membership of a community and provides protection, rights, empowerment, a sense of acceptance and inclusion" (European Network on Statelessness 2015, 7). Without this legal bond and access to functioning citizenship, stateless children face severe challenges to acquiring documentation and legal identity; they experience obstacles to education and healthcare, forced movement, harsh living conditions, sepa-ration from families, vulnerabilities to exploitation and human trafficking, social exclusion, and targeted discrimination (Lynch 2010). Although the problem of childhood statelessness remains under-researched, Jacqueline Bhabha (2011) contends that statelessness is a particularly important child rights issue because minors are "peculiarly dependent on states" to provide basic services and to offer support when families fail them (13). Statelessness is "potentially devastating for a child because it jeopardizes the child's automatic claim to inclusion by and attention from the state," she writes. "It is therefore a key indicator of vulnerability, a proxy for problematic access to essential resources, services, and protections. Statelessness in children . . . has profound human rights repercussions" (3). Indeed, children who have some form of legal status—such as legal nationality or refugee status—have been found to enjoy "considerably greater access to rights," such as education and healthcare, compared to their stateless counterparts (Blitz 2011, 61). While legal identity alone does not guarantee a good life, "its absence is a serious impediment to it" that "interferes with many fundamental encounters between the individual and the state. It affects the individual's capacity to make claims on the state, and it disrupts the state's ability to plan and provide resources and services to the individual" (Bhabha 2011, 1).

International human rights law and frameworks establish principles for preventing and reducing statelessness, which in turn are meant to stem the negative consequences related to lack of legal status. The "right to a nationality" outlined in Article 15 of the UDHR (United Nations General Assembly 1948) is closely connected to the concept of "effective nationality," or legal nationality as the foundation of exercising other rights. These principles have been developed with landmarks such as the 1930 Hague Convention on Certain Questions relating to the Conflict of Nationality Laws and the 1997 European Convention on Nationality, as well as re-inforced by international law such as the 1966 International Covenant on Civil and Political Rights, the 1957 Convention on the Nationality of Married Women, the 1979 Convention on the Elimination of all Forms of Discrimination against Women (CEDAW), and the 1989 Convention on the Rights of the Child. The key international legal instruments addressing statelessness, however, are the 1954 Convention relating to the Status of Stateless Persons and the 1961 Convention on the Reduction of Statelessness. The 1954 Convention defines a stateless person as someone who is "not recognized as a national by any state under the operation of its law" (United Nations High Commissioner for Refugees 1954, Article 1.1). It seeks to ensure that stateless people enjoy a minimum set of human rights, including those related to education, employment, housing, identity, and travel documentation (United Nations High Commissioner for Refugees 1954). The 1961 Convention aims to prevent statelessness, as well as to reduce it over time by requiring states to safeguard their nationality laws to prevent statelessness at birth and later in life (such as in cases of state succession or denationalization) (United Nations High Commissioner for Refugees 1961).

Although the international community tends to focus on de jure statelessness (the condition of having no legal nationality), the term "de facto statelessness" is frequently used to describe those facing similar human rights challenges. De facto statelessness implies that a person lacks an effective nationality and suffers from many of the same human rights consequences as the de jure stateless. The de facto stateless "are persons outside the country of their nationality who are unable or, for valid reasons, are unwilling to avail themselves of the protection of that country" (Massey 2010, 61). In cases of de facto statelessness, a person has legal nationality but is unable to enjoy the rights associated with such status. This may occur due to legal oversights or mistakes, but is often the result of crime (such as slavery and human trafficking) or state discrimination against minority groups (Weissbrodt and Divine 2016, 873). However, this terminology is increasingly problematized by statelessness scholars who contend that differentiating between de jure and de facto statelessness ignores important realities about effective citizenship in general. On the one hand, scholars such as Jason Tucker (2014) acknowledge the harms of ineffective citizenship but contend that statelessness should refer only to individuals without legal nationality—whether functioning or not. He warns against trying to broaden the definition of statelessness, arguing that it will possibly weaken advocacy efforts and attempts to forge appropriate international protections. On the other hand, some advocates warn that certain vulnerable populations require protections from an expanded understanding of statelessness, including those outside their country of nationality who face real risks of serious harm but who do not qualify for refugee status for a variety of reasons. Although the UNHCR continues to struggle with appropriate methods for identifying and measuring instances of de facto statelessness, it remains a category of concern (Massey 2010).

State nationality laws ought to reflect international principles, yet in reality these ideals often fall short. International instruments and approaches provide useful guidance for combating statelessness, but ultimately it is the state that grants legal nationality by operation of its domestic law and establishment of its parameters. The UNHCR estimates that at least 10 million people around the world lack legal nationality—of which approximately one-third are children—yet data gathering is difficult and the exact number of stateless people is unknown (United Nations High

Commissioner for Refugees n.d.d).[1] Carol Batchelor (1998) argues that "statelessness is not only a legal problem, it is a human problem"; she contends that rather than relying on preexisting legal structures and vastly different state approaches for determining legal nationality, the international system needs a "broader, more universal means of applying national legislation" to protect the right to a nationality outlined by international principles (182). Laura van Waas (2011) warns that specific protection needs for the stateless are unaddressed in international frameworks, providing states with vague guidelines for implementing domestic laws. These shortcomings suggest "a much more comprehensive crisis whereby the implementation and enforcement of the normative framework is failing" (37). For instance, there is an absence of agreement on the identification of "stateless persons," which includes confusion about the status of the de facto stateless, and states are left to devise their own procedures with little guidance. Without a supervisory agency to monitor and enforce the proper treatment of the stateless—and no way to offer diplomatic protection for a stateless person, since they do not have a legal relationship to a state—the international norms related to nationality are often difficult to implement at the state level (van Waas 2011, 37–39).

Remaining tension between universal rights norms and the privileging of state sovereignty create further challenges. For instance, nondiscrimination is inherent to universal rights but a few lawful exceptions are permissible in relation to state rights under international law. Human rights law generally prohibits discriminatory enforcement of human rights based on identity—including "race, colour, sex, language, religion, political or other opinion, national or social origin, property, birth or other status" (United Nations General Assembly 1948, Article 2). This principle provides human rights protections for stateless persons, who are rights claimants by virtue of their human existence. Yet the International Covenant on Civil and Political Rights allows states to distinguish between citizens and noncitizens in regard to some political rights (such as voting) and freedom of movement (United Nations High Commissioner for Human Rights 1966a). Similarly, the International Covenant on Economic, Social, and Cultural Rights allows developing nations to limit the provision of economic rights afforded to noncitizens (United Nations High Commissioner for Human Rights 1966b). Despite protections against discrimination

---

[1] Such limits on information is nothing new; Arendt (1966) deplored the lack of reliable statistics following the World Wars and argued that this data gap was tied to "the decision of the statesmen to solve the problem of statelessness by ignoring it" (279).

based on national or social origin, "there remains a disparity between prescribed rights and the realities noncitizens must face"—sometimes due to "economic inability or practical reality," or as a result of "geopolitics, nationalism, and/or outright racism" (Weissbrodt and Divine 2016, 873). When Arendt was critiquing international human rights after the World Wars, the prevailing assumption was that everyone had citizenship some-where; statelessness was cast "as an unwelcome yet anomalous condition" that "did not need to raise any questions about the ordering principles of the international system itself" (Gündoğdu 2015, 11). Today, broad ac-ceptance of human rights standards—including the universality of rights based on personhood rather than legal status—risks turning the human rights challenges faced by noncitizens into "unfortunate exceptions" to ideals that separate rights from legal nationality (Gündoğdu 2015).

In response to the problem of statelessness, the UNHCR and various NGOs have adopted a legalistic approach that emphasizes the ratification and enforcement of the statelessness conventions, universal birth registra-tion, and the provision of legal nationality to de jure stateless individuals. Plan International (n.d.), for instance, has helped register 40 million chil-dren and influenced birth registration laws in ten countries with its "Count Every Child" campaign. The European Network on Statelessness (n.d.) and the Institute on Statelessness and Inclusion (n.d.a.), both European organizations led primarily by legal scholars, advocate reformed na-tionality legislation and change within the United Nations system. The UNHCR has more than tripled its expenditures on statelessness since 2009, which includes the 2014 launch of its "I Belong" campaign to elim-inate statelessness within a decade (United Nations High Commissioner for Refugees 2014). Its Global Action Plan centers on actions to "resolve existing situations of statelessness, prevent new cases of statelessness from emerging, and better identify and protect stateless persons" (United Nations High Commissioner for Refugees 2014, 4). The UNHCR's cam-paign has set the global agenda for combating statelessness and focuses on ten strategic priorities—almost all centered on the legal acquisition of citizenship:

1. Resolve existing major situations of statelessness
2. Ensure that no child is born stateless
3. Remove gender discrimination from nationality laws
4. Prevent denial, loss, or deprivation of nationality on discriminatory grounds
5. Prevent statelessness in cases of State succession

6. Grant protection status to stateless migrants and facilitate their naturalization
7. Ensure birth registration for the prevention of statelessness
8. Issue nationality documentation to those with entitlement to it
9. Accede to the UN Statelessness Conventions
10. Improve quantitative and qualitative data on stateless populations (United Nations High Commissioner for Refugees 2014)

Such current approaches address statelessness as a human rights violation as well as a root cause of further abuse and marginalization—but they also perpetuate "thin" notions of citizenship that fail to address the ways in which statelessness serves as a symptom of wider, deeper marginalization (Kingston 2017b). Indeed, studies of statelessness tend to be "dominated by legal scholars and typically [evoke] an implicit liberal tradition of citizenship" that may ignore post-statelessness inequalities (Balaton-Chrimes 2014, 16). Liberalism's emphasis on the value of autonomy pays little attention to how a person's worldview and circumstances are influenced by others. As a result, liberalism holds a "thin" notion of citizenship that is primarily operationalized through legal status such as formal citizenship (Balaton-Chrimes 2014, 17), rather than participatory membership within a society. While current actions to eliminate statelessness are vital and well intentioned, their legalistic approaches "flatten" the problem of statelessness and posit the acquisition of legal nationality as their sole aim. Yet existing data show that the granting of citizenship "ameliorates many, but not all, of the complex problems that have roots in economic inequality, systemic discrimination and other forms of injustice" (Lynch and Blitz 2011, 207). These concerns require us to push beyond thin notions of citizenship to seriously consider what it means to truly be a member of a political community, including how statelessness is symptomatic of more pervasive challenges to the rights to place and purpose.

Symptoms of Marginalization

Statelessness is one tool of oppression that is utilized within a broader process—a process that did not start with statelessness and certainly won't end simply with the provision of legal status. To fully understand the entire scope of this problem, it is imperative to investigate both its causes and its consequences. While it is true that some technical causes of statelessness (such as oversights related to marriage, divorce, and state succession) are relatively easy to correct with policy changes, most cases are much more complicated and fraught with political tensions. Indeed, the causes of statelessness are often symptoms of broader issues within a given state—including marginalization against racial and ethnic groups, members of religious minorities, and political rivals. In their research on impacts of statelessness, Brad Blitz and Maureen Lynch (2011) argue that "elements of discrimination and inequality are common to all forms of statelessness, and it is therefore necessary to develop an understanding of the mechanisms that not only create statelessness but also perpetuate deprivation, as well as those common elements found in solving state-lessness and restoring nationality" (5). In her work on childhood state-lessness, Bhabha (2011) further contends that "children who are stateless end up without a state for a reason: they are considered dispensable, un-deserving, threatening, or dangerous" (22). In short, statelessness isn't a politically neutral occurrence that happens in a vacuum or could impact anyone; statelessness affects *certain* people because they were deemed unworthy of membership and rights protection in their community. Their lack of functioning citizenship—and the resulting protections on rights to place and purpose—is so fundamentally lacking that they are denied the most basic semblance of political identity: legal nationality.

Methods of rendering people stateless—which include denationaliza-tion, exclusionary citizenship laws, and inequalities that obstruct regis-tration and naturalization—highlight how lack of legal nationality serves as a symptom of social problems that run deep (Kingston 2017b). In the case of denationalization, or stripping a citizen of their previous legal na-tionality, the denial of status is often used in times of conflict to "purify" communities of minority groups or punish political opponents. This weap-onization of citizenship has been increasingly utilized since World War II, when Nazi Germany revoked legal nationality from minorities in the years leading up to the Holocaust. The German state defined a citizen of the Reich as an individual "of German or related blood" and limited the enjoyment of political rights to legal nationals under its German Reich Citizenship Law of 1935 (one of the so-called Nuremberg Race Laws). The Law for the Protection of German Blood and German Honor further asserted that "purity of German blood is the essential condition for the con-tinued existence of the German people" and outlawed marriage between Jews and non-Jews (United States Holocaust Museum n.d.). More recent examples abound: In the 1970s and '80s, similar discriminatory citizen-ship laws were used in Bhutan to exclude Bhutanese-Nepali citizens and others outside the new legal category of "genuine Bhutanese," prompting en masse migration to neighboring Nepal in 1990 under severe pressure from the government. Those who were categorized as "non-nationals" during a 1988 census were told to leave the country or face imprisonment; those who protested faced swift action such as arrests, torture, rape by security forces, and even death (Human Rights Watch 2007). Many families were forced to hand over identity papers, sign "voluntary" migration forms, and then sit for photos; they were told to smile for the camera as evidence that they were happy to leave their homes and start new lives in Nepal—which often meant years of living in refugee camps before finally attaining permission to resettle elsewhere (Kingston and Stam 2017). Confiscating or canceling passports has also been used to silence political dissent in countries such as Rwanda, where criticizing ruling parties and political leaders is not tolerated, as well as to limit protesters' activities in places such as China. In May 2012, for example, the National Police of Rwanda cancelled the passports of twenty-five Rwandans abroad—in clear violation of international law protecting the right to a nationality and prohibiting statelessness. Many of those affected were leaders (or relatives of leaders) of the Rwandan National Congress, an opposition movement, and the act came after allegations that the government had engaged in the attempted murder and harassment of exiled opponents (Holmes 2012; see also Kingston 2017a). In China, the outspoken activist-artist Ai Weiwei was banned from leaving the country for more than four years after his passport was confiscated during a major 2011 crackdown of political activism. Although not fully denationalized, the artist was denied freedom of movement—and by extension prevented from undertaking his work or visiting his child in Europe—through this denial of citizenship rights (Phillips 2015).

Notably, denationalization is increasingly being discussed as a tool in the West's "War on Terror." As noted in the introduction, French president François Hollande proposed to strip French citizenship from dual nationals convicted of terrorism; the measure was withdrawn in March 2016 but not before highlighting a growing tension between civil rights and national security goals (Nossiter 2016). Similar stances have gained increasing support in countries such as the United States, Canada, and Norway. US senator (and former presidential candidate) Ted Cruz sponsored the "Expatriate Terrorists Act," a failed attempt to strip American citizens of their legal nationality if they were suspected (but not necessarily convicted) of involvement with a designated foreign terrorist organization. The American Civil Liberties Union (2014) argued that the bill was "dangerous because it would attempt to dilute the rights and privileges of citizenship, one of the core principles of the Constitution"—and was unnecessary because existing US laws already punished acts of terrorism. In the United Kingdom, legislation was passed in 2014 allowing the government to strip terror suspects of their British citizenship—even if it renders them stateless, in violation of international law—in a move that extends that country's existing and extensive powers to revoke legal status. The new rule broadens so-called deprivation powers and can revoke legal nationality, effective immediately and without a public hearing, if the UK home secretary determines that such citizenship is against the country's vital interests (Bennhold 2014). Matthew Gibney (2013) links this political issue to the historical evolution of banishment, arguing that ethical scrutiny of denationalization is of central importance. As such, liberals have raised three major concerns related to such withdrawal of legal nationality. First, it can lead to statelessness—which is "unjust and cruel" from a liberal perspective; second, denationalization is "invidious" and violates the principle of equal respect by generating second-class citizenship; and third, denationalization is arbitrary—and thus an illegitimate exercise of state power (Gibney 2013, 651–652).

Exclusionary citizenship laws can also be used to block minorities from accessing legal nationality, even when they have a long history of living within state borders. These practices are often met with a state's refusal to recognize a group's history of residency, including the groups' accounts of migration or indigeneity. In Thailand, for instance, members of so-called hill tribe groups are denied status as Indigenous minorities in the area and are instead labeled as "illegal" immigrants. Many were left stateless due to limitations on *jus soli* nationality provisions enacted in 1972—including the requirement that parents have permanent residency status in order for children to qualify for Thai legal nationality, blocking hill tribe children born in Thailand from acquiring citizenship. A 2008 amendment to the Thai Nationality Law potentially closed that nationality gap, but it remains questionable whether families can fully satisfy the evidentiary requirements to access legal status—particularly since many lack birth certificates, which were routinely denied to them prior to a 2008 amendment to the Thai Civil Registration Act (Rijken et al. 2015). In the European Union, tens of thousands of ethnic Romani face widespread discrimination and situations of statelessness. Vulnerable populations include Romani families who fled the former Yugoslavia during conflict in the 1990s; they are unable to access citizenship in other European countries but are no longer counted as citizens in new states such as Bosnia and Herzegovina. Critics argue that such statelessness is part of a wider pattern of anti-Roma discrimination in Europe (de Verneuil 2014). The production of stateless Roma is "not an accident" but rather the combination of long-standing prejudices and forced displacement (Sigona 2016, 272). Similarly, statelessness in Estonia has been connected to discrimination against particular identity groups, including Russian speakers, despite anti-discrimination laws within the country (Vetik 2011).

Such discrimination is intimately tied to inequalities that obstruct access to birth registration and the provision of legal status to children. Birth registration is "the continuous, permanent and universal recording within the civil registry of the occurrence and characteristics of birth," which "establishes the existence of a person under law, and lays the foundation for safeguarding civil, political, economic, social and cultural rights" (United Nations Human Rights Council 2014, 9). Yet an estimated 230 million children under the age of five have never been registered (UNICEF, 2013), perpetuating statelessness and lack of documentation for future generations. In many cases, parents are required to present their own identity documents in order to register their children (thereby discriminating against the stateless and undocumented migrants), or states refuse to register the children of noncitizens (including stateless persons and asylum-seekers) (United Nations Human Rights Council 2014). Recent data also suggests that ethnic minorities living in isolated areas and/or facing poverty are less likely to access birth registration compared to their nonminority, wealthier counterparts (UNICEF 2013), in part due to the indirect costs of registration such as missed work or the costs of illegal bribery demands (United Nations Human Rights Council 2014). In India, children from marginalized groups—including street children, children from "backward castes," the urban poor, migrants, and nomadic children—face significant obstacles to birth registration and accessing state-issued documentation. These challenges make millions of children automatically vulnerable "to the quiet discrimination and dangers that come from being 'invisible'" (Plan India 2009, 14). Issues of discrimination are exacerbated in times of conflict and emergency, which has been starkly illustrated by the intersection of gender inequality and forced displacement stemming from Syria's civil war. Gender discrimination in nationality laws within Syria and neighboring countries (including Iraq, Jordan, and Lebanon) has already created unique challenges for women to access legal nationality and pass their status on to children, with laws and social practices relying on husbands to confer legal status to the children they fathered. The consequences of armed conflict—including dead and missing fathers, child marriages, lack of identity documentation, and the inability to access birth registration—puts new pressures on refugee mothers and threatens to create a "stateless generation" of Syrians (Osborne and Russell 2015, para. 1).

For many minority groups, the marginalization that prevents birth registration often creates obstacles for naturalization. Basic human equality is associated with full political membership (Marshall 1965), so the denial of citizenship represents yet another way to exclude minorities from state protection and further discriminate against oppressed groups. Blocking marginalized individuals from becoming naturalized citizens "is symptomatic of the structural violence leveled against minority groups that the government has deemed dangerous, impure, and/or unwanted within the territory," thereby building inequalities and hierarchies of recognition into the system (Kingston 2017b, 25). In the Dominican Republic, for instance, long-standing discrimination against Dominican-born people of Haitian descent culminated in a 2013 high court ruling that rendered many tens of thousands stateless. In a retroactive decision, the Dominican Constitutional Tribunal ruled that those born to undocumented migrants were not covered by *jus soli* citizenship provisions. Despite attempts to remedy the problem, Human Rights Watch (2015a) found that government agencies have refused to restore original nationality documents and caused bureaucratic delays that have prevented thousands from exercising citizenship rights. At the same time, military and immigration authorities continue to profile, detain, and forcibly expel Dominicans of Haitian descent (Human Rights Watch 2015a). Kristy Belton (2016) writes that such denials of legal status within a person's country of birth constitutes a form of "rooted displacement," a "peculiar and injurious form of displacement" that occurs while the stateless remain physically rooted in their country of birth (908). While the international community tends to think about displacement in relation to situations of armed conflict and emergencies, statelessness is a long-term, everyday human rights challenge where displacement occurs "in place." Using qualitative fieldwork in the Bahamas and the Dominican Republic, Belton (2016) finds that the sense of identity experienced by those who are stateless "is ambiguous at best or nonexistent at worst" and that their crisis is their "inability to choose to belong to the communities of their birth" (907–908).

Such examples highlight how statelessness fits into a broader, hierarchical system of discrimination and abuse; they also help to problematize the assumption that legal nationality will translate into human rights protection. Advocates attempting to eradicate statelessness through the provision of status—such as pressing for accession to the statelessness conventions, ensuring birth registration, and providing legal nationality to de jure stateless individuals—understand that citizenship matters greatly for protecting human rights in our state-centered system. Surely legal nationality is an important prerequisite for human rights protection; its provision is one way, among numerous options, that a government can signal a group's worthiness to political membership. However, human rights' enduring legal emphasis also limits our understanding of political membership and narrows our approach to tackling the problem of statelessness. With or without legal status, state-sponsored discrimination will endure in the form of denied functioning citizenship, to varying degrees and exhibited in a number of ways. Here we have the circular dilemma in which people are discriminated against because they are stateless—and they are stateless because they are discriminated against. It is a mistake to frame citizenship in thin terms such as a "fixed or static concept signifying passive legal relationships between individuals and their respective states" because citizenship is an evolving concept that involves politics and society—"a series of habits, dispositions, and practices" that an individual is politically situated within (Schattle 2012, 13–14). The current legalistic focus on the provision of legal nationality to eradicate statelessness, despite its incredible good intentions, ignores the protection gaps that it helps to create. People are bound by the complexities of their political situations and communities, including the prejudices and inequalities prevalent in their societies, and full membership requires more than legal status to protect against marginalization and rights abuse. Current actions aimed at combating statelessness remain vital, but they require additional, complementary approaches that address how statelessness fits into a broader picture of marginalization. As I've argued previously: "Critics may contend that focusing on legal status will at least reduce some of the ill effects of statelessness, but in the long-term I believe this strategy simply puts a temporary bandage on widespread issues of structural inequality" (Kingston 2017b, 29).

To address this problem, we must push beyond thin notions of citizenship to explore what it truly means to be a member of a political community. Rather than embracing the binary citizen-versus-noncitizen construction at the heart of so many contentious political debates, we must instead reframe our understanding of membership to acknowledge the concept of functioning citizenship. This means viewing statelessness not only as a lack of legal nationality but also as a consequence of structural discrimination that strips individuals of their citizenship or obstructs its acquisition from the start. Once that reality is acknowledged, the social good of citizenship goes beyond mere legal status to encompass a relationship between the state and the individual that respects human dignity and personhood—ideals that human rights norms are built on. As the next section illustrates, noncitizens around the world are already calling for functioning citizenship in various ways and in spite of a plethora of obstacles that stands in their way. The advocacy and activism of stateless people and other noncitizens remind us that legal nationality is indeed important, but that political voice is not reserved solely for citizens. Instead, we are reminded that a political community is made up of a diverse range of actors whose need for rights protections—and whose value as members of the human family—transcend passports and identity documents.

Noncitizenship and Political Agency

The dominant narrative about statelessness is that people without legal nationality are voiceless, powerless, and vulnerable to a range of rights abuses. The stateless are often invisible on paper, left off birth registries and census rolls because of the legal precariousness of their situation. They are frequently denied birth certificates, identity documents, passports, and even marriage and death certificates—all official ways of proving one's identity and, by extension, one's existence within a political community. This lack of legal status makes information on the true scale of statelessness difficult at best; indeed, a fundamental challenge in anti-statelessness action and advocacy is a lack of reliable data on how many people are stateless and where they are located. In its global survey on statelessness, the Institute on Statelessness and Inclusion (2014) acknowledged that "it is still difficult to get a full and reliable picture of the magnitude of statelessness in all countries" (40) because of definitional issues, gaps in data collection tools, lack of adequate or comprehensive data collection, unwillingness or lack of awareness among potential survey respondents to self-identify as stateless, and protection concerns related to the identification of stateless populations. In many countries, data on these "hidden" stateless populations is limited because "statelessness is not high on the political agenda" (Institute on Statelessness and Inclusion 2014, 41). Echoing the work of Arendt (1966) and Agamben (1998), the stateless are portrayed as "rightless" and trapped within "bare life" existences.

Yet while the stateless lack a variety of resources necessary for the full provision of functioning citizenship, it is important that we don't confuse *legal* invisibility with *political* agency. It is wrong to assume that the stateless—and noncitizens more generally—are voiceless or powerless when it comes to pursuing their basic human rights. In countless cases from around the world, the stateless engage in activism and status negotiations despite the massive obstacles to political participation that stand before them. Constructions of the "bare life" led by the stateless miss this important point because they rely too heavily on legal status alone, often assuming that anyone without the protections of legal nationality will be unable or unwilling to engage politically. To comprehend existing advocacy by stateless individuals as well as to consider their future potential for enacting positive change, we must expand our understanding of participation—and relatedly, our notions of citizenship and political membership. As Kelly Staples (2012) notes in her work on membership, it is imperative "to avoid the tempting, but self-defeating conclusion that people are not people if they are excluded from the wide-ranging benefits of belonging to some or other state" (6); we must reject the idea that the stateless are denied the human capacity to act in their best interests. In fact, Engin Isin (2009) argues that "time and again we see that subjects that are not citizens act *as* citizens: they constitute themselves as those with 'the right to claim rights'" (371). From this perspective, the "actors of citizenship" are not necessarily those who hold legal nationality and "the political is not limited to an already constituted territory or legal 'subjects'; it always exceeds them" (Isin 2009, 370).[2]

Activism among various stateless populations highlights how some stateless groups claim political agency despite their lack of legal nationality. In his qualitative research study of Roma families and Roma rights advocates in Italy, Nando Sigona (2016) found that stateless Roma people "are neither rights-less nor agency-less"; from their perspectives, "they repeatedly interrogate and challenge the reasons for their exclusion and negotiate precarious and contingent forms of inclusion" (275). For instance, the Roma build their everyday lives within the opportunity structures available to them, navigate complicated and ever-changing immigration rules in attempts to regularize their positions, and undertake travel when

---

[2] It's noteworthy that Isin (2009) does not equate citizenship with membership but instead defines it as "a dynamic (political, legal, social and cultural but perhaps also sexual, aesthetic and ethical) institution of domination *and* empowerment that governs *who* citizens (insiders), subjects (strangers, outsiders) and abjects (aliens) are and *how* these actors are to govern themselves and each other in a given body politic" (371). Citizenship "is a relation that governs the conduct of (subject) positions that constitute it. The essential difference between citizenship and membership is that while the latter governs conduct *within* social groups, citizenship is about conduct *across* social groups all of which constitute a body politic" (371).

it increases the likelihood of gaining passports or visas. While millions of people—including stateless Roma—live their lives without legal nationality and endure extreme disadvantage and marginalization as a result, Sigona (2016) argues that "they nonetheless exist and make claims, sometimes successfully, for rights and entitlements" (270). In Estonia, interviews with stateless Russian-speakers highlighted how individuals made instrumental calculations, as well as engaged in normative and affective considerations, when navigating the complexities surrounding their options for legal nationality. Unlike cases of extreme marginalization when the stateless have no access to citizenship, Russian-speakers in Estonia make decisions about which legal status to pursue based on practicalities of citizenship (such as residence rights, employment considerations, and freedom of movement) as well as on issues related to identity, emotional connections, justice, and mutual respect. Rather than citizenship being a "permanent condition of birth," this example shows that stateless individuals—when provided with options—consider a variety of factors and aim for citizenship choices that fulfill a variety of needs (Fein and Straughn 2014, 691). Despite threats of state-sanctioned violence, stateless hill tribe members in Thailand continue to campaign for Thai nationality and a host of other protections, including access to healthcare and education. The 2017 army killing of teenaged activist Chaiyaphum Pasae, an outspoken Lahu hill tribe advocate, sparked international outcry against extrajudicial killings in the uplands (Human Rights Watch 2017).

Conceptions of rightlessness and "bare life" ignore such examples of political agency and remain overly deterministic, privileging legal status—often without acknowledging the hierarchies of personhood encapsulated within the citizenry—while ignoring the potential of noncitizens as political actors. Reflecting on research among stateless Urdu-speakers in Bangladesh, Victoria Redclift (2013) argues that "the ambiguity of citizenship status is lived in the everyday" (170) and that discrimination based on race, ethnicity, age, class, and gender are routinely "hidden behind citizenship's beneficent façade" (7). Rather than accepting the terms "citizenship" and "statelessness" as stable identities of law and fact, she writes that they encompass "shifting assortments of exceptions, rejections, inclusions, and denials" (170). Indeed, " 'stateless' people can access 'rights' just as citizens can be denied them"; theories of citizenship must recognize the social relations within which rights are enabled, noting that legal status is not always enough to protect rights if one's social and spatial position is tenuous (Redclift, 2013, 170). From this perspective, it is noteworthy that most conceptions of noncitizenship become "reduced to a journey to citizenship," reinforcing the belief that legal nationality is of utmost value while losing any meaning and force behind the concept of noncitizenship (Tambakaki 2016, 928). Part of the challenge here, therefore, is to draw attention to "process, subjectification, agency and claims-making" without limiting discussion to the binary citizen/noncitizen construction (Tambakaki 2016, 933).

For some, the realities of marginalization—within the citizenry as well as outside it—require careful analysis of the power of noncitizenship, kept separate from calls for mere legal nationality. Heather Johnson (2016) defines noncitizenship as "a political status that is not simply the absence of citizenship, but that has political content in itself" (951–952). In her study of refugee and migrant protest across Europe—and particularly situated in refugee protest camps in Germany and Austria—Johnson (2016) argues that noncitizens are increasingly "making demands on the state that are tied directly to not only their living conditions, but to the quality of their political lives" (953). Using actions such as rallies, marches, hunger strikes, and protest encampments in public spaces, thousands of protestors are "asserting the legitimacy of their political voice as noncitizens" and asserting noncitizenship as "an autonomous and independent subjectivity rather than simply as an absence of citizenship" (953). This perspective requires more than simple inclusion in citizenship frameworks; it requires new conceptions of political agency across a variety of social constructs that divide people—including legal status. While citizenship and noncitizenship "stand as mirror opposites" if we limit our discussion to legal status categories, a substantive expansion of those terms reveals that the boundaries between them are "dynamic and porous" (Landolt and Goldring 2016, 854). While statelessness and other forms of noncitizenship are frequently (and correctly) tied to extreme vulnerability and exploitation, it is also true that variations, contingencies, and different experiences exist among stateless individuals. A study of migrants living in the Canadian city of Toronto, for example, highlights the importance of migrant agency and social learning; case studies show "the degrees to which migrants experience, meet, navigate, and try—or not—to change their formal or substantive conditions of presence and access over time" (Landolt and Goldring 2016, 858). From this perspective, the category of noncitizenship is not just absence of legal nationality but rather a category that acknowledges and challenges power relationships, political exclusion, and inequality. To consolidate the force of this category, "we need to start with the difficult task of attenuating its relationship with citizenship" (Tambakaki 2016, 933). In other words, we must resist the temptation of "collapsing noncitizen action back into citizenship frameworks" (Johnson 2016, 953).

The challenge here is to balance the potential for noncitizen political agency with an acknowledgment of the practical, devastating consequences of statelessness. Theorists Katherine Tonkiss and Tendayi Bloom (2016) reject treating noncitizenship as the mere negation of citizenship, calling for a "full and accurate conceptualization of noncitizenship" for inclusion in both theoretical and policy-oriented discussions (840).[3] Noting that the lack of attention to noncitizenship has created a gap in critical liberal theory that leads to the inability to fully address practical issues faced by those without legal status, Tonkiss and Bloom (2016) argue that these challenges are seen "most keenly" in the case of statelessness. Defining the stateless solely by their lack of legal nationality "has the effect of reinforcing the idea that there is no relationship and enabling their exclusion from even core rights protections" (841). Instead, they stress that noncitizenship is heterogeneous and complex, constructed by various actors in different places and through modes; it involves vulnerability to human rights abuses but may also involve circumstances in which noncitizens challenge that vulnerability and exhibit political agency (Tonkiss and Bloom 2016, 848–849). Yet this opening of theoretical space should not ignore the realities of statelessness as a cause and consequence of marginalization. While there are powerful and important examples of stateless groups exhibiting agency and fighting for their human rights, the majority of stateless individuals face extreme situations that often make such action impossible. Matthew Gibney (2011) warns "not to exaggerate recent changes in the distribution of rights across the citizen/non-citizen divide," since the major citizenship goods of voice and security are usually enjoyed by noncitizens in limited terms, at best (43). Indeed, there is widespread interdisciplinary agreement that lack of legal nationality leads to severe deprivations of the rights to place and purpose. The difficult balancing act, therefore, is to acknowledge and fight against such abuses of fundamental rights—while also acknowledging the potential for agency, empowerment, and indeed the expression of human dignity by stateless individuals.

Statelessness offers the starkest example of denied functioning citizenship, while at the same time offering powerful reminders about the

---

[3] Tonkiss and Bloom (2016) argue that political theorists are limited by the tools available for discussing membership and rights, which rely on a vocabulary centered on citizenship. This inadequate means of analysis is illustrated by the traditional hyphenated spelling of "non-citizenship," which they reject as scholars and editors (841). Following their example, this book also rejects the hyphenated construction of this term.

strength of human resiliency and the desire for political agency. The existence of at least 10 million stateless people around the world, despite international laws guaranteeing the "right to a nationality," forces us to examine Arendt's critiques about the efficacy of human rights norms and our current world system. Reliance on state duty-bearers leaves little political space for effectively responding to statelessness, instead offering another tool of marginalization and oppression to hold over minorities and political dissenters. The lived experiences of stateless people illustrate how rights to place and purpose are deeply impacted by lack of legal nationality; in that sense, legal status remains a human rights "prerequisite" in our current system. At the same time, it is naïve to assume that the acquisition of legal nationality will "solve" the problem. The underlying discrimination and marginalization that makes statelessness possible in the first place will not be eradicated by the issuance of citizenship papers and a passport—as many of those suffering from de facto statelessness know all too well. Rather, we must focus on the elusive goal of real, meaningful political membership and begin to question what truly functioning citizenship might look like. Stateless individuals around the world give us starting points on this intellectual journey, as their strategies to survive and be recognized reject the assumption that only citizens have political agency, and that only legal status makes one worthy of fundamental human rights.

CHAPTER 3 | Forced Displacement and
          | Broken Ties

THE SO-CALLED BALKAN ROUTE humanitarian corridor had supposedly been shut to displaced persons by the time I arrived in Belgrade, Serbia, in September 2016.[1] The route was formally shut down on March 8, when official border closures in Macedonia, Croatia, and Slovenia blocked passage by refugees and other migrants. By the end of April, those closures left approximately 54,000 people (including thousands of Syrians) stranded in Greece (Danish Refugee Council 2016, 5). Yet while politicians applauded the fact that irregular migration flows in the region had ended, some argued that border closures and desperation drove the displaced into the arms of human smugglers—with tens of thousands still passing through the Balkan Route, albeit in more dangerous and exploitative ways (Kingsley 2016). Indeed, signs of ongoing human movement were everywhere during my visit to Belgrade: city parks transformed into informal refugee camps, lines of men waiting to use public sinks and toilets, families taking a short rest before resuming their long treks westward. In conversation, Serbian officials and nongovernmental organization (NGO) workers scoffed at the idea that the Balkan Route was indeed "closed," noting that desperate people always find a way—and that in the Balkans, with its still recent history of war and displacement, people felt empathy for refugees and were inclined to allow them safe passage. Yet regional pressures to close the

---

[1] The route became a popular passageway into the European Union in 2012, when visa restrictions were relaxed for five Balkan countries (Albania, Bosnia and Herzegovina, Montenegro, Serbia, and Macedonia). Approximately 20,000 people crossed the Hungarian border illegally in 2013 and nearly all applied for asylum after crossing, but those numbers rose dramatically in the following years due largely to the arrival of asylum-seekers from war-torn countries such as Syria and Somalia. Most displaced persons who claimed asylum in Hungary headed on toward other EU countries, particularly Austria and Germany, where many again applied for asylum (Frontex n.d.).

Balkan Route reflected a broader trend of closing borders and preventing displaced persons from seeking international protections. While border fences were being erected to prevent entry via the Balkans, for instance, borders surrounding Syria were also closing to migration. Very few legal routes remained for displaced Syrians by 2016, when tightly controlled land borders and strict visa requirements provided few migratory options; by the end of May, an estimated 165,000 people were stranded in Syria along the Turkish border (Danish Refugee Council 2016, 4).

The United Nations High Commissioner for Refugees (UNHCR) warns of an "unprecedented" global crisis in forced displacement, with 65.3 million people displaced in 2015. That figure includes 21.3 million border-crossing refugees—more than half of whom were children under the age of eighteen. As a result of armed conflict and persecution, the UNHCR estimates that nearly 34,000 people are forcibly displaced every day. These figures also include internally displaced persons (IDPs) who often flee their homes for the same reasons as refugees but who lack the same international protections, since they do not cross international borders and are not covered by the UNHCR's original mandate (United Nations High Commissioner for Refugees 2015a). Although most displaced persons are legal nationals of a state, they lack functioning citizenship with their governments; in fact, their governments are often responsible for the human rights abuses and conflict that prompted their displacement to begin with. While some protections under international law are meant to fill the gaps created by these broken ties, in reality refugees and IDPs suffer widespread human rights abuses in the absence of a reliable state duty-bearer. Indeed, increasing anti-refugee sentiments and a growing reliance on securitized practices of refugee detention highlight how the forcibly displaced are often unable to access basic human rights entitlements afforded to them under international law. Without functioning citizenship to a state government—and without effective provision of the refugee rights intended to alleviate the harms of that absence—refugees face growing threats of denied rights to place and purpose. Similarly, the norms of state sovereignty mean that IDPs are often left defenseless in the absence of state allies.

Human rights, including the right to seek asylum, are meant to serve as a backup when functioning citizenship fails, "a sort of legal parachute that ideally should open in an emergency" (Follis 2015, 43). Yet the trend of closing borders against the forcibly displaced—as well as the troubling rise of anti-refugee sentiments, refugee detention, and the stubborn refusal to acknowledge many so-called illegal immigrants as asylum-seekers—highlights how human rights norms fail to fill this protection gap. Indeed, persistent threats to rights of place and purpose illustrate how the forcibly displaced are deemed less worthy of basic rights than state citizens within host countries (or potential sites of asylum, if people can actually reach them). On the hierarchy of personhood, the displaced are often viewed with suspicion as potential threats to national security, economic stability, and even cultural identity. Already reeling from the effects of broken ties with their country of origin, the forcibly displaced may escape the horrors of war but find themselves without equal recognition as human beings deserving of fundamental rights. This reality points toward the inadequacies of refugee rights, which provide limited legal protections for the displaced despite the international community's persistent failure to act on their behalf. And while the world continues to view forced displacement as an exception to the norm, cases of protracted displacement and enduring refugee flows around the world show that displacement is not a temporary problem in need of solution but rather an ongoing human rights need. Without functioning citizenship to a state—and without a reliable, rights-protective international community to fill this devastating protection gap—the forcibly displaced suffer severe deprivations of their rights to place and purpose, as exemplified by issues such as refugee detention and obstacles to education in displacement.

The Inadequacies of Refugee Rights

Forced displacement is conceptualized by the international community in legalistic terms as well as more broadly in response to new rights challenges. The most widely accepted, narrow definition of "refugee" comes from the 1951 Convention Relating to the Status of Refugees (Refugee Convention), which defines the term as a person who, "owing to well-founded fear of being persecuted for reasons of race, religion, nationality, membership of a particular social group or political opinion, is outside the country of his nationality and is unable or, owing to such fear, is unwilling to avail himself of the protection of that country" (United Nations High Commissioner for Refugees 2010, Article 1.A.2). More broadly, discussions of forced migration increasingly consider anyone whose flight stems from significant threats to basic subsistence, security, or liberty—including those deemed "survival migrants" and IDPs, who are covered by the non-binding UN Guiding Principles on Internal Displacement. In many cases, this shift acknowledges how the circumstances of forced migration have changed since the creation of the refugee regime in the 1950s; factors such as generalized violence, environmental change, and food insecurity drive displacement around the world (Betts 2013, 2). The conceptual connection between these narrow and broad categories of the forcibly displaced is that "the assumed relationship between state and citizen is likely to have broken down" (Betts and Loescher 2011, 6), meaning that any semblance of functioning citizenship has ceased to exist. Measures have gradually been enacted to address forced displacement outside the narrow definition of the Refugee Convention—including various protections in regional human rights frameworks and an emerging range of jurisprudence that applies international law to the protection needs of broadly defined displaced persons. These complementary protections are severely limited in scope and application, however, and remain an inadequate response to the immense scale of forced displacement (Betts 2013, 15). Jennifer Hyndman (2000) argues that "a smaller and smaller proportion of refugees meet the formal Eurocentric post-World War II requirements," and discrepancies between narrow and broad definitions of displacement "[have] generated a geographically unequal system of refugee protection and assistance" (12).

It is notable that the international community relies on foreign states to step in and fill protection gaps left by lack of functioning citizenship despite growing reluctance to directly engage in matters of forced migration. Rights protection during displacement remains rooted in whether a person can secure the protection of a state government, regardless of norms related to asylum and refugee rights. "In the absence of the ability or willingness of the country of origin to provide protection, the rights of those people are only likely to be met when another state or collection of states is willing to stand-in as the substitute provider of rights—whether temporarily or permanently," explain Alexander Betts and Gil Loescher (2011, 6). Ongoing controversy over refugee resettlement and rising anti-refugee sentiment around the world, however, highlight how many governments are unwilling to undertake that stand-in role. Those states who have championed the rights of displaced persons in the past are also changing their position in the face of the Syrian refugee crisis. Sweden—which had taken in more refugees per capita than any country in Europe, admitting more than 80,000 refugees in recent years—finds itself grappling with the financial, cultural, and security ramifications of such intense refugee resettlement. A 2016 *Foreign Policy* article thus announced "the death of the most generous nation on earth" (Traub 2016). The UNHCR (2002), which acknowledges that the "safety net" of government protection disappears when civilians are forcibly displaced, assists states in their responses to forced displacement but ultimately is a supranational organization that cannot be considered "a substitute for government responsibility" (para. 3). While state governments are the duty-bearers of the right to asylum and corresponding refugee rights, the UNHCR provides critical responses where no state apparatus actually exists, transforming national funding into a "multinational rapid-reaction force" to meet unexpected migration needs (Hyndman 2000, 173). Made up of member states that pay its bills, the United Nations thus assists in the "devolution of responsibility for refugees and displaced persons from states to such multilateral organizations as UNHCR," representing a "reinvention of states in different guises" that minimizes state obligations, partly as a means of political survival for the state itself in response to lack of political will to assist refugees (Hyndman 2000, 173).

Indeed, hesitant responses to recent refugee crises fuel growing concerns that attention to refugee and asylum rights are based on political calculations rather than respect for global norms. This is partly due to a fundamental shift in the nature of displacement; during the Cold War, refugee admissions were in the interest of most developed states. In recent years, however, increasing numbers of refugees have led to a prioritization of intake restrictions in order to maintain border control (Orchard 2014, 2). The displaced are often discussed with a "crisis vocabulary" that is "subsumed within discourses of crisis and danger," made more complex by a "complicated configuration of political, socioeconomic, and environmental forces that have conjoined to create a crisis situation" (Nyers 2006, 4). The immediacy of such crises leaves little time for the critical self-reflection needed to eliminate discrimination within response systems, focusing on refugees as short-term problems in need of immediate solutions (Nyers 2006, 4–5). Within the field of humanitarian aid, assistance is increasingly centralized, authorized, and politicized; Hyndman (2000) writes that "there is no pure, apolitical humanitarian solution to the politically charged events of mass human displacement." Instead, "humanitarianism is an increasingly well-funded and politicized process of balancing the needs of refugees and other displaced persons against the interests of states" (Hyndman 2000, 3). While a rise in NGO-led humanitarian efforts correlates with the decline of conventional protections of asylum, geopolitical interests prioritize flight that is motivated by pro-Western political values—including privileged political and civil rights protections over persecution related to economic, cultural, and social rights (Hyndman 2000, 4, 9). When it comes to resettlement, case studies highlight how these programs are intensely politicized and generally used as political tools to meet state goals. "The result is a process which rests on an illusion of equity, belied by a reality in which refugees' resettlement prospects are measured not only in terms of their protection needs, but also in terms of their 'potential for integration' and political affiliations," writes Katy Long (2011), citing "difficult" resettlement cases such as various Muslim groups from Somalia that are viewed as unlikely candidates for social integration abroad (18).

As is often the case with human rights protection, weak or nonexistent enforcement mechanisms thwart the full protection of refugee rights. Although border-crossing refugees tend to be viewed as problems for the international community, solvable only through international cooperation (Orchard 2014, 3), the international community has not adequately addressed questions of responsibility. A case in point is a 2011 Mediterranean Sea disaster that left sixty-three of seventy-two passengers dead after they attempted the perilous journey from Libya to Lampedusa, Italy. These migrants were ultimately left to die at sea after military and coast guard vessels, as well as NATO and Frontex officials, failed to offer aid. A Council of Europe inquiry into the incident resulted in unenforceable "lessons for the future" and relied on diplomatic language of "omissions" and "failures," without actually pinpointing who is responsible for implementing those lessons or holding states accountable. Karolina Follis (2015) writes that these approaches perpetuate ideas of collective responsibility, or "obligations distributed so widely that no one agent can be held to account" (55). Despite universal human rights and the principle of equality of survival, which is implicit to the obligation to provide rescue at sea, the increasing death toll of migrants in the Mediterranean shows that "practice fails to meet aspiration" (56) and the survival of some displaced persons is less politically important than others. In response, Follis advocates a robust notion of responsibility that includes concepts of duty and guilt in relation to state action (or inaction). More broadly, the international community has signaled at least a marginal interest in expanding norms of responsibility; the Responsibility to Protect (R2P) doctrine has garnered much discussion within the UN community as a means of preventing and responding to the mass atrocity crimes of genocide, war crimes, crimes against humanity, and ethnic cleansing (see Office of the Special Adviser on the Prevention of Genocide n.d.). An "unbundled" approach to this concept, including an emphasis on "sovereignty as responsibility," has been advanced as an opportunity for combating structural violence—including statelessness and internal displacement in states where the government is unable or unwilling to act as an effective duty-bearer (Kingston and Datta

2012). The Guiding Principles on Internal Displacement also outline the rights of IDPs and stress responsibilities even when displacement does not result in cross-border migration (see United Nations Office for the Coordination of Humanitarian Affairs 2004), but again, enforcement of these principles is often a key challenge.

These failures of enforcement and responsibility also extend to protracted situations of displacement, which represent long-term challenges to human rights but rarely attract sustained attention from the international community. The UNHCR (2009) defines a protracted refugee situation as one in which refugees have been displaced for five years or more after their initial displacement, without "immediate prospects for implementation of durable solutions" (para. 4). These situations represent long-term lacks of functioning citizenship without clear solutions in sight, with states often viewing refugee populations as nuisances rather than vulnerable bearers of human rights. Host, origin, and donor states "have chosen to understand *their* refugee problem in demographic terms, as the physical presence of unwanted foreign residents on *their* territory," writes Long (2011). "Their solution is the removal of such interlopers" (1). This assertion is highlighted by the situation of Rwandan refugees, who fled genocidal violence and harsh repression between 1959 and 1998—including during the 1994 genocide that claimed up to 1 million lives. Nearby African countries tend to see Rwandan refugees as competition for resources, segregating them into refugee camps and regularly creating push factors such as cutting food rations and limiting access to farmland in order to force repatriation (O'Connor 2013). The UNHCR-invoked Cessation Clause came into effect in 2013 as part of renewed attempts to bring refugees "home" from neighboring countries, nullifying recognized refugee status and encouraging the repatriation of approximately 70,000 refugees despite reports of increasing state-sanctioned persecution in Rwanda and beyond. Refugees unwilling to return to Rwanda face situations of statelessness, partly because they rarely have opportunities for integration into host societies (Kingston 2017). A historical view of global refugee responses highlights how a declining quality of asylum—including increasingly restrictive conditions—exacerbates suffering during prolonged displacement and prevents refugees from resuming their "normal life" (Long 2011, 2).

Reliance on state sovereignty and the government duty-bearer of human rights not only creates protection gaps for the forcibly displaced but also perpetuates the myth that such displacement is abnormal within the international system. In reality, displacement represents a common situation around the globe, despite being framed as emergency or crisis. In working to secure the "normality" of citizenship and the state, modern statism produces the "accident" of the refugee; the category of refugee has been invented and naturalized as a crisis situation in stark contrast to the normalcy of the citizen (Nyers 2006, 9). The privileging of sovereignty means that refugees are excluded from the political realm, "included in the discourse of 'normality' and 'order' only by virtue of their exclusion from the normal identities and ordered spaces of the sovereign state" (Nyers 2006, xiii). By viewing the displaced as problems in need of solutions—rather than, first and foremost, as people in need of human rights protection—the international community focuses on immediate emergency response but ignores the longer term responsibilities necessary for providing protection and filling some of the void left by lack of functioning citizenship. For instance, the displaced are often denied agency and voice and are instead viewed solely as recipients of emergency humanitarian aid. At the same time, working within this crisis mode means that many well-intentioned actors lack critical self-assessment and fail to gain a deeper understanding of the realities of forced displacement as a political category, rather than a temporary state of emergency. These inadequacies of refugee rights—including the misguided view of displacement as anything less than a normal feature of our international system—leads to the continued denial of functioning citizenship and glaring gaps in the protection of rights to place and purpose.

Mistrust, Migration, and the Rights to Place

Various international laws and frameworks are meant to fill protection gaps and ensure at least temporary rights to place. The forcibly displaced, stripped of functioning citizenship, are meant to access the rights to place *somewhere* while more permanent solutions are identified. The 1948 Universal Declaration of Human Rights (UDHR) outlines "the right to seek and to enjoy in other countries asylum from persecution" in Article 14(1), setting the foundation for the 1951 Refugee Convention and the rise of the UNHCR as its "guardian." Today's refugee regime—which includes the UNHCR, state governments, and a host of NGOs tasked with providing vital humanitarian aid and resettlement assistance—centers on the ideals of freedom from persecution and international cooperation. The core principle of non-refoulement, for instance, asserts that no refugee should be returned to a country where they face serious human rights threats; this principle is considered a rule of customary international law and is meant to guide decision-making processes in relation to displacement around the world, including those related to solution-building. The UNHCR (2003) outlines three "durable solutions" for refugees: voluntary repatriation to the country of origin, local integration into the country of asylum, or re-settlement to a third country (5). In theory, a durable solution "repairs the tear in the state system fabric by ensuring that no individual goes without membership in some state" (Aleinikoff 1995, 260). While IDPs and other "persons of concern" are not entitled to the same durable solutions as refugees, attempts have been made to define and respond to their protec-tion needs. The Guiding Principles on Internal Displacement, for instance, identify the rights of IDPs in all phases of displacement. Although non-binding, the Principles reflect and are consistent with international law; they "provide protection against arbitrary displacement, offer a basis for protection and assistance during displacement, and set forth guarantees for safe return, resettlement, and reintegration" (United Nations Office for the Coordination of Humanitarian Affairs 2004, 5). Other persons of concern displaced by "weighty or humanitarian reasons" or where "exceptional hardship" would result from their return home—even while falling out-side the legal definition of a refugee—continue to require a new protection framework, however (United Nations High Commissioner for Refugees 1992, III.A.14). At the bare minimum, temporary protection for these populations might include respect for the right to leave one's country, cor-responding access to a country where safety may be sought, respect for basic human rights (including humane treatment in the country of refuge), and respect for the right to not be forcibly returned to danger (United Nations High Commissioner for Refugees 1992, III.B.18). At their core, these laws and frameworks reflect an acknowledgment that the rights to place are vital necessities; the forcibly displaced must enjoy the right to a safe haven, even if that right to place is a temporary one while more long-term remedies are identified.

Despite existing frameworks for providing rights to place during times of crisis, however, the forcibly displaced are often denied the most basic protections of their fundamental human rights. The global refugee regime has effectively created hierarchies of personhood within processes of asylum as well as in relation to the provision of durable solutions. These hierarchies are supported and perpetuated by forces of globalization, in-cluding increasing emphasis on border security and fears about globalized terror networks. The forcibly displaced are categorized not only according to the veracity of their claims for asylum but also on features such as re-ligious affiliation, ethnic background, country of origin, language, and political beliefs. Developed countries including the United States, Canada, and Australia "have become caught up in an instrumentally rational process of desperately defending their borders against certain kinds of embodied movement," focusing on "categories of persons" who cross borders and seek asylum (Paul 2014, 210). Processes of managing migration—as well as the status of persons within borders, both citizens and migrants—are more stringent than ever before, with responses to migration increasingly rationalized and paths to naturalization ever more contingent (Paul 2014, 216). Indeed, legal solutions to displacement are "profoundly state centered" and often focus more on the "containment" of migration than on improved protection capacities; such state-centeredness within legal discourse "has shown disturbingly little concern with the actual experiences and desires of refugees themselves" (Aleinikoff 1995, 258). Alexander Aleinikoff (1995) warns that policies of containment—which include detention, visa restrictions, limited options for resettlement, push-backs, and return—basically represent an attempt to "keep third world refugee problems from inconveniencing the developed states" (265–266). Furthermore, "the risk here is that a politics of containment will have the ugly result of abandoning refugees to the very states from which they fled in search of assistance and protection" (266).

In Europe, governments that had once welcomed refugees during the Cold War became less accepting of Kurds, Sri Lankans, and other refugees from developing states beginning in the 1990s. These vulnerable populations were increasingly labeled "economic migrants" by politicians and the media. Matthew Carr (2012) writes that these "invasion narratives" were often based on "hypotheses and fantasies" rather than actual numbers, and that reliable data were often ignored or inflated in the "xenophobic anti-immigrant climate" that spread through Europe in recent decades (23). In his work on *Fortress Europe,* Carr (2012) explains:

By the end of the Cold War, "asylum-seeker" was firmly enshrined in European political and media discourse as a subcategory of refugee whose legitimacy had yet to be proven and whose claims were frequently assumed to be suspect. These suspicions were often steeped in racialized assumptions, as "asylum-seeker" became code for Third World immigrants in general. But they were also fueled by the belief that Europe's immigration restrictions were being violated on a massive scale. To many Europeans the refugees from the Balkan wars, the African "board people" arriving on Mediterranean beaches, and the impoverished Albanians who arrived on commandeered hulks at the ports of Brindisi and Bari were the most visible expression of an invisible and limitless tide of impoverished and desperate migrants that threatened to engulf the continent. (22)

The rhetoric of humanitarianism is frequently at odds with policies and practices more closely aligned with goals related to security and border control. The international community increasingly militarizes human-itarian initiatives and abandons universal norms related to asylum and human security. "Geopolitical sovereignty is modulated into moral sover-eignty and responsibility," explains Maurizio Albahari (2015) in his work on Mediterranean migration—including interceptions at sea, militarized deterrence, detention, and deportation (20). He argues that a "military-humanitarian continuum" is established in the midst of such emergencies, relying on a humanitarian "crimes of peace" whose system has "proven crumbling and volatile and that *keeps proving* unjust, violent, and unequal" (21). A migrant shipwreck at Lampedusa in October 2013 drew interna-tional attention to the Mediterranean migration crisis and resulted in a bi-partisan resolution within the European Parliament that some hoped would be a turning point for European immigration policy. In reality, however, these political processes have done very little to change the continent's closed border policies. On the contrary, writes Giuseppe Campesi (2014), "it has led to further hardening of border control policies, increasing the dangers faced by migrants and potential asylum seekers. . . . [There are] few openings for regular migration, forcing foreigners to rough paths in an attempt to circumvent the 'barrier' erected to protect the borders of Europe" (127). Those who benefit from this "migration diplomacy" are not migrants themselves but rather security bureaucracies who garner po-litical power, material and financial resources, and public visibility as the legitimate solution for recurring "migration emergencies" (Campesi 2014, 127). And although international human rights law guarantees the right to asylum and affirms freedom of movement, in reality it leaves categories of migrants with insecure legal standing because it also affirms the prin-ciple of territorial sovereignty, which includes border control and security measures. Ayten Gündoğdu (2015) writes that "border controls, justified as legitimate acts of sovereign statehood, end up creating divisions within humanity itself, thereby rendering the rights of migrants (asylum-seekers and undocumented immigrants in particular) vulnerable to discretionary decisions and uncertain sentiments such as compassion" (93).

For those who reach their destination countries, systems of detention are often used as a deterrence tool that effectively serves as a punishment for human movement—even if that is not necessarily its intended function.

In Italy and nearby states such as France and Spain, governments notably avoid any reference to "detention" per se, using terms such as *retention, trattenimento*, and *internamiento* (Campesi 2015, 428). Illegal immigration in Italy was a misdemeanor crime punishable with a fine until April 2014, when Law no. 64/2014 decriminalized it. However, Campesi (2015) writes that immigration detention was always meant to be an administrative measure (to keep migrants at police disposal pending deportation) rather than a form of criminal punishment (445). The main difficulty for the state, however, is that migrants are able to resist and undermine deportation measures; if a receiving country such as Italy cannot locate a migrant's travel documents, for instance, it may be near-impossible to deport that person. "Migrants seen perfectly aware of the difficulties that receiving countries face in identifying them and exploit the situation hindering the deportation machine," writes Campesi (2015, 446). A detainee in an Italian immigration facility told him: "In Morocco I have never had an identity card, nor a passport, nor even have I ever had my fingerprints taken. I cannot be identified. The Moroccan consulate does not accept me. . . . Detaining me here is completely useless" (446). This liminal zone of de facto statelessness may thwart deportation efforts but leaves migrants vulnerable to prolonged detention.[2] Immigration detention is increasingly handled as a deterrence tool, "becoming a measure whose only aim appears to be that of destroying foreigners' resistance by convincing them to accept the failure of their migration project" (Campesi 2015, 447). The normalization of detention in the context of asylum and immigration "demonstrates that the perplexities of human rights have not been fully resolved with their codification in law"; human rights norms may guarantee the right to asylum and regulate the conditions of detention, but there is still ongoing debate about the maximum acceptable duration of detention and what constitutes "arbitrary" detention (Gündoğdu 2015, 121).

Reliance on systems of detention to manage forced displacement, including the maintenance of long-term refugee camps, holds troubling human rights possibilities and exacerbates the negative impacts stemming from lack of functioning citizenship. Rather than serving as temporary

---

[2] Italian reforms in November 2014 mean that migrants there can no longer serve prolonged periods of detention in a single instance, but they may still serve repeated short-term detentions that prevent them from building a life in Italy (Campesi 2015, 447). In other countries around the world, the inability for receiving states to deport de facto and de jure stateless migrants often leads to prolonged, indefinite periods of detention. This includes detention in Egypt, where stateless migrants may be held in detention for years (McBride and Kingston 2014).

spaces for refugees and asylum-seekers on a path toward durable solutions, detention facilities and camps are becoming liminal spaces where unwanted populations can be contained and segregated from the citizenry. If this current trend continues, Michel Agier (2011) argues that "camps will no longer be used just to keep vulnerable refugees alive, but rather to park and guard all kinds of undesirable populations" (3). Indeed, this movement is already under way in Europe, where there is growing acceptance of camps at state borders. In many cases, the displaced are less readily accepted as refugees or internally displaced but instead are framed as "rejected" and "illegal," redefined and stigmatized as illegal immigrants much like the category of the *sans papiers* in France. "This general term criminalizes in an indistinct fashion any displacement of individuals who are undesirable under one heading or another," writes Agier (2011, 31). Although European and Australian refugee warehousing garners the most international attention, it is important to note that the United States government has been quietly operating an immigration detention facility in Guantánamo Bay, Cuba, since 1991 as part of the US Migrant Interdiction Program (MIP). Although the vast majority of undocumented immigrants interdicted at sea ("interdictees") are returned to their point of origin, the US Coast Guard identifies a small percentage with a credible fear of persecution or torture and transfers them to Guantánamo for further processing. Those with a substantiated fear remain there until they are resettled; US policy stipulates that they cannot be paroled or admitted to the mainland, so most must be resettled to a third country. Azadeh Dastyari (2015) contends that this is "the oldest extraterritorial interdiction, processing and detention regime in the world," predating the European Border and Coast Guard Agency (Frontex) and Australia's processing and detention regime, yet few scholars know of its continued existence (6).

These threats to asylum rights can only be understood in the context of discrimination against immigrants, who are regularly viewed as criminals and national security threats even though their motivations for migration often include severe violations of their economic rights and threats to human security. Legal mechanisms that block citizenship rights in the United States, for instance, play key roles in patterns of exclusion, establishing new patterns of social stratification based on legal status. In contrast to racial discrimination, these patterns of legal exclusion "stress individual and moral culpability for exclusion and discrimination" (Waters and Kasinitz 2015, 117). Data show that intensive policing in poor US communities is related to the rise in deportations, immigration detention, and the imprisonment of Latinos—made possible by integrating federal immigration authority data systems with local and state police records. A misdemeanor offense, such as a traffic violation, could expose an undocumented immigrant and facilitate that person's detention and/or deportation (Waters and Kasinitz 2015, 125). In Switzerland, an analysis of the country's Der Bund/ Newsnet media showed that a "rather clearly structured membership category device" sorted migrants in news coverage immediately following the Arab Spring revolutions, with migrants categorized according to their current location relative to Switzerland. Outside of state borders, the displaced were referred to as "refugees," but within borders they were either "asylum-seekers or approved refugees." This stood in contrast to migrants from Tunisia, who are represented in the Swiss media as economic migrants and "benefit scroungers" who are draining resources with their claims for special treatment (Rellstab 2015, 130). Again, it is noteworthy that the distinction between refugee and irregular migrant is made not based on fears of persecution of human rights abuses but rather against the backdrop of state-centered interests and political calculations.

Forcible displacement is perhaps the most extreme case of denied rights to place, but it cannot be fully understood without acknowledging the complexity of the process it represents. It begins with a first instance of forced movement, such as fleeing one's home in the midst of a violent attack, but that initial event begins a long process that continually threatens, transforms, and problematizes our understanding of the right to place. Moving among various temporary shelters or camps, attempting to cross international borders, anxiously applying for asylum, awaiting durable solutions such as resettlement or integration—all of these events in the process of forced displacement reflect a precarious right to belong or remain within a territory, much less within a political community. For displaced persons, the rights to place necessitate freedoms of movement and asylum despite challenges stemming from discrimination, security concerns, and state-centric interests that increasingly construct refugees and other persons of concern as suspicious, illegal, and unworthy foreign others. Yet despite these human rights challenges, the displaced also impact the places they inhabit throughout this process—including countries of refuge and resettlement. "The history of displacement is by definition a history of place—of departure and of arrival, sometimes of multiple journeys, and also of staying put," writes Peter Gatrell (2013). "Refugees left their mark on destinations such as Beirut, Kokkinia, Marseille, Bourg-Madame, Chandigarh, Karachi, Hong Kong, Shatila and Masindi. Their descendants too imaginatively reconstructed the places they left behind, investing them with notions of beauty, pleasure, fecundity and stability"

(289). For displaced persons, the right to place represents a safe haven but also a broader community that represents "home"—and a home is something far more precious and complicated than mere shelter.

Purpose in Displacement: Obstacles to Education

Denied functioning citizenship and unable to access basic rights to place, the forcibly displaced struggle to enjoy rights to purpose. Frequently portrayed as the epitome of "bare life," refugees and other displaced persons certainly face extreme hardship related to the human rights we often connect to a life of dignity—including rights to education, employment, family unity, and freedom of expression. This rights violation combines with a denied capacity to trust—"the capacity to tame chance, especially the chance of being hurt" that people outside of conflict zones take for granted (Valentine and Knudsen 1995, 2). For the displaced, "it is this capacity that is rendered powerless; individual and groups have little else to do than to flee" (2). These vulnerabilities lead Agier (2011) to ask whether a politics of the displaced (which he equates here with statelessness) is possible; "Does a political right exist that includes the right to 'protection' outside the protection of a nation-state? Can citizenship be exercised by the stateless?" This raises the "endlessly repeated question of the relationship of individuals to the state" (15).

Forced to prioritize the immediate needs associated with human survival during their initial flight, displaced persons often find that their rights to purpose remain seriously compromised after they achieve relative levels of safety in camps and other places of refuge. Even in established camps, which often grow to resemble cities rather than temporary shelters, the gradual provision of schools and commercial areas often cannot replicate the feeling of living in a secure home. In Jordan's Zaatari camp, for instance, more than 80,000 Syrian refugees have access to schools, churches and mosques, hospitals, and the "Champs-Elysée" shopping street—including a variety of shops, restaurants, coffee houses, and even a pizza delivery service. In 2015, there were an estimated 2,500 refugee shops, and approximately 60 percent of the camp population earned some income from this economic system. Yet, despite the hard work and agency that made much of this progress possible, refugees living in Zaatari remain eager to return home (Weston 2015). Children talk about becoming engineers and lawyers to help rebuild Syria, while adults acknowledge that many young people will struggle to find ways to channel their potential while they live in the camp; "despite an air of permanence [refugees] have created, many know this place is not home" (para. 20). In other vast camps, such as Kenya's Dadaab camp near the Somali border—the world's largest refugee camp before the Kenyan government scheduled its closure in late November 2016—ongoing security concerns continued to plague residents, despite establishment of a long-term community. In Dadaab, ration cuts by the World Food Programme (due to funding limitations) and threats from the militant group Al-Shabab drastically increased vulnerabilities to malnu-trition and starvation, physical attacks and murder, rape, and the forced recruitment of child soldiers (Schwarz 2016). It is worth noting that Kenya was sharply criticized for forcibly returning refugees to Somalia, despite ongoing violent conflict there, prior to the scheduled November 30 closure date. Amnesty International (2016) estimated that 280,000 displaced per-sons were affected by the camp closure, although other organizations have reported much higher numbers.

Perhaps one of the most striking examples of threatened rights to pur-pose in displacement, however, stems from the human right to educa-tion. The UNHCR estimates that of the 6 million primary and secondary school-age refugees under its mandate, 3.7 million have no school to at-tend. Refugee children are five times more likely to be out of school than are non-refugees. Only 50 percent of refugee children can access primary education (compared to the 90 percent global average) and just 22 per-cent have opportunities to attend lower secondary school (compared to the 84 percent global average) (United Nations High Commissioner for Refugees 2016c, 4). In Syria, the civil war has "reversed more than a decade of progress in children's education," with the country's estimated 4.8 million school-age children suffering from a collapse of the public education system; approximately 2.2 million students inside Syria are out of school, while more than 500,000 refugee children do not attend school outside the country (UNICEF et al. 2013, 5). In a 2013 joint report, four major child protection actors—UNICEF, World Vision, the UNHCR, and Save the Children—noted that Syrian children are "learning in free fall" and argued that access to education "is an essential platform for protec-tion, social stabilization and economic recovery, and one the world cannot ignore" (UNICEF et al. 2013, 3). UNICEF et al. (2013) offered four key recommendations: engage in long-term educational planning for displaced Syrian children, support host countries and double international invest-ment, "scale-up success and innovation" (for instance, by creating informal learning centers and addressing trauma in schools), and end the destruction of Syria's education infrastructure (9). In their report on refugee education capacities in the host countries of Lebanon, Turkey, and Jordan, Shelly Culbertson and Louay Constant (2015) argue that the Syrian civil war has created an "education crisis for the Middle East" that has strained the capacities of neighboring countries and created severe risks to individual education rights and society at large (x). Their policy recommendations center on improving access to education, coordinating the management of refugee education, promoting social stability and planning refugee education in the midst of political constraints, and ensuring quality education for refugee students and their host country peers (x–xi). Many of these recommendations center on responding to strained resources; for instance, creating effective "double shift" classrooms to compensate for lack of teachers, inadequate space and overcrowding, and other limited resources (Culbertson and Constant 2015; also see Chapter 5).

Within camps, the control of refugee populations and limited educational opportunities highlight the impacts of lack of functioning citizenship. Susan Banki (2013) notes that the provision of education (and other forms of aid) in refugee camps is a way to "count, control, and hold accountable refugee populations" during situations of protracted displacement (135). The restrictions placed on camp residents make these spaces "semi-closed systems," which impact education in four key ways: a highly limited supply of teachers and school administrators; a relatively immobile student population; a limited flow of capital and other resources to camp schools; and limited access to innovation, including curriculum reform (135–136). In cases where mass resettlement eventually takes place, it is noteworthy that those "left behind" in camps experience serious negative impacts that further reduce their educational capacities. Following mass resettlement and resulting declines in student populations, camps experience a shift in resources (goods, labor, and capital) and diminished motivation levels among students and teachers, reducing the possibility for a healthy learning environment in the camp schools (Banki 2013, 134).

After resettlement, refugee children continue to experience severe challenges to their educational rights that obstruct broader rights to purpose. Existing research on educating resettled refugee students tends to focus on trauma, welfare, and social and cultural adjustment rather than on pedagogy and academic achievement. In Australian public schools, for instance, the low literacy of refugee-background students is widely recognized yet there is little research on how teachers are responding or what students' complex needs are (Windle and Miller 2013, 198). In their qualitative study of three Australian secondary schools, Joel Windle and Jennifer Miller (2013) found that teachers serving refugee populations often focused on students' social welfare, trying to alleviate some of the pressures associated with a lack of resources. Teachers were also often required to teach outside of their areas of training, overlooking aspects of language development as a direct result of their lack of English as a Second Language (ESL) specialization. "The consequences for students are that they remain on the fringes of the education system in terms of academic success, social integration, and transition—that is to say, schooling is not a transformative process in terms of social power," explain Windle and Miller (2013). "Although they are not excluded from school, most students do not matriculate with scores that allow further tertiary education, and therefore access to stable and higher paid professions and careers" (208). Similar issues have been raised in countries of resettlement such as Canada, where lack of adequate ESL teacher training and program funding leads to high dropout rates among immigrant and refugee students (Rossiter and Derwing 2012). In European countries of refuge and resettlement, the literature again focuses on social integration and the provision of basic welfare rather than academic achievement—for instance, centering on the need to provide healthcare and mental health counseling, job training to help young refugees quickly enter the work force, and resources for cultural adaptation (see Eklund et al., 2013; Ingleby et al. 2013; Krasteva 2013). While these are certainly important issues for educators, they fail to adequately address the full scope of the problem. In many cases, the nature of conflict and displacement means that refugee children are blocked from accessing their full rights to purpose—including accessing education and later enjoying the rights to work, expression, and livelihood that follow.

Armed conflict in the Middle East has created a refugee crisis in higher education, as well, interrupting many students' university educations or blocking young people from beginning their studies in the first place. Worldwide, only 1 percent of refugees attend university—compared to a 34 percent global average (United Nations High Commissioner for Refugees 2016c, 4). More than a quarter of Syria's population was enrolled in higher education in 2011, before conflict disrupted everyday life; today, there is a substantive demand for higher education among Syrian refugees, as well as Iraqi refugees who have endured protracted displacement (United Nations High Commissioner for Refugees 2015b, 2). Within conflict states themselves, intellectual communities have been decimated by war; in Syria, many university students and academics joined anti-government protests in 2011 and were arrested, martyred, or forcibly displaced as a result of their political activism. Notably, it seems that the Syrian government aims to ignore that reality; its Ministry of

Higher Education claims that students remain in Syrian universities and that somehow the number of enrolled students has increased during the last several years—despite the ongoing conflict and data to the contrary (Al Ahmad 2016). Access to higher education in countries of refuge such as Jordan, Lebanon, and Turkey is often obstructed by severe financial challenges (including tuition and cost of living expenses), lack of travel and academic documents, and sometimes language barriers. "The problem is snowballing," explains James King, a senior research and communications manager at the Institute of International Education's (IIE) Scholar Rescue Fund. "You now have 25-year-olds who would have gone to university when they were 22 but have never been able to access it" (quoted in Redden 2015, para. 2). Yannick Du Pont, the director of the Dutch educational NGO SPARK, highlights the impacts on rights to purpose: "The first inclination is 'OK, we should provide food and drink and shelter', and of course we should; it's essential. But people want to develop themselves, especially the youth" (quoted in Redden 2015, para. 4).

In response to forced displacement from Syria and Iraq, an increasing number of university scholarship programs have been created in countries of asylum and in other third countries—yet they are inadequate to meet the scope of demand. The UNHCR (2015b) advocates a "do not harm" approach for ensuring that refugee access to higher education is inclusive, non-discriminatory, and rights-protective. The agency notes that scholarships should cover the full course of study as well as living costs for students and perhaps close family members, with an acknowledgment that "intensive, long-term support" will be necessary for these students to meaningfully benefit from higher education (3). Scholarship initiatives should not jeopardize the legal status or well-being of refugee students; universities should carefully manage expectations and be sure that initiatives are durable, solution-driven, and mindful of students' need for effective integration into the academic environment (United Nations High Commissioner for Refugees 2015b, 3). Indeed, experts working in the field warn that tuition scholarships are not enough. Allan E. Goodman, president of IIE, notes that "it's relatively easy to get compassionate universities and colleges to say we'll forgo tuition, but what we have to come up with is the airfare and ticket to get them out of Syria or out of the camp to the U.S. or to Europe and the living expenses while they're a student" (quoted in Redden 2015, para. 13). And despite the grants and scholarships that have been allocated to Syrian refugee students, educators warn that there is an enormous gap between opportunities and demand. Several thousand scholarships have been offered, compared to approximately 100,000 potential Syrian refugee students and another 120,000 IDPs without access to higher education or existing scholarships (Al Ahmad 2016).

Despite these glaring protection gaps, it is important to recognize the ways that displaced persons act as advocates for their rights to purpose and attain at least some level of empowerment—often *in spite* of government duty-bearers, rather than because of them. Gatrell (2013) writes that refugees are "habitually portrayed as if they are without agency, like corks bobbing along on the surface of an unstoppable wave of displacement" (9), while Peter Nyers (2006) notes that the prevailing attitude in analyses of refugee flows "provides no place for refugees to articulate their experiences or struggles or to assert their (often collectively conceived) political agency" (xiv). Rather than this silence being natural or inevitable, he contends that it is "something that is produced by power relations that require explanation and critical analysis" (Nyers 2006, xiv). In the context of refugee education, some students identify and take advantage of new opportunities ironically made possible by their forced displacement. Marion Fresia and Andreas Von Känel (2015) argue that refugee children embody both the figure of the innocent victim and hopes for a better world. For instance, Somali women and girls had among the lowest literacy levels in the world before their country's 1991 civil war, but they found new educational opportunities in their displacement. In a study of refugee women and girls in Dadaab, Patricia Buck and Rachel Silver (2013) found that participation in schooling served as a key marker of gender difference, negotiation, and change in Dadaab. Increasing access to education and expanding earning power gave Somali women "new prospects, powers, and possibilities" that fostered and indicated gender change, highlighting that they were not "passive recipients" but rather leaders of change in their communities (130).

For border-crossing refugees, the very act of migration represents an act of empowerment in extreme, devastating circumstances—often undertaken with the hope of asylum guiding their journey. "Rather than waiting for permission from the state to move, a refugee often waits instead for permission to reside," explains Heather L. Johnson (2014, 6), who calls refugee migration a "rupture" that represents the limit of regular migration. Yet by exploring the ways in which displaced persons face threats to place and purpose, we uncover the varied ways such migration denies people the worth afforded to many citizens. On the hierarchy of personhood, it is apparent that refugees and other displaced persons are often viewed with suspicion and concern; they are problems in need of solution rather than people who are equal in human dignity and rights. Meanwhile, the global

refugee regime clings to universal norms and centers its work on the notion of the state as the duty-bearer of human rights. The criteria set forth by
the Refugee Convention, for instance, are "clearly based on a framework
of the state and nationality" by requiring that refugees cross a state border
and be unable or unwilling to avail themselves of the protection of their
home country (O'Sullivan 2012, 89). Notably, some scholars contend that
limiting refugee status to those facing persecution fails to capture the full
issue of refugeehood; Andrew E. Shacknove (1985), for example, writes
that persecution is but one manifestation of the broader phenomenon of
"the absence of state protection of the citizen's basic needs" (277). These
more inclusive perspectives create openings for discussing functioning
citizenship in the context of displacement, yet existing challenges to a
person's claiming refugee status (in the most legal, narrow sense of the
term) highlight how difficult this journey will be. As countries continue to
close borders to asylum-seekers and states insist on classifying persecuted
migrants as "illegal" immigrants, displaced persons and their advocates
face the reality that universal rights such as those to asylum, physical security, and education do not provide any semblance of functioning citizenship, even within the confines of temporary international protection.
These inequalities—this ordering of human worth, with many citizens
outranking displaced persons on the hierarchy of personhood—leads to
"crimes of peace" encompassing state negligence, ill-conceived policies,
and the flourishing of criminal networks engaged in human trafficking and
smuggling (Albahari 2015, 22).

And like many human rights debates, current approaches to forced
displacement are also guilty of relying on the fiction that functioning citizenship is a usual state of being. Displacement is approached as a temporary problem—a rift in the relationship between citizen and state that
can, for a limited duration, be addressed by stopgap protections from
the international community. From this perspective, what is "normal"
and healthy is a stable and positive relationship between the government and its citizenry; normality is posited as functioning citizenship,
(falsely) assuming that this ideal occurs regularly. Atle Grahl-Madsen
(1966), for instance, assumes that "the normal mutual bond of trust,
loyalty, protection, and assistance between an individual and the government of his home country" is commonplace, except when it has
been broken (or simply does not exist) among political refugees (79).
Similarly, Shacknove (1985) notes that the "normal basis of society"
is "a bond of trust, loyalty, protection, and assistance between the citizen and the state"—yet this bond has been severed in the case of the

refugee (275). For the forcibly displaced, as well as stateless persons discussed in Chapter 1—and for a great many other populations, who will be explored throughout this book—there is nothing usual about the ideal of functioning citizenship. Instead, the ordering of personhood and human worth is a fundamental feature of the international system, including its refugee rights regime.

CHAPTER 4 | Irregular Human Movement and the Creation of Liminal Spaces

A PLUME OF DARK gray smoke rose from the "Jungle" two days after French authorities began emptying the migrant camp located outside Calais, serving as a visible reminder that many former residents were not leaving willingly. The camp had become a key symbol of Europe's migration crisis, where desperate migrants awaited their opportunity to reach the United Kingdom—often by hiding themselves in cargo vehicles entering the Channel Tunnel. Estimates vary, but the camp was home to 6,000 to 10,000 asylum-seekers and migrants before French authorities began dismantling the informal settlement in October 2016. Adults were transferred to centers around the country with options for claiming asylum in France, while unaccompanied minors were sent to shipping containers converted into temporary accommodations. Others disappeared before demolition began, seeking shelter in the countryside or in neighboring towns (BBC News 2016; *Guardian* 2016). Human rights advocates warned that the demolition left hundreds—and possibly thousands—of unaccompanied children at risk (Bochenek 2016). Almost a year later, the Calais camp was gone and many of its former residents slept on the streets without access to essential services. "We are literally trying to get drinking water to people. We don't have water, we don't have food—and no sanitation," said Clare Moseley, founder of the aid organization Care4Calais, in June 2017. "There's skin disease, gum disease. It really, really is the absolute basics of life here. . . . When we were in the Jungle, we were trying to get clothes to people and even some kinds of social care. It really was a step up from where we are now" (quoted in McAuley 2017, para. 7–8).

By demolishing the Jungle without adequate provisions for its residents, the French government—much like other states facing waves of irregular human movement—emphasized economic and security[1] priorities rather than the protection of human rights. In the beginning, critics contend that the Jungle was "really just a way to get refugees out of town proper," setting up a "dirty, disease-prone, shanty town rife with crime" that would hopefully make the displaced so miserable that they would simply leave (Samuel 2016, para. 4). When those attempts failed, the camp's closure was framed as an action necessary for securing the international border, protecting drivers and the ground transportation of goods to market, and (ironically) protecting the human dignity of camp residents who lacked humanitarian services within the Jungle. First sequestered in the squalid camp and then denied even that small semblance of home, migrants faced a clear message: You are not welcome here. Irregular migrants (who may or may not qualify for protections under the UN Refugee Convention) are thus viewed as suspect and criminal, denied any semblance of functioning citizenship despite international protections of universal rights—including the right to claim asylum. On the hierarchy of personhood, irregular migrants represent yet another category of people whose worth is not valued as equal to that of nationals—or as fully human. Efforts to segregate and drive away migrant populations not only deny rights protections but also refuse migrants recognition of their basic humanity and membership within the human community.

The Jungle camp in Calais is but one example of how irregular human movement creates liminal spaces where full personhood is denied and rights are routinely violated. Various forms of illicit human movement leave many individuals without functioning citizenship, often because they are outside their country of legal nationality and cannot claim rights for fear of arrest, deportation, or some other form of retribution. These categories

---

[1] Notably, heightened border security measures have served, in some instances, to create a level of desperation that breeds security threats. Migrants attempting to cross the Channel into the United Kingdom have blocked roads leading to the Calais ferry port, for instance, in hopes of slowing vehicles long enough to jump onboard and hide. In June 2017, a van driver crashed near Calais after Eritrean migrants blockaded a motorway with tree trunks, causing a crash and subsequent vehicle fire (Willsher 2017). These events perpetuate the idea that irregular migrants are dangerous threats to the citizenry, strengthening security responses to migration that devalue rights protections. This emphasis shapes the way states and citizens view migrants, in France and elsewhere. Examples abound: A French farmer named Cédric Herrou was fined after helping African migrants cross the border from Italy into France on humanitarian grounds (Chrisafis 2017), thus treated as an accomplice to criminal activity. Frustrated refugees whose camp in Dunkirk was destroyed by fire were met with riot police, not social workers or aid providers, in April 2017 (Gentleman 2017). It is little wonder that migrants engage in complicated cross-border strategies to pursue their own livelihoods and survival, which includes managing networks and identities while reacting to changing security situations (Sassen 2013, 34).

of migration include irregular migration—which is often called "illegal" or "undocumented" migration, and includes a recent increase in cases of unaccompanied child migrants—as well as those who, often as part of this process, cross borders via human smuggling or trafficking. Here we see definitional lines blurring; there are debates about who counts as a migrant versus a refugee, at what point smuggling becomes trafficking, and so forth. In some cases, lack of functioning citizenship is what necessitates migration in the first place; consider marginalized stateless groups and citizens of corrupt, oppressive governments. Yet these forms of illicit movement also create liminal spaces where migrants and trafficking victims exist outside of the law, beyond the reach of functioning citizenship where they are dangerously vulnerable to rights abuses. These abuses include narrowed possibilities for the right to place as well as constant threats of deportation and ever-tenuous rights to purpose.

Irregular Movement

Migration has been an element of human civilization since our humble beginnings, but the rise of the state system and globalized conceptions of state security have increased the focus on borders and made space for a distinction between regular and irregular movement. Although there is no universally accepted definition of irregular migration, it is generally viewed as movement that occurs outside the norms of sending, transit, and receiving countries. For instance, irregularity from the perspective of a sending country includes cases when an individual crosses borders without a passport or valid travel documents, while a receiving country focuses on lack of authorization to enter, stay, or work within its borders under domestic immigration regulations (International Organization for Migration n.d.). "To be 'irregular' in migration is to experience mobility in ways that are outside of the strict policies and procedures of management and control governing border regimes," writes Heather Johnson (2014, 3–4). "Becoming irregular involves crossing a border without permission or in a way that is outside of the provided frameworks; it involves bypassing all check-points and lacking valid papers" (4). While this form of movement is often called "illegal migration," Johnson (2014) argues that these movements and resulting identities are shaped by the state as it seeks to "cordon off groups and individuals marked by their migration strategy as 'outside' (of the law, particularly)"—thus enabling their continued exclusion and criminality, while justifying restrictive policies and state control

(4). In a broad legal sense, "irregularity" refers to a "multiplicity of liminal statuses" including illegal entrants, those who overstay visas, and migrants who drift between different statuses but often lack real control over their legal right to remain within a territory (Costello 2016, 65).

The boundaries between irregular migration and forced displacement are often both blurred and interconnected. Irregular migration frequently occurs as a result of human rights abuses and deprivations ranging from valid fears of persecution to pervasive threats to economic, social, and cultural rights. Denied functioning citizenship at home, individuals undertake irregular migration in hopes of claiming rights elsewhere. In some cases, obstacles to obtaining political asylum lead to alternative forms of human movement—including illegal entry and residence abroad. Since the mid-1970s, for instance, European policies aimed at curtailing legal entry and residency have driven many potential asylum-seekers "underground," forcing foreigners already living within EU territories to become illegalized in various ways and to different degrees (Krause 2011, 22). In times of human rights crises, immigrant- and refugee-receiving countries may use high-profile events to implement restrictive measures aimed at controlling migration and in turn facilitate the rise of irregular migration, such as human smuggling. Alison Mountz (2010) writes that widespread human smuggling prompts states to develop narratives to justify their day-to-day work and promote vague security agendas. "In crisis, nation-states pit protection of their own citizens against a broader commitment to protect human rights," writes Mountz. "The crisis-driven discourse is accompanied by a corresponding geography where states manipulate space to subvert human rights, alter legislation, and extend their reach beyond territorial borders" as part of the securitization of migration (xvi–xvii). Left with few legal options for immigration or asylum, many desperate migrants thus undertake irregular movement in attempts to protect their basic rights. Ironically, the rise in irregular migration prompts further restrictions on human movement—curtailing legal opportunities and fueling irregularity rather than stemming the tide. Frequently portrayed as "illegal" immigrants, in fact the distinction between immigrant and displaced person is often an arbitrary one created for state interests rather than for human rights protection.

Challenges to legal migration spur irregular movement, including creating dangerous opportunities for the proliferation of human trafficking and smuggling. The United Nations addresses the issues of human trafficking and smuggling in its Convention against Transnational Organized Crime. The Protocol to Prevent, Suppress and Punish Trafficking in Persons, especially Women and Children, stresses the use of force or coercion to facilitate to human movement and exploitation. It defines human trafficking as "the recruitment, transportation, transfer, harboring, or receipt of persons, by means of the threat or use of force or other forms of coercion, of abduction, of fraud, of deception, of the abuse of power or of a position of vulnerability or of the giving or receiving of payments or benefits to achieve the consent of a person having control over another person, for the purpose of exploitation" (United Nations Office on Drugs and Crime 2004, 42). Such exploitation may include sexual exploitation, forced labor or services, slavery or similar practices, servitude, or the removal of organs (United Nations Office on Drugs and Crime 2004, 42). Relatedly, the Protocol against the Smuggling of Migrants by Land, Sea and Air defines human smuggling as "the procurement, in order to obtain, directly or indirectly, a financial or other material benefit, of the illegal entry of a person into a State Party of which the person is not a national or permanent resident" (United Nations Office on Drugs and Crime 2004, 54–55). In addition to violating state and international law, both human trafficking and smuggling represent lucrative opportunities for transnational criminal networks and severe human rights challenges for the international community. In many cases, processes of trafficking and smuggling are intricately connected, with instances of smuggling regularly crossing over into problems of human trafficking. Even when trafficking does not occur, paid smugglers are often neglectful or outright abusive of their "clients" as they undertake dangerous, illegal voyages to their destination countries.

Unfortunately there are countless examples of human trafficking and smuggling stemming from lack of functioning citizenship and restricted avenues to legal immigration around the world, including in Southeast Asia and North America. In Burma,[2] the Rohingya—members of a Muslim ethnic minority group—have suffered government oppression, including statelessness, for decades. Called "the world's most persecuted minority" by the United Nations and human rights advocates, the Rohingya face state-sanctioned violence that has been described as ethnic cleansing and even genocide (Popham 2012). Direct violence since June 2012 has forced tens of thousands of Rohingya to seek safety outside of Burma, even though neighboring countries such as Bangladesh and Thailand also harbor discriminatory views of the group, and many Rohingya undertake

---

[2] The country's military-led government officially changed the state's name from "Burma" to "Myanmar" in 1989, but I continue to use the term "Burma" in solidarity with Burmese human rights advocates and the country's pro-democracy movement.

treacherous voyages to other countries with the aid of human traffickers and smugglers. Those who can afford smugglers' fees might find themselves transported down the Bay of Bengal, over Thailand's southern coast, and into Malaysia. Along the way, displaced Rohingya face threats, such as lack of food and water, as well as abuse by smugglers who are known for killing or abandoning those who could not pay their fees. In some cases, Rohingya face "soft deportation" by the Thai government; they are moved from detention cells onto wooden boats, headed toward the Andaman Sea, where they are often picked up again by smugglers—who may be working in league with Thai officials. Those who cannot pay ransom for passage to Malaysia are often forced into indentured servitude on Thai farms and fishing vessels, thereby becoming victims of human trafficking (Perlez 2014).

Similarly, migrants fleeing government corruption, gang violence, and poverty in Central America and Mexico endure serious risks related to human smuggling and trafficking into the United States. Human Rights Watch (2014) contends that US immigration officers issue deportation orders to irregular migrants at the US-Mexico border that offer only a cursory screening for fears of persecution or torture, or the intention to apply for asylum; this process fails to effectively identify those who are fleeing serious risks in their home countries. Mexican drug cartels have seized the opportunities created by migrants' desperation and restrictive US immigration policies, exploiting Central Americans by exacting smuggling fees from them or trafficking them into dangerous situations. Migrants, including unaccompanied children, face threats of sexual exploitation, assault, forced labor, and even forced recruitment as soldiers in the region's drug wars; these threats are perpetuated by a widespread lack of law enforcement within Mexico, government corruption, and the absence of effective mechanisms for combating trafficking (Davila 2015).

In many cases, the negative consequences resulting from lack of functioning citizenship prompt unaccompanied children to undertake dangerous irregular migration. Older children who smuggle themselves across state borders in search of safety and/or livelihoods find themselves in a dangerous limbo since they often lack the state documentation that provides them with a legal identity—and they certainly don't possess the visa or residency statuses necessary for fully enjoying the rights to place and purpose. While unaccompanied child migrants experience the same vulnerabilities as adult irregular migrants, they also face the "acute need that comes from the deprivation of key elements of childhood"—including a consistent education, a secure home, and a supportive family and community (Bhabha 2011, 16). Indeed, many of these children "lack the common protections afforded to children generally by parents, family, or community members in the society at large" while their absence of legal residency status denies them the "fall-back guarantees" and the "safety net" of public or state rights that are essential for the protection of minors (Bicocchi 2011, 109). Luca Bicocchi argues that while most undocumented child migrants in Europe are not legally stateless, their lack of status prevents them from accessing their social rights or making rights demands on their country of origin; this "complex package of rightlessness and compromised access to the protection of family or state" renders them de facto stateless (110). Undocumented child migrants face a situation of "triple vulnerability" as children, as migrants, and as undocumented individuals outside their country of origin (112)—all leading to serious deprivations of rights to place and purpose, including access to education, healthcare, and housing (113–119). A troubling example of this vulnerability occurred in the United States, when the US Department of Health and Human Services placed more than a dozen migrant children in the custody of human traffickers. According to a Senate report, state officials failed to conduct background checks of caregivers tasked with caring for them during their immigration proceedings (Huetteman 2016).

The issue of unaccompanied minors became a migration crisis in the United States beginning in 2011 with a surge in child migration from Central America, while armed conflict and poverty has intensified the problem in Europe. Central American child migrants experience long-standing "push" and "pull" factors in the region, including the need to escape violence and economic woes and to reconnect with family members already living in the United States (Rosenblum 2015, 10). The increased migration of unaccompanied minors has been supported by networks of human smugglers, who promise "door to door" services while misrepresenting US immigration policies and falsely assuring parents that children will be granted lawful permission to remain in the United States on entry (15). In May 2016, US Customs and Border Protection data showed that apprehensions of unaccompanied child migrants involved children primarily from Guatemala (9,383), El Salvador (7,914), and Honduras (4,224) during the first six months of fiscal 2016 (October 2015 to March 2016). In that time period, apprehensions of unaccompanied children totaled 27,754—showing an increase of 78 percent from the year before. Relatedly, there were 32,117 apprehensions of family members—defined as children traveling with at least one parent or guardian—during that time, more than double the rate from the previous year (Krogstad 2016). In Europe, unaccompanied child migrants arrive from war-torn states such as Syria, Afghanistan, and Iraq or travel in hopes of escaping discrimination and poverty back home, but they are often denied adequate treatment on arrival. A lack of suitable accommodations and protection mechanisms for unaccompanied children in Greece has led to arbitrary and prolonged periods of detention. Detention has included unsanitary and degrading conditions, ill-treatment by police, detention with adult inmates, and the inability to access essential services such as medical treatment, psychological counseling, and legal aid (Human Rights Watch 2016a). Ashley Gilbertson (2016), a photographer who was granted entry into two Sicilian refugee shelters as part of a UNICEF team, noted that "the [Italian] state is having an especially hard time taking care of all the kids traveling alone," with many children without "much of anything to do as they wait for a decision on their asylum status" (para. 12). A seventeen-year-old boy from Gambia named Sanna told her: "We are not at school—if we were, we could say we have a normal life. But we are here, and all we do is eat and sit. They had a football before, but the ball is flat now" (para. 14). In the United Kingdom, a 2015 report by the Law Centres Network's Principles to Practice Project noted that despite government assurances, the asylum and care process did not reflect adequate understanding of child rights or allow child migrants to provide input about their needs. Researchers concluded that the British asylum process "merely pays lip service to children's best interests" (Law Centres Network 2015, para. 4).

A Place within the Global Mobility Regime

The processes of global migration are increasingly marked by an emphasis on securitization, politicization, and privatization that narrow possibilities for functioning citizenship and challenge the right to place. These concerns are most prevalent for irregular migrants and the forcibly displaced, but the impacts of these trends are felt at some level by anyone who engages in cross-border movement. The term "global mobility" refers to the movement of people across international borders for any length of time or purpose. It offers a more inclusive concept than the term "international migration" since it extends beyond immigrants, asylum-seekers, and refugees to include lesser-considered categories of travelers who cross borders for tourism, business, education, or temporary work abroad (Koslowski 2011, 2). While many countries support ease of travel for lucrative business and tourism purposes, the growth of the global mobility regime also favors migration policies that privilege highly educated and skilled workforces while preventing irregular migration and controlling displaced populations (Häkli 2015, 87). For instance, border security is one of the oldest and most basic functions of the state, but the nature of security has changed dramatically. Once focused on the military defense of territory against external threats, national security today has been reframed in terms of transnational phenomena such as migration, terrorism, economic flows, and cybercrime. As a result, security issues are seen as separate from the state and more directly connected to everyday life—including threats to the identity of social groups and security within routine activities. "The result of this shift in the meaning of security has been the penetration of security policies and practices deep into the fabric of society to the level of the individual," writes Gabriel Popescu (2015, 101). Borders play an important role in risk management strategies stemming from this perspective, emerging as security guarantors that have "uncritically become part of everyday life" while actively producing the perception of social and human security risks (102).

The border is a site of contestation that highlights how the historical territorial markers of citizenship are being reshaped by the forces of globalization. Anne McNevin (2011) writes that the prioritization of transnational market relations has disrupted the territorial frame of citizenship, prompting border policing of irregular migrants to enforce a territorial account of membership that is otherwise challenged by globalization. For irregular migrants, this situation requires political strategies to stake claims on community membership where they live and work; these are "struggles for legitimate presence and political equality" that are "contestations of citizenship that both undermine *and* reinscribe the conventional form of citizenship and the state's power to enforce it" (2). Johnson (2014) argues that irregularity directly challenges sovereign states both to "define the territorial nation-state as the only political space and place in the international order and to assert citizenship as the only status embodied with political agency" (4–5). From this perspective, irregularity represents a "rupture" and an "interruption" in dominant discourses, with migrants asserting their presence and changing political space (5). Interestingly, discussions of migration often rely on the existence of firm borders; the border is "always assumed rather than questioned" while scholars often fail to recognize how many borders are delegitimized or actively ignored. Brad K. Blitz (2016) notes that this subversion "raises a normative challenge to the exclusion of certain groups" and also highlights how the erection of borders does not guarantee the prevention of mobility (14). State interests in protecting the territorial markers of citizenship have prompted governments to build walls in places such as the United States/Mexico, South Africa/Zimbabwe, and Israel/Palestine, yet Wendy Brown (2010) contends that these walls often amount to little more than frequently breached theatrical props that blur the distinction between law and lawlessness. This drive to strengthen and securitize borders has led to the rise of a "business of noncitizenship," allowing for-profit private entities to play an increasing role in migration control—including the enactment and development of policy. Private visa processing companies, border guards, surveillance technology providers, transportation and detention firms, and deportation companies all represent private entities involved in decision making and the use of force related to migration control. "This contributes to a commodification of the construction of noncitizenship, which in turn emphasizes economic consideration, illegality, security and risk," writes Tendayi Bloom (2016, 892).

The importance of passports and state-issued documentation, as well as the growing use of biometric identification, is central to the securitization of the global mobility regime. Passports serve as a technology of "borderity," or the regulation of mobility, which has become naturalized and embedded in border control practices (Häkli 2015, 86). Indeed, passports and related documentation have become crucial for distinguishing between citizens and noncitizens—including the delineation of rights, social goods, and the enjoyment of freedom of movement in particular (Torpey 2000). Although wealthy countries have advanced systems of documentation and border control, it is noteworthy that irregular migrants are often able to obtain fraudulent documents quite easily in developing states such as India and Malaysia. Kamal Sadiq (2009) argues that the "documentary citizenship" expressed by these "paper citizens," while illegal, blurs the borders of political membership and raises questions about the true nature of citizenship. Is a passport, for instance, a true representation of citizenship within a political community? This question is complicated by the use of biometric technologies, which have gained increasing acceptance as yet another tool of documentation and border security; they are often posited as a "solution" for documenting migrant populations, including the forcibly displaced. Biometric systems measure physical or behavioral characteristics—such as fingerprints, faces, irises, and DNA—and are used for identity management, either to determine a person's identity or to verify their identity claim (Jain et al. 2011; Ashbourn 2014). Critics of biometric documentation warn of potential negative consequences, however, including the denial of humanitarian aid, limitations on coping mechanisms to survive displacement, and threats to basic protections.

Legal and ethical concerns include worries about privacy rights, "function creep", and misuse of data, and the prioritization of security over refugee and migrant rights (Kingston 2018).

The experiences of irregular migrants and asylum-seekers often overlap in detention facilities and processing centers situated in remote locations. The securitization of migration and its related discourse of crisis results in heightened surveillance and enforcement in the name of national security, increasingly exercised in detention facilities far away from the sovereign territory. Migration crises thus occur at the margins of state borders—on islands, in airports, at sea, and in offshore detention facilities. "These sites are hypervisible during crises and yet simultaneously obscured from view of the general public and human rights monitors," argues Mountz (2010). "This paradoxical location makes them ideal sites for enforcement activities where states manipulate geography" (xvii). And although refugee camps and migrant detention centers are frequently conceptualized as different sorts of spaces—the refugee camp a humanitarian space focused on protection while the detention center represents a mechanism of border control and security—the experiences of those contained within these spaces highlight striking similarities. "In both sites, migrants are there because they resisted the state border regulation; they are irregular," explains Johnson (2014, 126). Administrative structures are meant to separate migrants from the citizenry, political agency is "tightly circumscribed" (if not outright denied) and viewed as "dangerous and unwelcome," and those who live within these spaces "live in a space of territorial and temporal exception where their futures are held in abeyance, indeterminate and in the control of the authorities that govern the space" (126). These facilities serve to limit or deny functioning citizenship, physically separating migrants from legal citizens and effectively criminalizing human movement through the securitization of state borders. It is notable that this applies not only to irregular migrants, but also to asylum-seekers invoking their fundamental rights to protection against persecution.

Australia hosts one of the world's most controversial offshore programs, operating detention and processing facilities for irregular migrants and asylum-seekers in neighboring island nations rather than on Australian soil. The country's "Pacific Solution" began in 2001 in response to increasing dangerous migration by boat, often aided by networks of human smugglers. Subsequent agreements with the governments of Nauru and Papua New Guinea support Australia's tougher border policies, ensuring that all migrants who arrived by boat would be processed and settled outside of Australian territory. The Australian government argues that processing asylum-seekers in other countries is necessary for a variety of reasons, including the prevention of human smuggling, ensuring border security, preventing overcrowding in detention facilities, and creating a safe and orderly process for migrants. According to May 2016 statistics, 77 percent (915) of the 1,194 detainees in Nauru were found to be refugees, while 98 percent (541) of detainees in Papua New Guinea qualified as refugees (Karlsen 2016). Human Rights Watch (2015c) calls Australia's transfer policy "harsh," however, arguing that it focuses on returning migrants rather than protecting their human rights. Citing similar criticisms from the United Nations High Commissioner for Refugees (UNHCR), the organization notes that this "return-oriented" policy results in overcrowded and dirty detention facilities, slow and unfair asylum claims processing, disregard for detainees' physical and mental health, persecution of gay asylum-seekers, threats of sexual assault, and even offers by the Australian government to entice asylum-seekers to return to unsafe home countries. Human Rights Watch (2016b) argues that these actions represent an outsourcing of human rights obligations to "poorer, less well-equipped, and unsafe countries" (para. 4). In 2015, this process included returning migrant boats to Sri Lanka and Vietnam despite their poor human rights records as well as reportedly paying more than $30,000 USD to human smugglers to return a boat to Indonesia (Human Rights Watch 2016b). Current policy discussions hint at worse treatment to come; in October 2016, Australian prime minister Malcolm Turnbull announced his support for a new law banning irregular migrants—including those who could be categorized as refugees under international law—from obtaining any visa to enter Australia. The retrospective law could be applied to nearly 1,300 already detained on Manus Island and Nauru; notably, 72 percent of camp detainees have been assessed as genuine refugees (Conifer 2016). Turnbull argued that the ban would send a strong message to human smugglers and irregular migrants: "They must know that the door to Australia is closed to those who seek to come here by boat with a people smuggler. It is closed. Those passengers will never settle in this country" (quoted in Conifer 2016, para. 5–6).

Within its state borders, however, Australia is one of various developed countries that has expanded its population of legal noncitizen residents through the expansion of temporary visa programs. While temporary visas constitute legal migration and therefore don't fall into the category of "irregular" migration, it is worthwhile to note how these schemes disrupt traditional processes toward full legal citizenship and obstruct functioning citizenship. Australia reflects a global shift from permanent settlement to temporary mobility, providing a range of different visas that include employer-sponsored temporary migrants, international students, graduate workers, and tourist-workers on holiday work schemes. This diversification of migrant statuses creates a "patchwork" of rights and entitlements, often without clear pathways to permanent status that leaves many migrants in "precarious" situations (Robertson 2016, 940). Requirements for permanent status are ever-changing and unequal, with the "promise of citizenship" often subjecting noncitizens to systemic violence and intense state regulations; a migrant's financial and personal investments in Australia "can be severely disrupted by the state's ever present power to exclude" (946).

Similar criticisms have been directed toward temporary visa programs in other countries. In the United States, the American Federation of Labor and Congress of Industrial Organizations (AFL–CIO) argues that guest worker programs undermine immigrant rights, creating "a system that allows employers to hire people who *by law* have virtually no rights and are therefore easy targets for exploitation and abuse" (Lederer 2015, para. 1). Elizabeth F. Cohen (2015, 2018) further argues, as noted in Chapter 1, that the US government has slowly devalued immigrant time over the past half century. It has rendered time-in-residence politically valueless while using actions such as deferred departure to create and legitimize a class of permanent "semi-citizens" who lack fully functioning citizenship (see also Cohen 2009). In Canada, critics say the country's seasonal agricultural worker program denies workers labor rights and leaves them vulnerable to deportation if they complain. "This program is a form of apartheid," said Chris Ramsaroop, an organizer with Justicia for Migrant Workers. "Migrant workers are employed and live under a different set of legal rights than Canadians. The very existence of temporary foreign worker programs enables the Canadian government to deny basic freedoms and protections as a result of their immigration status" (quoted in Levin 2017, para. 7–8). Within Europe, countries such as Germany partially built their economies with the labor of guest workers; 750,000 Turkish citizens worked in Germany between 1961 and 1972 to fill vacant jobs. The presence of these workers explains why some German neighborhoods—such as Berlin's Kreuzberg—are "palpably Turkish" (Mekhennet 2011, para. 4), but a lack of appropriate integration programs for these seemingly temporary migrants also limited their abilities to engage in Germany society, advocate for their rights, and access functioning citizenship. "Neither Turkey as the sending country nor Germany as receiving country did enough, for a long time, to take care of these people," said Cem Özdemir, the son of

Turkish guest workers who came to Germany during the 1960s (quoted in para. 17).

Indeed, many migrants' rights to place—including their ability to access legal residency and perhaps attain legal naturalization one day—is dependent on their assigned "market value" in the global labor market and their perceived social fit within a state's dominant society. Aihwa Ong's (2006) influential work on "neoliberalism as exception" makes the case for an emerging mode of citizenship that organizes people according to marketable skills rather than political membership. This has serious repercussions for rights protections, since the distribution of rights and benefits "are now malleable," configured in large part by "market-driven modes of governing" (27). Relatedly, Sébastien Chauvin and Blanca Garcés-Mascareñas (2012) argue that migrant "illegality" does not typically serve as an absolute marker of illegitimacy but instead serves as a "handicap" on a spectrum of probationary citizenship. Within this system, an "emerging moral economy of deservingness" encourages irregular migrants to gather proofs of presence, reliable conduct, and other emblems of good citizenship with an eye toward future naturalization. However, these demands are made at the same time that states are intensifying restrictions and controls on immigration, making it difficult for migrants to gather official documentation while they have "illegal" status (243). Blitz (2016) notes that successful migration depends on "structural constraints, social barriers and individual factors, including ethno-national affiliations; age, sex, gender; educational level and linguistic ability; job status and occupational profile; social and professional networks; and residency. These constraints, in turn, serve to define a range of migrants whose personal identities, social and official status are often shaped by their degrees of access" (13).

Deportation and Tenuous Rights to Purpose

For individuals whose market value and personhood are not recognized by the state, the widespread use of deportation holds irregular migrants' rights to place under constant threat. Such expulsions limit migrants' ability to enjoy rights to purpose while clearly identifying them as less worthy of rights protections compared to legal citizens. Deportation—the forced removal of "illegal" aliens from the "physical, juridical, and social space of the state"—has emerged as the presumably natural government response to irregular migration (Peutz and De Genova 2010, 1).

Examples abound, including well-known cases of detention and deportation across the Mediterranean region (see Andrijasevic 2010) and along the US-Mexico borderlands (see Talavera et al. 2010). In Switzerland, "suspicious" sub-Saharan African migrants are frequently identified as "illegal" migrants and deported whereas Portuguese construction workers or domestically employed Slovak nurses without work visas are relatively free from fears of deportation; immigration practices and policies control the distinction between "good illegals" and "bad illegals" (Wicker 2010, 224–226). In Israel, the government shifted its policy on unauthorized migrant workers who were once welcomed to take jobs formerly held by Palestinian workers. Beginning in 2002, the Israeli government initiated a mass deportation campaign targeting an estimated 100,000 irregular migrants in response to rising unemployment within the state (Willen 2010, 262–263).

The rise of the deportation regime forces us to consider questions of *freedom,* in the most basic sense of the word: "the freedom to traverse space and to make a place for oneself in the world" (Peutz and De Genova 2010, 3). Nicholas De Genova and Nathalie Peutz (2010) write that "deportation . . . is premised on a normative division of the world into territorially defined, 'sovereign' (nation-)states, and within these states, the ubiquitous division enacted between more or less 'rightful' members (citizens) and relatively rightless nonmembers (aliens)" (7). While in reality deportation is usually time-consuming, expensive, controversial, and ultimately ineffective for halting irregular migration, the deportation regime is profoundly effective at producing and maintaining the illegality of irregular migration. With this wide acceptance of "illegal" status come legal, financial, and human rights consequences—as well as a "deeply interiorized mode of being—and of being put in place" (14). Unlike the stateless, who struggle to protect their rights in the absence of the state, deportable migrants become the object of sovereign state power to exclude while being at the same time included in the purview of state's power (15). For many deported individuals, the act of deportation represents a departure from their home—not a return to it. Consider the case of Alex Sanchez, a former gang member and the director of a gang violence prevention program in Los Angeles, who had re-entered the United States after being deported to El Salvador in 1994. Deported as a "criminal alien," Sanchez found himself in an unfamiliar and hostile environment that prompted him to undertake irregular migration; his so-called home country of El Salvador was now a place of foreignness and stigma. Indeed, deportees with criminal convictions face discrimination and illegality in both countries, with deportation serving to exacerbate lawlessness rather than combat it (Coutin 2010).

Despite the existence of universal rights, in reality "aliens" face state scrutiny that challenges their fundamental rights to purpose; subject to immigration laws and under threat of deportation, irregular migrants "never quite reach the position of comfort" allotted to them by the idealistic promise of post-national membership (Joppke 2010, 84). Certain rights are often out of reach for irregular migrants—including political rights, absolute protection from expulsion, the rights of diplomatic protection, and a variety of social rights (84 and 90). Matthew Gibney (2011), who uses the term "precarious residents" to describe irregular migrants and other vulnerable groups, argues that the "very limited social, economic and political rights of precarious non-citizens are often a consequence of deliberate policy on the part of the state" (44). He continues: "The withholding of rights is motivated by a desire to encourage their departure from state territory or, according to some, to keep them vulnerable to economic exploitation. The state cannot therefore be counted on to be an ally in the search for social and economic security [for these people]" (44). Indeed, the securitization of migration and the "othering" of foreigners that it perpetuates fuels the criminality of human movement while at the same time denying legitimate/legal avenues that could ensure rights to place. Without the protection of place—both in terms of legal rights to remain within a territory as well as membership within a political community—irregular migrants experience uncertainty in their daily lives that challenges even the most fundamental rights to purpose.

Salient rights to purpose vary by individual, but in the context of the United States, three basic entitlements are often denied to or are unequally accessed by irregular migrants: rights to education, family, and fair employment. First, irregular migrants face severe challenges to education despite universal rights to primary education as well as protections for higher education and technical training.[3] The 1982 US Supreme Court decision *Plyler v. Doe* ensured that undocumented students have access

---

[3] Article 26(1) of the Universal Declaration of Human Rights (UDHR) outlines the human right to an elementary education, noting that technical and professional education will be "generally available" and that higher education "shall be equally accessible to all on the basis of merit." Article 26(2) further contends that education "shall be directed to the full development of the human personality and to the strengthening of respect for human rights and fundamental freedoms," with the aim of promoting understanding, tolerance, and friendship among nations and identity groups (United Nations 1948). These norms, like other articles of the UDHR, are reinforced by binding international law, and education is addressed by Article 13 of the International Covenant on Economic, Social and Cultural Rights (United Nations High Commissioner for Human Rights 1966) and Article 28 of the Convention on the Rights of the Child (United Nations High Commissioner for Human Rights 1989).

to free K–12 public education because it is necessary for achieving any meaningful degree of individual equality. The Court ruled that children should not forfeit their education because their parents had decided to migrate irregularly, and forcing them to do so would impose a lifetime hardship on them. However, many undocumented students continue to suffer inequalities during their K–12 years despite legal protections. In many cases, whether an undocumented student succeeds in school is dependent on social factors that extend far beyond the provision of free education. Social and emotional hardships include migration stressors (including the loss of close relationships, a sense of isolation, and the necessity to learn English), anxieties and depression associated with one's undocumented status, and socioeconomic challenges. Some students manage to maintain high levels of optimism and perseverance in spite of these obstacles—often if they are able to form positive relationships with teachers and school counselors—but undocumented youth endure significant issues that can greatly impact their school attendance, grades, and academic involvement (Pérez 2012, 8–12). "Historically, public schools have wielded the power to either replicate societal inequalities or equalize the playing field," writes Roberto Gonzales (2016, 13). Unfortunately, many large urban school districts lack the human resources to meet student needs; school stratification often disadvantages migrant children when it comes to accessing higher-level curricula or receiving much-needed support. A perception that such resources are provided according to merit, rather than race or class-based discrimination, normalizes the achievement gap between migrant and native children (Gonzales 2016, 13).

Additionally, the pressures of undocumented legal status often create challenges for migrant parents that negatively impact their children's early development and can adversely influence their future educational achievement. In his ethnographic study of irregular migrants raising their young, American-born children in New York City, Hirokazu Yoshikawa (2011) argues that parents' undocumented status can harm children's development in their early years—regardless of whether their children are US citizens. The exclusion of irregular migrants impacts developmental contexts directly experienced by children, as well as indirect contexts that influence their well-being, while documentation status also impacts potential assimilation into neighborhoods and peer networks that can facilitate learning. Yoshikawa offers a model outlining four kinds of development contexts that can transmit the impact of parents' undocumented status on early childhood development: (1) Interactions with legal and illegal authorities—ranging from government agencies to human smugglers—that may limit access to resources: Fears of deportation may force parents to avoid governmental agencies that provide childcare subsidies or food stamps available to their American citizen children, for instance, while debts to smugglers can adversely affect a family's financial well-being. (2) Experiences embedded in more informal social ties that highlight key differences between undocumented migrant families and documented ones: In most households, *all* adults were undocumented—meaning that entire households lacked access to essential resources such as bank accounts and driver's licenses. New arrival parents also had less social support to assist with raising their children, often living in neighborhoods with few organizations serving the needs of undocumented families. (3) Adverse work conditions: These often included exploitation, high numbers of hours worked, wage stagnation, lack of benefits, and low levels of autonomy. (4) These three sets of experiences result in a fourth set related to the intimacy of home and childcare settings, where infants and toddlers spend the most time. In turn, these contexts all lead to parental stress and mental health issues, the inability to access resources for child development, and lower levels of skilled childcare—all of which negatively impact early childhood development (Yoshikawa 2011, 22–24).

Irregular migrants who succeed in K–12 despite such obstacles are nevertheless routinely denied equal access to higher education in the United States, as well as technical and professional education. Equal access to education ends with high school graduation, and federal law has greatly curtailed access to higher education by making financial aid unavailable to irregular migrants for postsecondary education. Undocumented students are far less likely to attend college compared to their native-born peers; although some states have provided undocumented students with financial aid opportunities and in-state tuition rates, those students are unable to work legally to support themselves while in school—or after graduation (Pérez 2012, 5–7). In a study of 110 undocumented Latino high school, community college, and university students from across the United States, William Pérez found that students faced a wide range of educational, social, and institutional challenges as a direct result of their lack of legal status. Despite these obstacles, however, results indicated high levels of academic performance (including extensive extracurricular participation and leadership activities) and civic engagement. Access to community college served as an important educational gateway for some, but students who were eventually able to gain legal status enjoyed dramatic educational gains compared to those who remained undocumented. For many undocumented students, coming of legal age at eighteen represents a transition to illegality—"a process that not only shapes their lives socially and emotionally but also redefines their rights, access, and ability to stay in the country" (Gonzales 2016, 12). While one's lack of legal status may be less consequential in childhood, when US law protects the right to K–12 education, it becomes a "master status" in everyday life that trumps one's cultural identity, behavior, and educational attainment (15). Within the United States, polarized debates about immigration tend to pit hardliners against those who are supportive of legal pathways to citizenship, particularly for students who immigrated as babies and young children. The DREAM Act (Development, Relief, and Education for Alien Minors) was first introduced in the US Senate in 2001 with the aim of creating a path to citizenship for undocumented migrants raised in the United States, but several versions of this bill have failed to pass despite growing pressure from a youth movement of so-called DREAMers. Passage of the DREAM Act would open up opportunities for higher education and legal employment, as well as protect migrant students' right to place within the United States, but the 2016 election of Donald Trump made this an unlikely possibility in the near future.

Second, undocumented families endure hardships related to their irregular migration that threatens their fundamental rights of the family—"the natural and fundamental group unit of society" (United Nations 1948, Article 16.3) that has special protections within human rights frameworks and law.[4] The tightening of immigration laws and increasing threats of deportation from the United States serve to harm the family lives of irregular migrants, including relationships between parents and children, as well as between siblings. In her book *Divided by Borders*, Joanna Dreby (2010) tells the story of Mexican migrants who leave their children with caregivers in Mexico so the parents can work long hours in the United States, hoping to enhance their children's opportunities through their own labor. Drawing from interviews with more than 140 family

---

[4] Article 12 of the UDHR guards against "arbitrary interference" with one's privacy, family, and home, while Article 16(3) stipulates that the family "is the natural and fundamental group unit of society and is entitled to protection by society and the State" (United Nations 1948). The Convention on the Rights of the Child stresses the key importance of family and identity, noting that children have the right to preserve family relations without unlawful interference (Article 8), to not be separated from their parents against their will except in particular cases of abuse or neglect (Article 9.1), and to special state protections when temporarily or permanently deprived of their family environment (Article 20.1). Notably, Article 9(4) recognizes the possibility of detention or deportation; states should supply children (or family members, where appropriate) with essential information about the whereabouts of the absent family members unless that information would be harmful to the child's well-being (United Nations High Commissioner for Human Rights 1989).

members in New Jersey and south-central Mexico, Dreby considers how migrant parents adapt to immigration policies and make the decision to migrate without their children. Interviews show the emotional fallout that results from these choices: unmet expectations, tensions and hurt feelings in parent-child relationships, parental (especially maternal) guilt, and children's resentment of their parents' absences. Ultimately, Dreby finds that separation transforms power dynamics within families and places severe challenges on the family unit. In the "sequel" to her research, Dreby (2015) focuses on the experiences of families who are internally divided while living together. Interviews with 201 Mexican families living in Ohio and New Jersey highlight how "illegality is more than a legal status: it is a social one" (5). She argues that the US immigration "had crystallized and become so strict and far-reaching that legal status had begun to divide even families residing together in the United States" (3). Dreby contends that enforcement policies have created a culture of fear akin to a public health crisis, manifesting in symptoms including severe anxiety among parents and children. Interviews show that restrictive immigration policies sometimes force women to remain with manipulative and/or abusive partners; traditional gender roles are often reinforced as illegality impacts power negotiations within families. Inequalities arise between siblings with different legal statuses, as well, with illegality marking differences in daily routines and future opportunities. Legal status also shapes children's identity formation, and illegality—"just like race and class disadvantages—is likely to have unexpected long-term consequences for children's social mobility" (11).

Irregular migrant families share commonalities but also achieve varying levels of success. In her study of transnational families split between El Salvador and the United States, Leisy Abrego (2014) seeks to better understand the discrepancies that arise in family well-being by focusing on immigration policies and gender. She argues that the production of illegality in the United States "determines the life chances and well-being of people beyond its territorial borders. From determining who is eligible for a visa and who can regularize his or her status to how long immigrants must wait to file a petition for their close relatives to join them in the country, policies and enforcement practices produce illegality with consequences that are not easily contained by borders" (9). Abrego also contends that gender ideologies, structures, and practices shape migrant opportunities and family behavior as well as labor markets and other social institutions/ spaces. Unquestioned gender inequalities perpetuate social problems such as the uneven burden of childcare and higher moral expectations faced by women migrants. Structural barriers and socioeconomic inequalities "can prevent poor and working-class parents from fulfilling their social expectations"—often leading to increased disadvantages for migrant mothers, absentee fathers, and highly gendered differences in access to jobs and the resulting ability to send remittances home (10). "Families all around the world are expected to provide much of the emotional and economic support necessary for children's healthy development" and transnational Salvadoran families are no different, explains Abrego. "Parents make the decision, with a limited set of options, to pursue migration as a way to provide for their children. They are hopeful at the outset, but not everyone is successful" (23). In the end, there are often long-term consequences of family separation that impact individual family members as well as the societies in which they live. For instance, family separation has been linked to children's school performance and their feelings of belonging within their country and their community. Abrego notes that many migrant youth "had developed a lack of concern for the world around them" as they waited to be reunited with their parents, existing within "suspended lives" (168).

Third, rights to fair employment are often inaccessible to irregular migrants.[5] In the United States, modern migration was significantly marked by the *bracero* program—a series of agreements between Mexico and the United States that gave temporary work visas to Mexican men between 1942 and 1964, allowing them to work on American farms. The program was intended to employ Mexicans to do difficult "stoop labor" that US workers mostly refused to do (Cohen 2011, 9); eventually the imported workers were to return home to Mexico. *Braceros* formed complex identities across the two countries that made them "simultaneously national, alien, transnational, and modern" (Cohen 2011, 7). Once encouraged to (temporarily) immigrate to the United States to do work that most Americans found unappealing, many Mexican laborers today are often cut off from legal employment opportunities.[6] The US civilian

---

[5] Article 23 of the UDHR contends that everyone "has the right to work, to free choice of employment, to just and favorable conditions of work and protection against unemployment," without discrimination, and with rights to equal pay and to "just and favorable remuneration" that ensures an existence "worthy of human dignity." Article 4 provides protection against slavery or servitude (United Nations 1948). The International Covenant on Economic, Social and Cultural Rights reinforces these protections, highlighting the "right to work" in Article 6(1)—which includes "the right of everyone to the opportunity to gain [their] living by work which [they] freely chooses or accepts" (United Nations High Commissioner for Human Rights 1966).

[6] Mexicans made up 52 percent of all irregular migrants within the U.S. in 2014, although their numbers had been declining in recent years, and 59 percent of irregular migrants were found in six states: California, Texas, Florida, New York, New Jersey, and Illinois. About two-thirds

workforce included 8 million unauthorized workers in 2014, representing 5 percent of the total American workforce. These irregular migrants were overrepresented in farming (26 percent) and construction (15 percent), although in these industries (and all others) they were significantly outnumbered by US-born workers (Krogstad et al. 2016). It is notable that even among documented immigrant workers, who make up 17 percent of the American workforce, employment patterns contrast sharply with those of native-born workers. Even legal immigrants are more likely than their US-born peers to work in industries such as administrative services, agriculture, extraction, construction, leisure/hospitality, and manufacturing (PEW Charitable Trusts 2015), all jobs that generally entail long hours, difficult and sometimes dangerous working conditions, and low pay. Foreign-born workers are less likely to be employed in education, finance and real estate, healthcare, information industries, and various professional services (PEW Charitable Trusts 2015). For irregular migrants, their precarious legal status provides opportunities for unscrupulous employers to exploit them in various ways, including paying them at rates lower than minimum wage requirements, exposing them to dangerous working conditions, requiring them to work long shifts without overtime pay or adequate break time, and a host of other labor law violations. These issues occur despite the fact that irregular migrants hold legal rights under state and federal law (with some exceptions, mainly related to unemployment insurance and union organizing) (Legal Aid Society—Employment Law Center n.d.).

The political and economic factors that force many migrants to undertake irregular movement, thus giving up rights to place in their home communities, often create little sympathy or motivation in host communities to provide avenues for legal employment. Journalist David Bacon (2008) argues that globalized systems create illegality "by displacing people and then denying them rights and equality as they do what they have to do to survive—move to find work" (vi). His interviews with hotel workers in California and meatpackers in North Carolina, for instance, highlight how immigration enforcement harms irregular laborers and the workers around them. At the same time, Bacon notes that the economic system that causes labor displacement—including the corporatization of the Mexican economy, promoted by the North American Free Trade Agreement (NAFTA), that slashed many Mexican wages and harmed

---

(66 percent) of adult irregular migrants in 2014 had been in the United States for at least a decade (Krogstad et al. 2016).

small businesses—benefits from labor displacement and the undocumented labor it creates (see Chapter 3).

The US state of Arizona offers a case study for understanding the complicated economic impacts of irregular migration on a host community. Arizona passed a series of tough anti-immigration laws, and its population of undocumented workers dropped by 40 percent between 2007 and 2012, which was by far the biggest percentage decline in any American state. Some contend that this move financially benefited Arizona while others argue the opposite; indeed, it is difficult to measure the costs of irregular migration and labor because so much activity is left off the record books. Immigration opponents argue that taxpayers are burdened with education, medical, and even incarceration costs of irregular migrants while advocates point out that irregular migrants contribute annual tax revenue that boosts state and federal programs. Arizona's "immigration surplus," or the economic activity produced by migrants, certainly shrank as a result of immigration legislation. As the state's economy recovered between 2010 and 2014, some employers complained that they were unable to find laborers to work in the agricultural and construction sectors—thereby limiting Americans' abilities to undertake profitable work and expand their businesses (Davis 2016). Jeremy Barbosa, president of Precise Drywall Inc. in Phoenix, would send fifty laborers to help build luxury homes before the immigration crackdown. "I could pull out phone books where I had 300 or 400 guys' numbers," he said. "Now you have to put out feelers, buy ads, go on Craigslist, tap job agencies just to get a few men. Growth is based on the ability to hire" (quoted in para. 28–29). Such concerns have done little to weaken the anti-immigrant fervor in the United States, however, as many conservatives increasingly call for the deportation of undocumented migrants and withdrawal from trade agreements such as NAFTA.

Despite the pervasive threats that irregular migrants face in the United States, many young people have been surprisingly active in campaigning for their rights. The undocumented youth movement, comprised of so-called DREAMers, transformed the US immigrant rights debate in unexpected ways during Barack Obama's presidency. It is generally assumed that hostile environments that stigmatize immigrants and stress nationalism offer few opportunities for social movement mobilization. Yet the DREAMers took strategic steps—including identifying niche openings, creating compelling representations, forming strategic alliances, and disciplining messages and their messengers—to produce "a legitimate voice" calling for legal status and rights protections for young, undocumented migrants who called the United States "home" (Nicholls 2013, 15). For years, these undocumented youth had given up their aspirations for higher education or successful careers because they were limited by their status; in many cases, this lack of documentation was a carefully guarded secret that thwarted attempts to organize. The proposed DREAM Act provided a pivotal focus for mobilizing against these long-standing issues, however. An organizational structure was formed with the help of immigrant rights associations, college campus support groups, online networks, and national organizations, providing an inclusive environment for young people to "come out" and finally talk about their status with those who shared their experiences. DREAMers rejected the hierarchy of personhood that had been inscribed by their lack of legal status and collectively asserted that they were "undocumented, unafraid, and unapologetic. They publicly rejected a life in the shadows and demanded the right to be recognized as rights-deserving human beings" (4). These efforts show that political participation among irregular migrants is not impossible, although it is complicated; the DREAMers and other migrants have vulnerabilities that many other activists do not, such as the threat of deportation.[7]

The distinction between regular and irregular—legal and illegal—migration often constructs categories of membership, worthiness, and personhood. As the boundaries between irregular migration and forced displacement continue to blur and overlap, the international community grapples with hierarchies of personhood that privilege citizens while denying basic protections to individuals seeking physical security and livelihoods abroad. These divisions deny functioning citizenship and perpetuate international crime such as human trafficking and smuggling, fueling dangerous global trends such as the migration of unaccompanied children. Securitized and privatized processes of global migration narrow possibilities for political membership, challenging the right to place as migrants struggle to meet growing demands related to documentation, surveillance, and border protection. Those who are not deemed worthy of membership and its resulting protections face the threat of deportation

---

[7] Many who registered for the Deferred Action for Childhood Arrival (DACA) program—an executive action by President Obama to allow certain young immigrants to secure renewable two-year work visas and exempt them from deportation—fear that the personal information they provided to the US Citizenship and Immigration Services will be used against them if handed over to Homeland Security enforcement agents. Following the election of Donald Trump, DREAMers worried that they would again be denied legal avenues toward higher education and employment, as well as threatened with family separation (Preston and Medina 2016).

and detention, constraining rights to purpose such as those related to education, family, and fair employment. Trapped within liminal spaces outside the law and beyond the reach of human rights protection, irregular migrants grapple with a troubling lack of functioning citizenship where their basic claims to place and purpose are often derided and ignored.

PART III | Marginalized Nations and Minorities

CHAPTER 5 | Nomadic Peoples and Alternate Conceptions of Place

WITHIN THE HIERARCHY OF personhood, nomadic peoples are frequently relegated to an inferior status marked by devalued cultural identities, livelihood strategies, and capabilities. Often viewed as remnants of the past who are unable (or unwilling) to adequately care for themselves and the land resources around them, nomadic peoples are pressured by majority populations to give up their ways of life and conform to "modern" sedentary ideals. In Europe, for instance, efforts to assimilate traditionally nomadic groups such as Roma and Travellers have become increasingly prominent since the nineteenth century—focusing in large part on behavioral change and ideals of "respectable" society that led to conversion efforts to embrace both market economics and Christianity (Smith and Greenfields 2013, 14–15).[1] Discrimination against and dehumanization of Roma fueled genocide by the Nazis during World War II, known in Romani as *Porrajmos* (the "Great Devouring"). Today, human rights advocates cite widespread abuses throughout Europe, including ineffective state responses to violence and hate speech against Roma, segregated public schools, forced evictions, and ongoing coercive sterilization (see European Roma Rights Centre n.d.). These violations perpetuate historical

---

[1] In many ways, processes of sedentarization were successful; while modern stereotypes characterize "Gypsies" as nomadic peoples, the majority are settled with some form of permanent dwelling—although long-standing discrimination means they lack strong emotional attachments to particular states. Ironically, many Roma families in modern times have forcibly undertaken migration as a result of persecution, extreme hardship, and armed conflict rather than because of nomadic instincts. (For an interesting short discussion on this topic, see Sampson 2000.) Yet the Roma's historical reputation for nomadism, combined with cultural styles that tend to differ from that of the majority sedentary population, means that Roma communities today face ongoing challenges to their rights to place and purpose similar to the threats confronted by other, more "traditional" nomadic groups.

processes of discrimination against nomadic peoples in Europe, where the Roma are viewed as suspicious strangers outside the state protection afforded to the "legitimate" citizenry. Indeed, Jacqueline Bhabha (2017) argues that the Roma are excluded from national, regional, and global citizenship mechanisms for claiming their rights.

Such stark denial of functioning citizenship was grimly illustrated in 2008, when the image of two drowned Roma sisters in Italy—and the beachgoers who continued to enjoy their day at the beach, just feet away from the bodies—sparked international outrage. Eleven-year-old Violetta and thirteen-year-old Cristina Djeordsevic had drowned in the Bay of Naples, in sight of their young cousins Manuela and Diana. After they were recovered and pronounced dead, their bodies lay covered with beach towels for three hours before being taken away. In the meantime, a troubling photograph of the bodies showed beachgoers continuing nonchalantly with their seaside picnics and games of Frisbee. The photograph drew intense condemnation from critics of Italian prime minister Silvio Berlusconi, who had won a third term in office with anti-immigrant rhetoric and support for a fingerprinting program to document the country's 150,000 Roma—including many families who had been in Italy since the Middle Ages. Violetta and Cristina, both Roma children who had been born in Italy, became human faces for the "endless procession of marginalization and prejudice" facing the estimated 10 million European Roma—the majority of whom suffer enduring poverty, statelessness, and "official indifference and reluctance" from governments to address their human rights challenges (McDougall 2008, para. 12). Cardinal Crescenzio Sepe, the most senior Catholic clergyman in Naples at the time, noted solemnly that "Cristina and Violetta had faced nothing but prejudice in life and indifference in death; an unforgivable truth" (quoted in McDougall 2008, para. 9).[2]

---

[2] Outrage over Cristina's and Violetta's deaths has not quelled the persecution against Roma communities in Italy, however, and examples of denied rights to place and purpose abound. For instance, in 2013, the municipality of Rome was accused of segregating 4,000 Roma in overcrowded, substandard social housing. Relocated following forced evictions, Roma families were placed in pre-fabricated or mobiles homes located far from essential services, places of potential employment, and Italian residential neighborhoods (Amnesty International 2013). In 2017, hundreds of Roma were forcibly evicted from the Gianturco informal settlement in Naples. Some displaced families were placed in a segregated container camp, Via del Riposo; the site was targeted by arsonists in a 2011 hate crime, and graffiti proclaiming "No Roma, enough" was still visible nearby (Motoc 2017, para 11). The evictions prompted criticism of the European Commission for its refusal to open an infringement case against Italy for discriminating against Roma in fair housing (Motoc 2017).

This lack of functioning citizenship among nomadic peoples is not limited to Europe, however. In African countries such as Tanzania and Kenya, pastoralist nomads such as the Maasai face challenges from land privatization, the subdivision of communal lands, and conservation activities that all tend to benefit sedentary citizens while ignoring the needs of nomadic populations (Homewood et al. 2009). "Land grabbing" practices (which are often facilitated by government corruption and rights abuse) privilege sedentary development plans and threaten nomadic rights to place and purpose, threatening to end the nomadic way of life in many Maasai communities. Bedouin in the Middle East and North Africa (MENA) region face similar concerns, often regarded as primitive savages unable to effectively manage and sustain land resources. In Israel, Bedouin communities have been stripped of traditional lands and denied the functioning citizenship afforded to Jewish Israeli citizens. In these cases and countless others, nomadic peoples are deemed inferior to majority populations and subjected to policies aimed at "civilizing," settling, and controlling them. As governments increasingly deal with limited natural resources, including the land conflicts this scarcity engenders, an emphasis on sustainable development is often used to portray nomadic peoples as unworthy of rights to property and movement.

While it is difficult to gain a clear estimate of the number of nomadic peoples worldwide—with various sources offering the broad range of 50 million to 250 million globally—there is widespread agreement that the nomadic way of life is in danger of cultural extinction (Gilbert 2014, 9). Focusing on three case studies—European Roma and Travellers, the Maasai in Tanzania and Kenya, and the Bedouin in the Middle East and north Africa—this chapter argues that nomadic peoples are frequently denied functioning citizenship, in part, because their alternate conceptions of place are not valued (and perhaps not understood) by sedentary majority populations. Indeed, their differing views on land—and by extension, on community and the nation—position them outside the political community of the majority citizenry. While each case study has its unique history and challenges, each illustrates the threats nomadic peoples are experiencing to their essential rights to place and purpose. Their perspectives often ignored in decision making and their identities devalued by pervasive discrimination, these groups are relegated to unequal positions vis-à-vis sedentary citizens.

Eliminating Nomadism

Conflict between settled and nomadic populations has contributed to violent conflict throughout much of human history,[3] resulting in bias and persecution that continues to threaten vital livelihood strategies central to nomadic identities. Colonial powers considered nomadic peoples more "backward" than other so-called savages, and today nomadism continues to be viewed as something to be abolished; nomadic populations face a variety of legal pressures to integrate within the majority settled society (Gilbert 2007, 681). Colonial settlers around the world classed nomadic peoples as "primitive" subhumans akin to parasites rather than full human beings, viewing them as obstacles to "progress" and "civilization." At the same time, settlers' need for land and territory meant that the extermination of nomadic populations created opportunities for the control and exploitation of resources (Gilbert 2014, 29). Nomadic peoples have traditionally been viewed as incapable of engaging in "effective occupation" of land because of their mobile lifestyles as pastoral nomads, hunter-gatherers, or peripatetic service nomads. Yet being able to travel through traditional territories is crucial for nomadic survival, making freedom of movement essential for protecting nomadic peoples' cultural modes of being. In fact, identity among nomadic peoples is often intricately linked to their patterns of mobility and livelihood. Rather than living nomadic lifestyles because they have not yet "discovered" the benefits of settlement, many nomadic peoples choose to retain their traditional practices— or adapt those practices according to their needs and preferences—partly to express and protect their identity. In the face of increasing threats to those nomadic lifestyles, many groups are fighting for their cultural survival.

Nomadism "denotes a mobile way of life organized around cyclical or seasonal patterns" and refers to "groups of people who practice spatial mobility to enhance their well-being and survival" (Gilbert 2014, 3). It represents a management strategy for sustainable land use as well as a powerful source of cultural identity. Often viewed in the past as "wanderers" without purpose, nomadic peoples today are widely regarded by specialists as having "a rational and efficient strategy for harvesting scarce resources spread unevenly across wide territories" and aligning

---

[3] Recently, for instance, tensions between nomadic and sedentary peoples have been linked to conflict in the Darfur region of Sudan, where tribes compete for resources as a result of desertification. These tensions are also linked to the creation of colonial distinctions between ethnic Tutsis and Hutus that later contributed to the 1994 Rwandan genocide (Gilbert 2007), as well as the enaction of discriminatory policies against Bedouin nomads in the Middle East and Maasai tribes in East Africa that are explored later in this chapter.

with a cultural identity that is greatly informed by these processes of migration and survival (Gilbert 2014, 3). Writing about his childhood home in Kenya's Maasai Mara, Stephen Muntet (2016) notes that "a cow is life" for his pastoralist nomadic family. Cattle are "a source of food, pride, prestige, wealth, and status"; they are a marker of traditional identity that is threatened by frequent droughts and resource-driven conflicts that are "changing the dynamics of these communities more than ever before" (para. 1). Furthermore, many nomadic and semi-nomadic groups migrate seasonally according to their traditions, sometimes crossing international borders that represent current political realities but do not reflect historical territories and land use patterns (Stavenhagen and Amara 2012, 159).

In his study of the uplands of Southeast Asia, James Scott (2009) argues that people on the margins have adapted their lifestyles to evade state capture and state formation; they are "political adaptations of nonstate peoples to a world of states that are, at once, attractive and threatening" (9). Although Scott's (2009) analysis focuses on hill peoples in Zomia (a mountainous region that spreads across seven Asian countries), his broader argument about people living in the "periphery" of the state is vital for understanding the situation of nomadic peoples. While today it is difficult to imagine living outside the purview of the state, for much of human history people had a choice as to whether they lived within or outside the state, or in an intermediate zone, and that choice could be revisited according to one's circumstances (Scott 2009, 7). The founding of agrarian states created a distinction between settled, state-governed citizens and a "frontier penumbra of less governed or virtually autonomous peoples" (Scott 2009, 3–4). The state had incentives to enclose people at the periphery in the zone of governance; this enclosure movement represents an effort "to integrate and monetize the people, lands, and resources of the periphery" and ensure that they contribute to the gross national product and to foreign exchange—as well as to ensure that their economic activity was "legible, taxable, assessable, and confiscatable, or, failing that, to replace it with forms of production that were" (4–5). This ungoverned territory represented both a challenge and a threat to the state. Scott notes: "[The periphery] was home to fugitive, mobile populations whose modes of subsistence—foraging, hunting, shifting cultivation, fishing, and pastoralism—were fundamentally intractable to state appropriation. The very diversity, fluidity, and mobility of their livelihoods meant that for an agrarian state adapted to sedentary agriculture, this ungoverned landscape and its people were fiscally sterile" (6). Portrayed as less-advanced "barbarians" and enemies of the state, people at the periphery—including nomadic peoples, some of whom endure today—faced discrimination, persecution, and threats to their physical and cultural survival. Yet Scott notes that once we "entertain the possibility" that these people *chose* their autonomous location on the periphery, rather than simply being "residue" left over from civilizing projects of the state, "the standard civilizational story of social evolution collapses utterly" (8).

With the rise of modern human rights and declining acceptance of violence against nomadic populations, states have adopted legal approaches to eliminating nomadism that often occur alongside other influential processes. Governments increasingly turn their attention toward the integration and assimilation of nomadic peoples through the process of sedentarization, which is often violently imposed on those who do not voluntarily agree to settlement. Sedentarization is "the establishment of a human group in a fixed territory; it is a settling process"—one that requires abandoning the nomadic way of life (Gilbert 2014, 2). Policies are often directed toward nomadic populations deemed uncivilized or inferior to majority populations, with the aim of encouraging settlement by volunteer or forced means. In some cases, policy-induced settlement happens alongside settlement prompted by other factors. In Mali, drought-induced sedentarization has occurred in recent decades as an adaptive strategy for nomadic populations coping with the loss of livestock. More recently, forces such as conflict, forced migration, refugee camps, and repatriation have furthered the settlement agenda within parts of Africa (Randall and Giuffrida 2006). Notably, the impacts of forced settlement often include severe social and cultural disruptions of traditional life. In a study of the Negev Bedouin Arab tribes in Israel and the Maasai tribes in Kenya, for instance, new trends of substance abuse emerged following settlement. In Bedouin society, lack of employment opportunities and alteration to traditional tribal and patriarchal family structures contributed to drug and alcohol consumption, as well as the highest school dropout rates in Israel (Abu-Saad and Mburu 2001, 16–18). Among the Maasai, research shows that heavy drinking among teenagers and increased drug use is connected to rapid social change and social frustrations (21).

International human rights norms provide some opportunities for combating these threats, but their reach remains limited. Many nomadic communities have aligned themselves with the Indigenous rights movement in recent years, arguing that their ties to ancestral lands, ethnic identities, and cultural traditions qualify them as recognized Indigenous populations.[4] Indigenous rights frameworks—including the 2007 United

---

[4] Although there is no universally accepted legal definition of Indigenous peoples, a definition by the UN Special Rapporteur Martinez Cobo (1986) is often accepted as authoritative: "Indigenous

Nations Declaration on the Rights of Indigenous Peoples—are further explored in Chapter 6; they include special protections related to self-determination, land rights, and rights to cultural integrity. However, many governments refuse to recognize minorities as "Indigenous" and to grant resulting special protections; this is the case among nomadic populations in China, Thailand, and Tanzania (as discussed later in this chapter), to name a few. Many states do not recognize nomadic communities' traditional use of land and deny the legal recognition of collective forms of land ownership, thus necessitating the transfer of common grazing land to private individual ownership. There are also questions as to whether nomadic pastoralism still constitutes "traditional" land usage if nomadic communities adopt modern techniques (see Gilbert 2007). Jérémie Gilbert (2007) contends that there needs to be a "legal arsenal" protecting nomadic land usage that includes two specific sets of rights: rights that are accessories to nomadic lifestyles, such as hunting or gathering rights, and rights that enlarge our existing approach to freedom of movement to encompass nomadism. While Gilbert applauds the promotion of nomadic rights under the banner of Indigenous rights, he also stresses the need to emphasize nomadic perceptions of mobility and land usage. This approach requires states to recognize that cultures evolve and change over time; nomadic communities have the right to engage in self-determination and change their practices as they so wish, but those changes do not strip them of their identities as nomadic peoples.

These legal approaches are important tools for combating human rights abuses, but legal change must happen alongside broader steps toward social inclusion. Suspicion and persecution of people who move "too much" profoundly impact nomadic communities, and this bias helps us understand why functioning citizenship is routinely denied those on the margins of majority society. Previous chapters on the forcibly displaced and irregular migrants illustrate this point, but these biases also create hierarchies

---

communities, peoples and nations are those which, having a historical continuity with pre-invasion and pre-colonial societies that developed on their territories, consider themselves distinct from other sectors of the societies now prevailing in those territories, or parts of them. They form at present non-dominant sectors of society and are determined to preserve, develop and transmit to future generations their ancestral territories, and their ethnic identity, as the basis of their continued existence as peoples, in accordance with their own cultural patterns, social institutions and legal systems" (para. 379). Other key definitions are often drawn from the International Labor Organisation (ILO) Convention No. 169 on Indigenous and Tribal Peoples, the World Bank, and Erica-Irene Daes (Chairperson of the United Nations' Working Group on Indigenous Populations) (see Gilbert 2007, section 3; International Work Group for Indigenous Affairs n.d.).

of personhood within citizen populations. Hagar Kotef (2015) argues that subject-positions, or identity categories, and the political orders that give them meaning cannot be separated from human movement. We cannot understand poverty without considering a history of vagrancy, migratory work, and homelessness, for instance, while we cannot fully consider racism in the United States without knowing about the slave trade (3). Despite a liberal concept of freedom that privileges the ideal of "freedom of movement," movement has nevertheless been "constructed as a threat rather than an articulation of liberty" in most societies (4). "Paradoxically, the predominant settled society has a dual approach to nomadism, with a romanticized and idealistic view of a life of freedom and mobility but also a fundamentally entrenched attitude of superiority which links nomadism with primitivism and backwardness," writes Gilbert (2014). "An overarching perception is that nomadism was a primitive form of civilization and that humankind has developed a more 'civilized' sedentary way of life"; this view has led to discrimination and racism against nomadic peoples that includes their legal marginalization (2). Looking back at historical perceptions of the American poor and Indigenous peoples, for instance, Kotef (2015) notes that their portrayal as a political problem rests on the simple fact that "they move too much"; their movement "becomes surplus and, therefore, can no longer encapsulate freedom" but rather "it has become a threat to order" (110). This problem of "excessive" movement has long framed migrants and nomadic peoples as uncivilized, savage, and suspect.

Indeed, the persecution of those who fail to conform to settlement norms is visible in almost every major city in the world with the ongoing criminalization of homelessness. People who are homeless and those facing housing exclusion experience threats to their rights of dignity and equality as well as curtailed access to justice.[5] The social stigma related

---

[5] Sometimes described as "urban nomads" (Spradley 1970), people who are unhoused occupy a complicated position within our discussion of the right to place. On one hand, homelessness can be viewed as a social problem that reflects a variety of rights abuses and injustices; many people live on the street as a direct result of poverty, foreclosure, declining work opportunities, lack of public assistance and affordable housing, domestic violence, mental illness, addiction, and lack of affordable healthcare (National Coalition for the Homeless 2009). Even in resource-rich countries such as the United States, the problem of homelessness endures. In January 2015, an estimated 564,708 people were homeless on any given night in the United States—including more than 200,000 people in families and more than 47,000 veterans of the armed forces. About 15 percent of the US homeless population is considered "chronically homeless," which makes them most vulnerable for severe mental health illnesses and substance abuse disorders (National Alliance to End Homelessness 2016). (The US Department of Housing and Urban Development defines

to their "rooflessness" encourages discriminatory policies concerning public order and security, degrading treatment by officials, lack of privacy in emergency shelters, and various restrictive regulations that block the access of the homeless to rights otherwise enjoyed by citizens (Kenna and Evangelista 2013, 42). In Hungary, for instance, recent legislation has made it a criminal offense to live in public spaces or "dumpster dive" in search of food. The law imposes fines, community service, and even jail time on people who are homeless. An earlier version of the law was struck down in November 2012 as a violation of the right to human dignity, but a March 2013 constitutional provision paved the way for discriminatory policies aimed at the country's 30,000 homeless people (Gall 2013). This antagonistic response to the issue of homelessness is nothing new; an analysis of the historical archetypes of the "vagabond," the "transient," and the "stranger" highlights the way excessive movement has been portrayed as deviance for centuries (see Amster 2008, 3–6). Randall Amster writes that "when we consider the nomenclature of 'homelessness' . . . it becomes apparent how intertwined our notions of identity are with the stability of 'place,' or more precisely with things being in the 'right place.' Homeless people now and throughout history have quite literally been defined as people without a 'right place' to be" (6). Demonized as diseased and socially deviant, the homeless are targeted for eradication by a plethora of laws that criminalize their existence in public spaces (see Amster 2008, chapter 3). A 1994 decision by voters and the city council in Berkeley, California, helped spark this trend; the city approved an anti-panhandling

---

the chronically homeless as an "individual or family that is homeless and resides in a place not meant for human habitation, a safe haven, or in an emergency shelter, and has been homeless and residing in such a place for at least 1 year or on at least four separate occasions in the last 3 years. The statutory definition also requires that the individual or family has a head of household with a diagnosable substance use disorder, serious mental illness, developmental disability, post-traumatic stress disorder, cognitive impairments resulting from a brain injury, or chronic physical illness or disability" [Federal Register 2015, 75792]).

On the other hand, many advocates and scholars warn against equating homelessness with powerlessness. In some cases, urban homeless enclaves exhibit "inherent intentionality" and "conscious resistance" to mainstream norms (Amster 2008, 8). Various studies of homeless populations have shown that homelessness can be a lifestyle choice that reflects self-determination, survival calculations, and independence. David Wagner (1993), for instance, argues that these street communities represent a form of social movement action that resists dominant institutional structures of work, family, and public social welfare. In an attempt to reassert the human dignity of homeless individuals and acknowledge their right to self-determination, advocates increasingly reject the charity-based model for responding to homelessness and instead emphasize a human rights–based approach (HRA). An HRA stresses a person's rights to a variety of goods—including food, physical security, and healthcare—and the corresponding duties required of states, while need-based charity models instead center on generosity and voluntary humanitarian responses (Kenna and Evangelista 2013).

law that prohibited. "aggressive" panhandling, begging at night, asking people for money as they got in and out of their vehicles, begging within a ten-foot "bubble" around bank ATM machines—and later even sitting on the sidewalk (Mitchell 2003, 161–162). These laws have been replicated throughout the United States. "The current restrictions on homeless people's behavior in public spaces are clearly an effort to regulate space so as to eliminate homeless people, not homelessness," argues Don Mitchell (2003), who calls this process "the annihilation of space by law" (167) and an attempt to "make sure homeless people have no right to the city—even when the laws [politicians] construct turn out to be as constitutionally invalid as they are morally repugnant" (199).

In the remaining portion of this chapter, three case studies—of the European Roma and Travellers, the Maasai in Tanzania and Kenya, and the Bedouin in the MENA region—broadly illustrate how this prioritization of settlement norms facilitates the denial of functioning citizenship around the world. These case studies share important commonalities related to exclusion and persecution, yet they are dissimilar in many ways: The Roma have a long history of human movement, yet their recent migration tends be forced rather than voluntary. While Roma communities are often culturally distinct from the state society they are situated within, many Romani advocates strive for a variety of rights protections—such as access to public education and social housing—that would serve to integrate this group more fully within the majority population. Maasai and Bedouin activists also work for an array of rights protections, but their priorities also include access to resources and freedoms that make nomadism possible. In places such as East Africa and the MENA region, vital land and water resources—as well as the ability to enjoy freedom of movement—are necessary for sustaining nomadic livelihood strategies and maintaining cultural traditions. In all three cases, however, nomadic peoples face denials of their fundamental freedoms as a result of their perceived unworthiness and their history of moving "too much." Situated among powerful sedentary majority populations, nomadic peoples struggle to gain recognition of their full personhood and their entitlement to human rights. This includes not only rights to place—including the ability to live within communities without fear or discrimination, as well as protections related to land use and freedom of movement—but also the rights to purpose that follow from sustained cultural identities.

European Roma and Travellers

Historically most commonly termed "Gypsies," Europe's nomadic peoples include a diverse group who are identified today as Roma, Gypsies, Travellers, Manouches, Ashkali, Sinti, and Boyash (European Commission n.d.).[6] Traditionally "peripatetic" nomads, these groups have moved among settled populations offering a craft or a trade (see Gilbert 2014, 7). The term "Roma" is frequently used within the European Union, where approximately 6 million Romani individuals reside—often as EU citizens but sometimes as stateless individuals.[7] Although EU countries have banned such discrimination, Roma living within their borders continue to face prejudice and social exclusion (European Commission n.d.; Bhabha 2017). Images and stereotypes of Roma and Travellers have been institutionalized within cultural traditions, making them "irrefutably 'fixed' within the public imaginary" and leaving little space for cultural change, adaptation, or assimilation into sedentary populations (Ó hAodha 2011, 4). Indeed, these groups are frequently defined by their nomadism and set apart from so-called settled society, thus "hiding both the fluid nature of settled society and the increasing tendency among Travellers to settle" (Taylor 2008, 5). The roots of this discrimination can be traced to myths rooted in Judeo-Christian traditions, which called on sedentary society to exclude nomadic peoples and their lifestyles. For instance, one legend says that a "Tinker" or "Gypsy" made the nails used to crucify Jesus on the cross, thereby cursing the tradesman to a life of wandering (Ó hAodha 2011, 106). Mícheál Ó hAodha writes that the derogatory status associated with "Travellers" and "Tinkers" within Irish folklore traditions has not only contributed to discrimination against nomadic peoples but has negatively influenced their own cultures. "The pseudo-religious nature of these folktales which provide an explanation or alleged justification for the outcast position occupied by Travellers in Irish society has had a profound

---

[6] In the United Kingdom, the term "Gypsy" is commonly used to describe an ethic group with origins in India, while "Traveller" describes nomadic groups of predominantly European origin. Yet in some cases, English and Welsh nomadic groups are described as "Gypsies" while Scots and Irish ones are "Travellers." Notably, the blanket term "Gypsy" has historically been used to describe nomadic populations in Europe and the term is closely tied to racialized and pejorative definitions (Taylor 2008, 4–5).

[7] Tens of thousands of stateless Roma live within Europe, often because poverty and exclusionary practices prevent them from accessing documentation such as birth certificates. Situations of armed conflict, forced migration, and state succession have also created statelessness among Roma communities in Europe, blocking many individuals from accessing essential services and effectively claiming rights (Council of Europe 2012, 183–184).

effect on Traveller self-identity and on the self-confidence of Travellers," argues Ó hAodha, noting that this "probably acted as a partial explanation as to why they were, and continue to be, the subject of prejudice from Irish society" (103–104).

The modern history of Europe's Roma and Travellers is one marked by pervasive human rights abuses. Deep-seated discrimination against nomadic peoples led to a series of German laws that prohibited encampments and irregular employment among Sinti and Roma "Gypsies," as well as involuntary sterilizations and the detention of nomadic peoples beginning in the mid-1920s through World War II. During the war, the Roma were targeted for forced sterilization, medial experimentation, internment at concentration camps, and genocidal elimination by the Nazi German government (Amnesty International n.d., 4; see also Bhabha 2017, 46–48). Tens of thousands of Sinti and Roma were killed by the Nazis throughout German-occupied Europe, prompted by the beliefs that Gypsies were "asocials" outside of "normal" society and racial "inferiors" who threatened the purity of a "superior Aryan" race (United States Holocaust Memorial Museum n.d.). European nomadic peoples became increasingly defined as "social problems" in need of remedy following World War II, leading to laws against unauthorized encampments and begging by the 1950s (Bhreatnach 2006; Smith and Greenfields 2013). A variety of factors influenced this shift toward modern, state-sanctioned discrimination. For instance, in Ireland the decline of markets and fairs meant that settled people saw little purpose to Travellers' visits, while these groups lost opportunities to earn money and reunite with scattered families and friends. Greater control over street trading and public housing led to heightened regulation of the urban poor in Ireland and elsewhere, while compulsory school attendance and criminalized informal labor habits led to a growing gap between Travellers and settled populations. Nomadism and illiteracy also meant that Travellers were less likely to utilize social welfare programs, or they faced discrimination from the local authorities tasked with providing benefits (Bhreatnach 2006, 141–143). Widespread poverty among nomadic populations—and the perception that these groups were problems in need of fixing—led to programs that sought to reduce, and perhaps eliminate, these minority groups from Europe. Roma women in the former Czechoslovakia were offered financial incentives to undergo medical sterilization from the early 1970s until 1990, for instance, with doctors systematically and coercively sterilizing Romani women with support from policymakers, government structures, and social workers (Tritt 1992, 32; Cahn 2015, 266). In 2014, the United Nations acknowledged that "Anti-Gypsyism" remains a major challenge for Roma's social inclusion and human rights protection as part of a global survey on Roma rights (Izsák 2015).[8]

Ironically, some approaches aimed at protecting nomadic peoples' rights to place in Europe often serve to directly violate their rights to purpose—and represent a fundamental lack of understanding of how one's ideal "place" is culturally constructed. Policies motivated by humanitarian concerns, such as the elimination of homelessness and the provision of public education, are solidly grounded in a sedentary worldview that fails to recognize the economic, social, and cultural values of nomadism. Those who seek to secure a physical "place" for nomadic populations in Europe by encouraging (or forcing) settlement do so by creating barriers to nomadic movement, cutting off opportunities to access a "place" that exists in multiple sites and sometimes across state borders. David M. Smith and Margaret Greenfields (2013) argue that long-term processes of settlement and sedenterization have occurred alongside broader processes of urbanization and industrialization in the United Kingdom, prompting the settlement of nomadic communities there. They write that "the enforced immobilization of the majority of Britain's Gypsies and Travellers and their continuing marginalization highlights a number of basic contradictions in what is purported to be a diverse yet socially inclusive nation while raising fundamental questions over the nature of inclusivity and 'tolerance'" (Smith and Greenfields 2013, 197). In their study of Gypsies and Travellers in the United Kingdom, Smith and Greenfields found that many respondents who had settled in housing estates felt increased concentrations of social exclusion; institutionalized racism, negative stereotypes, and suppressed nomadism combined with insufficient site capacity and enforced settlement to create gross "intersectional disadvantages" experienced by many community members (200).

Rather than supporting rights to purpose, this forced "protection" of place leads to a variety of further abuses. In many cases, settlement also threatens the group's cultural identity and recognition of their minority status. For instance, Travellers in Britain have been denied their identity in recent decades—sometimes in court, as a result of a 1968 law defining Gypsies as people of a "nomadic habit of life"—if they did not fit the

---

[8] The United Nations considers "Anti-Gypsyism," as defined by the Council of Europe, "a specific form of racism, an ideology founded on racial superiority, a form of dehumanization and institutional racism nurtured by historical discrimination, which is expressed, among others, by violence, hate speech, exploitation, stigmatization and the most blatant kind of discrimination" (quoted in Izsák 2015, 5; see also Council of Europe 2012).

unrealistic ideal of perpetual nomadism (Taylor 2008, 221). As the gap between "Gypsy" folklore and everyday life widens, these nomadic peoples lose their separate identity status within the popular imagination and potentially miss out on special rights protections enjoyed by other minority groups (Taylor 2008, 224). Since 2006, Italian "Pacts for Security" have given local authorities increased power to monitor camps, collect data, and identify camp inhabitants in response to situations of so-called nomad emergency or Roma emergency, often resulting in forced evictions without the provision of adequate alternative housing. Simultaneously framing nomadism as a security threat while barring Roma and Sinti communities from viable options for settlement—particularly due to housing segregation, discriminatory identification procedures, and the perpetuation of poverty and social exclusion—the Italian government denies these groups rights to purpose associated with living standards and family protections (Nolan 2011), as well as education (Rozzi 2017).

The Maasai in Tanzania and Kenya

Maasai communities are made up of pastoralist nomads[9] whose livelihoods shift between mixes of herding, farming, and hunting/gathering—and whose perspectives on land use often clashes with mainstream conceptions of place. Maasailand [10] straddles the Tanzania-Kenya border, along a broad section of the Great African Rift Valley that is famous among tourists for its impressive wildlife reserves. While most Maasai remain in rural areas and have livestock-dependent livelihoods, there is a growing shift away from traditional subsistence patterns—driven in large part by land privatization and the subdivision of communal lands (which block access to resources and prevent free movement), and conservation activities that set aside lands for wildlife protection (Homewood et al. 2009, 1–3). Although some government policies aim at protecting pastoralist livelihoods, these

---

[9] Nomadic pastoralist communities rely on livestock as a livelihood strategy, depending on access to grazing lands to support their animals and requiring mobility to avoid overgrazing. Some pastoralists are not fully nomadic but are transhumant (they move livestock from one grazing area to another) or even sedentary. A key feature of pastoralist nomads is that their communities have social and cultural ties to the maintenance of their herds and use periodic mobility to sustain their livestock (see Gilbert 2014, 5).

[10] The term "Maasailand" denotes a "loosely bounded area of East Africa whose rural population is dominated by Maa-speaking communities which, despite their diversity, self-attribute to Maasai ethnicity. It is not a formal term and does not denote an administratively recognized region" (Homewood et al. 2009, 1).

moves have primarily benefited sedentary populations while ignoring nomadic perspectives. General land law views pastoralist rangelands as "empty," for instance, leaving vital grazing grounds open for government reallocation. The control of hunting licenses and game viewing in wildlife management areas has also been centralized, running counter to prevailing attitudes about best practices in community conservation and providing little (or no) income at the local and individual household levels. Although Tanzania and Kenya have approached land tenure issues differently from colonial times to the present day, they have nevertheless arrived at similar outcomes in Maasailand: "many rural poor find themselves with few or no rights to the land they live on, paradoxically at the same time laws are being passed that are supposed to increase security of tenure of rural communities. As a result, Maasai are increasingly excluded from resources central to livelihoods, in ways that impact on land use and well-being" (Homewood et al. 2009, 7).

The problem of "land grabbing" in Maasailand has exacerbated challenges to place and purpose in recent years. In Laikipia County, Kenya, Maasai communities face ongoing court battles over the "sale" of communal lands; these cases are frequently marked by reports of harassment, police brutality, arrest, torture, and theft as local officials and businesses pressure Maasai to give up legal rights to their traditional lands. In addition to threatening Maasai rights to place, these actions endanger rights to purpose that center on practices of pastoral nomadism and related cultural traditions. For instance, Kenyan nongovernmental organizations (NGOs) Eng'ape E Maa Association and IMPACT (2015) emphasize the case of a Maasai community in Segera, which was notified in 2014 that a 2,300-acre piece of land had been sold to the North Tetu Cooperative Society. The Maasai were given notice to leave their lands while fences, a house, and a deep trench were constructed in part to block access to a nearby river; the community had lived on that land for more than thirty years. The Maasai stopped construction and destroyed the fence, and those actions were met with escalating violence that resulted in one person being killed by drowning (reportedly in front of his ten-year-old child), with dozens of arrests and beatings by police and private ranchers. "Laikipia is called Laikipia because of us, its people. How come that we are now homeless and landless?" asked Lerantoi Parkusa (quoted in Eng'ape E Maa Association and IMPACT 2015). "I keep wondering what government means. They say government belongs to the people. Which people? I do not feel this government belongs to me because of its actions. We are children of a lesser wife. We are illegitimate."

In Tanzania, land grabbing cases have attracted international attention to Maasai communities near world-renowned wildlife reserves such as the Serengeti and Tarangire national parks. Communities in Loliondo, just east of the Serengeti, faced years of conflict over land access and use when the government allocated land use to a foreign hunting company in the early 1990s, without account for existing Maasai community needs that included support for traditional livestock grazing practices. Human rights groups criticized the Tanzanian government for evicting several hundred Maasai households from the area in 2009, and then again in 2013 when officials announced plans to convert 40 percent of the Loliondo area (including six Maasai villages) to wildlife reserve, thus evicting up to 20,000 people (Ngoitiko and Nelson 2013). Global media attention and activism led to a reversal of those plans in September 2013, but the case highlights the way business interests are often prioritized over the rights of the Maasai people. Maasai leader Edward Loure, whose family lost their ancestral lands to what is now Tarangire national park, argues that giving communities legal title to their land is key to reducing human-wildlife conflicts and stimulating sustainable development. Without legal title, the Maasai faced ongoing risks of land loss to safari companies and multinationals; a shift from customary rights to legal title is necessary to avoid land grabs (Vidal 2016). "People had no legal documents, no security," said Loure, reflecting on his own experiences and activism. "Nothing was documented. We had to make sure people had security. Many villages had lost huge amounts of land and received no compensation. Now they can show that the land belongs to them. Until now, government or anyone could claim that it was not owned by anyone and do what they want" (quoted in Vidal 2016, para. 7).

Advocacy efforts to protect the rights of the Maasai further highlight complexities associated with defining nomadic identities in a largely sedentary world—including how these communities fit within international development models. In response to threatened land rights and a host of other human rights concerns, Maasai activists became involved with the international Indigenous rights movements in the 1990s and enjoyed increased visibility and donor funding as a result. However, their alignment with Indigenous rights backfired when it came to the Maasai's relationship with state governments. Leaders in most African states, including Tanzania, regard all citizens (except perhaps some of Asian heritage) as "Indigenous" and reject claims that minorities face discrimination because of their cultural distinctiveness, modes of production, or political-economic marginalization. Maasai activists and NGO leaders reframed their efforts from the language of Indigenous rights to that of "pastoralist livelihoods," seeking to be less confrontational with the government (Hodgson 2011, 157). This has happened alongside a push for development, spurred by the UN Millennium Development Goals (MDGs) and the subsequent Sustainable Development Goals (SDGs). In Tanzania, for instance, these global initiatives have translated into the key policy documents Tanzania Vision 2025 (outlining the country's social and economic vision) and a poverty reduction strategy called MKUKUTA. Yet these moves generally don't address the needs of pastoralist nomads; rather, they stress increased competition and encourage the growth of business practices that destroy traditional practices. Privatized industries, revised land regulations and land sales, large-scale commercial agriculture, wildlife tourism and big game hunting industries, and limited opportunities for healthcare and education have all harmed Maasai communities. Indeed, government development strategies encourage pastoralists to "replace transhumant pastoralism with more 'productive' and less 'environmentally harmful' modes of livestock 'farming' (as opposed to 'herding')" (Hodgson 2011, 183). As a result, the Maasai have witnessed increased alienation of their lands (especially for drought and dry-season grazing land), competition for water and other livestock-related resources, declining use of health services, and increased impoverishment (Hodgson 2011, 183).

The Bedouin

The term "Bedouin" is used to describe nomads (or nomadic pastoralists) in the MENA region; it is largely used to differentiate between people whose livelihood depends on raising livestock with "graze and browse" methods and populations who have an agricultural or urban base (Chatty 2006, 6).[11] In recent history, MENA governments have regarded the Bedouin as "anachronisms" and "throw-backs to a past era," attempting to subdue and assimilate them into modern agricultural and industrial ways of life in a process that is aligned with ideals related to nation-building and "modernization" (Chatty 2006, 1). In Saudi Arabia, for instance, Bedouins are generally regarded as "primitives" and even "savages" who are largely

---

[11] This is a simplified definition of the term "Bedouin," which is indeed a contested one among scholars. For instance, some use "bedouin" (with a lower case "b") as a descriptive term indicating those who live on semi-arid lands and raise livestock. Others use "Bedouin" (with an upper case "B") to describe a nomadic community of people, a tribe, or an ethnicity. For discussion of the history of this term and the debates surrounding it, see Chatty 2006.

restricted to folklore, particularly following state actions to "detribalize" these communities through processes of sedentarization aimed at denying nomadic rights to control and manage their resources (Fabietti 2006). In many cases, development schemes aimed at reducing or eliminating nomadism center on the degradation of arid steppe land and global interests in preserving biodiversity. Sedentarization pressures emphasize the need to protect lands and limit grazing, yet they rarely recognize (at least officially) the traditional knowledge and sustainable practices of Bedouin communities (see Chatty 2006, 12–13). Nomadic pastoralism is often seen as a special problem for conservationists, since large herds need access to large areas of grazing land to survive. Only recently has this view begun to change, with greater acceptance among researchers that nomadic pastoralists have "special knowledge and understanding of land resources and their sustainable use" (Rowe 2006, 760). However, this view is not widespread in the Middle East's conservation sector, where suspicion of nomadic groups "may also be politically motivated" (Rowe 2006, 760). Yet Bedouin societies have always utilized adaptive strategies for pursuing their livelihoods, just as they have connected with non-pastoral communities for economic, social, and political relations (Chatty 2006, 10); today, some Bedouin have commercialized their culture to meet tourism needs or have settled and become less mobile than their ancestors. Desert tourism has been advanced as a substitute for (or a complement to) nomadic pastoralism among the Tuareg in the Algerian Great South and the Bedouin in southern Jordan, for example, leading to social changes and growing dependency on state governments (Chatelard 2006). Although case studies of nomadic peoples throughout the MENA region vary in significant ways, research throughout the region highlights how mobility and migration "has created an under-class of people who reject the sedentist outlook and economy," instead using their "mobility, adaptive responsiveness and opportunism" as survival strategies (Chatty 2006, 25).

Bedouin Arabs living in the Naqab (Negev) Desert in southern Israel[12] have experienced a particularly dramatic change in lifestyle, including

---

[12] In the Israeli context, "Bedouin" defines an ethnic group that is part of the Arab minority, not a way of life. Rather than dealing with the Arab community, Israeli policies focus on sub-ethnic groups according to religious and cultural affiliations, geographic location, and local governance structures (Shmueli and Khamaisi 2015, 6). Most of today's Bedouin in the Naqab are descended from three groups: Tarabin (Indigenous Arab nomads), Tiaha (fellaheen from cultivated areas who became nomadic), and Azazmah (those brought from Africa as slaves). Most Bedouin in the area came from the Sinai, but some migrated from lands east of the Jordan River or from Yemen. Prior to modern state borders, the Naqab, Sinai, and Jordan were one open space utilized by Bedouin according to their customary law and traditions (Shmueli and Khamaisi 2015, 23).

threats to their place and purpose. Traditionally these communities were organized into nomadic or semi-nomadic tribes who were widely dispersed throughout the Naqab to tend to herds and engage in seasonal agriculture, but those lifestyles have been viewed as incompatible with the modernization of Israel. Processes of displacement and land expropriation have reduced the Bedouin's area of land use in Israel from more than 2 million dunams (494,200 acres) to less than 386,000 dunams (95,383 acres) (Abu-Saad and Creamer 2012, 20). In its process of nation-building, the Israeli government enacted laws and military regulations that enabled the state to confiscate Bedouin lands and settle communities into higher density towns, including creating residential developments in the Naqab to concentrate Bedouin populations in permanent settlements (28–31). Yet almost half the Bedouin Arab population (around 84,000 people) live in towns and localities that are unrecognized by the Israeli government, representing resistance to state-sponsored urbanization programs (38). These unrecognized villages lack local addresses and thus prevent Bedouins from voting in local or municipal elections, but nevertheless the Bedouins have formed "a recognized political element that has had practical visibility," including engaging in leadership practices that continue traditions of local self-rule (Champagne 2012, 273). In response, the government frequently denies services such as paved roads, transportation, garbage disposal, electricity, running water, telephone service, community health services, and even schools (Abu-Saad and Creamer 2012, 38; see also Shmueli and Khamaisi 2015, 69)—all essential public services necessary for establishing a functioning town or territory (place) and pursuing goals related to livelihoods, education, and community-building (purpose).

Indeed, current living conditions of the Naqab Bedouin Arabs include pervasive threats to an array of fundamental human rights. Bedouins face severe challenges to their right to healthcare, for instance, a reality particularly visible when their health status is compared to that of Israeli Jews: they suffer from higher rates of infant mortality and lower levels of health services (see Abu-Saad and Creamer 2012, 50–51). Lack of adequate housing is a widespread concern that has been linked to gender-based discrimination and violence against women in these communities (Manjoo 2012). Yet the state continues to fund "law enforcement" activities such as evictions and house demolitions rather than focusing on the development of Bedouin areas (Abu-Saad and Creamer 2012, 49). Human Rights Watch (2013) and other rights advocates have called for a moratorium on the demolition of "illegal" Bedouin homes, which are destroyed because they are built without permits; even so, the government refuses to legally recognize these communities or allow residents to gain title to their ancestral lands. The year 2016 saw a dramatic rise in forced evictions across the West Bank and the demolition of a record number of Palestinian and Bedouin structures (Farha 2016). These actions continue a long history of state discrimination, including the government's ignoring Bedouin land rights and community needs; it is little wonder that many Bedouins respond to government planning with "mistrust" and see resolutions as "a government tool to limit their development" (Shmueli and Khamaisi 2015, 53).

Indigenous rights frameworks offer the Naqab Bedouin, similar to the Maasai, some opportunities for human rights claims and protection, but this advocacy approach is limited by the government's refusal to acknowledge indigeneity within its borders. Bedouin are culturally distinct from the Israeli Jewish majority and suffer ongoing marginalization and discrimination as a collectivity, providing them with sufficient grounds to claim protections as an Indigenous group under international law. Indeed, the Bedouin share a variety of common traits with Indigenous peoples elsewhere in the world, including semi-pastoralists in North Africa (Stavenhagen and Amara 2012, 181–182). However, the Israeli state has not recognized the continuity of the Bedouin or their rights as Indigenous peoples; relying on a liberal democratic modernization argument, it rather emphasizes that the Bedouin's best future is entwined with urbanizing and achieving national economic plans. If they will not modernize on their own, so the argument goes, the state can enforce policies forcing Bedouin communities to modernize—without their consent and without recognition of their right to self-determination (Champagne 2012, 268). While Israel has not formally recognized Indigenous peoples, it has sometimes used practical recognition of intermediary traditional local leadership, often to maintain social order and stability (266). Oren Yiftachel (2012) contends that studies of the Naqab should be resituated within an "internal colonial scholarly paradigm" that defines Bedouins as "an Indigenous community subject to a process that began as colonialism imposed from the outside and has continued as 'internal colonialism' since the end of the military government in the late 1960s" (289). He argues that current scholarship ignores a central factor since 1948—"Israel's ethnic internal colonialism of the Naqab"—and resulting negative effects of "dispossession, displacement, and constant struggles with Israeli authorities for land, development, and housing rights" (293). Bedouins have particularly suffered from these policies for reasons of land and demography; the state seeks control over vast expanses of Bedouin land in what some scholars have called "ethnic cleansing" of the region, while fears about their "dangerously" high fertility rates prompt racist discourse stressing modernity and positing the Bedouin as inferior citizens (294).

These three case studies illustrate how human movement is of central importance to nomadic livelihood strategies and cultural identities, yet these practices are often derided by sedentary majority populations who view people who move "too much" with distrust. Different ideals about territory, homeland, and community are often misunderstood—or outright rejected—by wider society, thus relegating nomadic peoples to inferior positions on the hierarchy of personhood. Nomadic peoples are thus viewed as less deserving of land and resource rights (in places such as Maasailand and the Naqab Desert) as well as the social services necessary for the enjoyment of functioning citizenship. Nomadic peoples' rights to place and purpose—which are bound to their alternate conceptions of place itself—are often systematically denied, with sedentary ideals privileged at the expense of nomadic communities. These situations remind us that territory plays a central role in the provision of functioning citizenship, but with the caveat that territory is used in socially approved ways; even in cases where a group has long historical ties to the land, they are expected to use it in ways that support sedentary ideals. Thus, functioning citizenship is at least partially dependent on a group's embracing sedentary perspectives on territory—and, by extension, on community and the nation.

CHAPTER 6 | Indigenous Nations and Tribal
Sovereignty

By our ancient treaties, we expected the protection of the government.
The white man had obtained most of our land and we felt he was
obliged to provide something in return, which was protection of the
land we had left, but we did not want to be absorbed and assimilated
into his society. United States citizenship was just another way of
absorbing us and destroying our customs and our government. . . .
We feared citizenship would also put our treaty status in jeopardy and
bring taxes upon our land. How can a citizen have a treaty with his
own government? . . . This was a violation of our sovereignty. Our
citizenship was in our own nations.

—Tuscarora Chief Clinton Rickard (1973, 53)

FUNCTIONING CITIZENSHIP TAKES ON new complexity in relation to
Indigenous nations, which offer alternative pathways to political membership that exist separate from—or perhaps alongside—that of state society.
Calls for tribal sovereignty problematize the international community's
central focus on state governments for legitimizing human rights
claimants, framing Indigenous tribes as political actors whose authority
predates that of the state. For many native communities, state membership often comes second to the ties that bind one to an Indigenous nation.
(The Onondaga Nation, for instance, maintains a legally distinct territory
just outside Syracuse, New York; some members reject the social goods
associated with US citizenship and instead rely on tribal political membership and documentation.) The growing recognition of Indigenous rights
has led to increased interest in Indigenous sovereignty and nation-building

as frameworks for protecting minority rights and reasserting the political power of Indigenous communities, who have long been relegated to dangerously low positions within state-supported hierarchies of personhood. Yet Indigenous nations represent a fundamental challenge to the modern human rights regime, which relies on states as both duty-bearers and the foundations of the international system. Negotiating how Indigenous nations can fit within this framework—and indeed, how they can engage in meaningful political activity—is something that requires ongoing engagement and critical discussion.

The Indigenous rights movement galvanizes support for alternative understandings of political membership that reassert Indigenous sovereignty and create political space outside or alongside the traditional state structure. The movement's principles culminate in the 2007 United Nations Declaration on the Rights of Indigenous Peoples (UNDRIP), which sets international standards for recognition and for protecting Indigenous rights as conceptualized by Indigenous activists around the world. Importantly, the UNDRIP prioritizes rights to place and purpose that reflect Indigenous worldviews and priorities, and these sometimes differ dramatically from the conceptions of settler states. The UNDRIP makes clear that "historic injustices" such as colonization and land dispossession have prevented Indigenous peoples from exercising their "right to development in accordance with their own needs and interests," and that there is an "urgent need" both to respect and to promote their inherent rights, which are affirmed in treaties and other agreements with states (United Nations 2007, 2). Rights to place emphasize spiritual and cultural connections to land, as well as the rights to remain within Indigenous communities and territories.[1] Rights to purpose include rights to self-determination (Article 3), to autonomy or self-governance (Article 4), to nationality (Article 6), to religious and cultural traditions (Article 12) as well as the rights to transmit cultural knowledge to future generations (Article 13), to establish and control appropriate educational systems (Article 14), to establish their own media in their own languages (Article 16), to participate in decision making

---

[1] Article 25 notes that Indigenous peoples "have the right to maintain and strengthen their distinctive spiritual relationship with their traditionally owned or otherwise occupied and used lands, territories, waters and coastal seas and other resources and to uphold their responsibilities to future generations in this regard." Article 26 expands on rights to traditional lands, including the right to "own, use, develop and control the lands" and be treated with "due respect" concerning legal recognition and protection of lands and resources. Article 10 protects against forced removal from Indigenous lands, and Article 9 stipulates that "Indigenous peoples and individuals have the right to belong to an Indigenous community or nation" without discrimination (United Nations 2007).

(Article 18), and to engage in economic and social activities and development (Articles 20, 21, and 23). Notably, Article 5 contends: "Indigenous peoples have the right to maintain and strengthen their distinct political, legal, economic, social and cultural institutions, while retaining their right to participate fully, if they so choose, in the political, economic, social and cultural life of the State." Indigenous nations are thus recognized as occupying a political space that doesn't fit within the state model; not only does the UNDRIP stress the validity of treaties, which are agreements between sovereign political actors (usually assumed to be states), but it also provides a reconceptualization of membership that allows Indigenous persons to exist simultaneously in both Indigenous nations and settler state societies. This re-frames our ideas about citizenship and political membership, de-emphasizing the role of the state as the sole legitimate authority.

At the same time, this assertion depends on recognition from the duty-bearing settler state, thus bringing us full circle in a scenario where Indigenous sovereignty and rights depend on recognition from other sovereign actors who, in many cases, have directly benefited from the oppression of native communities. The UNDRIP attempts to break apart the hierarchies of personhood that have historically oppressed Indigenous nations; but the protection of Indigenous rights—and indeed, the legitimacy of Indigenous nationhood and sovereignty—is a complicated and politically fraught task. To better understand the challenges to functioning citizenship within native communities, this chapter explores the historical trajectory leading to modern Indigenous rights concerns—including the erosion of Indigenous nationhood historically experienced by the Haudenosaunee Confederacy[2] and other Indigenous communities. Processes of claiming Indigenous rights and recognition challenge the reliance on state citizenship for recognizing personhood and claiming human rights, thereby offering alternative pathways for conceptualizing identification, legal status, and political membership. Increasingly, discussions related to Indigenous recognition emphasize processes of tribal nation-building that center on

---

[2] The Haudenosaunee Confederacy—sometimes called the Iroquois or the Six Nations—is made up of the Mohawk, Oneida, Onondaga, Cayuga, Seneca, and Tuscarora nations. Founded with the goals of uniting the nations and creating a peaceful means of decision making, the Confederacy is one of the first and longest lasting participatory democracies in the world. Most of the Haudenosaunee nations were originally located in what is now New York State (the Tuscarora, who later joined the Confederacy in the early 1700s, were originally located in North Carolina). The Haudenosaunee are often commonly referred to as the Iroquois; a term given to the Haudenosaunee nations by the French. I have chosen to refer to these Indigenous nations by the name their ancestors chose for their confederacy, rather than by the name chosen by European colonizers. "Haudenosaunee" means "People of the Long House" (see Onondaga Nation n.d.b.).

the broad themes of self-determination and Indigenous knowledge systems, reclaiming tribal sovereignty from the ward relationship, and economic development. The complicated, unique positions of Indigenous nations thus question reliance on state governments for the provision of functioning citizenship, offering possibilities to· resist hierarchies of personhood—as well as resulting violations of rights to place and purpose—and highlighting inadequacies in existing approaches to rights protection.

Claiming Indigenous Rights, Recognition, and Nationhood

The global history of Indigenous peoples is marked by the pervasive denial of self-determination—including the loss of ancestral lands, processes of physical and cultural genocide, and the relegation of once-sovereign Indigenous nations to the position of wards of settler states (see, for example, Coates 2004; Woolford et al. 2014; Smith 2015). The slaughter of Indigenous populations by colonial forces slowly gave way to "civilizing projects" aimed at forcibly assimilating native groups into Western cultural practices, including Christianity and settler capitalism. Genocidal processes of physical violence have often shifted to exterminating cultural and national identities, including recent (or ongoing) government actions such as the killing of Inuit sled dogs in the Canadian Arctic, wildlife and land use policies that fail to account for Indigenous livelihoods and traditions, and reliance on government recognition of tribes in order to access rights protections (Kingston 2015). The European principle of individual ownership based on labor also legitimized the dispossession of Indigenous people from their traditional territories, thus reconstructing their status "from sovereign nations to dependent populations within international law, where they were recognized at all" (Stewart-Harawira 2008, 161). Among other things, these processes included the loss of Indigenous land rights, the invalidation of treaties signed between sovereign nations, the designation of sovereign Indigenous nations as "populations" within states, and the use of targeted strategies to transform Indigenous peoples into docile, productive laborers in service to the settler state (Stewart-Harawira 2008, 162–163). Indigenous persons also came to depend on state-issued documentation for their freedom of movement. In the United States, for example, the passport as an identification document transitioned from a political letter of introduction to a "certificate of citizenship" (Robertson 2010, 126) in the late 1800s and early 1900s—early precursors to the post-9/11 security environment that impacts Indigenous movement today. Those without formal status lack the "durable identities" expressed through citizenship, which states encourage in order to "discourage people from choosing identities inconsistent with those validated by the state" (Torpey 2001, 166). These combined factors constitute a worldwide erosion of Indigenous sovereignty and nationhood that has only recently garnered widespread attention from the international community, thanks to the persistent dedication of the Indigenous rights movement.

Indigenous leaders utilize the language of modern human rights to make significant political gains worldwide—although the recognition of Indigenous rights is far from universal and was certainly not a priority of the international human rights regime from the start. Key rights frameworks such as the Universal Declaration of Human Rights (UDHR) and the UN Convention on the Prevention and Punishment of the Crime of Genocide (Genocide Convention) made no reference to Indigenous peoples, and these issues remained low on political agendas of world leaders within the United Nations, as they were within its predecessor, the League of Nations (Coates 2004; Burger 2016). The social movements of the 1960s gave rise to Indigenous organizations such as the US American Indian Movement, however, and centered on the language of decolonization and racism (Coates 2004, 239). Ken Coates (2004) argues that "a broader reconsideration of the nature of human rights and the rights of ethnic minorities brought about, indirectly, significant shifts in the political power of aboriginal groups" (231). At the same time, activists began to connect their local and regional protests to a broader "reality of shared experiences" that helped them connect with other groups to share resources and logistical support, as well as identify an intellectual context in which to situation their struggle—including a shared pattern of dispossession (241–242). Indigenous communities increasingly rely on international law for the protection of human rights; when domestic laws are not in place (or there is no will to enforce them), some turn toward regional bodies such as those within the Inter-American human rights system (see Pasqualucci 2006). Within the UN system, activists "formed a particular path of Indigenous resistance and transformative politics" that sought to advocate rights within the state-structured system while at the same time seeking to alter that system in the long term (Lightfoot 2016, 254). For instance, independent experts from the Working Group on Indigenous Populations met from 1982 to 2005 to share rights recommendations with a twenty-six-member Sub-Commission and the Commission on Human Rights (Burger 2016, 317). In 2007, the adoption of the UNDRIP by the

UN General Assembly not only added new Indigenous rights to the international consensus but also "challenge[d] some fundamentals of the human rights system and the Westphalian system of sovereign states" by calling on governments to protect *both* individual and collective rights, including rights to land and self-determination (Lightfoot 2016, 254).

The UNDRIP is often approached as a necessary starting point, but certainly not a complete victory for Indigenous rights and recognition.[3] The Declaration extends rights to the additional category of "peoples," thus challenging the territorial concept of a people in international law and instead focusing on ethnic, cultural, and religious identities (Quane 2011, 285). It represents growing acceptance of the value of cultural membership; ultimately, "respect for Indigenous peoples presupposes respect for their culture" (Xanthaki 2007, 14). Yet the UNDRIP's inherent recognition of Indigenous self-determination also raises questions about the very nature of sovereignty; Marco Odello (2016), for instance, argues that the UNDRIP "is an instrument that may improve some specific rights related to Indigenous populations, but it may also create certain conditions for segregation and accentuation of differences" as a result of "the contrast between liberal individualistic approaches to rights and collective rights" (52).[4] Ulf Mörkenstam (2015) notes that challenges to traditional state-centered conceptions of political rights and democracy lead to a "gap in the contemporary political debate between this recognition [of Indigenous self-determination] on the global level and an institutionalization and legal recognition of these rights in political practice on the nation-state level" (634). In this sense, self-determination is still a contested concept—although it's vital to note that Indigenous peoples' claims "to existence as societies differentiated from mainstream national societies are taken nowadays as valid arguments in the dialogue with the states, while in the

---

[3] Questions remain, for instance, regarding whether the concept of property may be reconceptualized as a community right in response to growing recognition of rights to cultural heritage—including in relation to cultural sites and artifacts (see Macmillan 2015)—even though respect for culture and land rights remain at the center of calls for Indigenous self-determination. Economic self-determination (including sustainable development and enjoyment of natural resources) is often viewed as a legal basis for protecting Indigenous land claims to territory (Xanthaki 2007, 238), yet nomadic Indigenous peoples face continued threats to their land rights by settled agriculturalist societies; international human rights law is still evolving to respond to these challenges (Gilbert 2007) and the UNDRIP is viewed as a beginning step toward protecting Indigenous land rights (Gilbert and Doyle 2011).

[4] Helen Quane (2011) notes that potential far-reaching negative consequences (such as secessionist claims and inter-communal violence) are avoided or at least limited because the UNDRIP is restricted in its sphere of application, and also because it recognizes only a limited right to internal self-determination within communities (285).

recent past they were regarded as the sad laments of peoples destined to disappear within a fully Westernized planet" (de Oliveira 2009, 13). For many scholars, frameworks such as the UNDRIP represent a foundation for negotiating rights protections and demanding recognition. Mörkenstam (2015) argues that

> Indigenous self-determination primarily is to be understood as a way to balance the power between Indigenous peoples and the nation-states in which they live. Without a solid legal foundation for Indigenous peoples to define self-determination in their own languages and to negotiate the conditions of their relation with the nation-states on their own terms, the colonial past (and present) of violent conquest and domination might continue. In this perspective, Indigenous peoples' right to self-determination ought to imply recognition of Indigenous peoples as having a standing equal to nation-states, i.e. *as if* they were sovereigns. Only after negotiations between two (or more) equal political entities could any answers be given to the questions of nature of the domain of independent control, the extent of its control and of its particular political institutions. In this way, the right to self-determination has to be interpreted procedurally rather than substantially. (635)

The promise of Indigenous nationhood is complicated, however, by definitional constraints. First, there are no universally accepted criteria for claiming indigeneity and ensuing rights. The United Nations relies on two key definitions that depend on ancestral links to territory and particular cultural and religious distinctiveness (see Martínez Cobo 1987; Daes 2001). Generally, the principal criterion is self-identification; that is, communities determine whether they consider themselves as Indigenous peoples (Lennox and Short 2016, 2). Yet some scholars contend that these definitions—while good starting points—are too simplistic; they are frequently constructed by non-Indigenous society and distort the complexity and ever-changing nature of Indigenous identity (Axelsson and Sköld 2011, 6–7). Indeed, "colonization, political policies and cultural processes have often excluded or devalued representations of Indigenous peoples in official statistics" (Axelsson and Sköld 2011, 1)—including Aboriginal populations in Australia (Smith et al. 2011) and the Maori in New Zealand (Kukutai 2011). Today many self-identified Indigenous groups are denied recognition by state governments, thus preventing them from accessing special protections and resources afforded to Indigenous peoples. Examples include the San (Bushmen) in Botswana (Sapignoli 2016) as

2016) as well as federally unrecognized "ghost tribes" throughout the United States (Miller 2008; Dadigan 2012).

Second, the meaning of the term "nationality" sometimes deviates from that of citizenship, often becoming muddled when associated with identity groups that may or may not have their own state. Anthony D. Smith (1991) defines a nation as "a named human population sharing an historic territory, common myths and historical memories, a mass, public culture, a common economy and common legal rights and duties for all members" (14). He notes that a nation is not the same as a state; in some views of the nation, common descent or customs may play a much more vital role than the legal-political community that is so important in most Western conceptions. In fact, several nations may reside within the borders of one state, as is the case with multiple indigenous tribal "nations" located throughout states such as the United States and Canada (Kymlicka 1995, 79). From this perspective, the term "nationality" connotes a historical relationship to a specific ethnic, linguistic, or racial group. This definition contrasts sharply with current usage that is synonymous with citizenship, which uses nationality as a legal term describing membership in a state-based political community. In the United States, the term "nation" within indigenous communities generally centers on a combination of kinship, government, shared territory, worldview, and spiritual community (Champagne 2008). It is important to recognize, however, that the broad category of "indigenous peoples" represents a plethora of cultures, identities, and governance models with varying priorities and understandings of political membership.

With these limitations and complexities in mind, it is no wonder that global claims for indigenous sovereignty, self-determination, and autonomy are routinely denied when "nations" are conceptualized as being beyond the confines of state society and governance. The Tohono O'odham Nation in Arizona and their obstacles to free movement, for instance, serve as another example of the growing importance of citizenship to a recognized state. Their ancestral lands were divided between the United States and Mexico through the Gadsden Purchase in 1853, separating the Tohono O'odham people by an artificial line created by outside forces (Osburn 1999/2000). Members of the Nation often transported members from Mexico to the United States through traditional border crossings in order to access tribal medical care and engage in cultural exchange, but enhanced security measures by the US government challenged this movement and stepped up requirements on using official US documentation rather than tribal IDs (Osburn 1999/2000; Luna-Firebaugh

2000).[5] A declaration of citizenship in the Tohono O'odham—or Mohawk, Blackfeet, Yaqui, Kickapoo, Cocopah, Kumeyaay, or other indigenous nations—often results in extended delay and intensive interrogation, prompting many indigenous people to simply respond "US," "Mexico," or "Canada" at the border (Luna-Firebaugh 2002). Eileen M. Luna-Firebaugh (2002) writes that such enhanced and restrictive border crossing procedures are "an assault on indigenous sovereignty as well as an assault on the cultural integrity of native societies." Inevitably some choose to ignore the legalisms of the official border, yet militarization of the border by US agencies increases the danger of traditional crossings. Indigenous people have been detained, arrested, or forcibly returned across the international border. Ceremonial objects have been disrespectfully handled, and ceremonial participants have been subjected to intense questioning and even ridicule (Luna-Firebaugh, 2002; see also Schertow 2013). Despite Article 36 of the UNDRIP—which asserts that indigenous peoples have the right to maintain and develop contacts across borders, and states are obligated to take effective measures to ensure the implementation of this right (United Nations 2007)—the easiest and safest way for indigenous persons to cross international borders is by utilizing state-issued passports, often requiring them to claim a nationality they do not view as valid. It seems that although the nature of the colonial project has shifted, political processes continue to erode indigenous nationhood—even as states increasingly acknowledge their unique positions within the international community.

The Haudenosaunee Confederacy

Challenges to indigenous sovereignty were sharply highlighted in 2010, when the Iroquois Nationals lacrosse team (whose ancestors are credited with inventing the sport of lacrosse) was prevented from traveling to the World Lacrosse Championship in Manchester, England, using their tribal passports. Although members of the Haudenosaunee Confederacy are eligible for American or Canadian passports, some have been traveling abroad with their own tribe-issued passports since 1977. Stricter security regulations under the 2004 Intelligence Reform and Terrorism Prevention Act limited the United States' once-broad interpretation of passport law,

---

[5] It is understandable, then, that the Tohono O'odham voiced strong objections to US president Donald Trump's proposed border wall, rejecting construction on tribal lands bordering Mexico (Rickert 2016).

however, tightening regulations and requiring indigenous people to produce US-issued passports in order to gain re-entry into the country. On July 13, the team was prevented from boarding an international flight at New York City's John F. Kennedy Airport, thus beginning a "Kafkaesque nightmare" involving the US State Department, Great Britain, and the US Department of Homeland Security (Haygood 2010, para 4). The US State Department offered to expedite passport processing so that the team could travel to the championship, but players decried the offer and argued that the rejection of their sovereign passports belittled their cultural pride (Haygood 2010). Although the team garnered the promise of one-time waivers for members born in the United States on July 14, a similar deal could not be reached with the Canadian consulate; half of the team members were from the Canadian side of the border. The British government also refused to honor the waivers, insisting on the use of US or Canada-issued official passports for entry into the country. Twenty-three team members were ultimately unable to participate in the championship games as a result of the passport dispute (McAndrew and Mariani 2010). The Federation of International Lacrosse, it should be noted, considers the Haudenosaunee Confederacy to be a full member state, like the United States or Canada, with a lacrosse team ranked fourth in the world at the time of the incident (Merkelson 2010). This passport debacle illustrates how the principle of indigenous sovereignty faces practical implementation challenges within the modern state system.

With this precipitating event in mind, let us consider the erosion of indigenous nationhood from the perspective of the Haudenosaunee nations in North America. This case study cannot encapsulate the experiences of all indigenous peoples, but it does illustrate important issues that are central to modern debates about indigenous sovereignty and membership. Politically, the Haudenosaunee have long asserted their sovereignty in response to European colonization. Prior to US independence, the Haudenosaunee met with delegates from England, France, and the Netherlands. The Confederacy made at least fifty treaties with European powers during the colonial era, most of which expressed peace and friendship—not the transfer of sovereignty to another nation. After the Revolutionary War, US statesmen acknowledged the international status of indigenous nations and made treaties with them. Eventually, the United States government entered into three major treaties with the Haudenosaunee Confederacy; two of these treaties have never been abrogated by either side and remain in effect today, while a third—the 1789 Treat of Fort Harmer—was superseded by the Treaty of Canandaigua in 1794. Even now, the Haudenosaunee receive annuities from the Canandaigua Treaty in the form of bolts of muslin cloth and a $4,500 payment allocated each year from the US Treasury. Although the US government ceased treaty-making with indigenous nations in 1871, the Haudenosaunee Confederacy asserts that previous treaties remain binding. Nations of the Haudenosaunee, therefore, have never relinquished their sovereignty or transferred sovereignty to another entity, such as the United States (Onondaga Nation n.d.d.).[6]

Despite their strong efforts to preserve indigenous sovereignty, the Haudenosaunee nations have faced numerous challenges from the United States as the government sought to assimilate indigenous peoples and enforce stricter control over its perceived territories. The General Allotment (Dawes) Act of 1887, for instance, allotted tribal land to individual tribal members, but held the land in trust by the US government. After a person established "competency" as a private property holder and member of American society, theoretically the trust period would end, the land would become taxable, and the allottee would become a US citizen. Although the Dawes Act was touted as a positive path toward full and unqualified citizenship, indigenous responses to the legislation reflected a drift toward what Kevin Bruyneel (2004) calls an "ambivalent form of American citizenship" (32). That is, indigenous people came to define themselves as neither fully inside nor fully outside the political, legal, and cultural boundaries of the United States. This response to the Dawes Act was compelled not only by the forced acculturation of indigenous people and the ethnocentric view that tribal members were not "civilizing" fast enough to be full citizens, but also from frustration over non-indigenous Americans taking advantage of the allotment process to get easy and cheap title over tribal land (Bruyneel 2004).

In 1924, the Indian Citizenship Act (ICA) conferred US citizenship on indigenous people en masse and secured indigenous rights to tribal property, thereby implicitly codifying a form of dual citizenship for indigenous people living within US borders. Approximately 125,000 people were granted citizenship (another 175,000 had acquired citizenship previously), and those who maintained enrollment in a recognized tribe were guaranteed rights to communally held tribal property (Bruyneel 2004). People who are excluded from American political life usually see the codification of citizenship status as a positive development; in fact, Jeffrey Sissons (2005) writes that most indigenous people today would favor a

---

[6] For a broader discussion of treaties between the United States and indigenous nations, see Harjo 2014.

form of dual citizenship over an exclusive indigenous citizenship that positioned them outside of the "post-settler nation" (such as the United States or Canada). In the case of the ICA, however, few indigenous people viewed the conferral of US citizenship as an unambiguously positive step. In fact, during the 1920s "no group of indigenous people more vocally and consistently refused U.S. citizenship than did those tribes and citizens of the Haudenosaunee nations" (Bruyneel 2004, 38). A few weeks after the ICA's passage, Haudenosaunee leaders sent letters to President Coolidge and Congress respectfully declining US citizenship, rejecting dual citizenship, and stating that the act was written and passed without their knowledge or consent. Tuscorara chief Clinton Rickard was the most prominent Haudenosaunee leader to mobilize resistance to the ICA. His foremost message was that the Haudenosaunee did not want US citizenship—whether dual citizenship or citizen-ward status—and that citizenship in any form amounted to political integration at the expense of indigenous citizenship. He saw American citizenship as leading to cultural assimilation within American society and the loss of the Haudenosaunee nations' government-to-government relationship to the United States (Rickard 1973; Bruyneel 2004).

Tensions increased further with the passage of the Immigration (Johnson) Act of 1924, which imposed immigration quotas and affected indigenous border crossings between the United States and Canada. Section 13(c) asserted that aliens ineligible for citizenship could not be admitted to the United States, which meant that North American Indians coming into the United States from Canada were denied entry.[7] Bruyneel (2004) writes that the combination of the Johnson Act and the ICA amounted to an effort by the US government to "firm up" their boundaries and declare all indigenous people residing within their borders to be "citizen-components of this solidified American political space" (39). Indigenous people living within US boundaries were legally distinguished and separated from other indigenous people within North America, thereby containing their political identities within the nation-state. Although this may not have immediately impacted those residing at a distance from international borders, it affected the Haudenosaunee nations and their citizens' abilities to express political identity (Bruyneel 2004). The Akwesasne Mohawk, for instance, are split

---

[7] This was a marked shift from provisions of the Jay Treaty, signed by the United States and Great Britain following the American Revolutionary War, which provided free movement for indigenous groups living on either side of the border. US courts have held that the Jay Treaty was abrogated by the War of 1812, although these decisions are controversial (Osburn 1999/2000).

between the American state of New York and the Canadian provinces of Ontario and Quebec.

Throughout the years, the Haudenosaunee have also been impacted by various US court cases. Although the Confederacy does not ordinarily seek justice in the American court system—leaders note that the nations have their own methods for of "deciding matters"—some cases strike directly at the issue of indigenous sovereignty. Focusing here on the Onondaga Nation in central New York State, various court cases have questioned the legitimacy of Haudenosaunee sovereignty and decision making. The Haudenosaunee nations successfully refused to accept treaty payments in one lump sum through the 1946 Indian Claims Commission Act. Haudenosaunee representatives note that "as long as the annuities remain, we know that the treaties are still in use" (Onondaga Nation n.d.a.). During the 1960s and 1970s, various court cases upheld indigenous sovereignty; court decisions established that New York State cannot collect taxes on stores located within Onondaga territory, that the New York State Department of Transportation does not have powers of eminent domain on the Onondaga Nation, that state income taxes cannot be collected on Haudenosaunee lands, and that state agencies have no jurisdiction on these lands (Onondaga Nation n.d.a.). These decisions reinforce the assertion that Haudenosaunee nations enjoy sovereignty and are not under the jurisdiction of the US government.

Representatives of the Onondaga Nation—and, in turn, the Haudenosaunee Confederacy itself—clearly define indigenous sovereignty and their relationship to governments such as the United States and Canada. Like the US federal government, the Haudenosaunee is a constitutional government that has the power to resolve differences between member nations and to add legislation to a collective set of laws, called the Great Law. In the past, treaties with European governments and later the United States required approval from the Grand Council. "Haudenosaunee sovereignty was not granted by the United States, any more than U.S. sovereignty was granted by the English crown in the eighteenth century," the Onondaga assert. "Sovereignty is an inherent right that, in the case of the Onondaga Nation, was established with the formation of the Haudenosaunee and adoption of the Great Law of Peace" (Onondaga Nation n.d.d., para 10). Individual nations possess sovereign authority as both a nation and as part of the Confederacy. The Onondaga, for instance, consider their 7,300-acre territory in New York state to be the land of a sovereign, independent nation that exists outside the jurisdiction of the US government. The nation is governed by a council of chiefs, selected in accordance with their traditional democratic system. As an independent government, the Onondaga Nation does not pay taxes to the state of New York or to the US federal government—and it asserts that it does not receive the benefits paid for by these taxes (Onondaga Nation n.d.c.).

Although the Haudenosaunee have substantially secured various indigenous rights within the United States, their procedural recognition as an independent nation is called into question when powerful members of the international community refuse to accept their passports, as was the case in 2010. In a practical sense, then, Haudenosaunee political sovereignty exists only if an established nation-state acknowledges it through court cases and legislation, at passport control, and even through government assistance programs that supplement indigenous economies. After all, the Haudenosaunee do not have the military might or economic leverage to defend their sovereignty without outside assistance. These criticisms have been raised against other examples of indigenous sovereignty, including the case of Nunavut (a Canadian territory largely controlled by the Inuit) and the world's smallest country, Niue (an island nation in the Pacific Ocean). All of these cases raise the question previously highlighted by Sissons (2005): If indigenous groups are economically and politically dependent on a larger nation-state, can these cases of dependent independence be accurately described as indigenous sovereignty? He admits that the sovereignty of every nation is limited by the sovereignty of other countries, but in cases such as the Onondaga (and in Nunavut and Niue), indigenous sovereignty is "directly funded by another nation and is, in part at least, an expression of that other nation's political will" (115).

In her work on identity recognition, Nancy Fraser (2003) proposes an alternative analysis that treats recognition as a question of social status. She contends that misrecognition is not necessarily about the depreciation of group identity but rather the social subordination of an individual in the sense of being prevented from participation as a peer in social life. Her status model, therefore, encompasses a politics "aimed at overcoming subordination by establishing the misrecognized party as a full member of society, capable of participating on par with other members" (27). From the perspective of the Haudenosaunee, "society" should be understood not as the nation-state but rather as a geographical area where Americans and indigenous peoples live together. Respect for indigenous sovereignty— including indigenous passports and mobility rights—is a necessary step toward more equitable social status. This is a step that requires equal partnerships between states and indigenous nations; although these entities have varying political and economic resources, at a fundamental level these groups must interact as peers rather than majority/minority or colonizer/colonized.

If this relationship is viewed from a multinational perspective, rather than from the view of minority rights that simply posits indigenous peoples as a minority group living within the American state, then the importance of status becomes more obvious. For the Haudenosaunee, "status" is directly linked to respect for indigenous passports and the wider issue of indigenous sovereignty. Multicultural theorist Will Kymlicka (1995) writes that "the aim of self-government is to enable smaller nations to interact with larger nations on a more equitable basis" (104). He argues that common citizenship strategies (for instance, requiring Haudenosaunee members in New York to utilize US nationality) tend to fail and increase conflict in multination states. A regime of common citizenship "means that the minority has no way to limit its vulnerability to the economic and political decisions of the majority, since the boundaries and powers of internal political units are defined to suit the administrative convenience of the majority, not the self-government claims of the minority" (Kymlicka 1995, 183). Furthermore, Kymlicka warns that it is not possible to eliminate nations and identities. He writes, "If anything, attempts to subordinate these separate identities to a common identity have backfired, since they are perceived by minorities as threats to their very existence, and so have resulted in even greater indifference or resentment" (185). From a multinational perspective, therefore, indigenous sovereignty must be respected in order to create a more equitable relationship between the state and indigenous peoples. Rather than requiring peoples such as the Haudenosaunee to rely on state citizenship (and state-issued passports) for rights protection, the respect for their own sovereignty and social status provides a political space for addressing their unique needs and priorities.

Iris Marion Young (1990) contends that rights aren't "things"; they are relationships (25). This statement takes on new meaning in the cases of the Haudenosaunee and countless others, whose relationships with state governments—which I argue center on whether or not they enjoy functioning citizenship—impact their ability to protect the rights of their members. The 2010 passport dispute involving the Iroquois Nationals lacrosse team drew attention to this issue and illustrated the practical implications of absent state citizenship. As state policymakers and indigenous leaders think more critically about legal nationality and rights, the real question is whether relationships will serve to advance or deny the rights of indigenous peoples. The challenges are bigger than mere passports, as identity and status play a major role in determining how to solve practical issues while protecting indigenous sovereignty. As indigenous leaders continue to push for rights recognition and protection, they face central challenges related to tribal nation-building. In a system that privileges the political power of states, where do indigenous nations fit—and how can they carve out the necessary space for engaging in meaningful self-determination?

Tribal Nation-Building

To answer these key questions, we turn to the promising—and often frustrating—concept of nation-building. Tribal, or indigenous, nation-building is frequently approached in one of two ways: through either an economic-development lens or via an emphasis on legal, political, cultural, economic, health, and educational aspects. Both models place sovereignty, self-determination, and community autonomy as "the driving force for nation building" (Brayboy et al. 2012, 13). Rights to place are of vital importance in these models, which stress the necessity of land for the enjoyment of rights to purpose—including purpose related to education and knowledge, political self-determination, and livelihoods. Bryan McKinley Jones Brayboy and his colleagues (2012) outline approaches to tribal nation-building along three broad themes: (1) self-determination and indigenous knowledge systems, (2) reclaiming tribal sovereignty from the ward relationship, and (3) economic development. Each of these approaches is discussed here in turn.

Self-Determination and Indigenous Knowledge Systems

The right of self-determination is a fundamental principle under international human rights law, asserting that all peoples should "freely determine their political status and freely pursue their economic, social and cultural development" (United Nations High Commissioner for Human Rights 1966, Article 1.1). For indigenous peoples, protecting the right to self-determination is inherently connected to defending and strengthening aboriginal knowledge systems. Although such indigenous "ways of knowing" are diverse, they share "the notion of an interrelationship between all forms of existence"—including interconnected conceptions of the physical world, metaphysics, and the worlds of both matter and spirit (Stewart-Harawira 2008, 163). Vine Deloria Jr. (1999) of the Lakota Nation, for instance, contends that indigenous knowledge is connected to the lives and experiences of individuals and communities, respecting all data and knowledge as relevant to all things. Indigenous peoples "have persistently explained their conceptualization of [indigenous knowledge] as an inter-dependent and integrated whole, as opposed to the compartmentalization imposed by the legal regime that has the tendency to distinguish culture from knowledge" (Fan 2016, 238). Knowledge systems lie at the heart of indigenous identity and membership, thus providing the foundation for decision making related to the economic, social, and cultural development associated with self-determination.

Debates about indigenous knowledge span a variety of concerns, in-cluding issues of intellectual property rights and the protection of bio-cultural diversity that often align with calls to protect rights to place—particularly indigenous land rights. Rebecca C. Fan (2016) writes that the ongoing "displacement and dispossession faced by indigenous peo-ples . . . continues to undermine their capacity to maintain, control, pro-tect and develop their emplaced knowledge" (246), thus presenting a key challenge for protecting the right to self-determination and the survival of indigenous knowledge. Although international law considers land as a re-source for food and agriculture, Johanna Gibson (2011) notes that less at-tention is paid to land "as a mechanism for the transmission of knowledge including that of traditional cultural expressions" (433–434). She argues that land is "a critical and contested zone in interpretations of the right to self-determination and indeed in the meaningful realization of that right for indigenous people"—and she questions whether indigenous cultural rights can be fully realized if traditional knowledge is lost (435–434). In response to these concerns, indigenous educators increasingly focus their energies on sharing traditional knowledge about traditional land and nat-ural resource use. In the Canadian Arctic territory of Nunavut, Inuit leaders advocate a return to hunting not only to pass on traditional knowledge sys-tems but also as a means of survival in times of economic scarcity. Facing the lowest levels of food security in Canada, the Nunavut Food Security Coalition announced a strategy in 2014 to help more people hunt and share "country foods" such as caribou and seal (CBC News 2014). Similarly, a growing number of indigenous nations in the United States—including the Oglala Sioux on the Pine Ridge Reservation in South Dakota—are prioritizing community education about traditional food production, as well as food-based business development, as a way to spark entrepreneur-ship and respond to food shortages (Spanne 2015). Around the world, indigenous communities are also striving to reassert "food sovereignty"[8] with the growth of farming and gardening projects, as well as through the assertion of hunting and fishing rights, heritage seed saving, and the promotion of native cuisine and traditional ingredients. These actions are not only about promoting and protecting indigenous knowledge but are also direct responses to the negative health consequences of replacing indigenous foods with processed foods—including the rapid increase of metabolic disorders like Type II diabetes (Hoover, 2018).

The protection of indigenous knowledge systems is closely connected to broader education challenges facing native students, thus raising questions about how best to ensure equity in indigenous schooling. A 2016 report in the *Chronicle of Higher Education* highlights the devastating consequences of discriminatory US policies toward indigenous nations such as the Blackfeet nation in Montana—including pervasive historical trauma, social ills that thwart educational goals (such as domestic violence and substance abuse), and often a low regard for mainstream education. American Indian and Alaska Native students have the highest high school dropout rates in the United States (6.7 percent, which is double the national average) and the lowest graduation rate (70 percent); they are least likely to enroll in college and second-least likely to graduate (behind Black students), but their low population numbers mean they are often overlooked in national discussions about educational achievement gaps (Field 2016, A21). To fill these voids, scholars contend that specific strategies must be enacted to respect indigenous cultures and acknowledge their histories of oppression. Marlene R. Atleo (2009), for instance, writes that strategies for ensuring educational equity requires dialogue between educators and indigenous peoples: "The forging of new relationships takes time and effort and often a baring of the heart as we move to new relationships between indigenous peoples and the settler societies" (132). This includes appropriate indigenous education aimed at battling the long-term effects of colonization and developing a "new language of and for indigenous history" (Harris et al. 2011, 326). Taiaiake Alfred (2004) advocates "warrior scholarship" that resists imperial power and renews indigenous education. This scholarly ethic requires that students and educators honor knowledge from indigenous traditional cultures, fight for political independence in

---

[8] "Food sovereignty is the right of peoples to healthy and culturally appropriate food produced through ecologically sound and sustainable methods, and their right to define their own food and agriculture systems" (Nyéléni 2007).

the face of state sovereignty, and denounce and confront false claims of authority and legitimacy that have co-opted indigenous scholars (95–96).

Reclaiming Tribal Sovereignty from the Ward Relationship

Indigenous sovereignty is "the inherent right of tribal nations to direct their futures and engage the world in ways that are meaningful to them." From this perspective, "self-determination is the engagement of sovereignty; put another way, self-determination is the *operationalization* of sovereignty" (Brayboy et al. 2012, 17). Yet the promise of tribal sovereignty is fundamentally challenged by indigenous relationships to the settler nation-state that are marked by histories of colonial control and domination. Despite growing international acceptance of indigenous rights and self-determination—in principle, at least—the political position of indigenous nations is a far second to that of the state. At the same time, current understandings of indigenous sovereignty are often understood only within the context of the settler state-indigenous nation relationship, positioning tribal sovereignty within a broader power framework that privileges state autonomy and treats indigenous peoples as wards of state governments. These hierarchies are enabled not only by fundamental power inequalities that privilege state sovereignty but are also perpetuated by confusion surrounding basic concepts necessary for reclaiming indigenous sovereignty and decision making. For instance, the notion of an international "right to autonomy" is "blurred and undetermined" (85), although the domestic recognition of various forms of indigenous autonomy are widespread around the world and are particularly concentrated in Latin America (Tomaselli 2016, 85 and 96). Such indigenous autonomies face severe implementation challenges regardless of constitutional guarantees, due in large part to lack of political will and the prioritization of economic interests over indigenous rights claims (95). There is also confusion about fundamental concepts of self-governance and political membership, including those related to self-identification and constitution. Processes of group formation among indigenous nations are ambiguous, since most models assume that groups are pre-constituted within identifiable communities and stable borders. Fundamental questions arise about the optimal inclusivity of indigenous communities as well as the circumstances by which a person could reasonably be excluded from one—and answers to these questions can have serious human rights consequences (Gover 2016, 36).[9]

---

[9] Examples abound to illustrate how these ambiguities impact indigenous communities and weaken solidarity. For instance, in 2013 the Nooksack nation in Washington State announced they

The very language of "sovereignty" uncovers inherent differences between indigenous nationhood and state models of decision making and power. Alfred (1999) warns against the assumption that sovereignty is the appropriate model for indigenous governance, noting that traditional nationhood contrasts sharply with dominant understandings of "the state" that emphasize absolute authority and hierarchy (56). "'Sovereignty' implies a set of values and objectives in direct opposition to those found in traditional indigenous philosophies," explains Alfred. "Non-indigenous politicians recognize the inherent weakness of assertions of a sovereign right for peoples who have neither the cultural framework nor the institutional capacity to sustain it. The problem is that the assertion of a sovereign right for indigenous peoples continues to structure the politics of decolonization, and the state uses the theoretical inconsistencies in that position to its own advantage" (57). Although arguing on behalf of indigenous nationhood within the dominant paradigm is thus self-defeating, it is noteworthy to remember the state has created incentives—such as allowing a small measure of self-administration and the allocation of some profits related to land exploitation—to integrate indigenous nations into its own sovereignty framework (60). Peter d'Errico (2009) notes that while the terminology is frequently used in discussions of indigenous sovereignty, "we will always want to keep in mind that the reality behind the names is what we are struggling over" (109). Under US federal law, for instance, "tribal" sovereignty is a lesser-form of authority and self-governance than the sovereignty associated with the state. d'Errico argues that it is "not really sovereignty at all, but dependence" (109) and that a fundamental premise of "American Indian sovereignty" is that it is, realistically, no such thing—but rather a form of "indirect rule" governed by tribal leaders loyal to the state (110–111). By following the model of state sovereignty—which indigenous nations are told they cannot do, since they are not states—they may ultimately sacrifice their ultimate goal of self-defined self-determination (116). He contends that indigenous nations must re-assert their conceptions of sovereignty to fit their belief models rather than to conform to the state structures imposed on them. This process is notably dependent on rights to place:

---

were expelling more than 300 members whose claims were suddenly deemed illegitimate (Jarvis 2017). In Canada, government legislation regulating the legal definition of Metis peoples has resulted in "intense suffering as well as ongoing undermining of basic Metis family structures and personal and familiar well-being" (Weber-Pillwax 2008, 203).

Ultimately it is land—and people's relationship to land—that is at issue in "indigenous sovereignty" struggles. To know that "sovereignty" is a legal-theological concept allows us to understand these struggles as spiritual projects, involving questions about who "we" are: beings among beings, peoples among peoples. Sovereignty arises from within a people as their unique expression of themselves as a people. It is not produced by court decrees or government grants, but by the actual ability of a people to sustain themselves in a place. This is self-determination. (d'Errico 2009, 119)

While the conceptualization of a universal definition of "indigenous territory" is problematic due to the diversity of indigenous cultures throughout the world, the indigenous rights movement has led to an increasingly coherent set of principles that stress spiritual connections to land (Gray 2009, 18). It's thereby no surprise that the breakdown of indigenous territorial control can lead to devastation among indigenous communities—including through the establishment of reservations, the privatization of land, the dispossession and forced relocation of indigenous peoples, and processes of transmigration that introduce new waves of colonization (37–38). In countries such as Chile, governments have abolished the legal legitimacy of collective property and, in the process, stripped indigenous peoples of their de facto minority status. The Mapuche, who were confined to approximately 3,000 reservations in Chile between 1884 and 1927, held fewer than 600 reservations by the 1980s (Calbucura 2009, 65). Yet the connection between indigenous land and sovereignty leads to another set of complications; it is noteworthy that many indigenous people are urban, even while most maintain strong links to their home communities. Limiting our understanding of indigenous nations to the confines of reservations and rural sites risks limiting the participation of urban members in decision-making processes (Sissons 2005, 124). Indeed, Sissons argues that such models "reinforce a separation between those who wish to remain on the land and those who don't" and risks creating hierarchies of indigeneity (126).

Economic Development

Indigenous nation-building requires "adequate and appropriate economic development" in order to achieve self-governance and equal political footing (Harris et al. 2011, 282), yet development projects often occur without indigenous support and to the detriment of native communities. Indigenous approaches to lands and resources are at odds with a global economic model that stresses the exploitation of natural resources and the expansion of infrastructures; despite human rights protections within the UNDRIP and other frameworks, economic development often occurs without respect for indigenous culture or priorities (Barelli 2016, 69). Article 32(2) of the UNDRIP recognizes that indigenous peoples should be consulted before development projects are authorized on their lands, stressing the principle of free, prior, and informed consent (United Nations 2007). The language of Article 32(2) does not specify exactly how this consent will be garnered, however. At a minimum it requires the state to consult with indigenous leaders in good faith and reach an agreement, but it could also mean that states should obtain consent before moving forward with proposed plans. Indigenous peoples do not enjoy "veto" power related to all issues that affect their lands, but the normative framework of the UNDRIP highlights increasing recognition that indigenous communities should have a say over development projects that are likely to have serious impacts on their cultures and lives (Barelli 2016, 78–79). Even in cases where development projects aim to improve the livelihoods of indigenous communities, well-intentioned proposals often fail to achieve their stated goals. A growing body of research shows that economic development needs to be controlled by tribes and their members, despite a prevalence of outside advice and programming aimed at alleviating poverty and un-employment within indigenous communities. Imposed programs that lack indigenous input and decision–making frequently fail, while those that are undertaken by indigenous peoples themselves or in full partnership with others are largely successful. A central challenge of this process is how to grow indigenous economies in ways that increase independence of na-tive communities and overcome the dependence created by colonialism (Harris et al. 2011, 286–287).[10]

Challenges to appropriate indigenous development are particularly ap-parent in cases of large-scale development projects that exploit natural re-sources, which often adversely affect indigenous communities. Frequently, traditional lands are viewed as "under-developed" regions prime for state and private investment, resource extraction, dam building, and other

---

[10] Recent controversies related to the widespread establishment of "Indian casinos" illustrate that adequate and appropriate economic development is a complex goal. In the US state of California alone, more than sixty Indian casinos earn billions in gambling profits each year. Some tribes have begun disenfranchising members, or stripping them of their status as members of a federally recognized indigenous tribe and thus barring them from sharing in the profits from these casinos. These actions have serious economic ramifications, leading some critics to contend that greed and power are motivating factors for disenfranchisement (see Dao 2011).

forms of "development" that benefit national interests (Errico 2011, 329). Notably, Article 26 of the UNDRIP recognizes indigenous peoples' right to own, use, develop, and control natural resources (United Nations 2007). In countries such as Brazil, however, indigenous concepts of space have often been reconstructed in ways that benefit colonial interests, including both the state and transnational corporations. The construction of the BR-174 highway through Waimiri-Atroari territory, for instance, and the use of "accelerated integration" plans to congregate indigenous survivors into controlled settlements had devastating consequences for indigenous nationhood in the Amazon region (Baines 2009, 50). Disseminating the rhetoric of globalization through intensive marketing campaigns, the Brazilian state identified indigenous spokespeople who legitimized harmful development programs and perpetuated the imposed construct of a "traditional" and "docile" Indian culture that was used as evidence of the state's respect for diversity (58). In the United States, ongoing indigenous resistance to the Dakota Access Pipeline (DAPL) and calls to sell off "vacant" federal land highlight tensions between indigenous views of appropriate economic development and dominant corporate/state economic approaches. The DAPL, a $3.8 billion project intended to cross below North Dakota's Lake Oahe (a water source upstream from the Standing Rock Sioux reservation) drew the ire of thousands of indigenous and non-native protestors alike in 2016 and 2017, who claimed the pipeline could contaminate drinking water supplies and desecrate sacred lands (Eleftheriou-Smith 2017). During that same time, conservationists and hunters rallied against a Republican proposal to sell 3.3 million acres of federal land—a proposed sale that was justified by politicians because the undeveloped wilderness served "no purpose for taxpayers" (Enders 2017, para. 2).

Indigenous nations and calls for tribal sovereignty raise important questions about the nature of political membership when state society is not the central site of authority, identity, or belonging. Indigenous nationhood offers an alternative site of citizenship and recognition that is simultaneously powerful and constrained; international frameworks for indigenous rights stress self-determination while relying on state governments for rights provision and protection. As native communities continue to formulate their approaches to nationhood and sovereignty—from within, alongside, or beyond state society—their discussions provide an opportunity for thinking through the value of political membership and how alternative processes of recognition might unfold. Self-determination and indigenous knowledge systems, reclaimed tribal sovereignty, and economic development offer three pathways toward indigenous nation-building that reject the hierarchies of personhood that have marked the global history of indigenous peoples for centuries. These approaches may offer new avenues toward functioning citizenship, thus prioritizing indigenous rights to place and purpose that have been routinely ignored by the very state governments tasked with their protection in recent years.

CHAPTER 7 | Second-Class Citizens in
the "Land of the Free"

POWERFUL INDICATORS OF SOCIAL stratification and inequality are all around me in the city of Saint Louis—and so are not-so-hidden messages about worthiness and hierarchies of personhood. "Don't be that guy," a bright red advertising poster reminds commuters at a local bus stop. "The Panhandler: Don't ask. Don't give. And help eliminate panhandling on Metro."[1] As I drive home, I stop at a red light and a carefully positioned corner road sign reminds me that "aggressive begging" is a crime. Indeed, I might be engaging in the criminal act of "impeding traffic" if I pause to share money or a kind word with a person who is homeless; local activists are warned not to feed people without a vending permit, even though the food is given for free.

I notice that "Black Lives Matter" (BLM)[2] signs are displayed in front yards and windows in predominantly Black[3] or racially diverse city

---

[1] Metro St. Louis launched its "Don't Be That Guy" campaign in November 2015 aimed at eliminating illegal or anti-social behavior such as engaging in vulgar language and shouting, selling items or gambling, and smoking. Metro St. Louis noted that it had "posted friendly messages" throughout its system—including inside MetroBus shelters, on walls in transit centers, and around MetroLink platforms—to encourage passengers to "steer clear of those behaviors" (Hibbard 2015, para 2). Motorists are also encouraged by road signage to "join the city's effort to end homelessness" by calling 9-1-1 if they witness "aggressive begging" or someone "impeding traffic."

[2] After the 2014 police killing of Black teenager Michael Brown in nearby Ferguson, Missouri, Saint Louis activists demanded acknowledgment that "Black Lives Matter" (BLM)—a phrase coined after the killing of unarmed teenager Trayvon Martin in Florida—and their mobilization has lived on as an intersectional continuation of the Black liberation movement. BLM leaders argue that they are "broadening the conversation around state violence to include all of the ways in which Black people are intentionally left powerless at the hands of the state. We are talking about the ways in which Black lives are deprived of our basic human rights and dignity" (Black Lives Matter n.d.a., para 4). The success of BLM and increasing social activism on a range of issues has spurred growing awareness of the need to engage with intersectionality—"efforts to think, analyze, organize as we recognize the interconnections of race, class, gender, sexuality" (Davis 2016, 18). For our purposes here, intersectionality requires us to consider the processes by which hierarchies of personhood are created within the American citizenry and how those hierarchies violate essential rights to place and purpose.

[3] Words are powerful because people create and transmit meaning through language—including the words we use to categorize groups of people. From a sociological perspective, we

neighborhoods such as Shaw, but these signs are rare in White suburbs like Webster Groves, where my university is located. And socioeconomic and racial lines are drawn block-by-block within city limits, dividing residents who live in close geographic proximity but are often socially and economically worlds apart. For instance, I live in Lafayette Square— a beautiful historic enclave of Victorian Painted Ladies nestled between neighborhoods where housing prices are far lower and crime rates are drastically higher than in other parts of the city. Despite pleas from community organizers asking residents not to engage in racial profiling, some of my White neighbors frequently send out electronic emergency alerts about young Black boys wandering the park or streets looking like they are "up to no good." When Black teenagers repeatedly stole the tip jar from a local ice cream shop, several neighbors advocated shooting at the teens—or at least believed this crime was worthy of "life in prison" to discourage such reckless behavior in the future. ("Or maybe you could just get a heavier tip jar," another neighbor retorted.)[4]

For those following the story of Saint Louis (or of Detroit, New Orleans, Milwaukee, Chicago) from afar, the human suffering in urban

---

see that some terms "perpetuate differences in the historical and lingering advantages, power, and privilege between different racial and ethnic groups" (Koch 2015, 260). Terminology used to discuss race in the United States has changed markedly over the last century, and certainly terms such as "colored" and "Negro" are no longer acceptable. However, the terms "Black" and "African American" are often used interchangeably but stem from different historical perspectives. The term "Black" gained widespread usage starting in the 1960s, viewed as a logical antithesis to "White" and connected to strength and power as exemplified by the slogan "Black power" (501). "Black" gained general acceptance by the 1970s, having lost its connections to so-called radical activism. Rather than being seen as a substitute for the word "Negro," "the term [Black] had helped to instill and maintain a sense of group consciousness, racial pride, and a hope for racial justice" (Smith 1992, 503). Beginning in the late 1980s, "African American" was advanced as a term that connected people with their ancestry, thereby placing the group within a global perspective and aligning it with a broader cultural heritage. The term also aligned closely to White ethnic identifiers (such as "Italian American") and could perhaps appeal to allies positioned against ethnic (but not necessarily racial) intolerance (Smith 1992, 507). Today, the terms "Black" and "African American" are both used to discuss race in the United States, while the term "White" also has widespread acceptance. For the purposes of this chapter, I have opted to use the term "Black" (except when "African American" is used in direct quotes) because it is the identifier embraced by activists in the Saint Louis area, including leaders of the "Black Lives Matter" movement. (I capitalize Black and White unless they are un-capitalized within direct quotes; again, both styles are widely used.) I acknowledge the power and value of the term "African American," however, and I regret the inadequacies of language in this instance.

[4] I hesitate to write these stories for fear of perpetuating an image of Saint Louis that centers on poverty and racial division, yet sharing these encounters is the only way to uncover the hierarchies of personhood they represent. The full story of Saint Louis—and the stories of so many American cities, which people often claim to understand because they've read a few magazine articles about urban decay—is complicated and messy, never conforming to binary categories that separate Black and White or rich and poor. Too often our narratives of postindustrial decline ignore the diverse

centers is an exception to the norm, a blemish on the American Dream. More than depicting suffering, however, these stories reflect a state of neglect and abandonment that has become pervasive within American cities—a failure of citizenship that the world was confronted with, at least temporarily, with the arrival of Hurricane Katrina in New Orleans in 2005 or the acknowledgment of lead-poisoned drinking water in Flint, Michigan, in 2014. A humbling reminder that human rights violations happen everywhere, including in our own backyards, lack of functioning citizenship denies many Americans the "right to have rights" that we commonly associate with stateless persons and refugees. Despite *jus soli* nationality laws that afford legal nationality at birth, lack of functioning citizenship within the United States creates a category of second-class citizens who suffer from structural violence and oppression throughout their lifetimes.

In this chapter, I return "home" to focus specifically on the cities of Detroit, Flint, and Saint Louis to discuss the denial of functioning citizenship within the United States. While every city has its own history (and such violations of rights certainly occur in rural and suburban areas, in addition to urban centers), I contend that these case studies offer important lessons for understanding how structural inequalities construct hierarchies of personhood that are reinforced, perpetuated, and sometimes passionately defended over the course of generations. Beginning with Margaret Somers's (2008) "contractualization of citizenship" and the possibility of "internal statelessness" despite the provision of legal nationality, I argue that high rates of housing evictions and heated battles over healthcare illustrate how the rights to place and purpose are often deeply impacted by the prioritization of markets over fundamental protections. At the same time, wealth gaps are deeply rooted in the country's history of racial inequality even while perceptions of race and belonging hardly conform to strict identity categories. Using these three cities as case studies, this chapter argues that some American citizens— much like the de jure stateless and other vulnerable people highlighted throughout this book—lack the functioning citizenship necessary to protect their fundamental rights to place and purpose. As Americans debate how to revive blighted urban centers, I further argue that development efforts must prioritize the rights of existing residents, and that all citizens

---

array of determined activists and committed citizens who are the true heroes of these stories, hell-bent on resisting the hierarchies of personhood that are so profoundly connected to issues of racial and socioeconomic equality in the United States.

deserve equal recognition and protection by their duty-bearing government. As civil rights icon Angela Davis (2016) rightly notes: "Whenever you conceptualize social justice struggles, you will always defeat your own purposes if you cannot imagine the people around whom you are struggling as equal partners" (26).

Race, Class, and the Contractualization of American Citizenship

The failed 2005 government response to Hurricane Katrina represented a shocking and deeply troubling moment in the history of US citizenship.[5] Yet for many New Orleans residents—and indeed, residents of many American urban centers—the situation came not as an unexpected shock but rather as a poignant reminder of how a hierarchy of personhood existed within the American citizenry. Although Katrina's victims were not de jure stateless, their lack of functioning citizenship rendered them "internally stateless" (Somers 2008, 5) and unable to access the protections that should follow from nationality—particularly to one of the world's wealthiest and most powerful states. Rather than viewing Hurricane Katrina as a single event, Somers (2008) contends that it was part of an ongoing story related to the "contractualization of citizenship" that shifts the rights and obligations central to the social contract (2). She writes that market ideologies have broken down the social contract between governments and citizens in "an effort to reorganize the relationship between the state and the citizenry, from noncontractual rights and obligations to the principles and practices of quid pro quo market exchange," thereby collapsing the boundaries that protect the public and civil society from the market (2).

Although Somers (2008) acknowledges that market fundamentalism is not the sole cause of today's social exclusions, she asserts that it has "radically exacerbate[d] the exclusions of race and class" since the 1970s by

---

[5] But certainly not the only deeply troubling moment. Lest we forget, for instance, the legal construction of race vastly affected US citizenship law for most of the country's history. Ian Haney López (2006) investigates the role of law in defining racial categories, arguing that racial prerequisites helped determine who was fit (or unfit) for naturalization and American citizenship—and that the notion of the "White nation" was (and is) used to restrict immigration to preserve a supposed national identity (11–13). As highlighted by a variety of critical race theorists, the social construction of race impacts American identity, citizenship, and the protection of right; these issues are hardly limited to the binary construction of "Black versus White" (see Delgado and Stefancic 2014).

delegitimizing affirmative action and then cloaking discrimination with the fiction of a "color-blind" market (5). The outcome, she argues, "has been an ever-growing superfluous population, no longer accommodated by a regime in which market value is the chief criterion for membership. This population makes up America's socially excluded and internally stateless who have lost the right to have rights" (Somers 2008, 5).[6] Basic necessities for livelihood—such as food, water, healthcare, and shelter—hence shift from the language of universal human rights to that of market commodities, where only those who are able to pay for these "goods" are worthy of accessing them. Reflecting on Hurricane Katrina and its aftermath, Somers (2008) writes:

> The sight of so many forgotten New Orleanians without the resources to evacuate the city was but a momentary snapshot in a steady process of increasing social exclusion and an eviscerating of the public sphere. On the surface it began with the government's failure to adequately construct and maintain the city's levees. At the core, however, it was driven by an ideational assault on the idea of poverty as a social problem, and poisoned with the stigmatizing venom of personal blame and cries of dependent immorality. . . . [Only by reconstructing this much longer story] can we understand how and why those left behind in New Orleans to face the storm alone were *already* a rightless, stateless, and expendable population deemed unworthy of the mutual recognition due moral equals. That's why they had been left behind in the first place. (11)

In the United States, obstacles to the rights to shelter and healthcare offer two examples (among many) of how market fundamentalism impedes the enjoyment of place and purpose. Perhaps there is no clearer manifestation of the right to place than the human right to adequate shelter—the right to housing "which ensures access to a safe, secure, habitable, and affordable home with freedom from forced eviction" (National Economic & Social Rights Initiative n.d., para. 1). Yet millions of Americans are evicted each year because they can't pay their rent. In Milwaukee, a city of fewer than 105,000 renter households, approximately 16,000 adults

---

[6] This perspective was poignantly illustrated in 2018 when the *New York Times*, responding to the arbitrary arrest of two Black men at a Philadelphia Starbucks, asked readers: "What do you do to feel safer in public spaces?" A reader from Chicago, Christopher Scott, responded: "I keep my Platinum American Express card near my driver's license so that law enforcement can see that I am a 'citizen,' someone in the upper middle class, without overtly saying so" (quoted in Haque and Moore 2018).

and children are evicted each year (Desmond 2016, 4). In his study of eight American families facing the eviction process, Matthew Desmond argues that "eviction's fallout is severe"—destroying families, uprooting communities, and harming children—and that "we have failed to fully appreciate how deeply housing is implicated in the creation of poverty" (5). (Newer data assembled from about 83 million court records since 2000 shows this is an intentional, pervasive problem that often devastates poor, Black families; see Badger and Bui 2018). Desmond notes simply: "Not everyone living in a distressed neighborhood is associated with gang members, parole officers, employers, social workers, or pastors. But nearly all of them have a landlord" (5). While Desmond (2016) believes that solutions are possible, he contends that they depend on the answer to a single question: "Do we believe that the right to a decent home is part of what it means to be an American?" (300). If the answer is "yes," it creates a moral imperative to reject the market fundamentalist approach to shelter and instead affirm that housing is a basic right. This shift further requires us to think differently about another "right" that is embraced by market capitalism: "the right to make as much money as possible by providing families with housing—and especially to profit excessively from the less fortunate" (305).

Rights to purpose rely on the foundational right to health; put simply, bodily health is a bare minimum requirement for pursuing a "dignified and minimally flourishing life" (Nussbaum 2011, 33). An emphasis on healthcare as a market commodity rather than a right, however, has led to a healthcare crisis in which many Americans lack health insurance, cannot afford essential medicines and doctor's visits, and/or struggle to pay rising insurance premiums. This includes not only poor Americans but also the working- and middle-class who critics argued would lose federal benefits under (failed) Republican healthcare reform proposals in 2017 (Ehrenfreund 2017). This is not a new issue, however; the American healthcare debate traces back to at least 1945, when US president Harry Truman recommended healthcare for every American as part of the country's existing social insurance system. The American Medical Association (AMA)'s public relations charge against such reforms helped coin the term "socialized medicine," which was "political dynamite" in an anti-communist age; the policy was subsequently dropped and instead the government used tax breaks to encourage companies to offer their workers private insurance plans, thus entwining healthcare provision with employment (*Economist* 2016, para. 4). Recent political furor over "Obamacare," or the Affordable Care Act (ACA), highlights how this emphasis on market fundamentalism remains strong within US culture—and particularly among conservative Republicans who favor a "small government," oppose redistributive economics, and balk at legislation requiring citizens to carry health insurance. In 2013, New Hampshire state representative Bill O'Brien said the ACA was "as destructive to personal and individual liberties as the Fugitive Slave Act," a nineteenth-century law that required runaway slaves to be returned to their owners (quoted in Isquith 2013, para. 4). From this perspective, citizenship is equated with individual liberties—such as the ability to purchase or decline health insurance—and privileges market fundamentalism rather than the protection of universal rights. This emphasis on personal choice assumes, incorrectly, that everyone has the resources necessary to enjoy a true range of options. Those who cannot afford unsubsidized healthcare in a market-driven system are effectively cut off from medical services, denied a universal human right because they cannot afford to pay for it.

Inequality in the United States does not abide by definitive categorizations, but it is impossible to consider hierarchies of personhood without acknowledging the vital connections between race, socioeconomic class, and lack of functioning citizenship. "Every conversation about resources in the United States is also about race and racism," explains Tressie McMillan Cottom (2015, para. 1). "Freedom—from being stopped and frisked; from predatory criminal justice fines; from cells—is arguably the resource from which every other resource flows: education, marriage, income, wealth, happiness, actualization" (para. 2). Indeed, Kristin Perkins and Robert Sampson (2015) contend that the intersection of individual and contextual forms of deprivation—including the combination of racial and economic inequality—often have devastating consequences for young Black people. Their study of Chicago adolescents, based on four waves of longitudinal data from 1995 to 2013, illustrates how a "poverty trap" can have lifelong and inter-generational impacts. They argue that "compound deprivation" (the intersection of individual with contextual forms of poverty—including but extending beyond material conditions like income to social forms of deprivation, such as weak social support networks or low collective efficacy) is difficult to escape, particularly for Black youth (para. 2). Their data show that Whites are far better able to overcome early severe deprivation, thereby escaping the ongoing severe poverty that ensnares many Black communities. Even in the most basic financial terms, government census data support the assertion that Black households are underprivileged in US society: In 2015, the real median income of Black households ($36,898) was significantly lower than that of Whites ($62,950), and the poverty rate for Black people was a startling 24.1 percent, compared to 9.1 percent among Whites (Proctor et al. 2016, 7, 12, and 14).

Yet perceptions of racial equality—and the future of race relations in the United States—vary widely among the country's citizenry. In 2016, during the height of the US presidential election, research highlighted deep racial divides among Black and White Americans. Black respondents were far more likely to believe that Black people were treated unfairly in a variety of ways—including dealing with the police, applying for loans and mortgages, voting, and securing employment—and an overwhelming majority (88 percent) said the country needed to make changes to ensure racial equality, compared to 53 percent of White respondents who believed more work was needed. Notably, 43 percent of Black respondents were skeptical that such changes would ever occur, compared to 11 percent of Whites (Pew Research Center 2016, para. 2, 3, and 5). In fact, a growing number of White Americans believe that bias against White people is more of a problem than bias against Black people—even though this assertion stands "in stark contrast to data on almost any outcome that has been assessed" (Norton and Sommers 2016, para. 9). This lack of awareness about enduring racial inequalities illustrates why Davis (2016) warns that we cannot assume that the eradication of the legal apparatus of racism equals the abolition of racism. Legal segregation may be over, for instance, but "racism persists in a framework that is far more expansive, far vaster than the legal framework" (16–17). Rather than focusing on identifiable racists as perpetrators, Davis stresses the need to root out racism that is embedded in institutional structures and to acknowledge how racism at home connects to broader and intersecting processes of oppression (18).

The intricate link between race and socioeconomic class is perpetuated by narratives of political membership and worthiness. In her research at a Detroit homeless shelter, for instance, Aimee Meredith Cox (2015) found that young Black women are expected to "shapeshift" into "manageable and respectable members of society whose social citizenship is always questionable and never guaranteed, even as these same institutions os-tensibly encourage social belonging" (7). She describes these women's interactions with state institutions and practices as "choreography" and contends that this shapeshifting reveals destructive, normative ways of life that "valorize white supremacy, patriarchy, and modes of production that render young Black women at best superfluous and at worst valueless" (28 and 9). Clarissa Rile Hayward (2013) contends that people "reproduce identities, not just by telling and retelling the stories from which they were constructed, but also by *institutionalizing* those stories: by building them into norms, laws, and other institutions . . . that give social actors incentives to perform their identities well" (2). She argues that the construction of the Black ghetto (and conversely, the White enclave) institutionalized stories of racial difference. The concentration of joblessness, poverty, and a variety of social problems in "black places" transformed collective problems into what became regarded as "black problems" within the popular consciousness (Hayward 2013, 45). Indeed, Michelle Alexander (2012) makes a compelling argument that the US criminal justice system has been used to change the language of racial discrimination, using one's status as a convicted felon as grounds for the denial of fundamental rights (including the right to vote) rather than explicitly citing race. She argues that "the arguments and rationalizations that have been trotted out in support of racial exclusion and discrimination in its various forms have changed and evolved, but the outcome has remained largely the same" (1).[7] In her acclaimed book *The New Jim Crow,* Alexander writes:

> What has changed since the collapse of Jim Crow has less to do with the basic structure of our society than with the language we use to justify it. In the era of colorblindness, it is no longer socially permissible to use race, explicitly, as a justification for discrimination, exclusion, and social contempt. So we don't. Rather than rely on race, we use our criminal justice system to label people of color "criminals" and then engage in all the practices we supposedly left behind. Today it is perfectly legal to discriminate against criminals in nearly all the ways that it was once legal to discriminate against African Americans. Once you're labeled a felon, the old forms of discrimination— employment discrimination, housing discrimination, denial of the right to vote, denial of educational opportunity, denial of food stamps and other public benefits, and exclusion from jury service—are suddenly legal. As a criminal, you have scarcely more rights, and arguably less respect, than a black man living in Alabama during the height of Jim Crow. We have not ended racial caste in America; we have merely redesigned it. (2)

To understand how hierarchies of personhood are constructed within the American citizenry, we must consider the pervasive denial of functioning

---

[7] The 2016 documentary *13th,* which features interviews with Alexander, argues the mass incarceration of people of color has simply provided a new form of legal bondage and disenfranchisement. The Oscar-nominated film is titled after the 13th Amendment to the US Constitution, which prohibits slavery—unless involuntary servitude is punishment for a crime (DuVernay n.d.).

citizenship that exists within US cities such as Detroit, Flint, and Saint Louis. As these case studies illustrate, perceptions of worthiness often hinge on racial and class-based divides that posit some Americans as more deserving of rights protections than others. For many, such denials of full state protection constitute a denial of full personhood. In his historical analysis of racial oppression in the United States, for instance, Christopher Alan Bracey (2016) argues that "a core founding principle of this nation was the belief held by whites that blacks did not possess equal humanity and therefore did not deserve equal treatment" (2). Today, human rights issues such as widespread poverty, lack of clean drinking water, and police brutality exemplify gaps in functioning citizenship that limit rights to place and purpose in the so-called land of the free.

Detroit City and the Flint Water Crisis

Growing up in Metro Detroit (the area of Southeast Michigan surrounding Detroit) in the 1980s, my city had the dubious honor of being the murder capital of the country and for making national news for its Devil's Night fires, a pre-Halloween tradition that burned thousands of inner-city buildings to the ground. My grandparents told me stories of glamorous shopping trips to Hudson's department store and movie nights at the Fox Theater many years ago, but my view of Detroit was one informed by pervasive homelessness and violent crime, crushing poverty and lack of social services, and crumbling houses and buildings that were remnants of their former glory. As Mark Binelli (2012) writes in his book *Detroit City Is the Place to Be: The Afterlife of an American Metropolis*: "For people of my generation and younger, growing up in the Detroit area meant growing up with a constant reminder of the best having ended a long time ago. We held no other concept of Detroit *but* as a shell of its former self. Our parents could mourn what it used to be and tell us stories about the wonderful downtown department stores and the heyday of Motown and muscle cars. But for us, those stories existed as pure fable" (11). And while I knew that Detroit suffered from serious social ills, it was only in adulthood that I fully understood the severe human rights implications of this situation. Looking at Detroit through the lens of human rights, I saw its variety of problems—including a failing public school system and a lack of emergency first responders—as direct violations of universal and inalienable rights. Some argue that "Detroit's social contract was torn to shreds long ago"; residence receive "paltry" public services from the local government and nearly half of all property owners don't pay taxes (Uberti 2014, para. 14). The question among many outsiders is simply: Why does anyone still live in Detroit? (Uberti 2014). The answer, in all honesty, is that many people *don't* want to live there; its population rank in 2016 was its lowest since 1850 as it fell out of the country's list of top twenty most populous cities. Detroit's population in the summer of 2016 was 677,116—a loss of 3,107 residents from the previous year (MacDonald 2016).[8]

In 2014, national attention shifted from Detroit—a city that had earned almost perverse and voyeuristic attention from the international community as a symbol of postindustrial decline—to the nearby city of Flint, where lead-contaminated public water sources poisoned the city's largely Black and low-income population. The city of Flint had temporarily switched its drinking water source to the Flint River in April 2014, but it did not implement corrosion control of iron pipes. Ten months later, water samples showed progressively rising lead levels in the water, coinciding with noticeable water discoloration. A state of emergency was declared in September 2015 when tests revealed spiking lead levels in the blood of Flint children (Pieper et al. 2017). As people complained about illness, hair loss, and rashes, the city government sought to minimize the concerns—and failed to swiftly respond to the public health crisis. Civil rights advocates argued that the situation in Flint reflected "environmental racism," when Blacks and other racial minorities are disproportionately exposed to polluted air, water, and soil (Eligon 2016, para. 4). "The fact that Flint residents have not had regular access to safe drinking water and sanitation since April 2014 is a potential violation of their human rights," warned Léo Heller, the UN Special Rapporteur on the human right to safe drinking water and sanitation,

---

[8] To be fair, exceptions to this rule certainly exist; rental rates have increased dramatically in now-trendy Detroit neighborhoods such as Midtown, Corktown, and Woodbridge (Burns 2017). Developers are moving ahead with new construction and historical renovation projects in "The District Detroit"—fifty blocks of businesses, restaurants, bars, and sporting venues popping up around Detroit's existing entertainment hub (The District Detroit n.d.). Yet excitement over such developments tends to focus on creating new housing and entertainment opportunities for already privileged citizens with little attention paid to improving the human rights situation of the city's residents, including funding the public school system, offering essential services, and providing safe and affordable housing. In the 1990s, Detroit residents were enticed by similar promises of urban renewal and voted to approve commercial gaming in 1996. The first casino license was issued to MGM Grand in July 1999 and was followed by two others. Reported contributions include more than $1.9 in casino revenue for public education and $2.6 billion in wagering taxes, in total, to the city of Detroit by 2017 (Michigan Gaming Control Board 2017). Although casino revenue has certainly aided the city, promises of widespread revitalization have fallen woefully short. Time will tell whether additional downtown developments can provide more far-reaching impacts for Detroit's existing residents.

in May 2016. "Serious problems reported on water quality, particularly high concentrations of lead, are also concerning human rights issues" (quoted in United Nations Human Rights 2016, para. 7). Leilani Farha, the UN Special Rapporteur on adequate housing, cautioned that "the impact on housing and living conditions for an already vulnerable group is clear and devastating" (quoted in United Nations Human Rights 2016, para. 9). Once again, southeast Michigan offered a stunning example of how the most basic rights and protections can be violated, even among citizens in one of the world's most "developed" countries, and how hierarchies of personhood construct some nationals as more worthy rights claimants than others.

Although Detroit has garnered far more scholarly attention than Flint (which most of the world only became aware of in 2014 thanks to the water crisis), the two southeast Michigan cities share similar histories—and their residents face similar denials of functioning citizenship. In his study of postwar Detroit, Thomas Sugrue (2005) argues that its urban crisis emerged as a consequence of "the most important, interrelated, and unresolved problems in American history: that capitalism generates economic inequality and that African Americans have disproportionately borne the impact of that inequality" (5). Arguing that the mutual reinforcement of race, economics, and politics from the 1940s to 1960s set the stage for today's crises, Sugrue points to problems such as residential segregation and perceptions of racial inferiority as causes of Detroit's devastating 1967 race riots.[9] He contends that ultimately the combination of deindustrialization, White flight, and hardening ghettoization was devastating and made residence within the inner city a "self-perpetuating stigma" (8).

Karen R. Miller (2015) expands this discussion with the concept of northern racial liberalism, or "the notion that all Americans, regardless of race, should be politically equal, but that the state cannot and indeed should not enforce racial equality by interfering with existing social or economic relations" (4). This perspective became popular among Detroit's White liberal leaders during and immediately after World War I, and then was increasingly embraced by mainstream White politicians by the end of

---

[9] The 1967 Detroit race riots began on July 23 with the police bust of an illegal after-hours "blind pig" saloon on Twelfth Street in the center of one of Detroit's largest Black neighborhoods. Five days of violence left forty-three people dead (thirty killed by law enforcement personnel), with 7,231 people arrested on riot-related charges. By the time the riot was suppressed by a combined force of nearly 17,000 police, National Guardsmen, and federal troops, rioters had looted and burned 2,509 buildings at a loss that included $36 million in insured property—not counting millions more of uninsured damages, as well as lost wages and government costs (Sugrue 2005, 259). The majority of rioters were young Black men who felt severe impacts related to unemployment, segregation, and various forms of racial discrimination (see 260–262).

the 1920s. Miller argues that many didn't believe in racial justice, but they saw this as a way to conceal their support for subordination. Racial liberal ideology "helped to reinforce and mask the enduring power of existing hierarchies and to contain African Americans' growing demands for citizenship and equality," she writes (Miller 2015, 5–6). "At its worst, rather than undermining racial inequalities, northern racial liberalism could and did function as an instrument for subduing the aspirations of the growing African American population and for casting their demands for equality as irrelevant and disruptive" (6). Indeed, Miller contends that American racism is not simply about a legacy of southern slavery; the origins of colorblind racism are "northern, urban, and modern" (17). Both northern racial liberalism and color-blind racism extend and affirm racial inequality alongside a commitment to the language, at least, or interracial understanding and race neutrality (7); they allow cities like Detroit to look racially progressive, yet to uphold existing relations of power and maintain the status quo (9).

Unfortunately, much attention to the postindustrial decline in southwest Michigan reinforces binary racial categories of difference and ignores histories of political resistance. Heather Ann Thompson (2001) warns that it would be a "tragic mistake" to simply see American urban centers in the 1980s as "doomed" places, or to see these sites as "symbolic battlefields on which American liberalism died an ugly death" (219). She notes that Black Americans certainly faced postwar discrimination but they were never passive victims; in fact, a full-fledged civil rights movement grew in the North—much like its southern counterpart—from 1945 to 1960 (20). Thompson argues that scholars cannot minimize the political complexity and determination of American Blacks and Whites alike; instead they must acknowledge postwar political and racial goals as well as alliances. In doing so, we uncover the reality that cities such as Detroit saw an unprecedented rise of African American political power that must be acknowledged and understood (219). Indeed, Sugrue (2005) argues that the stigma surrounding urban centers such as Detroit often reflects racial narratives that portray Black Americans in stereotypical tropes of inferiority, appealing to discourses in popular culture rather than true reflections of Black culture. Meanwhile, Whiteness is associated with "Americanism, hard work, sexual restraint, and independence"—all characteristics that many newly arrived European immigrants in postwar Detroit aspired to (9). In short: "To be fully American was to be white" (9). Looking to modern-day activism and the potential future of cities such as Detroit (and Flint), Sugrue writes: "What hope remains in the city comes from the continued efforts of city residents to resist the debilitating effects of poverty, racial tension, and industrial decline"—but the rehabilitation of Detroit will require "a vigorous attempt to grapple with the enduring effects of the postwar transformation of the city" (271). That includes facing the realities of race, residence, discrimination, and industrial decline head-on (271).

These cities struggle to regain their footing within a complex social and political structure; to put it mildly, that won't be easy. Rebecca Kinney (2016) writes that the "beautiful wasteland" of Detroit has captured the imagination of many journalists, scholars, and artists as a site of economic and social decline and that its potential as a "comeback city" has created a space for possibility (x–xi). Yet she argues that "the idea of Detroit as a postindustrial frontier is meant to be a racially neutral neoliberal project— a project that relies on a postracial outlook—yet it is steeped within the race-saturated rhetoric of the frontier. Ultimately, the racialization of place is not a symptom of capital but is produced by and in relationship to capital" (x). From this perspective, the new discourse about twenty-first-century Detroit and its potential is "a redeployment of long-standing American narratives of hard work and determination as a race neutral project; it is indeed privileges of whiteness that enable it to be cast as racially neutral" (xxii). Miller (2015) further argues that Detroit has an important place in the story of US postindustrial decline, and this narrative has always had a "racial cast" (21). "When the city was largely white, its working class was celebrated for its affluence; now that Detroit is majority-black, its population is maligned for its impoverishment" (21). At the same time, however, John Hartigan Jr. (1999) rightly reminds us that American poverty—and crumbling urban centers—also include White residents whose White racialness is often "distinctly objectified" with labels such as "hillbilly," "gentrifier," and "racist" (19). In his study of three predominantly White Detroit neighborhoods (Briggs, Corktown, and Warrendale) from July 1992 to February 1994, Hartigan found that such labels evaluate the racial content of communities and interests as well as police boundaries of status and privilege; ongoing class dynamics impact the White urban poor and leave them far differently positioned "in relation to the privileges that whiteness is assumed to ensure" (19). He writes:

> In order to think differently about race we need to pay attention to the local settings in which racial identities are actually articulated, reproduced, and contested, resisting the urge to draw abstract conclusions about whiteness and blackness. Rather, we need to take these situations as examples of a

different sort—as insights into the daily processes by which people make sense of racial matters in particular locales. The assertion that race is culturally constructed will remain a stunted concept unless it is linked to a heightened attention to the ways people actually construct meaningful lives in relation to race. (4)

In Flint, charges of human rights violations and environmental racism have done little to hasten effective government action or to spur solution-seeking for long-term change. When US president Barack Obama made a long-awaited visit to Flint in May 2016, he assured frustrated and angry locals: "We can turn this into an opportunity to rebuild Flint even better than before," arguing that the water problems reflected the broader issues of lost resources, a shrinking tax base, depleted services, and lack of capacity. "And so our goal here is to use this moment in which everybody's attention is focused to see if we can start rebuilding and moving Flint in a better direction," Obama said (quoted in Chuck and Bacon 2016, para. 32–33). Yet less than a year later, in February 2017, a government aid policy that provided water usage credits for homes and business ended, signaling the desire to wrap up the crisis and resume business as usual. Flint residents began once again paying the full price for water, even though it was still not safe to drink without filtering (Biryukov 2017, para. 1–2). Mayor Karen Weaver further noted that not all homes can be fitted with filters and that many residents were skeptical of data showing decreased lead levels (para. 7). In April 2018, the state of Michigan announced the end of its Flint bottled water program, even though home water lines weren't scheduled to be fully replaced until 2020; a federal judge denied a request to order Michigan officials to resume distribution of free water to residents (Associated Press 2018).

In Detroit, residents have become involved in urban self-provisioning—that is, finding alternatives to the "abandonment that had already overtaken so much of their city" (Kinder 2016, 5). Most feel compelled to do this "out of necessity, since existing market practices and government policies did not meet their basic needs" (6). Kimberly Kinder notes that some urban self-provisioners might simply hope to engage in countercultural lifestyles, but the residents she interviewed in Detroit simply wanted to live in a functional city; their self-provisioning was much more expansive than creating trendy pop-up coffeehouses. Residents became informal realtors trying to fill empty housing; they adopted or destroyed vacant structures to avoid theft and vandalism; they cleaned trash, cut grass, shoveled snow from public and abandoned land; and they monitored street activity to keep their communities safe (28). And Detroit isn't alone in this. Kinder writes:

> The rise of market-based governance has made basic services unavailable or unaffordable in urban areas nationwide. Countless residents now rely on household labor and neighborhood volunteerism to coordinate land use, maintain public spaces, and control social behavior. These practices provide meaningful, local, short-term 'fixes,' but Detroit's ongoing decline—despite ample evidence of widespread self-provisioning—challenges political ideologies that favor individual solutions to structural problems. Regrettably, more-lasting social reforms are slow in coming and may never arrive. In the meantime self-provisioning reflects a new social role vulnerable residents increasingly play in coordinating the logic and life of the neoliberal city. (24)

Detroit and Flint represent spaces of second-class citizenship where basic human rights protections are denied to "less worthy" Americans, with functioning citizenship frequently allotted along racial and socioeconomic lines. Indeed, worthiness is socially constructed through the use of historical tropes and stereotypes, as well as an emphasis on market fundamentalism that strips poor citizens of their full recognition as rights claimants.

Saint Louis and the Rise of Black Lives Matter

Just a few months after the Flint water crisis began, my current home—the city of Saint Louis—was shaken to its core by the killing of eighteen-year-old Michael Brown on August 9, 2014. The Black teen had been fatally shot by White police officer Darren Wilson in the city of Ferguson, Missouri—technically part of Saint Louis County but for all intents and purposes a part of Saint Louis (STL) city's neighborhood sprawl. Although Brown did argue with a convenience store clerk before the shooting, he was approached by Officer Wilson simply for walking down the center of the street (in violation of a municipal ordinance related to "manner of walking"). There are conflicting accounts of what happened next, but Brown lay dead within two minutes of their initial encounter. His body lay out in the hot summertime sun, in view of friends and family, for hours before being transported to the morgue. In the days that followed, Ferguson made international headlines as protestors—both violent and nonviolent—expressed their rage at the death of yet another young Black man. Two months later, thousands engaged in marches and other forms of protest as part of "Ferguson October," demanding police reform that included demilitarization, the end of racial profiling, and the arrest of Officer Wilson (who was later cleared by a grand jury). Brown's killing also marked the beginning of BLM, a movement identified as "an ideological and political intervention in a world where Black lives are systematically and intentionally targeted for demise" (Black Lives Matter n.d.b., para. 1).

Brown's death illustrated a long American history of lynching and racial oppression, bringing key issues related to equality before the law and freedom from discrimination to the fore. A 2014 white paper by ArchCity Defenders—a nonprofit civil rights law firm that provides legal advocacy to combat "the criminalization of poverty and state violence against poor people and people of color" in Saint Louis (ArchCity Defenders n.d., para. 1)—found that the municipal court system in Ferguson and surrounding areas directly impacted citizens' rights to place and purpose. A comprehensive survey of sixty courts found that half engaged in illegal and deeply harmful practices; three municipal courts (in Ferguson, as well as Bel-Ridge and Florissant) were specifically identified as "chronic offenders" whose practices violated the rights of the poor and undermined confidence in the judicial system (ArchCity Defenders 2014, 3). Revenue-driven practices (such as indiscriminate ticketing and fining) severely impact poor citizens—often leading to job loss and homelessness, among other things. Many people are incarcerated because they cannot afford to pay the fines levied against them. The result, according to ArchCity Defenders (2014), is that "the poor St. Louisans watch an unnecessarily expensive and incredibly inefficient network of municipal courts siphon away vast amounts of their money to support a system seemingly designed to maintain the status quo, no matter how much it hurts the communities the system is supposed to serve" (2).

In March 2015, the US Department of Justice (DOJ) (2015) issued a scathing report reaffirming these findings in Ferguson, noting that the Ferguson Municipal Court showed a pattern of prioritizing revenue over public safety and imposing particular hardships on the city's most vulnerable residents. The DOJ noted that minor offenses often led to crippling debts, jail time due to the inability of the person found guilty to pay fines, loss of driver's licenses, unemployment, and loss of housing. The report further concluded that the Ferguson Police Department engaged in practices of conduct that violated rights guaranteed by the US Constitution, including violating freedom of expression (First Amendment); conducting stops without reasonable suspicion and arrests without probable cause (Fourth Amendment); and using unreasonable force (Fourth Amendment). The harms stemming from police and court practices disproportionately impacted Black Americans and were due, at least in part, to intentional discrimination that was linked to direct evidence of racial bias and stereotyping about Black Americans by officials (United States Department of Justice 2015).

Ferguson was (and is) a predominantly Black city dominated by a White political power structure. When Brown was killed, Ferguson was approximately 70 percent Black but its mayor, five of six city council members, and fifty of fifty-four police officers were all White—as were its prosecutor, municipal court judge, and almost all of its court administrative staff (Norwood 2016, xix–xx). Kimberly Jade Norwood (2016) argues that on one level, protests were certainly about Brown's death resulting from the simple act of jaywalking. On the broader level, however, the protests were about much more: "They were also about police use of force against Black people; they were about the excessive tickets for traffic, quality of life and housing code violations that preyed on the most vulnerable; they were about unemployment and underemployment; they were about inadequate health care and public health concerns; they were about inadequate housing; and they were about substandard schools" (xx). Bracey (2016) writes that Michael Brown's death becomes part of "that familiar rhythm": "Whether black lives are snuffed out by an officer's bullet, choked out by an officer's bare hands, or defiled by an officer's nightstick, the message delivered and received is the same now as it has been before: black lives are not worthy of equal dignity" (2–3). For decades, Black people complained of these ills to no avail. "They simply were not believed," Norwood writes (2016). "It took a killing, it took outrage, it took property destruction, it took social media, to open the collective eyes of the world to see the 'cancer' of injustice that had been spreading in the community for years" (xx–xxi).

Indeed, Ferguson—much like urban centers throughout the United States—is made up of White spaces and Black spaces. Brown died in a predominantly Black east side neighborhood where residents cite worries such as police harassment and high crime rates among impoverished Section 8 renters.[10] Clustered around the city's business district only two miles away, pockets of affluent and predominantly White neighborhoods

---

[10] Colloquially referred to as a Section 8 voucher, the Housing Choice Voucher Program is a rental assistance program funded by the US Department of Housing and Urban Development (HUD) that provides subsidies for low-income families, elderly, and disabled households.

offer decidedly safer, more comfortable daily lives (Eligon 2015, para. 10). By various measures, "the St. Louis region remains among the most segregated places in the country, where most blacks and whites, though sometimes separated by only a short walk, live in different worlds," writes journalist John Eligon (para. 9). Such segregation is no accident; rather, it is the result of harmful economic and social policies that perpetuate racial inequalities and urban decline. Missouri was one of the first states to offer "home rule" to its cities, sealing modern boundaries between the city and its suburbs in 1876. The city of Saint Louis is now one of hundreds of local political units, part of a politically fragmented metropolitan area that is fiercely segregated along racial and socioeconomic lines (Gordon 2008, 10). The urban crisis in Saint Louis became particularly severe following demilitarization after World War II and deindustrialization, in part, because its local economy was so intricately rooted in commerce along the Mississippi River. While other Midwestern cities were also struggling, at least the automobile industry "belonged in the twentieth century" (Gordon 2008, 10). Saint Louis's population grew westward, toward the suburbs, and postwar programs to save the city through urban renewal and economic development often exacerbated problems and failed to assist the residents who most needed help (12; see chapters 4–5 in Gordon 2008). Colin Gordon contends that there is also an "iron law of urban decay"—a pattern that was identifiable in Saint Louis as early as 1919: "Rising incomes breed suburbanization. Suburbanization robs inner cities of their tax base. Inner city concentrations of poverty widen gaps between urban residents and substantive economic opportunities, and between suburban residents and urban concerns. And all of this encourages more flight, not only from the metropolitan core, but from decaying inner suburbs as well" (8). The combination of suburbanization and urban crisis led Saint Louis toward a segregated future where the city has "starker and simpler racial demographics than its peers" (10; see also Gordon 2016).

Yet after Brown's death, Mayor James Knowles III rejected the idea that Ferguson was racially divided and told reporters: "We're all brokenhearted, regardless of our race. This is not representative of our community" (quoted in CBS St. Louis 2014, para. 14–15). While it was certainly true that Ferguson protests drew participants from across racial and socioeconomic lines, the assertion that racial inequality is not a central problem in Ferguson fuels a dangerous political narrative. It plays into the sort

---

Vouchers are administered locally by public housing authorities (Housing Authority of St. Louis County n.d.).

of "colorblind racism" that led many Americans to rebuff "Black Lives Matter" with the retort "All Lives Matter"—that is, to insist on a post-racial version of the United States where race does not confer status or access to rights protections; where poverty is simply the result of laziness; or "you shouldn't be afraid of the police if you didn't do anything wrong." In the days and months following the death of Mike Brown, I heard these arguments from White neighbors, colleagues, and even students regularly. As protests continued in Ferguson and throughout the city of Saint Louis—and critical conversations about racial equality and American identity played out in many college classrooms—crowds of White protestors waved "Support the Police" and "We Love Darren Wilson" signs outside my usual grocery store on weekends. While Black Americans and their allies raised their voices (at great personal risk)[11] and called attention to America's enduring legacy of racial inequality, a substantial number of fellow citizens tone-deafly insisted that race no longer mattered. Yet in reality, as Norwood (2016) poignantly argues, "There is a different treatment of people in our society based on the color of their skin and their socio-economic status. There are two Fergusons as there are two Americas. We cannot change this reality unless we first acknowledge it" (xxi).

America's Internally Stateless

The international community so readily equates "bare life" with the plight of stateless persons and refugees, seemingly so far removed from those with legal nationality in the Global North, that my decision to include some American citizens within this discussion may seem strange indeed. Yet the cases of Detroit, Flint, and Saint Louis show that legal nationality does not guarantee equal rights protection—and that hierarchies of personhood within even the most privileged societies can lead to disastrous human rights consequences. With their denial of functioning citizenship, residents of these cities (much like poor and minority citizens throughout the United States) face threats to their place and purpose based on their perceived lack

---

[11] A 2014 report on Ferguson from Amnesty International USA found—in addition to concerns related to racial discrimination and excessive use of police force—that rights abuses and policing failures were commonplace during protests related to Brown's death. A delegation of international human rights observers concluded that law enforcement's response to protests imposed undue restrictions on the right to protest, that protestors faced intimidation and illegal dispersal, that the media and legal/human rights observers faced severe restrictions, and that law enforcement personnel were not held accountable for their actions in policing protests (Amnesty International USA 2014).

of worthiness and full personhood. Similar to the plight of stateless persons discussed in Chapter 2, some Americans are simply not recognized as rights-bearers or afforded corresponding protections. While the cases of these US cities rarely (if ever) include de jure statelessness, the systematic violation of rights renders some Americans "internally stateless" (Somers 2008, 5) because they lack a meaningful, mutually respectful relationship with a state government. These cases, like the examples presented throughout this work, force us to confront the questions of what it means to be a citizen and how we recognize claimants of fundamental human rights. In turn, how do we construct worthiness? And (I ask this final question as an American citizen examining her own society) how do we justify such hierarchies of personhood in the midst of such vast resources?

In cities such as Detroit, Flint, and Saint Louis, these questions should remind us to view calls for urban renewal through a critical, human rights-informed lens. Too frequently, "bringing back" cities is equated with economic prosperity and gentrification that reinforces the status quo but does little to fill rights gaps. Development schemes often focus on rebuilding a city for the benefit of those who can afford luxurious new housing and trendy restaurants, tailoring communities to wealthy future residents while pushing existing residents out. As developers promote high-rise apartment buildings in up-and-coming sections of Detroit, for instance, critics argue that grand visions for the city embrace the idea of a White Detroit—not a revitalized city that retains its Black core. In a telling example, a 2017 outdoor advertisement asked viewers to "See Detroit Like We Do." The ad featured the image of a predominantly White crowd as representative of the city of Detroit—which, in reality, is approximately 80 percent Black (CBS Detroit 2017). In Saint Louis, the city continues to criminalize homelessness—as well as providing aid to the unsheltered—citing the need to protect the well-being of wealthier residents with little alternative planning to meet the needs of displaced homeless populations. The 2017 shuttering of Saint Louis's largest homeless shelter was justified by reports of drug abuse and violence surrounding the downtown site, which created sometimes dangerous nuisances for residents living in nearby luxury lofts (Gray 2017). By having fewer shelter options—combined with laws against aggressive begging and loitering, as well as prohibitions against feeding the homeless—the city continues to dole out legal punishments for perceived unworthiness, all while government resources for combating the root causes of homelessness (such as mental illness, drug abuse, domestic violence, and lack of affordable housing) are severely limited and even reduced.

Of course, heroes exist in these daunting scenarios—although rarely do they come from the actual state duty-bearer of human rights. In Saint Louis, for instance, lack of government protections for homeless citizens often requires members of the community to step in and provide essential resources. STL Winter Outreach (n.d.) is an informal collection of concerned citizens who organize patrols when winter temperatures fall to twenty degrees or below (and volunteers have recently begun working during extreme summer heat). Volunteers rely on community donations to distribute blankets, food, and other essential items, and they often help transport people to shelters or seek emergency medical care, as needed. Holly Schroeder, an STL Winter Outreach volunteer organizer, described her experience after a typical—but nevertheless deeply troubling—night of assisting the homeless community of Saint Louis in April 2017. She noted that such volunteer work puts her at legal risk, while lack of resources threatens the human dignity of those she tries to help:

Street outreach tonight was fast and furious. We had to dodge police and city workers who didn't want us to feed people who were hungry. I've never dealt drugs, but I imagine making covert exchanges in plain view feels about the same—except my drugs were turkey sandwiches and bottled water. I'm still trying to wrap my head around how it's possible to break the law by feeding a hungry person.

We would have quick hellos and then I would tell them to move along quickly before we got spotted. It felt like that whack-a-mole game.

I saw a woman who was sobbing and so clearly pained I thought she was going collapse. I jumped out of the car to check on her. She had just found out her friend was raped, murdered, and left dead underneath a nearby bridge. The anguish was almost unbearable to witness and my offer of tissue and a sack lunch was woefully inadequate. I patted her arm and listened and reminded her to breathe.

Earlier in the evening I got a quick look inside the city overflow "shelter" and I am disgusted and horrified at the conditions. A huge plywood wall has been erected blocking out almost all the natural light and it's jam-packed with cots in rows on a concrete floor. There is no running water and no toilets. Two portable toilets are the only facilities. The large room is dimly-lit and "depressing" doesn't adequately convey the vibe of the place. Our pet shelters are more cheerful and have more creature comforts. It reminded me of the renderings of slave ships—no regard for the humans that would occupy the space. No acknowledgement that the homeless are actual humans.[12]

Schroeder's last sentence—that there is no acknowledgment that the homeless are actual human beings—speaks volumes about how perceived worthiness impacts the provision of rights to place and purpose. While the impetus for this book began with de jure statelessness, its case studies end here—with legal nationals of the United States of America, who are rendered "internally stateless" by a lack of functioning citizenship that excludes them from the protections usually afforded to American citizens. More broadly, their lack of recognition as worthy rights claimants further denies them access to the fundamental rights afforded to human beings; they are deemed less worthy—and by logical extension, less human—than fellow citizens whose race and/or socioeconomic status affords them a more privileged position within this hierarchy of personhood.

---

[12] Online communication, April 17, 2017. Shared with permission.

PART IV | Creating Inclusive Forms of Membership

CHAPTER 8 | Conveying the Problem(s) and Representing Personhood

MY FIRST IMAGES OF statelessness came from northern Thailand, where I learned about the intricate connection between human trafficking and lack of legal nationality while I was working as an intern and volunteer English teacher. When I began, my experiences with stateless hill tribe communities were a blend of happiness and heartache—barefoot kids, sometimes with hunger-distended bellies, in thatched roof houses, playing games and tickling each other; children singing nursery rhymes and play-acting skits, with others too traumatized from sexual abuse to interact with most adults. Worried that my academic studies of citizenship theory and social movement literature would dull the memory of what I had seen in Thailand, I taped photos above my desk back home. As I wrote my doctoral dissertation, one little face in particular stared back at me: Lu Tah, a six-year-old girl without a family who had happily clung to me whenever I visited her—but whose statelessness meant that she couldn't travel internationally, be adopted, attend public school, or enjoy the vast array of rights to place and purpose afforded to those with some semblance of functioning citizenship. Those images propelled forward my work on statelessness, a constant reminder that this complex and legalistic issue had real-life consequences for people I counted as my friends.

For human rights advocates around the world, making that sort of connection and convincing people to care about—and to truly see—human rights issues remains a central challenge. Indeed, Clifford Bob (2009) argues that "there are numerous human needs, grievances, and problems, the majority of which go unnoticed most of the time" (8). When I began researching the issue of statelessness in 2005, for instance, I was struck by how little attention the problem had received from the international community. Statelessness was largely ignored by leading human rights advocacy NGOs and was rarely discussed in the media; when lack of legal nationality did come up, it was usually in relation to other human rights concerns (such as human trafficking) or incorrectly equated with undocumented migration or forced displacement. Frustrated by this glaring omission, I began to explore the concept of issue emergence—the twin steps of constructing and accepting a specific problem as an international issue in the first place (Carpenter 2007a). Interviews with decision makers at leading nongovernmental organizations brought out the key challenges of statelessness, including those related to imagery and issue framing, despite the fact that the issue itself had characteristics that usually contribute to successful emergence.

More than five years after those initial interviews, I attended the First Global Forum on Statelessness coordinated by the United Nations High Commissioner for Refugees (UNHCR) in the Hague, the Netherlands. During that September 2014 meeting, I met with statelessness experts to follow up on the matter of statelessness's potential issue emergence. What I learned at the Global Forum—and what I've observed in anti-statelessness advocacy since that pivotal event—offers important lessons for mobilization aimed at dismantling hierarchies of personhood and promoting functioning citizenship around the world. Those experiences raise fundamental questions about how such vulnerabilities are communicated in the quest for full issue emergence and for garnering the support necessary to combat rights abuses. Issue experts know that problems such as statelessness exist and represent dire threats to people's fundamental rights—but how these issues are translated, how these stories are told and shared around the world, matter immensely.

Chapter 8 explores the international community's responses to hierarchies of personhood by considering how individuals' violated rights to place and purpose have been communicated and interpreted. The example of statelessness highlights the complexities surrounding issue emergence and reminds us that such emergence has serious implications for the protection of basic human rights, including every person's right to a nationality. While the factors that play into issue emergence vary by circumstance, it is clear that compelling visual narratives and framing are important factors in whether an issue successfully emerges onto the international agenda. The imagery associated with forced displacement, for instance, and the issue framing related to indigenous rights and environmental justice offer examples of how human rights stories are told to a global audience—for good and for bad. Although the existing literature on social movements and transnational advocacy provides a foundation for successful mobilization strategies, attention to the concept of functioning citizenship pushes us to reconsider how some of these actions may inadvertently reinforce hierarchies of personhood and constructions of worthiness. While issue emergence is certainly of dire importance, the supporting processes of providing visual narratives and issue framing require us to acknowledge that representation matters significantly—not only for the success of a campaign but also for determining how we discuss human rights protection and political membership. Critical consideration of these issues highlights the need to empower vulnerable populations to voice their perspectives and share their knowledge, while also remaining aware of how existing hierarchies of personhood impact advocacy decisions—including how we construct problems and tell stories. Ultimately, this chapter argues that we must reevaluate the ways that we *see* problems related to lack of functioning citizenship.

Issue Emergence: Statelessness as a Case Study

Issue emergence is the step in the process of mobilization when a preexisting grievance is transformed from a problem into an issue, attracting the attention and funding necessary to advance itself onto the international agenda.[1] Charli Carpenter (2007a) writes that this emergence "is the conceptual link between the myriad of bad things out there and the persuasive machinery of advocacy politics in world affairs" (102). Existing literature related to transnational mobilization, social movements, and agenda-setting offers limited lessons for understanding the process of issue emergence. This scholarship is organized around four key themes: issue characteristics, organizational characteristics, strategic characteristics, and

---

[1] Drawing on Margaret Keck and Kathryn Sikkink's work on transnational advocacy networks (TANs), Charli Carpenter (2007a) argues that issues emerge (1) when advocates name a problem as a rights violation and (2) when major human rights NGO gatekeepers begin referencing the issue in advocacy materials, which could lead to the creation of campaigns and/or coalitions aimed at solving the problem. Defining the issue involves showing "that a given state of affairs is neither natural nor accidental," identifying the responsible party, and proposing credible solutions (Keck and Sikkink 1998, 19), while issue adoption occurs when an issue is "championed" by at least one major player within the network—often exemplified by a shift in resources. Issue emergence represents a crucial step for understanding TANs in world politics because no effective advocacy is possible if an issue withers and fails at this early stage; all subsequent action depends on an issue's being defined and accepted as such by a critical mass of activists and gatekeepers (Carpenter 2007a, 2007b).

environmental characteristics (see Kingston 2013). First, issue characteristics focus on an issue's ability to fit into the international community's existing discussions, priorities, and moral standards.[2] Second, organizational characteristics emphasize an issue's connection to an organization's culture, ethics, and tactics (Bob 2005). The availability of issue entrepreneurs who are willing and able to champion a particular issue is also important for propelling a cause forward (Finnemore and Sikkink 1998). Third, strategic characteristics highlight the role of issue framing and marketing so as to attract attention and funding. Fourth, environmental characteristics refer to factors such as shifting political alignments and current events, which may affect an issue's chances of successfully emerging. Sidney Tarrow (1998) argues simply that "opportunities matter" (72), noting that changes in the political environment—such as increasing access to decision making, divided elites, or influential allies—all impact the likelihood that an issue will gain attention and support.

Yet these explanations cannot always predict which issues will emerge onto the global stage; while a "rash of literature" in recent decades acknowledges the impact of transnational advocacy networks in norm development and governance, much less attention centers on why those networks "gravitate toward certain issues and reject or dismiss others at any particular time" (Carpenter 2014, 2). Carpenter (2007b, 2010) prompts further discussion of issue emergence with her work on the matter of children born of rape, leading her to refute common explanations within the literature. While issues such as child soldiering have received substantial attention from child protection advocates, children born of rape—who frequently face widespread social stigma and related human rights abuses—are often ignored, despite sharing striking similarities in terms of issue characteristics. Carpenter (2014) argues that issue survival is not determined by merit of the issues themselves or by the receptivity of the external environment but rather is a result of relationships with global issue networks (ix).[3] In short, scholars are still struggling to understand why

---

[2] For instance, issues that involve "ideas about right and wrong" are amenable to issue emergence "because they arouse strong feelings, allow networks to recruit volunteers and activists, and infuse meaning into these volunteer activities" (Keck and Sikkink 1998, 26). Some scholars contend that advocates choose issues that align with preexisting moral standards, grafting on to normative justifications of related issues. Richard Price (1998) highlights this in his work on weapons taboos, arguing that the laws of war and humanitarianism helped make efforts to ban land mines intelligible. Issues that match with existing agendas (Bob 2005) or organizational "branding" (Hopgood 2006) are also more likely to emerge on the international agenda.

[3] Noting that global civil society is composed of "hubs" of core organizations (with the largest budgets and name recognition), Carpenter (2014) contends that the most significant role of political entrepreneurs is not teaching or persuading states but rather "selling their ideas to the advocacy

some issues "make it" onto the human rights agenda while others do not. This research has very practical consequences; overcoming the major hurdle of achieving issue emergence is necessary for advancing advocacy goals and facilitating global change.

These theories have practical implications for advocacy related to functioning citizenship and the rights to place and purpose. The issue of statelessness, for instance, has struggled for years to successfully emerge onto the international human rights agenda. Until very recently, statelessness served as an example of a social problem that had not yet fully emerged—yet reasons for its slow progress were rarely discussed. Despite the ratification of 1954 and 1961 statelessness conventions and some forward movement within the UN system, the problem has not garnered widespread attention or become "mainstream" enough to warrant campaign adoption from a major human rights NGO (Kingston 2012). Similar to the problem Carpenter (2010) described in her work on children born of wartime rape, statelessness's non-emergence could not be adequately explained by the existing literature. In a 2009 study, I conducted twenty-one semi-structured interviews with decision makers at leading US human rights and humanitarian NGOs to discover the reasons that statelessness had not come to universal attention. Few respondents had worked on the issue directly; some called statelessness a "particularly overlooked issue" that didn't garner attention within their organization, or saw it as something they "sort of stumbled upon" while researching related problems (Kingston 2013, 79). Interview data showed that statelessness encountered obstacles related to strategic characteristics, including absence of a clear problem, misunderstood issue basics, unclear consequences and lack of data, lack of compelling images, and a missing "CNN factor" that allowed the issue to be easily translated for mass media consumption. Also holding statelessness back from the international stage, it lacked widely recognized global solutions and there was a lack of overall political will to address the problem (Kingston 2013). These findings led me to recommend that advocates focus their energies on framing and information sharing at public and elite, policymaking levels; strategically building leadership within governments and international organizations; providing educational opportunities to expand knowledge of statelessness; and supporting community organizing to ensure grassroots mobilization (Kingston 2013).

---

elites who can carry their messages to governments" (12). Ultimately, "network structure does not merely position some organizations as 'gatekeepers': it also helps to constitute gatekeepers' preferences, and thus the advocacy agenda" (41).

Several years later, statelessness is no longer an emergence failure, but it still faces serious obstacles.[4] My research follow-up at the 2014 Global Forum highlights these very real challenges. For statelessness to achieve sufficient visibility to be addressed seriously, advocates of finding solutions must frame problems in understandable and relatable ways, raise awareness among the public and policymakers, and overcome the discrimination and political hostilities that often facilitate rights violations in the first place. In semi-structured interviews and group discussions I held with more than forty statelessness experts, these respondents expressed frustration regarding how statelessness is currently framed by the media, noting, for instance, that journalists force the issue into ready-made narratives about refugees or immigrants. Respondents also criticized scholars for narrowly defining it as a legal issue and/or assuming that lack of legal nationality is the most salient concern that stateless people face, while noting that policymakers often fail to see statelessness as a structural and transnational problem. The resulting lack of awareness results in limited existing research to draw from, lack of funding and increasing competition for resources among the core group of statelessness researchers, and a dearth of civil society engagement that prevents scholars from sharing information outside their like-minded communities. At the policy and implementation levels, hostile political climates continue to stifle action to eliminate statelessness and ensure the provision of truly functioning citizenship. Racism associated with anti-refugee and anti-migrant sentiments is part of the problem. Indeed, one negative consequence of the UNHCR campaign is that statelessness is conflated with forced migration. "Migration agencies all around the world are the same," noted one researcher. "They are about keeping people out, not letting them in." From this perspective, lumping

---

[4] Impressive advocacy efforts have led statelessness to enjoy partial, but not full, issue emergence. The 2014 launch of the UNHCR's "iBelong" Campaign to End Statelessness represented the most impactful development for bringing statelessness into visibility so far, complemented by the creation of issue-specific NGOs such as the European Network on Statelessness (ENS) and the Institute on Statelessness and Inclusion. These developments point toward successful issue definition, and certainly the UNHCR represents a significant issue champion within the international network. However, it is important to note that most mainstream human rights NGOs continue to reference statelessness only in relation to other issues, particularly forced displacement—if they mention statelessness at all. The same holds true for media coverage of statelessness, which generally focuses on lack of identification and birth registration in the wake of armed conflict and displacement. As noted in Chapter 2, the UNHCR campaign and associated advocacy efforts also focus primarily on legal solutions to statelessness, which are important but fail to identify the full range of responsible actors or credible solutions. While statelessness is finally achieving some much-needed international attention, its full emergence requires continued action—including focusing on existing recommendations related to framing, leadership, education, and community organizing (see Kingston 2013).

statelessness together with migration issues means it suffers from the same lack of political will that impedes durable solutions for refugees. (Keep in mind, however, that many are unaware of statelessness to begin with. When asked if the immigration debate colored discussions of stateless-ness, a human rights lawyer told me simply: "I think it would if people knew what statelessness was.")

The case of statelessness's slow and partial issue emergence shows that the severity of human rights abuses does not necessarily guarantee wide-spread attention. For a variety of reasons, serious violations of rights to place and purpose may be ignored or misunderstood by the international community, thus blocking access to resources, media coverage, public sup-port, and political will. These challenges highlight the need for a targeted advocacy strategy for exposing the rights abuse people are subjected to from a lack of functioning citizenship. Issue emergence usually doesn't "just" happen; rather, it results from long-term planning and coordina-tion. Yet the social and political inequalities underpinning hierarchies of personhood also mean that there are challenges built into this process— and sometimes those challenges come from within. Existing scholarship on issue emergence emphasizes the importance of imagery and framing, for instance, but advocates must remain aware of how those strategies fit within existing structural hierarchies. The goal is to convey the problem(s) and lobby for positive change, but without reinforcing dehumanizing and disempowering narratives that construct vulnerable people as undeserving, incapable, and inherently different.

Show and Tell: Conveying the Problem(s)

Didier Fassin (2012) writes that for human rights violations to resonate, narratives must go beyond blood; people must witness human suffering (25). Human rights advocates are deeply aware of this imperative, from those early stages of issue emergence to the sustained, long-term push for political support, resources, and news coverage. In the face of devastating conflicts and human rights abuses, some issues or events prompt outrage while others are ignored; some causes "go viral" while others fail to attract even passing public notice. In 2016, for instance, journalist Amanda Taub asked why some wars get more attention than others. Reflecting on why Americans were aware of the Syrian civil war but less likely to know about conflict in Yemen or the Congo, she noted bleakly: "The truth is that inat-tention is the default, not the exception" (para. 6). Indeed, Taubman (2016) argues that "conflicts gain sustained American attention only when they provide a compelling story line that appeals to both the public and political actors, and for reasons beyond the human toll. That often requires some combination of immediate relevance to American interests, resonance with American political debates or cultural issues, and, perhaps most of all, an emotionally engaging frame of clearly identifiable good guys and bad guys" (para. 7). More broadly, Matthew Powers (2016) writes that "human rights news" involves a growing number of newsmakers and increasing opportunities to introduce rights issues into media coverage, yet these possibilities are nevertheless limited by "an intense battle for limited public attention" (319). As a consequence, he acknowledges a tendency toward "simplified and misleading coverage" (319).

While statelessness highlights the complexities associated with issue emergence, other denials of functioning citizenship face associated challenges related to images, visual narratives, and issue framing. All of these examples illustrate the great importance of how human rights violations are represented; words and images matter. Indeed, the stories we tell about denied functioning citizenship and violated rights to place and purpose directly impact how the international community views worthiness for rights protections. Images have the capacity to build empathy and inspire positive action, for instance, but they may also serve to dehumanize and disempower vulnerable populations while constructing narratives about which people are legitimate claimants of human rights. Similarly, issue frames may build support and mobilize resources, but they may also de-prioritize certain core objectives in the quest for a simplified and compelling issue narrative. At the same time, dangerous counternarratives can be used to thwart advocacy attempts and reassert hierarchies of personhood that deny equal rights and recognition.

Images and Visual Narratives: Refugees

Heart-wrenching images of the Syrian refugee crisis earned the *New York Times* and Thomson Reuters a shared 2016 Pulitzer Prize for breaking news photography. The award-winning collection of photographs illustrated the devastating impacts of forced migration: bloodied asylum-seekers fleeing police brutality at a Serbian border crossing; families sleeping in human piles on bus floors and under train stations; parents trekking hundreds of miles with their possessions and children in tow (see Gonzalez and Estrin 2016). But the photograph that punched me in the gut—the one that overwhelmed me with emotion—was Daniel Etter's image of Laith Majid, an Iraqi man who had broken into tears after safely arriving in Greece on a rubber boat. The image of this man, weeping as he clutched his young son and daughter in his arms, forced me to stop and stare—and cry. Advocates of humanitarian photography would argue that this is exactly the intended effect: Make a human connection with the audience so they care about distant suffering, which will hopefully result in increasing political will to support human rights protection. Notably, Sharon Sliwinski (2011) writes: "The notion of universal human rights was born and is carried, in part, in the minds of distant spectators" (5). These images are frequently paired with moral arguments and ethical pleas to help; columnist Nicholas Kristof (2016a, 2016b) asked readers, "Do you care more about a dog than a refugee?" and asserted that "Anne Frank today is a Syrian girl" in the midst of the Syrian war. Such media coverage fits within a broader visual narrative of forced displacement, facilitated by humanitarian agencies and NGOs seeking to spread awareness and garner support for refugee protection. Yet while this use of humanitarian photography is powerful and well intentioned, it is fraught with ethical challenges and complexities that may sometimes hinder—rather than help—attempts to understand displacement in the context of functioning citizenship.

Humanitarian photography[5] has long been used to capture the suffering of forced displacement, drawing international attention to the plight of refugees while keeping them notably separate from the citizenry. Since 1945, images of the "lone suffering child" have become "ubiquitous" in UNESCO and UNICEF publications, in Western media coverage of conflict and humanitarian crises, and in fundraising campaigns (Fehrenbach 2015, 167). The UNHCR and other humanitarian organizations rely on visual imagery to ask the question: What is it like to be a refugee? While the UNHCR's visual catalog highlights the sheer scope and complexity

---

[5] Humanitarian photography is "the mobilization of photography in the service of humanitarian initiatives across state boundaries" (Fehrenbach and Rodogno 2015, 1). It is produced and disseminated by a variety of actors concerned with providing "aid, relief, rescue, reform, rehabilitation, and development," historically conforming to sensational strategies of commercialized mass culture and political propaganda in order to garner attention (7 and 11). Once the international community began to acknowledge "atrocity" crimes stemming from armed state conflict, for instance, governments and reformers began producing atrocity imagery that relied on an extant language of moral outrage. Christina Twomey (2015) writes that photographic technologies have historically "both collapsed distance between the subject of suffering and the viewer, and also created greater space between them—a sense of difference—that was essential to the empathetic or sympathetic response" (60). But critics contend that such photos often serve as rhetoric that focuses attention on specific cases of suffering, which is framed as undeserved and necessitating action while rarely gesturing at political causation—or, at least rarely conveying the political and social complexities at hand (Fehrenbach and Rodogno 2015, 6).

of forced displacement, the organization also emphasizes a "common underlying identity that is universally shared among all refugees" (Nyers 2006, 14). That identity is defined by photographic representations with themes of absence and lack; critics suggest that this discourse tends to "codify displaced people with empty, invisible, and voiceless identities" (16). "The representational practices of the UNHCR reinforce an image of refugeeness that negatively establishes the refugee as the inverted mirror image of the citizen," writes Peter Nyers (2006). "These practices are not only consistent with but also reproduce sovereign accounts of the location and nature of 'authentic' political identities and spaces" (18). These representations thus reinforce binary divisions between citizen and noncitizen, holding the refugee up as an example of "bare life" that is separate from (and opposite to) the citizen. Even while viewers may approach humanitarian images with empathy, these identity constructions serve to perpetuate hierarchies of citizenship that exclude refugees from the political community. Refugees are largely viewed as objects of sympathy and perhaps charity—but not full claimants of human rights on par with the protected citizenry.

Visual narratives are of vital importance because they help construct our views on worthiness and belonging. The impact of such constructions is perhaps no more glaring than in representations of the "pure" refugee, which are viewed as vastly different from the criminalized migrant.[6] The ideal of the "pure" refugee centers on universally understood themes of human suffering that justify worthiness for rights protections.[7] Representations of such forced displacement center on the story of innocent civilians fleeing violent conflict and cruel dictators; long lines of crying babies and desperate mothers on the long walk toward safety. This imagery of the "pure," legitimate refugee is well situated within the public imagination, even if that simplified issue frame is not wholly representational or accurate. Often this framing renders individual refugees

[6] As discussed in Chapter 4, for instance, migrants from Central America and Mexico frequently flee serious rights abuses related to government corruption and gang violence but are often unable to adequately access their rights to asylum in the United States (Human Rights Watch 2014). As a result, many migrants (including unaccompanied children) face threats to sexual exploitation, assault, forced labor, and even forced recruitment as soldiers in the region's drug wars (Davila 2015).

[7] Granted, many believe that it is often preferable when those special protections are provided elsewhere. As the world cheered on "Team Refugees" during the 2016 Rio Olympics in Brazil, Roger Cohen (2016) pointed out the hypocrisy of glorifying refugee athletes while vilifying refugees at home. The title of his op-ed column was simply "The World Loves Refugees, When They're Olympians."

indistinguishable:; "The unnamed individual embodies the condition of refugees everywhere who cannot avoid their amalgamation into a collective category of concern" (Gatrell 2013, 10). Indeed, Liisa H. Malkki (1996) argues that "in universalizing particular displaced people into 'refugees'— in abstracting their predicaments from specific political, historical, cultural contexts—humanitarian practices tend to silence refugees" (378). Yet in some cases the refugee is individualized, if only for a moment; he is, for instance, five-year-old Omran Daqneesh sitting dazed in the back of an ambulance after an airstrike in Aleppo (see Allen 2016; Narayan 2016). In all instances, however, visual representations of refugees in their "purest" form center on vulnerability and powerlessness—and represent a call for humanitarian action and empathy. The practicalities of how protections might be distributed are separate from the logic of the images themselves; the point is simply that the plight of the "pure" refugee has been successfully represented, albeit in very simplistic and easily understandable ways, that are generally equated with legitimacy and worthiness for special protection.

It is noteworthy that the hierarchies of personhood resulting from constructions of worthiness also tie into ongoing discussions of photography and its potential for exploitation and the "consumption" of others. By the 1980s, crises such as the Ethiopian famine of 1984-45 began raising important ethical questions about humanitarian photography within the global media. NGOs were accused of capitalizing on suffering and photographers of disrespecting the privacy rights of their subjects (Nissinen 2015, 297–298). The Ethiopian crisis led to a move toward positive imaging that reflected human dignity and self-determination, decisively linking practices of representation to those of development and intervention (Lidchi 2015, 293). These discussions led to various codes of professional conduct, including the 2006 Code of Conduct on Images and Messages that provides guiding principles for NGO-related photography. Yet ethics related to humanitarian photography remain fraught with tensions. For instance, Markus Lohoff (2015) argues that photography should be viewed with suspicion and critically scrutinized for representational bias, intention, and manipulation. "Wars are political and so are linguistic and figurative representations of war, whether their intention is propagandistic or progressive," he explains (82). As these images are more widely shared thanks to social networking platforms (Facebook, Twitter, Instagram) and digital media sources, there is also growing concern about a shallow "consumption" of images and the people they represent. Reflecting on the role of photography in storytelling throughout

US history, for example, Vinson Cunningham (2015) examines the role of modern technologies and criticizes the "cavalier consumption of others" facilitated by Facebook. Focusing on the popular project "Humans of New York" (which often uses photographic portraits and short personal stories to highlight social injustice), he cautions viewers against a "flattening humanism" that stresses human community without adequately addressing the structural barriers blocking genuine equality (para. 12). He warns that such storytelling "betrays shallow notions of truth (achievable by dialogic cut-and-paste) and egalitarianism"—made possible, in part, by the comfortable medium of your Facebook news feed (para. 12–13)

From a human rights perspective, these criticisms align with troubling concerns about the dehumanizing role of the "spectacle." Perhaps the best-known critic in this regard is Susan Sontag (2003), who argues that "being a spectator of calamities taking place in another country is a quintessential modern experience," and she goes so far as to equate journalists with "specialized tourists" (18). In an era of "information overload" with twenty-four-hour news cycles, she argues that photographs have a "deeper bite" and provide "memory freeze-frames" that allow viewers to mentally stock images for instant recall later (22); they lay down points of reference and serve as "totems of causes" (85). Yet Sontag warns that collective memory is a fiction—there is only "collective instruction" (85). "Photographs that everyone recognizes are now a constituent part of what a society chooses to think about, or declares that it has chosen to think about," she argues. "What is called collective memory is not a remembering but a stipulating: that *this* is important, and this is the story about how it happened, with the pictures that lock the story in our minds. Ideologies create substantiating archives of images, representative images, which encapsulate common ideas of significance and trigger predictable thoughts, feelings" (85–86). Ultimately Sontag (2003) contends that "our capacity to respond to our experiences with emotional freshness and ethical pertinence is being sapped by the relentless diffusion of vulgar and appalling images" (108–109)—and that we live in a "society of spectacle" (109).

These criticisms and concerns continue to shape ethical approaches to journalism, documentary photography, and other forms of visual representation—and they offer an important foundation for advocacy work aimed at dismantling hierarchies of personhood. In part, such criticism requires us to focus on the goals and priorities of vulnerable populations, while simultaneously acknowledging their capabilities and rights to self-determination. Indeed, critical reminders to respect equal personhood and inherent human dignity are central to the ultimate goal of promoting functioning citizenship and related rights to place and purpose. "I don't particularly want to show how the Rohingya are victimized by statelessness. . . . This group finds a way to adapt and to make it from one day to the next," explains Greg Constantine, a documentary photographer whose black-and-white imagery of stateless populations has garnered international acclaim. He argues that his goal is to provide the visual "ammunition" to help strengthen advocacy efforts, which includes giving a "human face" to the complex issue of statelessness;[8] his work is meant to be a resource for advocates and a visual record of human rights abuse, not a form of entertainment. Such processes of visual representation are deeply connected to issue framing, which continues the work of conveying the problem(s).

Issue Framing: Indigenous Rights and Environmental Justice

Issue framing—the process of assigning meaning to an issue and interpreting a cause—may lead to the mobilization of potential adherents and constituents, the achievement of bystander support, and the demobilization of antagonists (Snow and Benford 1988, 198). Some scholars argue that issue framing is also undertaken as a response to intense competition in the global "marketplace" of ideas, aimed at attracting attention and funding necessary for issue emergence and continued support. Indeed, the recent proliferation of NGOs worldwide, combined with limited resources such as funding opportunities and public attention, has created an environment of intense competition among even the most principled of actors. Alexander Cooley and James Ron (2002) note that growing numbers of international NGOs increase uncertainty, competition, and insecurity among groups working in the same sectors. In fact, global civil society has been called "a Darwinian arena in which the successful prosper but the weak wither" and where NGO support "is neither easy nor automatic but instead competitive and uncertain" (Bob 2005, 8 and 4). Across disciplines, scholars stress the intensity of issue competition and the necessity of strategies for securing limited resources. The construction of issues help people to define the social world, and framing techniques that provide clear understandings of problems and solutions are easiest for the public to accept (Edelman 1988, 12–13). As Sarah Pralle (2006) notes,

---

[8] Personal communications. October 29–30, 2012. Saint Louis, Missouri. Constantine's work is available online; see his personal website (www.gregconstantine.com) and the project "Nowhere People" (http://www.nowherepeople.org/).

advocacy groups must construct issues in a way that makes sense to potential participants and decision makers; they seek to get their framing of a problem accepted by policymakers and the general public "so that their solutions seem logical and desirable" (17–18).

An increasingly successful example of issue framing comes from the indigenous rights movement, which frequently aligns itself with calls for environmental justice. This framing was apparent in protests against the construction of the Dakota Access Pipeline (DAPL) on the Standing Rock Sioux Reservation in North Dakota, where calls for indigenous rights merged with environmental activism. Environmental justice has become an important issue frame for the global indigenous rights movement, including activism related to environmental degradation, land rights, sacred sites, food security, climate change, and local ecological knowledge. Such framing can "incorporate a range of demands for equity, recognition, participation, and other capabilities into a concern for the basic functioning of nature, culture, and communities" (Schlosberg and Carruthers 2010, 12–13). In their fight against the DAPL, protestors (identified as "water protectors") who were encamped on the northern edge of Standing Rock in 2016 and 2017 frequently expressed their goals in terms of environmental justice and solidarity that reached beyond current activism. "It's more than this pipeline, on this land, at this time. I see this movement continuing on," explained water protector Daphne Singingtree (quoted in Zambelich and Alexandra 2016, para. 17). Standing Rock protests resonated with indigenous peoples around the world; members of the Samburu community, a semi-nomadic indigenous tribe from Kenya, posted a photo online announcing "Samburu Stands with Standing Rock #NoDAPL" in January 2017 (Cultural Survival 2017). Environmental justice framing not only mobilized indigenous activists but also drew support from the broader international community. Even as the last Standing Rock protestors were cleared by police from the Oceti Sakowin Camp in March 2017 (following an eleven-month demonstration), journalists and activists tweeted #StandingRocksLastStand. Indigenous activists and a diverse range of allies then marched in Washington, DC, to "demand respect for indigenous rights, including their cultural rights and right to water, which for many indigenous peoples have a spiritual significance that bestows a responsibility to protect" (Motaparthy 2017, para. 3).

The links between indigenous rights and environmental justice—what Snow and Benford (1988) would call "frame bridging"—help mobilize support from a broader support base, but the framing consequences for the recognition of indigenous sovereignty are uncertain. This frame bridge posits indigenous peoples as natural guardians of the land and its limited resources, which appeals to a global community and de-prioritizes state borders and jurisdiction. (Indeed, problems such as climate change and rising sea levels are not limited to particular countries.) In their defense of treaty rights and sovereignty, indigenous peoples have become key leaders in the environmental justice movement, particularly in relation to climate justice and fishing rights (Norman 2017). Yet in some ways this is a double-edged sword; the combination of these two issues may confuse the issue narrative or de-prioritize the indigenous frame. Mainstream media coverage of Standing Rock illustrated this complex relationship; international attention came relatively late during the DAPL standoff—with coverage peaking as the situation at Standing Rock became more conflict-ridden and violent—and failed to reflect clear, authoritative narratives. In a study of DAPL media coverage from 819 sources, researchers found that "protestor" was more favored by media sources than "protector" and that media coverage tended to privilege a view of events that centered on defiance (Sehat 2017). That is, DAPL protests received international coverage when the situation became violent; coverage centered on conflict imagery and stories of defiance yet did not necessarily delve deeply into the issues of indigenous sovereignty or land rights. Media outlets struggled with terminology—including whether to use "protestor" or "protector" to describe participants—and researchers argue that those words matter. Indeed, "the language of protectors goes beyond a semantic argument to emphasize what these individuals and communities were fighting for, not fighting against" (para. 26). "In the end, perhaps the news coverage—which includes the earlier inattention and struggles over narrative—reflects the state of our national inexperience with discussions over Native American sovereignty," they contend (para. 27). Researchers further note that DAPL coverage has helped US citizens become "more practiced at thinking about continued relevance of land issues for Native Americans" (Sehat 2017, para. 28), yet it is unclear whether future coverage will push people to consider such issues with more "depth and complexity," as they hope.

At the same time, a comparison of government and media responses to 2016 protests highlights an underlying lack of respect for the indigenous rights frame—and a privileging of the White, non-native citizenry. Violent actions against Standing Rock water protectors prompted Maini Kiai, the UN special rapporteur on the rights of freedom of association and peaceful assembly, to denounce US security forces for their violent crackdown on nonviolent protestors as well as for the "inhuman and degrading conditions" many faced in detention (Bearak 2016, para. 1). Water protectors were subjected to rubber bullets, tear gas, mace, compression grenades, and beanbag rounds (para. 4). Meanwhile in Oregon, armed anti-government protestors led by Ammon and Ryan Bundy were acquitted of federal conspiracy and weapons charges following the takeover of a federal wildlife sanctuary (Sherwood and Johnson 2016). In their nearly six-week takeover of the Malheur National Wildlife Refuge headquarters, the primarily White militia was criticized for holding indigenous artifacts from the Paiute nation hostage—as well as for the group's long-standing disregard for, and sometimes destruction of, indigenous sites (Keeler 2016).[9] On the same day that seven armed occupiers were acquitted of all charges, 141 people were arrested in nonviolent anti-DAPL protests, thus highlighting a dangerous double standard (Tan 2016). Noting that the mainstream media used words such as "occupiers" and "armed activists" in their coverage of this event, journalist Janell Ross (2016) writes: "Not one seemed to lean toward terms such as 'insurrection', 'revolt', anti-government 'insurgents' or, as some on social media were calling them, 'terrorists'. When a group of unknown size and unknown firepower has taken over any federal building with plans and possibly some equipment to aid a years-long occupation—and when its representative tells reporters that they would prefer to avoid violence but are prepared to die—the kind of almost-uniform delicacy and the limits on the language used to describe the people involved becomes noteworthy itself" (para 2). Although the political circumstances surrounding these two protest sites are different, government and media responses to these events highlights how hierarchies of personhood were framed in ways that helped protect armed White protestors while exposing protection gaps for nonviolent indigenous ones.

Counterframes are often employed to offset successful issue emergence and to negate calls for social change. Equating activism with terrorism has become commonplace within the United States, where critics symbolically align with counterterrorism to delegitimize calls for human rights protection.[10] In 2017, a representative of the company building the

---

[9] Paiute tribal chairperson Charlotte Rodrique said she was offended by occupiers' statements that they were returning the land to its rightful owners by reclaiming the site from federal control. "You know, who are the rightful owners?" she asked. "It just really rubs me the wrong way that we have a bunch of misinformed people in here—they're not the original owners," alluding to Paiute legend claiming that the nation has lived in the area since before the Cascade Mountains were formed (quoted in Kennedy 2016, para. 3–5).

[10] This practice also occurred in response to Black Lives Matter (BLM) protests. Thousands of conservative Tea Party supporters, for instance, reacted to the destruction of property in Ferguson with comments "disparaging the rioters, bemoaning the state of our country and very much blaming skin color as the culprit of this debauched way of dealing with the state of our society" (Cunha 2014, para. 5). In a telling example, many accused BLM supporters of setting a firefighter's

DAPL equated protestors with terrorists in his written testimony before a US congressional panel of the House Energy and Commerce Committee. "I fear the aggressive tactics we have seen in North Dakota will soon be the norm—if they are not already," wrote Joey Mahmoud, an executive vice president for Energy Transfer Partners. "Had these actions been undertaken by foreign nationals, they could only be described as acts of terrorism" (quoted in Natter 2017, para. 2). As Standing Rock activists garnered national and international attention and support for their causes, critics launched powerful counterframes that equated social movement activism with engaging in terror activities. These counternarratives sought to delegitimize protestors, deny their human rights claims, and shift public opinion out of their favor. Critics argue that the media perpetuates these counterframes, giving nearly equal weight to narratives communicated by the police despite overwhelming evidence of police brutality aimed at silencing Standing Rock water protectors. By using words like "clash" and "riot," journalists "implicitly portray activists as committing violence, and police actions as warranted acts of self-defense, legitimizing and normalizing increasing levels of state-sanctioned violence" (Neilson 2016, para. 16).

To truly understand the consequences stemming from lack of functioning personhood—and to lobby effectively for rights to place and purpose—those involved must pay careful attention to representation. This assertion holds true not only for journalists and photographers seeking to spread awareness through narrative and visual storytelling but also for academic researchers and human rights practitioners. Imagery and framing are important tools for issue emergence and sustained advocacy, but recent examples remind us that representations can also have unintended consequences. Indeed, how we convey the problem(s) may reinforce harmful constructions of worthiness. Again, the words and images used to tell these stories matter immensely. With these lessons in mind, we must move forward with advocacy strategies that represent human rights claimants—empowering them to voice their perspectives and experiences, drawing on their knowledge for enacting positive change, and paying

---

home on fire in 2016 and spray-painting "Lie with pigs, fry like bacon" on the wall, noting that the home may have been targeted because of the "Blue Lives Matter" flag flying outside (Larimer 2016). Pro-police websites were quick to blame BLM "terrorists" (Gettys 2016), reinforcing the racist narrative that BLM activists were animals, losers, and criminals rather than legitimate rights claimants. (The firefighter, Jason Stokes, was later arrested for setting fire to his own home and accused of attempting to smear anti-police brutality activists.)

careful attention to the ways in which advocacy decisions factor into existing hierarchies of personhood.

Empowerment and Representation

The narratives that help us understand hierarchies of personhood must go beyond witnessing human suffering to acknowledge the capabilities of vulnerable groups, which includes listening to and respecting diverse perspectives. While a clear and understandable narrative is essential for effective advocacy and mobilization, that narrative must be informed by the views of those with a personal stake in the issue. We begin to expand possibilities for citizenship that extend beyond state recognition (including beyond legal nationality, residency permits, and refugee status) when we acknowledge political agency and resiliency. Reflecting on the limited political space available to refugees, for instance, Nyers (2006) writes that "the refugee is an aberration only when people accept as a matter of common sense that citizenship is the only authentic political identity of modern political life. Refugees are voiceless not in any essentialist way but only through the congenital disorder that comes with being classified as the absence of the sovereign voice capable of intervening in the public sphere" (17). He further argues that such space is "not just *there* in some timeless fashion. Rather, political space is created and sustained by ongoing human activity—much of it bloody, unfair, and prejudiced" (17).

Representations of vulnerable populations—including the forcibly displaced, who are frequently the focus of media accounts and scholarly studies—often portray such individuals as problems rather than as people with capabilities and opinions. Indeed, Peter Gatrell (2013) notes that the "making of the modern refugee" has rendered displaced persons anonymous, viewing them as "temporary and unique" and hence leaving them without a "clear footprint on the documentary record" of historical scholarship (11). In her work on the representation of refugees in Australia, for instance, Melinda McPherson (2007) argues that displaced women have been rendered invisible, infantilized, and paternalized (3). She contends that migrants and refugees to Australia are "automatically represented as problematic 'subjects' by government and media," which leads to narrow policies that respond accordingly, and that the stakes are higher for women whose discrete experiences are often not properly recognized (3). Yet she cautions advocates to beware of positing women and girls as the face of refugee victimhood, noting that we must "ensure [that] we are not simply replacing one form of disempowering representation (the absent or under representation of refugee women's issues and voices) with another (a victimized representation of refugee women that undermines agency)" (4). In Thailand, Pittaway et al. (2010) learned that some women felt researchers "stole" their stories of sexual abuse and made them suffer re-traumatization in the process. The researchers contend that such unethical research practices "firmly [place] refugees as 'objects' of research and [deny] their agency and capacity to respond to the serious issues affecting their communities" (236).

Yet new technologies and information-sharing opportunities are carving out spaces for vulnerable populations to create and share their own narratives on their own terms, including visual representations and political commentary. Young journalists in the Democratic Republic of Congo, for instance, have used Instagram to chronicle daily life in the conflict-ridden country and to tell stories that extend beyond standard narratives that ignore local capabilities and resiliency. "I want to show another image of North Kivu as many people have this image that in North Kivu it's always war and fighting," said Ley Uwera, a twenty-six-year-old photographer who also contributes photos for local news sources and NGOs (quoted in Berger 2016, para. 8). The potential of photography as a tool for empowerment is also being recognized by the international community; in 2015, for instance, a group of Syrian girls living in the Za'atari refugee camp in Jordan spent three months documenting their everyday lives as part of a media workshop. Their images and stories were featured in the documentary film "Waves of Childhood" (Sebastopol Documentary Film Festival n.d.; *Telegraph* 2016). Social media artist Khalid Albaih (2016), a Sudanese cartoonist who lives in Qatar, uses his "Khartoons" to draw international attention to human rights issues. One of his viral cartoons depicted two "choices" for Syrian children: "if you stay" (with an illustration of Omran Daqneesh, the Syrian child sitting dazed in an ambulance after his home was destroyed) and "if you leave" (with an image of Alan Kurdi, the three-year-old Syrian whose drowned body washed ashore on a Turkish beach). "I have quickly learned that the internet has a very short memory, especially when it comes to news," explains Albaih (para. 13). "In a world of memes, gifs and instant rolling news, the internet doesn't tolerate the usual or the expected. That means that to stand out, I have to work smarter, not harder, and to try to ask different questions" (para. 15).

Many human rights researchers return from their fieldwork reiterating this need for respecting local knowledge and including stakeholder voices in policy recommendations. Discussions with issue experts at the 2014 Global Forum on Statelessness, for instance, highlighted how issue framing by human rights elites may not always reflect lived experiences or priorities. "Framing [is happening] as if people exist in space, in a vacuum," explained one participant. "There are moments when statelessness matters and times when it doesn't. Circumstances and communities matter." Reflecting on her experiences conducting field-work among stateless populations, a researcher noted: "Statelessness kind of disappears when you are on the ground. People don't call them-selves that, organizations do. It's completely entangled with irregular mi-gration." She said that stateless children she works with talk "endlessly" about documents, which are linked to identity and belonging, as well as about public schools and freedom from police harassment. "Kids aren't so concerned with nationality, they're concerned with having a pass." Another specialist argued that too much attention was being focused on legal status and documentation rather than on the rights and protections they afforded. "What's the point of a document if schools are useless or don't exist, or if you can cross a border without them? What's the point?" Another participant argued that successful issue emergence will depend on building a "values-based narrative" to garner support and attract attention. "What's the story?" he asked. "Forget law—that's not what shifts attitudes."

Ongoing discussion of research and representational ethics is increas-ingly confronting these challenges, calling upon scholars and practitioners to respect the lived experiences of their participants and to work toward mutual exchange. Reflecting on participant claims that researchers "stole" their stories, for instance, Pittaway et al. (2010) recommend a new research framework that moves beyond principles of harm minimization to empha-size a negotiated reciprocal benefit. This requires researchers to justify their projects with reference to the benefits to the vulnerable groups them-selves (Pittaway et al. 2010, 247–248). By holding themselves account-able to the communities they seek to study, researchers must confront the hierarchies of personhood that perhaps constructed their participants as subjects/objects of research rather than as partners and stakeholders. This attitudinal shift is also emerging in other ways; discussions of ethical pho-tography and visual representation, for example, also stress the agency of those being photographed. Sanna Nissinen (2015) warns that it "is patronizing to discount the willingness of subjects to participate or their ability to confront and to alter self-representations," noting that subjects should be empowered rather than protected; anything less "disempowers subjects and denies their resiliency" (317).

The human suffering that results from lack of functioning citizenship is messy and complicated. The need to convey problem(s) in ways that facilitate issue emergence and sustained advocacy often impacts the ways that vulnerable populations are represented to the world. I argue that these decisions matter immensely; the words and images used to represent human rights violations may spur positive change, but they may also reinforce existing inequalities and perpetuate problematic constructions of worthiness. Constructions of the "pure" refugee, for instance, further devalue the personhood of the criminalized migrant while the "society of spectacle" (Sontag 2003, 109) often dehumanizes displaced persons and other vulnerable groups. Deciding to use the term "protestor" instead of "water protector" to describe activists at Standing Rock changes the narrative in important ways, while counternarratives threaten appeals to indigenous sovereignty and instead posit indigenous leaders as enemies of the state. The examples discussed in this chapter offer just a few glimpses of how representations impact our understanding of human rights—and how we construct perceived worthiness for rights protection in both intentional and unintentional ways. Advocacy strategies that empower claimants to share their perspectives and knowledge, while also remaining critical of how advocacy decisions might support existing structural inequalities, are vital first steps on the long road toward equal, just modes of representation. These actions must be taken if we are to truly uncover, and adequately represent, the hierarchies of personhood that facilitate violations of rights to place and purpose. Once that happens, we can meaningfully engage in strategies to provide functioning citizenship—or at least know where to start.

CHAPTER 9 | Actualizing the Ideal of Functioning Citizenship

MANY AMERICANS TOOK TO social media to express their frustrations in the days following violent clashes in Charlottesville, Virginia, between White supremacist groups and counterprotestors—and to share their grief over the death of thirty-two-year-old Heather Heyer, who was killed when a Nazi sympathizer intentionally drove his car into a crowd of people.[1] Amid the political debates (sometimes arguments) and calls to action, one meme stood out to me on my social networking feed. It read: "Equal rights for others does not mean fewer rights for you. It's not pie." While I agree in principle with this statement—that rights are not a limited resource—it occurs to me that this fight is not over some abstract recognition of rights or political membership. Instead, a vocal minority of White Americans were prompted to take up torches and swastikas in August 2017 because they feared a loss of privilege. As marginalized "second-class" citizens and migrants asserted their rights to place and purpose, some Whites feared their loss of status on the US hierarchy of personhood—not because they suddenly had fewer rights but because others were asserting their own claims and working to close the protection gaps that had primarily privileged White, straight, Christian men for so long. This serves as a poignant reminder that understanding the concept of functioning citizenship is not simply a theoretical or intellectual endeavor; rather, it helps us clearly see real-world political realities. While rights may be universal, hierarchies of personhood endow certain groups with benefits

---

[1] Two Virginia state troopers, Pilot Lt. H. Jay Cullen and Trooper-Pilot Berke M. M. Bates, were also killed when their helicopter crashed en route to the scene on August 12, 2017. Dozens of others were treated for injuries, including nineteen people who were injured in the car crash that killed Heyer (National Public Radio 2017).

that are made possible through the marginalization of others. Worthiness is socially constructed to support the values, norms, and identities of the majority. These constructions justify why some have financial resources while others do not, why some groups wield political power while others are denied equal representation, and why some identities constitute an "us" while others are a "them."

This book's discussion of hierarchies of personhood—inequalities that render some people more "worthy" than others for protections and political membership—fits within an ongoing scholarly conversation about the true nature of community and fundamental rights. Indeed, there is growing resistance to accepting at face value the idealistic notions of universal human rights and full citizenship. Instead, scholars push for realistic recognition of membership and its pitfalls, in large part to uncover the inequalities that perpetuate human suffering. As mentioned in the Introduction, Iris Marion Young (1990) uses the term "differentiated citizenship" to highlight injustices within the state social structure and to show that not all (supposedly) full citizens are treated as such; Elizabeth F. Cohen's (2009) concept of "semi-citizenship" illustrates how citizenship itself is a gradient category, with most people fitting on a spectrum somewhere between full and noncitizenship. More recently, Rhoda Howard-Hassmann (2015) considers the "slippery" concept of citizenship by noting how this supposedly universal right is often "contingent and insecure" as well as sometimes "partial, soft, obscured by political realities, or nonexistent" (2). "At the top of the slippery slope of citizenship are those who enjoy both de jure and de facto citizenship in wealthy, democratic countries—in effect, the lucky holders of hard citizenship rights," she contends. "At the bottom are those who are stateless, enjoying neither de jure nor de facto citizenship anywhere" (5). In the middle of this "slippery slope" are various types of migrants and refugees, trafficked and smuggled individuals, and vulnerable social categories who enjoy limited citizenship rights (Howard-Hassmann 2015, 5–6). Howard-Hassmann (2015) explains:

So citizenship is slippery, even though, legally speaking, you are a citizen or you are not, either a legally authorized migrant or an unauthorized one. Citizenship rights can vary by "race," ethnicity, gender, sexual orientation, stage of life, or social status. You can have one, several, or no citizenships depending on the laws of the countries where you and your parents were born; you can have hard or soft citizenship, depending on the wealth and power of the country or countries where you are legally a citizen. You may think you are a citizen when you are not; you may not realize the implications of not being a citizen, and it may not be in the government's interests to inform you of them. You may be forced by political and/or economic circumstance to become an undocumented migrant or worse, a refugee; you may even be denationalized because of your individual actions or your group membership. And it is much easier to slide down the slippery slope of citizenship rights than to climb back up again. War, civil war, natural catastrophe, poverty, marriage, travel, work: all may send you sliding down the slope. (17–18)

These gradations of citizenship impact one's ability to claim human rights protections from state duty-bearers, even while rights are supposedly universal, inalienable, and independent from citizenship status. As a result, issues of "semi-citizenship," "differentiated citizenship," and "slippery" citizenship translate into ranking people with various levels of human rights worthiness. Naomi A. Paik (2016) uses the example of the US prison camp to argue that the notion of universal rights is a "fiction" (5), with a spectrum ranging from the rightful to the rightless. This spectrum spans "from persons who enjoy protections of the law and rights, to prisoners who are subject to the law as convicted felons, to camp inmates who are swept into these spaces of removal—with many gradations in between" (3). "Rightlessness does not denote a strict legal status or essential set of identities. Rather, it is a condition that emerges when efforts to protect the rights of some depend on disregarding the rights of others," Paik argues (2016, 4). "The rightful—as worthy, deserving subjects—enjoy the protection of rights only because other, rightless subjects are so devalued that they are excluded from those protections. Put differently, the recognition of rights depends on the denigration of the rightless. Rightlessness is therefore necessary, and endemic, to rights" (4).

This book presents various manifestations of hierarchies of personhood, beginning with statelessness—the most direct and obvious lack of functioning citizenship—and progressing through the forcibly displaced, irregular migrants, nomadic peoples, indigenous nations, and "second-class" citizens in the United States. It challenges the binary construct between citizen and noncitizen, arguing that rights to place and purpose are routinely violated in the space between. Indeed, these violations help construct and support hierarchies of personhood that value some people as rights claimants more than others. By recognizing these realities, we uncover limitations built into our current international system—and hopefully begin to envision a path forward, toward the realization of human rights ideals founded on universality and inalienability. The ideal of functioning citizenship acknowledges the persistent power of the state and seeks to build mutually beneficial relationships between individuals and governments, yet it does not rely on traditional conceptions of citizenship that have proven too flawed and limited for securing true rights protection. In order to resist hierarchies of personhood—and thus, violations of rights to place and purpose—functioning citizenship necessitates the opening of political space for those who cannot be neatly categorized as "citizens" or "noncitizens." Only by recognizing that all people are inherently worthy of full personhood—and by advocating expanded forms of political membership and voice—can the ideals of modern human rights be realized.

"Practical" Recommendations for Filling (Some) Protection Gaps

Clearly, this book argues that legal nationality and identity documentation alone cannot guarantee the protection of human rights. However, a number of practical recommendations can help level the playing field, to a degree, and alleviate some human suffering. These recommendations alone are not enough to guarantee functioning citizenship, but they nevertheless provide necessary starting points in our movement toward positive change and more equitable rights protection. These steps are meant to complement a broader reassessment of recognition and political membership, as discussed in the following section, while recognizing that vulnerable people around the world require concrete actions to address their immediate concerns. Chapter 8 laid out possibilities related to making advocacy decisions—including constructing problems and showing/telling stories. In this chapter, I expand my recommendations to include encouraging state accession to human rights agreements and enforcing norms; providing identity documentation, including birth certificates; ensuring that processes for determining legal statuses and issuing documentation are conducted fairly and without prejudice; rejecting the use of denationalization as a weapon or form of punishment; utilizing best practices in refugee and migrant integration; fostering human rights education opportunities; empowering marginalized communities; and emphasizing rights entitlement rather than reliance on charity models.

Existing human rights law provides vital starting points for the provision of functioning citizenship, but **action is needed to encourage state accession to international agreements and to enforce human rights norms**. As discussed, this is already a priority of the United Nations

High Commissioner for Refugees (UNHCR), as demonstrated in the "iBelong" Campaign to End Statelessness; the campaign emphasizes accession to the 1954 Convention relating to the Status of Stateless Persons and the 1961 Convention on the Reduction of Statelessness (United Nations High Commissioner for Refugees, 2014).[2] Similar pressure is necessary to promote respect for the 1951 Convention Relating to the Status of Refugees (Refugee Convention), particularly in the face of the Syrian refugee crisis. Jordan, for instance, has a refugee population of approximately 1.1 million but is not party to the Refugee Convention or its 1967 Protocol. While the Jordanian Constitution has some provision for political refugees, it lacks a clear legal framework for dealing with refugees and asylum-seekers.[3] The influx of Syrian refugees has strained Jordan's overburdened infrastructure and resources, prompting the government to limit entry (and risk refoulement to Syria) and to limit freedom of movement within the country (Achilli, 2015). Researchers contend that many vulnerable families cannot afford the costs of a Ministry of Interior (MoI) Service Card necessary for refugees to access public healthcare and education services, while humanitarian assistance is increasingly controlled by the Jordanian government—with negative consequences for the displaced (Achilli 2015). In the case of indigenous rights (which sometimes overlaps with the rights of nomadic peoples), the most relevant binding international treaty for protecting indigenous rights is the 1989 Convention concerning Indigenous and Tribal Peoples in Independent Countries (ILO No. 169). The Convention contains provisions for respecting rights to land, livelihoods, culture, education, freedom of movement, self-determination, and other elements vital to indigenous sovereignty (see International Labour Organization n.d.a.). Yet its impact is severely limited by limited accession—including lack of ratification by the same countries that initially voted against the 2007 Declaration on the Rights of Indigenous

---

[2] Notably, Katja Swider (2017) outlines a number of normative issues that arise when the reduction of statelessness is prioritized over the protection of stateless persons. "If the interests and the human rights of the stateless are the guiding normative principle of the UNHCR's statelessness policies, the overemphasis on the elimination of statelessness needs to be reconsidered," she writes. "Instead of insisting that every person is a national of a state, the focus should be on maximizing access to rights by affected individuals" (206). I will revisit her criticism, among others, in the following section.

[3] Displaced persons in Jordan are subject to Law No. 24 of 1973 concerning Residency and Foreigners' Affairs, which does not distinguish between refugees and non-refugees. A memorandum of understanding (MOU) between Jordan and the UNHCR provides that Jordan accepts certain concepts from the Convention and allows the UNHCR to make status determinations, but refugees' stay in Jordan should not exceed six months (Saliba 2016).

Peoples (see International Labour Organization n.d.b.). (Many consider the Convention a forerunner of the more broadly accepted, but legally non-binding, Declaration. It is telling that the four states that voted against its adoption in 2007—Australia, Canada, New Zealand, and the United States—all have significant indigenous populations and violent histories of rights abuse against native populations.) Statelessness, refugee rights, and indigenous rights are three cases where existing international laws outline key protections yet remain limited by lack of state accession and enforcement of rights norms. While international law alone will not guarantee rights to place and purpose, these legal foundations are vital for establishing normative standards and building the global political will necessary to uphold them.

Targeted action is also necessary to provide identity documentation, including birth certificates. Research on statelessness and documentation discussed in Chapter 2 highlights legal nationality as an essential prerequisite for protecting a person's rights to place and purpose, and that identity documentation such as birth certificates are often vital for accessing basic entitlements. These needs are acute in Syria and neighboring countries, where the immediate pressures of displacement may make birth registration seem unimportant to families and officials alike. Yet later in life these children will need identity documentation to claim legal status and the protections that go along with it, including access to public education, legal employment, and passports. "Civil documents are important like food," explains a Syrian refugee living in Gaziantep, Turkey. "Like breathing" (quoted in Reynolds and Grisgraber 2015, 5). Existing guidelines for birth registrations in emergencies provide important starting points. For instance, Plan International (2014) argues that humanitarian agencies must ensure that birth registration "becomes an integral part of humanitarian assessments" and that it is incorporated into efforts aimed at "emergency preparedness, response, and recovery" (54). This requires funds to be specifically allocated for birth and civil registration; although birth registration may not be an "immediate, life-saving priority in humanitarian response," it remains an important protection tool in the long term (Plan International 2014, 54). Existing strategies for registering births in inaccessible places may also help to register babies born in the midst of displacement. For instance, birth registration rates in rural Pakistan have been boosted through the use of mobile phone technologies (Malik 2016). Modernized, computerized birth registration systems have increased registration in communities as diverse as the Roma in Europe and families in the war-torn Democratic Republic of the Congo (United Nations Children's Fund 2013).

At the same time, **bureaucratic processes for determining legal statuses and issuing identity documentation must be undertaken without prejudice** that reinforces existing hierarchies of personhood. In her study of the Aqcha (Akha) hill tribe in Northern Thailand, for instance, Amanda Flaim (2017) argues that situations of protracted statelessness may persist, paradoxically, "as a result of the bureaucratic practices and procedures that have been enacted to address it" (148). In Thailand, the forensic or evidence criteria used for assessing citizenship claims (seemingly rational evidentiary procedures) often "reproduce contingencies and discrimination in the application of otherwise progressive nationality law" (148). That is, no matter how strong the evidence is that someone is worthy of legal nationality under existing law, the acquisition of citizenship ultimately requires the "conferral of belief"—and this allows political biases of state officials to come into play, thus reproducing and reinforcing the condition of statelessness among hill tribe people who face ongoing social exclusion and discrimination (148). "In the end, [my research reveals] that no evidence, whether documents, data, or even DNA, can ever guarantee a place in the polity," writes Flaim. "In the case of citizenship conferral, even the smallest gap between (hi)story and evidence thereof must ultimately be bridged by the beliefs and thus the internalized national fantasies of the officials making these determinations" (163). Related criticisms might be raised in relation to the recognition of official refugee status among displaced persons, the differentiation between refugees and irregular migrants, the granting of visas and work permits for migrants, and the federal recognition of indigenous nations. In all of these situations, government officials are tasked with undertaking bureaucratic processes for determining political membership and, by extension, for assessing a person's worth and legitimacy in relation to state protections of fundamental human rights. Yet the processes that determine one's legal status and provide official documentation are processes that reflect the political priorities and biases of the state while they also create space for individual-level discrimination on the part of decision-making government officials. It is therefore imperative to safeguard these processes as much as possible by implementing clear and ethical standards, by monitoring the implementation of state policies, and by carefully screening and training officials tasked with carrying out such procedures.

Creating ethical standards related to recognizing legal status and political membership must also include **rejecting the use of denationalization**

as a weapon or a form of punishment. Stripping citizens of legal nationality is sometimes used to exclude minority populations and deny them state protections. Tens of thousands of Dominicans of Haitian descent were denied legal nationality in 2013, for instance, prompting concerns about the arbitrary deprivation of nationality, the denial of access to basic services, and risks of expulsion from the Dominican Republic (Human Rights Watch 2015b). Such policies express state-sponsored marginalization in legalistic terms, denying equal protection to citizens and embedding hierarchies of personhood within nationality laws. Even in countries with traditionally rights-protective policies, security concerns have prompted governments to utilize denationalization as a strategy to combat terrorism. In 2017, Khaled Sharrouf became the first to lose his citizenship under Australia's anti-terror laws. Sharrouf, one of his country's most notorious terrorists, has been accused of enslaving women from the Yazidi religious minority in Iraq and participating in the execution of pro-Syrian government soldiers—but has not returned to Australia to stand trial (Norman and Gribbin 2017). That same year, the European Court of Human Rights upheld a United Kingdom policy of stripping terror suspects of their British citizenship. The Court unanimously rejected the claim from a dual national—who was born in Sudan, migrated to the United Kingdom as a child, and became a naturalized British citizen in 2000—and accepted his denationalization as a legitimate act, since the man was suspected of participating in terror activities with the extremist group al Shabaab (Cowburn 2017). Similar measures have been considered in the United States, including the proposed Expatriate Terrorist Act (ETA) to strip suspected terrorists of their US citizenship. "The Expatriate Terrorist Act will ensure that any American who forfeits their country to intentionally join ISIS will have their citizenship stripped and won't be able to use a U.S. passport to come back and murder American citizens," said US Senator Ted Cruz (2017, para. 2), in contradiction to legal tradition where American citizenship is nearly unconditionally guaranteed.[4] However,

---

[4] Patrick Weil (2013), who prefers the term "denaturalization" to describe stripping a naturalized citizen of their legal nationality, notes that this practice became a "tool for the expulsion of those deemed to possess 'un-American' characteristics" during World War II (4). However, a series of Supreme Court decisions forged a new definition of citizenship in which the citizen "was no longer required to submit to a sovereign power able to change and nullify his or her status. American citizens, naturalized and native-born, were redefined as possessing sovereignty themselves. Citizenship had moved from an era when it was provisional, qualified, and unsecure to one in which it was nearly unconditionally guaranteed" (5). While denaturalization was used as "an instrument of racism, bigotry, and fear" in the 1940s, Weil notes that citizenship protections arose in the twentieth century as part of a US commitment to human rights (12).

Amnesty International Australia (2016) argues that revoking citizenship in such a manner can endanger a person's right to a nationality while failing to afford due process and the presumption of innocence. "Taking away a person's citizenship is one of the most severe actions a country can take against one of its own citizens," the nongovernmental organization (NGO) explains. "A government should not be able to do it automatically, without trial or conviction" (para. 6). Some states use denationalization as punishment following a guilty verdict, rather than as a preemptive measure. A Danish court stripped twenty-five-year-old Enes Ciftci of his citizenship, for instance, after he was convicted of fighting for ISIS in Syria. Ciftci, a Dankish-Turk, was born and raised in Denmark (Reuters 2017). Yet while those convicted of terrorism should certainly be punished, universal human rights norms require that prisoners maintain basic rights—including the right to a nationality. Rather than stripping a convicted terrorist of nationality and (quite frankly) pretending they aren't part of a state community, governments would be better served in their "war on terror" to acknowledge threats within their citizenry and identify ways to combat extremism from within.

Careful attention to best practices related to refugee and migrant integration is also vital for upholding rights norms and protecting human dignity. Although the term "integration" is often seen as a "chaotic concept: a word used by many but understood differently by most" (Robinson 1998, 118), useful tools exist for mapping out successful policies. In their conceptual framework, for instance, Alastair Ager and Alison Strang (2008) offer ten core domains (divided into four categories) reflecting normative understandings of integration: "markers and means" (employment, housing, education, health); "social connection" (social bridges, social bonds, social links); "facilitators" (language and cultural knowledge, safety and stability); and "foundation" (rights and citizenship") (170). It is notable that these domains fit within our categories of rights to place and purpose, which emphasize the essential elements necessary for a life of human dignity. Indeed, Ager and Strang contend that successful integration policies rely on a foundation of rights—albeit with space to accommodate a diversity of assumptions and values, depending on local and national contexts (185). "Articulating refugee rights . . . defines the foundation of integration policy, to which governments are accountable," they write. "These rights do not in themselves define integration, but they underpin important assumptions about integration" (175). Fieldwork data from sites of resettlement illustrate challenges to all four of these domain categories; in Central New York, for example, a study of resettled refugees living in

Utica showed widespread isolation and impoverishment, problems with communicating information from non-refugee populations to refugees, and inadequate efforts to share vital information with specific groups—including certain cultural groups and vulnerable refugee subgroups such as mothers, people with disabilities, and the elderly (Stam 2016). Kathryn Stam (2016) advocates the adoption of an "information abundance approach" to address many of these challenges, arguing that a more nuanced understanding of information-sharing practices (within the "information landscape") and cultural dynamics within particular refugee communities is central to successful integration efforts. This work highlights the need to assess refugee resettlement practices, including analyzing successes and challenges—particularly since refugee resettlement agencies often lose track of people after the initial period of government support has ended. In the United States, for instance, refugees frequently move or lose contact with agencies after their ninety days of resettlement assistance ends.

Opportunities for human rights education (HRE) must be expanded to uncover hierarchies of personhood and to foster advocacy as well as to make people aware of their rights (and of available resources for claiming them). Indeed, a newfound respect for HRE has emerged within the past thirty years as human rights educators push for the inclusion of HRE in school and university curricula, with growing recognition of its community-wide value for promoting peace and rights protection. In 2011, the United Nations General Assembly recognized the importance of HRE by adopting the Declaration on Human Rights Education and Training. The Declaration asserts that HRE represents a "lifelong process that concerns all ages" and encompasses the provision of knowledge related to human rights norms, principles, and protection mechanisms; learning and teaching in ways that respect both educators and learners; and empowering people to enjoy and exercise their rights while respecting and upholding the rights of others (United Nations General Assembly 2011, Articles 2.2 and Article 3.1). The UN has promoted HRE as a preventative tool aimed at strengthening respect for human rights norms (Gerber 2013). The United Nations defines HRE as

> all educational, training, information, awareness-raising, and learning activities aimed at promoting universal respect for and observance of all human rights and fundamental freedoms and thus contributing, inter alia, to the prevention of human rights violations and abuses by providing persons with knowledge, skills and understanding and developing their attitudes and behaviours, to empower them to contribute to the building and promotion

of a universal culture of human rights. (United Nations General Assembly 2011, Article 2.1)

A variety of educator-scholars offer data to support claims about the efficacy of HRE as well as pedagogical resources for integrating HRE into classrooms and communities. Studies in Liberia, Colombia, Sierra Leone, Senegal, and Mexico, for instance, have shown that HRE can play an integral role in peace-building (Holland and Martin 2017). In their survey of post-conflict HRE projects, Tracey Holland and J. Paul Martin note that HRE "conforms to the social reality of the place in which it is being taught"—and that peace-building HRE initiatives tend to focus on improving human security and meeting needs, improving communication, and leading learners to a greater awareness of the barriers impeding a human rights culture (276). Central to these teaching methods is the recognition of hierarchies of personhood—and the understanding that such inequalities foster conflict and perpetuate suffering. In the United States, Carol Anne Spreen and Chrissie Monaghan (2017) center their HRE practices on issues related to identity and belonging. "Despite our increasing diversification and global human rights movements, our ideas about citizenship and civic engagement are often simplistic and fail to address the complex notions of globalization, migration, and rights in meaningful and purposeful ways," they write (306). They integrate discussions related to power, empathy, and solidarity into their high school lesson plans, while using social action projects and community partnerships to help build students' advocacy skills (Spreen and Monaghan 2017). Lindsay Padilla (2015), who teaches at a US community college, writes that many of her students are likely to face human rights violations in their own lives and would most benefit from a "holistic, action-oriented pedagogy" (172). "With the most to gain from human rights recognition, these populations are more equipped to claim their rights if they know why they are excluded," she argues (170). "By emphasizing critical thinking, authentic dialogue, and creativity, HRE and service learning provide a worldview of emancipation necessary for restoring our humanness and assisting students in becoming agents of change" (177). Yet Padilla also notes that these lofty goals require fundamental changes; they necessitate a curriculum that not only discusses human rights but also works on "making human dignity a world reality" (178).

Relatedly, **ongoing action is necessary to help empower vulnerable populations and give voice to marginalized communities.** This issue is discussed in Chapter 8 in relation to visual narratives and issue framing, which I argue require the empowerment and representation of people most negatively impacted by hierarchies of personhood. I would add that such empowerment necessitates a genuine respect for self-determination and alternative cultural and/or national identities; in turn, this requires a real acknowledgment of histories that are often omitted from state narratives, including public school curricula and textbooks. Respect for indigenous knowledge systems (discussed in Chapter 6), for instance, serves to preserve native culture while strengthening tribal sovereignty. From an HRE perspective, learning from past events can strengthen current struggles for social justice. "Whoever seeks to act for change should also consider consulting the successful processes of emancipation and the acquisition of rights," notes Martin Lücke (2016, 49). He writes that history classes designed with an awareness of HRE, for instance, can critique power structures, visualize the forgotten, and empower marginalized groups (48–49). History teachers who integrate the premises of HRE into their existing courses can help students to develop a "consciousness of change" that is informed both by history (the realization that social change happened in the past and is thus possible) and human rights (envisioning and creating change to realize human rights in the present) (Engel et al. 2016, 68). Advocates of "African-centered learning" further contend that classes must confront historical realities—including tools and effects of exploitation stemming from slavery and colonialism—to seek paths toward the elimination of discrimination (Byrd and Jangu 2009).

Finally, **advocates must press human rights claims, always emphasizing entitlement rather than reliance on the charity model**. While it is true that NGOs and other nonstate actors play a powerful role in providing humanitarian relief and in making other rights-focused efforts, dependence on the generosity of donors and volunteers to fill protection gaps can inadvertently perpetuate hierarchies of personhood among those who are the focus of the NGOs' assistance. Rights to place and purpose—whether that entails rescue on the Mediterranean Sea or the provision of essential healthcare or affordable housing in the United States—should not be dependent on NGOs having the resources and interest to provide them. State duty-bearers and the international community as a whole must be subjected to continued pressure to respect the norms expressed by international human rights law and frameworks—for *everyone*, not just those who can afford social goods or who are deemed worthy of them. In his discussion of US evictions, for instance, Matthew Desmond (2016) argues that universal housing voucher programs should be developed to protect the right to adequate shelter among America's poor. The program would include measures preventing landlords from over-charging tenants as well as keeping families from renting more housing than they need; families would dedicate 30 percent of their income to housing costs, with the vouchers covering the difference. Looking toward successful voucher programs in the developing world as models, Desmond argues that universal housing would "change the face of poverty" in the United States (308). As noted in the Introduction, human rights violations should not support the pessimistic view that basic rights don't exist; instead, they highlight flaws in the international system that allow constructed hierarchies of personhood to endure. As we lobby for human rights—whether the right to shelter or the multitude of other entitlements linked to place and purpose— it is imperative that we remain aware that the provision of human rights should not and cannot be dependent on charity.

The "practical" recommendations in this chapter offer legal, bureaucratic, social, educational, and policy-related opportunities for filling some of the protection gaps in our current system. They are vital starting points aimed at alleviating human suffering while activists continue working within the state-centered rights regime. However, these recommendations are not enough—and they never will be. As discussed in detail, the protection of rights to place and purpose cannot rely on state duty-bearers and traditional conceptions of citizenship alone. Instead, targeted action for resisting hierarchies of personhood require attention to these "practical" recommendations as well as sustained work for imagining and implementing broader, more inclusive notions of political membership. As the next section illustrates, the task ahead is immense but necessary—and long overdue.

Expanding Our Notions of Citizenship

Despite guarantees of universal and inalienable human rights, in reality some people are deemed less worthy of recognition and respect than others. The persistence of hierarchies of personhood starkly uncovers the inadequacies of our current human rights regime, which relies on states as duty-bearers and falsely equates legal nationality with rights protection. In our current system, a functioning relationship between the state and the individual is often assumed, even while citizens routinely face state-sponsored discrimination and/or neglect, and so many others lack even the pretense of legal status. These situations force us to expand our notions of citizenship and move beyond legalities; we must fill protection gaps to ensure that states meet their obligations while also opening political space for those who do not fit neatly within traditional conceptions of the citizenry. Indeed, functioning citizenship requires us to partly work within the existing system by holding states accountable for upholding human rights norms while also seeking out new possibilities for membership. Realizing the ideal of functioning citizenship will take sustained activism and political will—and certainly there is no "one size fits all" solution to resisting hierarchies of personhood around the world. Yet recognizing the limitations of our current human rights regime, while acknowledging the alternate perspectives and identities that make up our human community, are vital steps forward.

This discussion began with statelessness, in part, because scholarship on this issue increasingly problematizes traditional models of citizenship and pushes us to reconsider our perspectives on political membership. These conversations question our reliance on the state system for rights protection, delinking legal status from a person's worthiness as a human rights claimant. Scholars such as Polly Price (2017), for instance, write that we must have a measure of "effective statelessness" as a necessary adjunct to the concept of de jure statelessness (28). "Without this conceptual pairing, we cannot judge the actual relationship between a state and those who belong to it," she notes (28). Kelly Staples (2017) argues that "understanding statelessness and the potential for limiting it will require us to acknowledge and challenge the myth that the state system can provide for even a basic universality of human status" (173). She writes that "the model of statehood which underpins many contemporary accounts of nationality and statelessness is still at odds with the reality in much of the world"—including state fragility and competition for resources among ethnic and social groups (173). And in her critique of the UNHCR's "iBelong" campaign, Swider (2017) acknowledges that although the policy goals of protecting stateless persons and eliminating statelessness will often complement each other, that is not always the case; when those goals conflict, "priority should be given to wider protection of the human rights of affected persons over the goal of eradicating statelessness" (191). "We are ultimately talking not about status but about rights (or at least the rights claims) of the stateless," writes Daniel Kanstroom (2017, 244).

Moving beyond statelessness (the starkest denial of functioning citizenship), the experiences of refugees and migrants illustrate that legal status is only one indicator of worthiness—for entry, residency, and even humanitarian aid. Before the world wars, for instance, the assumption at US entry points such as New York's Ellis Island was that "citizenship would be easily recognizable as such," with an emphasis on personal appearance and signals of wealth to determine worthiness for entry (Robertson 2010, 165). Craig Robertson writes that "race and class provided useful shorthand for establishing identity according to the categories [of legal status] created in the law," while immigrants traveling in the cramped and inexpensive steerage quarters were marked as poor—and thus "more susceptible to disease and the lack of morals which made their right to live and work in the United States questionable" (165). Later, passports provided entry documents but served to order migrants in other ways, privileging citizens from more wealthy and powerful countries—winners of the "birthright lottery" (Shachar 2009)—while denying movement and protections to others. Indeed, assessments of worthiness continue limiting freedom of movement, creating liminal spaces and fueling practices such as human trafficking and smuggling. Among the forcibly displaced, studies of refugee centers in Sicily show that Italian host populations constantly assess "deservingness" of displaced persons, regardless of their legal status (Casati 2017). Noemi Casati argues that refugees are categorized according to "informal hierarchies of merit" related to refugees' gratitude and trust, clothing and attitudes toward work, and reliance on welfare as an indicator of laziness and immorality (3, 5). Casati's research data show "that people's grids of evaluation are much more complex than simple oppositions between white and black, local and foreigner, citizen and refugee" (14). Political and economic configurations of host communities thus determine which people are most "deserving" of assistance and differentiate between "good" and "bad" forms of aid (2).

The cases of nomadic peoples and indigenous nations highlight how alternate conceptions of space and sovereignty can cast further judgments on perceived worthiness for rights protections, relegating groups who move "too much" and/or who hold national identities outside the state to lower positions within hierarchies of personhood. As discussed in Chapter 5, nomadic peoples are often viewed as suspicious strangers undeserving of the state protections afforded to "legitimate" citizens; this thinking has been used to justify the long-standing persecution of Europe's Roma and Travellers as well as the Maasai (in Tanzania and Kenya) and the Bedouin (in the MENA region, and particularly in Israel's Naqab Desert). Indigenous nations—some of whom also identify as nomadic peoples—face similar discrimination related to their differing views on land use and development, as well as their ongoing assertions of tribal sovereignty within a state-dominated international system. In a series of 2017 interviews with Native Americans about race, for instance, a number of interviewees linked government recognition of indigeneity with land/resource rights and ongoing marginalization. Noting that blood quantum rules violate matriarchal systems of assigning political membership, an Apache woman notes that her sisters are short one-sixteenth of a degree to qualify for recognized indigenous status that confers federal benefits.[5] "What does that mean?" she asks. "Does that mean their pinkies aren't Apache?" (Stephenson and Young 2017, 3:14–3:40). She further argues that such processes for determining indigenous status—and thus worthiness for indigenous rights and benefits—are created in a way meant to eventually erase indigenous claims, thereby nullifying the need to meet treaty obligations. When that happens, "then the land is available, the resources are available" (4:27–4:51). Another interviewee contends: "I think . . . that [the] essential point about our claim to sovereignty, our claim to land, our claim to a culture, our claim to resources, is one that gets lost if we don't insist upon the fact that we are nations" (4:52–5:06).

Hierarchies of personhood are further reinforced in US cities such as Detroit, Flint, and Saint Louis, where poor and minority Americans contend with a "second-class" citizenship status that denies them full rights protections from the state. Deeply entrenched opinions on worthiness and status are evident in ongoing racial conflict, debates about federal funding for basic rights such as affordable housing and healthcare, and lack of state responses to issues such as homelessness. Indeed, widespread lack of support for the "Black Lives Matter" movement highlights how politically fraught the task of claiming equal rights—and combating majority, White privilege—remains.[6] " 'Black Lives Matter' became a rallying cry to identify the places in which black life is cut short, whether it is in highly publicized instances of police brutality or through the slow suffocation of black communities facing poverty and economic inequality," explains Marcia Chatelain (Chatelain and Asoka 2015, para. 24). Yet, as noted in Chapter 8, BLM activists are frequently portrayed as domestic

---

[5] Blood quantum refers to defining bloodlines relating to ancestry by basing them on biological rather than cultural criteria. Following the 1934 Indian Reorganization Act, the majority of federally recognized indigenous tribes began using blood quantum requirements (as well as lineal descendancy or roll descendancy) as criteria for tribal membership and, thus, for federal protections and benefits. Indigenous nations that use blood quantum criteria require members to have at least one-half to one-sixteenth blood of their tribe; a Certificate Degree of Indian Blood (CDIB) is issued as documentation of tribal membership (Zotigh 2011; see also Ellinghaus 2017).

[6] Indeed, a 2016 national survey found that only ten percent of American voters believed that BLM had made racial issues in the country better; 48 percent said it had made things worse, while 36 percent said the movement had not resulted in any real change (Monmouth University 2016, para 4).

terrorists—reinforcing the racist narrative, also common during the 1960s, that civil rights activists are criminals rather than legitimate rights claimants. Although the "second-class" citizens discussed in Chapter 7 are indeed US nationals, processes such as the "contractualization of citizenship" and "color-blind" politics result in a form of "internal statelessness" (see Somers 2008), regardless of legal nationality in a rich and powerful state. As urban centers struggle to achieve economic renewal and equal rights protection, residents face threats to place and purpose frequently ignored in accounts of the "American Dream." Consider the last two stanzas of the poem "City Bleeding," in which Detroit-born poet Marge Piercy (2015) describes a city cut off from government protections and yearning for better times ahead:

> In blocks of zombie houses, crack
> houses, walls of gang graffiti,
> where packs of wild dogs turn back
> to wolves and the police never come,
> people still try with little help
> to remake community, to reach up
> and out of rubble into some venue
> of light, of warmth, of dignity, into
> whatever peace they imagine. Out
> of ruins eerie in their torn decay
> where people lived, worked, dreamed
> something yet begins to rise and grow. (21–22)

Once we accept the truth that legal nationality is not a guarantee of rights protection, we can more realistically assess its value—and even consider the ways that citizenship may hinder, rather than help, the enjoyment of rights in some cases. "Citizenship of a recognized State is often seen uncritically as the first and most important step in addressing the deprivations experienced as a result of statelessness," explains Tendayi Bloom (2017), yet she contends that claims of stateless and indigenous groups highlight the need to "significantly [reexamine the] liberal theoretical understanding of the State system itself" (153). Indeed, she contends that "citizenship regimes, in their assumption of binarity and mutual exclusivity, can in fact actively exclude, disenfranchise and subdue political claims of members" by giving and withholding status, as well as constructing and controlling group structures (Bloom 2017, 157). Bloom writes that state citizenship can therefore be "experienced as stifling, rather than only emancipatory and empowering" (157). Audrey Macklin (2015) uses the term "sticky citizenship" as a label that applies to "situations where a state seeks to *stick* citizenship on an unwilling recipient or where an individual is *stuck* with a citizenship she wishes to disavow" (223).[7] Moreover, Kanstroom (2017) warns that strengthening the protection of citizenship could have adverse consequences for future noncitizens, including rendering citizenship "still more precious and thus ever harder to achieve and to prove" and relegating noncitizens (especially the deported) to a "dangerous rightless realm" (245). "We must therefore do the harder, more basic work of defining and instantiating meaningful human rights protections for *all* people, regardless of status or location," he argues (245). Swider (2017) writes that we should do more than narrowly focus on the provision of legal nationality: "The fact that a status or condition leads to problems does not mean that this status or condition is a problem per se and needs to be eliminated. Sometimes the (legal) environment needs to be changed instead, so that affected persons no longer experience problems associated with their status without the phenomenon itself needing to be eradicated" (196).

If legal nationality cannot be equated with functioning citizenship and rights protection, we must ask the question, What makes an individual recognizable as a person worthy of rights in our state-centric system? Matthew J. Gibney's (2011) discussion of "precarious residents" (including unlawful migrants and asylum-seekers awaiting status determination) provides interesting starting points for conceptualizing political membership beyond the strict confines of state citizenship. First, one potential standard for defining membership is the principle of choice. He writes that membership should be available to anyone who chooses to live in a state. A second approach is to emphasize the role of individuals as subjects of state power; a state can only legitimately rule if the people consent to such rule. Third, the principle of societal membership contends that membership of a state should be composed of those who have a significant stake in the success and future of that society. All three of these approaches extend membership beyond legal notions of citizenship, which are often thin and unable to guarantee rights protection, and instead privilege the values of autonomy, democracy, and community. These alternative approaches to membership also extend the social goods of voice (freedom of expression

---

[7] This aligns with the perspective of Clark Hanjian (2003), who renounced his US citizenship in 1985 and chose to remain stateless. He argues that the choice to be stateless is a legitimate and reasonable option; this form of intentional statelessness makes a person both a sovereign and an alien, or a "sovrien."

and political participation) and security (security of residence or presence in a state), which are often limited for or denied entirely to those without functioning citizenship (Gibney 2011). Ultimately, engagement with such theoretical approaches helps facilitate discussions of political membership beyond legal nationality—and toward the aim of filling some of the protection gaps built into our current human rights system.

It is also useful to return to Benjamin Gregg's (2016) concept of the "human rights state," which was briefly discussed in the Introduction as a way to overcome the rights challenges inherent in state sovereignty. A human rights state is "a metaphorical community directed at a corresponding nation state," which advocates human rights as a "constituent element of that nation state" (24). Rather than relying on a state's generosity for human rights protections—since a government may indeed "decline to offer them" (25)—Gregg argues that self-recognition and group solidarity must combine to support the principle that "despite what a nation state claims, we claim human rights for ourselves" (33). Some transnational NGOs already intervene across state borders to create humanitarian zones that function as a form of human rights state (33), but a human rights state is different; rather than providing interventions that assume responsibilities from unwilling governments, a human rights state "pursues a nation state's eventual embrace of human rights" (34). It "aims to change state behavior and the behavior of groups within the political community" and is deterritorialized, yet it does not seek to leave the state out of its project (34). Instead, Gregg contends that "the physical nation state and the metaphorical human rights state coexist side by side, as the individual is a member of both" (33). This concept weakens state sovereignty "to the extent necessary to make domestic human rights possible"—with respect to the state's capacity to violate or deny rights—and requires participants to mutually recognize each other's "self-granted" human rights (36).

The human rights state requires transnational activism—a form of global activist-citizenship, if you will—in order to succeed. Gregg (2016) acknowledges that human rights "are resolutely political": "Their content and validity are socially constructed. Their universality is an aspiration to be achieved through social movements" (42). He contends that people must metaphorically "wear" human rights as one does a backpack, taking rights with them wherever they go (52). This requires the performance of citizenship, directing the proclamation of human rights at the nation-state as well as at other participants to build solidarity (47). Performance "means giving critical voice to the fact of being denied what the law, at least on paper, promises. A person claims toward others—performs for others—a right to have rights first of all as a right to oppose one's exclusion in practice from the law on paper" (48). This performance—what Gregg calls donning a human rights backpack—centers on the political advocacy of claiming, displaying, and sharing human rights. It delinks rights from legal nationality while at the same time acknowledging the power of the state system in its attempts to make governments eventual partners. Yet the overarching claim is clear: The state can no longer have the power to differentiate between rights bearers and non-rights bearers (53).

It is here that we must return to the concept of functioning citizenship, which acknowledges the persistent power of the state and the practical value of legal nationality but also recognizes the limitations of the state-centered human rights regime and the need for broader, more inclusive forms of political membership. The "practical" recommendations outlined earlier provide starting points for closing some protection gaps within the existing system, and those steps are vital within an international community that privileges legal nationality and the power of states. In an ideal world, these steps would be enough; all governments would adhere to human rights commitments under international law and strive to protect people's fundamental rights, universally and without prejudice. But we do not live in an ideal world, and, despite beautiful human rights frameworks and laws guaranteeing the rights and freedoms necessary for a life of human dignity, pervasive rights abuses continue. Hierarchies of personhood privilege some people above others, facilitating violations of rights to place and purpose that often happen in the absence of—or in spite of—legal status. These realities push us to think beyond traditional conceptions of citizenship and the duty-bearing state to seek out new forms of political membership that do not necessarily replace the existing state system, but serve to complement it—and perhaps also to keep it, at times, in check.

As such, the concept of functioning citizenship offers alternatives to existing perspectives that frame citizenship conversely as a right, an identity, and a commodity. As noted in Chapter 1, the "right to nationality" privileges state sovereignty and makes assumptions that limit the inclusiveness of seemingly universal human rights. Citizenship-as-identity models leave little space for multicultural perspectives, including those in which identities extend across borders or across multiple "national" categories. And the acknowledgment of citizenship as a commodity—a "good" that unlocks social, economic, and political opportunities that are frequently denied to noncitizens or nationals of poor/weak states—simply highlights how reliance on duty-bearing governments often falls short of human rights ideals. By focusing on the functionality of one's relationship to the state, the concept of functioning citizenship forces us to look beyond traditional, legal nationality to consider what benefits and outcomes citizenship *ought* to bring about. That is, it draws attention away from legal status/categorization and instead asks, What is the relationship here? Is it human rights protective—which includes providing opportunities for minorities to enjoy meaningful political membership? Honest and forthright answers to these simple questions help uncover shortcomings in our state-centric system, highlighting problems associated with statelessness and noncitizenship while also focusing on inequalities within national communities. In short, legal nationality in itself isn't sufficient to protect human rights; it isn't any guarantee that a person will be viewed as worthy, as fully human. Instead, attention to constructions of deservingness and hierarchies of personhood are vital for uncovering protection gaps and strengthening respect for fundamental rights.

Functioning citizenship is an aspirational ideal that moves beyond mere legal status to facilitate mutually beneficial, rights-protective relationships between the state and the individual while opening political space for those who do not fit within traditional conceptions of the citizenry—but who are nevertheless entitled to the same rights as all members of the human family. Much like Gregg's (2016) concept of the "human rights state," functioning citizenship works within and alongside the state system to put existing human rights norms into regular practice. Like Gibney's (2011) recommendations, functioning citizenship seeks to extend membership beyond the traditional confines of citizenship. This concept therefore walks the fine line between political reality and normative ideal; it acknowledges the pitfalls of the current international system while accepting that advocates, for now at least, must work within it. At the same time, it problematizes our reliance on states and legal nationality for protecting rights, constituting political communities, and ultimately determining one's worthiness as a fellow human being. Indeed, truly functioning citizenship requires political space for legal citizens and noncitizens; for nations whose sovereignty is separate from the state; for those whose territories extend beyond and through state borders; for those who represent a minority within the citizenry.

The necessary steps for facilitating this shift will differ greatly depending on circumstances, but they will all begin by acknowledging the fundamental limitations of our current system. Only by recognizing that hierarchies of personhood exist—and that every person is worthy of rights to place and purpose—can we move forward with filling the protection gaps that threaten human dignity. Personhood is not recognized by a passport any more than a political community is solely defined by a state government or its territorial borders. Instead, we must expand our notions of citizenship to include ways of belonging that do not fit neatly into state constructs—but which nevertheless have always existed, and will continue to exist, within our modern world system.

BIBLIOGRAPHY

Abrahamian, Atossa Araxia. 2015. *The Cosmopolites: The Coming of the Global Citizen.* New York: Columbia Global Reports.

Abrego, Leisy. 2014. *Sacrificing Families: Navigating Laws, Labor, and Love across Borders.* Palo Alto, CA: Stanford University Press.

Abu-Saad, Ismael, and Cosette Creamer. 2012. "Socio-Political Upheaval and Current Conditions of the Naqab Bedouin Arabs." In *Indigenous (In)Justice: Human Rights Law and Bedouin Arabs in the Naqab/Negev,* edited by Ahmad Amara, Ismael Abu-Saad, and Oren Yiftachel, 19–66. Cambridge, MA: Human Rights Program at Harvard Law School, Harvard University Press.

Abu-Saad, Ismael, and John Mburu. 2001. *The Influence of Settlement on Substance Use and Abuse among Nomadic Populations in Israel and Kenya.* NIRP Research for Policy Series 7. Amsterdam: KIT.

Achilli, Luigi. 2015. "Syrian Refugees in Jordan: A Reality Check." European University Institute, Migration Policy Centre, February 2015. http://cadmus.eui.eu/bitstream/handle/1814/34904/MPC_2015-02_PB.pdf?sequence=1&isAllowed=y.

Agamben, Giorgio. 1998. *Homo Sacer: Sovereign Power and Bare Life.* Palo Alto, CA: Stanford University Press.

Ager, Alastair, and Alison Strang. 2008. "Understanding Integration: A Conceptual Framework." *Journal of Refugee Studies* 21, no. 2: 166–191.

Agier, Michel. 2011. *Managing the Undesirables: Refugee Camps and Humanitarian Government.* Cambridge, MA: Polity Press.

Al Ahmad, Mohammad. 2016. "The Crisis of Higher Education for Syrian Refugees." Brookings Institution, June 17, 2016. Translated by Will Todman. https://www.brookings.edu/blog/education-plus-development/2016/06/17/the-crisis-of-higher-education-for-syrian-refugees/.

Albahari, Maurizio. 2015. *Crimes of Peace: Mediterranean Migrations at the World's Deadliest Border.* Philadelphia: University of Pennsylvania Press.

Albaih, Khalid. 2016. "Every Time My Work Goes Viral I Ask Myself: What Do I Do Next?" *CNN,* August 25, 2016. http://www.cnn.com/2016/08/25/opinions/khalid-albaih-in-his-words-trnd/.

Aleinikoff, T. Alexander. 1995. "State-centered Refugee Law: From Resettlement to Containment." In *Mistrusting Refugees*, edited by E. Valentine Daniel and John Chr. Knudsen, 257–278. Berkeley: University of California Press.

Alexander, Jessica. 2013. *Chasing Chaos: My Decade in and out of Humanitarian Aid.* New York: Broadway Books.gene

Alexander, Michelle. 2012. *The New Jim Crow: Mass Incarceration in the Age of Colorblindness.* Rev. ed. New York: New Press.

Alfred, Taiaiake. 1999. *Peace, Power, Righteousness: An Indigenous Manifesto.* Oxford: Oxford University Press.

Alfred, Taiaiake. 2004. "Warrior Scholarship: Seeing the University as a Ground of Contention." In *Indigenizing the Academy: Transforming Scholarship and Empowering Communities*, edited by Devon Abbott Mihesuah and Angela Cavender Wilson, 88–99. Lincoln: University of Nebraska Press.

Allen, Craig. 2016. "Photo Editors' Notebook: What Makes the Image of Omran Daqneesh Extraordinary?" *New York Times*, August 22, 2016. http://nyti.ms/ 2bB6za9.

American Civil Liberties Union. 2014. "Oppose Cruz Bill S. 2779, Expatriate Terrorists Act; S. 2779 Is Unnecessary and Dangerous." September 17, 2014. https://www.aclu.org/sites/default/files/field_document/140917_citizenship_ stripping_letter.pdf.

Amnesty International. 2013. "Italy: Double Standards: Italy's Housing Policies Discriminate against Roma." October 30, 2013. https://www.amnesty.org/en/ documents/EUR30/008/2013/en/.

Amnesty International. 2016. "Nowhere Else to Go: Forced Returns of Somali Refugees from Dadaab Refugee Camp, Kenya." November 14, 2016. http://www.amnestyusa. org/research/reports/nowhere-else-to-go-forced-returns-of-somali-refugees-from- dadaab-refugee-camp-kenya.

Amnesty International. n.d. "Human Rights on the Margins: Roma in Europe." https:// www.amnesty.org.uk/sites/default/files/roma_in_europe_briefing.pdf.

Amnesty International Australia. 2016. "Dangers of Revoking Citizenship." August 10, 2016. https://www.amnesty.org.au/dangers-revoking-australia-citizenship/.

Amnesty International USA. 2014. "On the Streets of America: Human Rights Abuses in Ferguson." http://www. amnestyusa.org/sites/default/files/onthestreetsofamericaamn estyinternational.pdf.

Amster, Randall. 2008. *Lost in Space: The Criminalization, Globalization, and Urban Ecology of Homelessness.* New York: LFB Scholarly Publishing.

Anderson, Benedict. 2006. *Imagined Communities: Reflections on the Rise and Spread of Nationalism.* Rev. ed. New York: Verso.

Andrijasevic, Rutvica. 2010. "From Exception to Excess: Detention and Deportations across the Mediterranean Space." In *The Deportation Regime: Sovereignty, Space, and the Freedom of Movement*, edited by Nicholas de Genova and Nathalie Peutz, 147–165. Durham, NC: Duke University Press.

Arango, Tim. 2015. "ISIS Transforming into Functioning State that Uses Terror as Tool." *New York Times*, July 21, 2015. http://www.nytimes.com/2015/07/22/world/ middleeast/isis-transforming-into-functioning-state-that-uses-terror-as-tool.html?_ r=0.

ArchCity Defenders. 2014. "Municipal Courts White Paper." http://www.archcitydefenders.org/wp-content/uploads/2014/11/ArchCity-Defenders-Municipal-Courts-Whitepaper.pdf.

ArchCity Defenders. n.d. "Our Mission & Story." http://www.archcitydefenders.org/who-we-are/our-mission-story/.

Arendt, Hannah. 1958. *The Human Condition*. 2nd ed. Chicago: University of Chicago Press.

Arendt, Hannah. 1966. *The Origins of Totalitarianism*. New ed. New York: Harcourt, Brace & World.

Arendt, Hannah. 1973. *The Origins of Totalitarianism*. New ed. San Diego: Harcourt Brace Jovanovich.

Ashbourn, Julian. 2014. *Biometrics in the New World: The Cloud, Mobile Technology and Pervasive Identity*. New York: Springer.

Associated Press. 1986. "S. Africa Refuses Passport for Anti-Apartheid Activist." *Los Angeles Times*, November 26, 1986. http://articles.latimes.com/1986-11-26/news/mn-15689_1_anti-apartheid-activist.

Associated Press. 2018. "Judge Won't Order Flint Bottled Water Program to Resume." *Detroit Free Press*, April 21, 2018. https://www.freep.com/story/news/local/michigan/flint-water-crisis/2018/04/21/flint-bottled-water-crisis/538864002/.

Atleo, Marlene R. 2009. "Strategies for Equities in Indigenous Education: A Canadian First Nations Case Study." In *Decolonising Indigenous Rights*, edited by Adolfo de Oliveira, 132–164. New York: Routledge.

Axelsson, Per, and Peter Sköld. 2011. "Introduction." In *Indigenous Peoples and Demography: The Complex Relation between Identity and Statistics*, edited by Per Axelsson and Peter Sköld, 1–14. New York: Berghahn Books.

Bacon, David. 2008. *Illegal People: How Globalization Creates Migration and Criminalizes Immigrants*. Boston: Beacon Press.

Badger, Emily, and Quoctrung Bui. 2018. "In 83 Million Eviction Records, a Sweeping and Intimate New Look at Housing in America." *New York Times*, April 7, 2018. https://www.nytimes.com/interactive/2018/04/07/upshot/millions-of-eviction-records-a-sweeping-new-look-at-housing-in-america.html.

Baines, Stephen. 2009. "The Reconstruction of Waimiri-Atroari Territory." In *Decolonising Indigenous Rights*, edited by Adolfo de Oliveira, 45–64. New York: Routledge.

Balaton-Chrimes, Samantha. 2014. "Statelessness, Identity Cards and Citizenship as Status in the Case of the Nubians of Kenya." *Citizenship Studies* 18, no. 1: 15–28.

Balibar, Étienne. 2011. *Politics and the Other Scene*. London: Verso.

Banki, Susan. 2013. "Refugee Camp Education: Populations Left Behind." In *Refugees, Immigrants, and Education in the Global South: Lives in Motion*, edited by Lesley Bartlett and Ameena Ghaffar-Kucher, 133–148. New York: Routledge.

Barak, Aharon. 2015. *Human Dignity: The Constitutional Value and the Constitutional Right*. Cambridge: Cambridge University Press.

Barelli, Mauro. 2016. "Development Projects and Indigenous Peoples' Land: Defining the Scope of Free, Prior and Informed Consent." In *Handbook of Indigenous Peoples' Rights*, edited by Corinne Lennox and Damien Short, 69–82. London: Routledge.

Batchelor, Carol A. 1998. "Statelessness and the Problem of Resolving Nationality Status." *International Journal of Refugee Law* 10, no. 1/2: 156–183.

Bauböck, Rainer. 1994. *Transnational Citizenship: Membership and Rights in International Migration*. Cheltenham, UK: Edward Elgar.

BBC News. 2014. "Malta Tightens Passport Sale Terms under EU Pressure." January 30, 2014. http://www.bbc.com/news/world-europe-25959458.

BBC News. 2016. "Calais 'Jungle': Fires Rage across Migrant Camp." October 26, 2016. http://www.bbc.com/news/world-europe-37771889.

Bearak, Max. 2016. "U.N. Officials Denounce 'Inhuman' Treatment of Native American Pipeline Protestors." *Washington Post*, November 15, 2016. https://www.washingtonpost.com/news/worldviews/wp/2016/11/15/u-n-officials-denounce-inhuman-treatment-of-north-dakota-pipeline-protesters/?utm_term=.49b50922d88b.

Belton, Kristy A. 2016. "Rooted Displacement: The Paradox of Belonging among Stateless People." *Citizenship Studies* 19, no. 8: 907–921.

Bennhold, Katrin, 2014. "Britain Expands Power to Strip Citizenship from Terrorism Suspects." *New York Times*, May 14, 2014. http://www.nytimes.com/2014/05/15/world/europe/britain-broadens-power-to-strip-terrorism-suspects-of-citizenship.html?_r=1.

Berger, Miriam. 2016. "Meet the Instagrammers Challenging How You See the Congo." *Buzz Feed*, August 13, 2016. https://www.buzzfeed.com/miriamberger/meet-the-instagrammers-challenging-how-you-see-the-congo?utm_term=.pg2LxAJy96#.pm1jyL0B2m.

Betts, Alexander. 2013. *Survival Migration: Failed Governance and the Crisis of Displacement*. Ithaca, NY: Cornell University Press.

Betts, Alexander, and Gil Loescher. 2011. "Refugees in International Relations." In *Refugees in International Relations*, edited by Alexander Betts and Gil Loescher, 1–27. Oxford: Oxford University Press.

Bhabha, Jacqueline. 2011. "From Citizen to Migrant: The Scope of Child Statelessness in the Twenty-First Century." In *Children without a State: A Global Human Rights Challenge*, edited by Jacqueline Bhabha, 1–39. Cambridge, MA: MIT Press.

Bhabha, Jacqueline. 2017. "The Politics of Evidence: Roma Citizenship Deficits in Europe." In *Citizenship in Question: Evidentiary Birthright and Statelessness*, edited by Benjamin N. Lawrance and Jacqueline Stevens, 43–59. Durham, NC: Duke University Press.

Bhreatnach, Aoife. 2006. *Becoming Conspicuous: Irish Travellers, Society and the State 1922–1970*. Dublin: University College Dublin Press.

Bicocchi, Luca. 2011. "Undocumented Children in Europe: Ignored Victims of Immigration Restrictions." In *Children without a State: A Global Human Rights Challenge*, edited by Jacqueline Bhabha, 109–129. Cambridge, MA: MIT Press.

Binelli, Mark. 2012. *Detroit City Is the Place to Be: The Afterlife of an American Metropolis*. New York: Metropolitan Books.

Birrell, Ian. 2016. "Dispelling the Myth of the Humane Refugee Camp." *Independent*, March 6, 2016. http://www.independent.co.uk/voices/dispelling-the-myth-of-the-humane-refugee-camp-a6915746.html.

Biryukov, Nikita. 2017. "Michigan Ends Flint Water Credit Amid Disagreement on Recovery." *NBC News*, February 28, 2017. http://www.nbcnews.com/storyline/flint-water-crisis/michigan-ends-flint-water-credit-amid-disagreement-recovery-n727276.

Black Lives Matter. n.d.a. "About the Black Lives Matter Network." http://blacklivesmatter.com/about/.

Black Lives Matter. n.d.b. "Guiding Principles: We Affirm that All Black Lives Matter." http://blacklivesmatter.com/guiding-principles/.

Blitz, Brad K. 2011. "Neither Seen nor Heard: Compound Deprivation among Stateless Children." In *Children without a State: A Global Human Rights Challenge*, edited by Jacqueline Bhabha, 43–66. Cambridge, MA: MIT Press.

Blitz, Brad K. 2016. *Migration and Freedom: Mobility, Citizenship and Exclusion.* Cheltenham, UK: Edward Elgar.

Blitz, Brad K., and Maureen Lynch. 2011. "Statelessness and the Deprivation of Nationality." In *Statelessness and Citizenship: A Comparative Study on the Benefits of Nationality*, edited by Brad K. Blitz and Maureen Lynch, 1–22. Cheltenham, UK: Edward Elgar.

Bloemraad, Irene. 2015. "Reimagining the Nation in a World of Migration: Legitimacy, Political Claims-Making, and Membership in Comparative Perspective." In *Fear, Anxiety, and National Identity: Immigration and Belonging in North America and Western Europe*, edited by Nancy Foner and Patrick Simon, 59–82. New York: Russell Sage Foundation.

Bloom, Tendayi. 2016. "The Business of Noncitizenship." *Citizenship Studies* 19, no. 8: 892–906.

Bloom, Tendayi. 2017. "Members of Colonised Groups, Statelessness and the Right to Have Rights." In *Understanding Statelessness*, edited by Tendayi Bloom, Katherine Tonkiss, and Phillip Cole, 153–172. London: Routledge.

Bob, Clifford. 2005. *The Marketing of Rebellion: Insurgents, Media, and International Activism.* Cambridge: Cambridge University Press.

Bob, Clifford. 2009. "Introduction: Fighting for New Rights." In *The International Struggle for New Human Rights*, edited by Clifford Bob, 1–13. Philadelphia: University of Pennsylvania Press.

Bochenek, Michael Garcia. 2016. "What Is Happening to the Children of the Calais 'Jungle'? Children Are at Risk if Authorities Continue to Rush Dismantlement of the Notorious Refugee Camp." Human Rights Watch, October 26, 2016. https://www.hrw.org/news/2016/10/26/what-happening-children-calais-jungle.

Bolongaro, Kait. 2016. "Palestinian Syrians: Twice Refugees." *Al Jazeera*, March 23, 2016. http://www.aljazeera.com/indepth/features/2016/03/palestinian-syrians-refugees-160321055107834.html.

Boroto, M. G. 2015. Conclusions of the Conference on Ensuring Everyone's Right to Nationality: The Role of Parliaments in Preventing and Ending Statelessness. Parliament of South Africa, the Inter-Parliamentary Union, and the Office of the United Nations High Commissioner for Refugees. November 26–27, 2015. http://www.ipu.org/splz-e/captown15/outcome.pdf.

Bouie, Jamelle. 2016. "How Trump Happened." *Slate*, March 13. http://www.slate.com/articles/news_and_politics/cover_story/2016/03/how_donald_trump_happened_racism_against_barack_obama.html.

Bracey, Christopher Alan. 2016. "Michael Brown, Dignity, and Déjà Vu: From Slavery to Ferguson and Beyond." In *Ferguson's Fault Lines: The Race Quake that Rocked a Nation*, edited by Kimberly Jade Norwood, 1–16. Chicago: American Bar Association.

Brayboy, Bryan McKinley Jones, Amy J. Fann, Angelina E. Castagno, and Jessica A. Solyom. 2012. *Postsecondary Education for American Indian and Alaska Natives: Higher Education for Nation Building and Self-Determination.* ASHE Higher Education Report 37, no. 5. Hoboken, NJ: Wiley Periodicals.

Brown, Wendy. 2010. *Walled States, Waning Sovereignty.* New York: Zone Books.

Brownsword, Roger. 2014. "Human Dignity from a Legal Perspective." In *The Cambridge Handbook of Human Dignity: Interdisciplinary Perspectives.* Kindle ed., edited by Marcus Düwell, Jens Braarvig, Roger Brownsword, and Dietmar Mieth. Cambridge: Cambridge University Press.

Brubaker, Rogers. 1992. *Citizenship and Nationhood in France and Germany.* Cambridge, MA: Harvard University Press.

Bruyneel, Kevin. 2004. "Challenging American Boundaries: Indigenous People and the 'Gift' of U.S. Citizenship." *Studies in American Political Development* 18: 30–43.

Brysk, Alison. 2002. "Conclusion: From Rights to Realities." In *Globalization and Human Rights*, edited by Alison Brysk, 242–256. Berkeley: University of California Press.

Buck, Patricia, and Rachel Silver. 2013. "Tradition, Enlightenment, and the Role of Schooling in Gender Politics among Somali Girls and Women in Dadaab." In *Refugees, Immigrants, and Education in the Global South: Lives in Motion*, edited by Lesley Bartlett and Ameena Ghaffar-Kucher, 116–132. New York: Routledge.

Burger, Julian. 2016. "From Outsiders to Centre Stage: Three Decades of Indigenous Peoples' Presence at the United Nations." In *Handbook of Indigenous Peoples' Rights*, edited by Corinne Lennox and Damien Short, 315–330. London: Routledge.

Burns, Gus. 2017. "Detroit Announces Largest Residential Development in 20-plus Years." *MLive*, May 30, 2017. http://www.mlive.com/news/detroit/index.ssf/2017/05/detroit_announces_largest_resi.html.

Byrd, Nola Butler, and Menan Jangu. 2009. "'A Past Is Not a Heritage': Reclaiming Indigenous Principles for Global Justice and Education for Peoples of African Descent." In *Social Justice, Peace, and Environmental Education: Transformative Standards*, edited by Julie Andrzejewski, Marta P. Baltodano, and Linda Symcox, 193–215. New York: Routledge.

Cahn, Claude. 2015. *Human Rights, State Sovereignty, and Medical Ethics: Examining Struggles around Coercive Sterilisation of Romani Women.* Leiden: Koninklijke Brill.

Calbucura, Jorge. 2009. "Legal Process of Abolition of Collective Property: The Mapuche Case." In *Decolonising Indigenous Rights*, edited by Adolfo de Oliveira, 65–78. New York: Routledge.

Calì, Massimiliano, and Samia Sekkarie. 2015. "Much Ado about Nothing? The Economic Impact of Refugee 'Invasions.'" Brookings, September 16, 2015. http://www.brookings.edu/blogs/future-development/posts/2015/09/16-economic-impact-refugees-cali.

Campesi, Giuseppe. 2014. "Frontex, the Euro-Mediterranean Border and the Paradoxes of Humanitarian Rhetoric." *South East European Journal of Political Science (SEEJPS)* 2, no. 3: 126–134.

Campesi, Giuseppe. 2015. "Hindering the Deportation Machine: An Ethnography of Power and Resistance in Immigration Detention." *Punishment & Society* 17, no. 4: 427–453.

Caplan, Jane, and John Torpey. 2001. "Introduction." In *Documenting Individual Identity: The Development of State Practices in the Modern World*, edited by Jane Caplan and John Torpey, 1–12. Princeton, NJ: Princeton University Press.

Carpenter, R. Charli. 2007a. "Setting the Advocacy Agenda: Theorizing Issue Emergence and Nonemergence in Transnational Advocacy Networks." *International Studies Quarterly* 51: 99–120.

Carpenter, R. Charli. 2007b. "Studying Issue (Non)-Adoption in Transnational Advocacy Networks." *International Organization* 61: 643–667.

Carpenter, R. Charli. 2010. *Forgetting Children Born of War: Setting the Human Rights Agenda in Bosnia and Beyond.* New York: Columbia University Press.

Carpenter, Charli. 2014. *"Lost" Causes: Agenda Vetting in Global Issue Networks and the Shaping of Human Security.* Ithaca, NY: Cornell University Press.

Carozza, Paolo G. 2013. "Human Rights, Human Dignity, and Human Experience." In *Understanding Human Dignity*, edited by Christopher McCrudden, 615–629. Proceedings of the British Academy, 192. Oxford: Oxford University Press.

Carr, Matthew. 2012. *Fortress Europe: Dispatches from a Gated Continent.* New York: New Press.

Casati, Noemi. 2017. "How Cities Shape Refugee Centres: 'Deservingness' and 'Good Aid' in a Sicilian Town." *Journal of Ethnic and Migration Studies* 44: 792–808.

CBC News. 2014. "New Strategy Promotes Hunting as Cure to Nunavut Hunger." May 5, 2014. http://www.cbc.ca/news/canada/north/new-strategy-promotes-hunting-as-cure-to-nunavut-hunger-1.2632602.

CBS Detroit. 2017. "Dan Gilbert Apologizing after Mostly-White Ad Declaring 'See Detroit Like We Do.'" July 24, 2017. http://detroit.cbslocal.com/2017/07/24/dan-gilbert-apologizing-after-mostly-white-ad-declaring-see-detroit-like-we-do/.

CBS News St. Louis. 2014. "Ferguson Mayor Addresses Racial Tensions, Number of Black Officers in City." August 13, 2014. http://stlouis.cbslocal.com/2014/08/13/ferguson-mayor-the-african-american-community-has-something-against-law-enforcement-in-many-ways/.

Champagne, Dwayne. 2008. "From First Nations to Self-Government: A Political Legacy of Indigenous Nations in the United States." *American Behavioral Scientist* 51, no. 12: 1672–1693.

Champagne, Duane. 2012. "Indigenous, Citizens and Human Rights: The Bedouins of the Naqab." In *Indigenous (In)Justice: Human Rights Law and Bedouin Arabs in the Naqab/Negev*, edited by Ahmad Amara, Ismael Abu-Saad, and Oren Yiftachel, 255–288. Cambridge, MA: Human Rights Program at Harvard Law School, Harvard University Press.

Chatelain, Marcia, and Kaavya Asoka. 2015. "Women and Black Lives Matter: An Interview with Marcia Chatelain." *Dissent*, Summer 2015. https://www.dissentmagazine.org/article/women-black-lives-matter-interview-marcia-chatelain.

Chatelard, Géraldine. 2006. "Desert Tourism as a Substitute for Pastoralism? Tuareg in Algeria and Bedouin in Jordan." In *Nomadic Societies in the Middle East and North Africa: Entering the 21st Century*, edited by Dawn Chatty, 710–736. Leiden: Brill.

Chatty, Dawn. 2006. "Nomads of the Middle East and North Africa Facing the 21st Century." In *Nomadic Societies in the Middle East and North Africa: Entering the 21st Century*, edited by Dawn Chatty, 1–29. Leiden: Brill.

Chauvin, Sébastien, and Blanca Garcés-Mascareñas. 2012. "Beyond Informal Citizenship: The New Moral Economy of Migrant Illegality." *International Political Sociology* 6: 241–259.

Chrisafis, Angelique. 2017. "Farmer given suspended €3,000 fine for helping migrants enter France." *The Guardian*, February 10, 2017. https://www.theguardian.com/world/2017/feb/10/cedric-herrou-farmer-given-suspended-3000-fine-for-helping-migrants-enter-france.

Chuck, Elizabeth, and Perry Bacon Jr. 2016. "Obama in Michigan: 'Turn This into an Opportunity to Rebuild Flint." *NBC News*, May 4, 2016. https://www.nbcnews.com/storyline/flint-water-crisis/obama-michigan-turn-opportunity-rebuild-flint-n568086.

Clenfield, Jason. 2015. "This Swiss Lawyer Is Helping Governments Get Rich Off Selling Passports." *Bloomburg Business*, March 11, 2015. http://www.bloomberg.com/news/articles/2015-03-11/passport-king-christian-kalin-helps-nations-sell-citizenship.

Coates, Ken S. 2004. *A Global History of Indigenous Peoples: Struggle and Survival*. New York: Palgrave Macmillan.

Cobo, Martinéz. 1986. *Study of the Problem of Discrimination against Indigenous Populations*. E/CN.4/Sub.2/1986/7/Add.4.

Cohen, Deborah. 2011. *Braceros: Migrant Citizens and Transnational Subjects in the Postwar United States and Mexico*. Chapel Hill: University of North Carolina Press.

Cohen, Elizabeth F. 2009. *Semi-Citizenship in Democratic Politics*. Cambridge: Cambridge University Press.

Cohen, Elizabeth F. 2015. "The Political Economy of Immigrant Time: Rights, Citizenship, and Temporariness in the Post-1965 Era." *Polity* 47, no. 3: 337–351.

Cohen, Elizabeth F. 2018. *The Political Value of Time: Citizenship, Duration, and Democratic Justice*. Cambridge: Cambridge University Press.

Cohen, Gerard Daniel. 2012. *In War's Wake: Europe's Displaced Persons in the Postwar Order*. Oxford: Oxford University Press.

Cohen, Roger. 2016. "The World Loves Refugees, When They're Olympians." *New York Times*, August 8, 2016. http://nyti.ms/2aOqOO5.

Comisión Técnica de Apoyo a la Implantación del DNI Electrónico. 2014. "DNI electrónico: Guía de Referencia Básica." http://www.dnielectronico.es/PDFs/Guia_de_referencia_basica_v1_4.pdf.

Conifer, Dan. 2016. "Manus Island, Nauru Refugees to Be Banned from Entering Australia, Malcolm Turnbull Says." Australian Broadcasting Corporation (ABC), October 29, 2016. http://www.abc.net.au/news/2016-10-30/manus-nauru-refugees-asylum-seekers-to-be-banned-turnbull-says/7978228.

Constantine, Greg. 2015. *Nowhere People*.

Constantine, Greg. n.d. "Nowhere People." Homepage. http://www.nowherepeople.org.

Cooley, Alexander, and James Ron. 2002. "The NGO Scramble." *International Security* 27, no. 1: 5–39.

Costello, Cathryn. 2016. *The Human Rights of Migrants and Refugees in European Law*. Oxford: Oxford University Press.

Cottom, Tressie McMillan. 2015. "Race Is Always the Issue." *Atlantic*, September 17, 2015. https://www.theatlantic.com/politics/archive/2015/09/race-is-always-the-issue/405295/.

Council of Europe. 2012. "Human Rights of Roma and Travellers in Europe." Commissioner for Human Rights. https://www.coe.int/t/commissioner/source/prems/prems79611_GBR_CouvHumanRightsOfRoma_WEB.pdf.

Coutin, Susan Bibler. 2010. "Exiled by Law: Deportation and the Inviability of Life." In *The Deportation Regime: Sovereignty, Space, and the Freedom of Movement*, edited by Nicholas de Genova and Nathalie Peutz, 351–370. Durham, NC: Duke University Press.

Cowburn, Ashley. 2017. "European Court Rules Theresa May's Policy of Stripping Terror Suspects of British Citizenship Is Lawful." *Independent*, March 9, 2017. http://www.independent.co.uk/news/uk/politics/uk-strip-terror-suspect-strip-british-citzenship-rule-european-court-human-rights-eu-judges-isis-a7620126.html.

Cox, Aimee Meredith. 2015. *Shapeshifters: Black Girls and the Choreography of Citizenship*. Durham, NC: Duke University Press.

Croucher, Sheila L. 2004. *Globalization and Belonging: The Politics of Identity in a Changing World*. Lanham, MD: Rowman & Littlefield.

Culbertson, Shelly, and Louay Constant. 2015. *Education of Syrian Refugee Children: Managing the Crisis in Turkey, Lebanon, and Jordan*. Santa Monica: RAND Corporation.

Cultural Survival. 2017. "African Samburu Tribe in Solidarity with Standing Rock." January 27, 2017. https://www.culturalsurvival.org/news/african-samburu-tribe-solidarity-standing-rock.

Cunha, Darlena. 2014. "Ferguson: In Defense of Rioting." *TIME*, November 25, 2014. http://time.com/3605606/ferguson-in-defense-of-rioting/.

Cunningham, Vinson. 2015. "Humans of New York and the Cavalier Consumption of Others." *New Yorker*, November 3, 2015. http://www.newyorker.com/books/page-turner/humans-of-new-york-and-the-cavalier-consumption-of-others.

Dadigan, Marc. 2012. "Without Federal Recognition, Tribe Struggles to Protect Sacred Sites." *California Watch*, July 16, 2012. http://californiawatch.org/environment/without-federal-recognition-tribe-struggles-protect-sacred-sites-17078.

Daes, Erica-Irene. 2001. Indigenous Peoples and Their Relationship to Land. Final Report. UN Doc. E/CN.4/Sub.2/2001/21. June 11, 2001.

Daniel, E. Valentine, and John Chr. Knudsen. 1995. "Introduction." In *Mistrusting Refugees*, edited by E. Valentine Daniel and John Chr. Knudsen, 1–12. Berkeley: University of California Press.

Danish Refugee Council. 2016. "Summary of Regional Migration Trends." http://reliefweb.int/sites/reliefweb.int/files/resources/DRC%20-%20ME%20Migration%20Trends%20May.pdf.

Dao, James. 2011. "In California, Indian Tribes with Casino Money Cast Off Members." *New York Times*, December 12, 2011. http://www.nytimes.com/2011/12/13/us/california-indian-tribes-eject-thousands-of-members.html?_r=0.

Dastyari, Azadeh. 2015. *United States Migrant Interdiction and the Detention of Refugees in Guantánamo Bay*. Cambridge: Cambridge University Press.

Davila, Ana. 2015. "Drug Cartels: Where Human Trafficking and Human Smuggling Meet Today." *Huffington Post*, June 16, 2015. http://www.huffingtonpost.com/ana-davila/drug-cartels-where-human-trafficking-and-human-smuggling-meet-today_b_7588408.html.

Davis, Angela Y. 2016. *Freedom Is a Constant Struggle: Ferguson, Palestine, and the Foundations of a Movement.* Chicago: Haymarket Books.

Davis, Bob. 2016. "The Thorny Economics of Illegal Immigration. *Wall Street Journal*, February 9, 2016. http://www.wsj.com/articles/the-thorny-economics-of-illegal-immigration-1454984443.

Delgado, Richard, and Jean Stefancic, eds. 2014. *Critical Race Theory: The Cutting Edge.* 3rd ed. Philadelphia: Temple University Press.

Deloria, Vine Jr. 1999. *Spirit and Reason: The Vine Deloria, Jr., Reader.* Golden, CO: Fulcrum..

d'Errico, Peter. 2009. "American Indian Sovereignty: Now You See It, Now You Don't." In *Decolonising Indigenous Rights*, edited by Adolfo de Oliveira, 105–121. New York: Routledge.

Desmond, Matthew. 2016. *Evicted: Poverty and Profit in the American City.* New York: Crown.

de Oliveira, Adolfo. 2009. "Introduction: Decolonising Approaches to Indigenous Rights." In *Decolonising Indigenous Rights*, edited by Adolfo de Oliveira, 1–16. New York: Routledge.

de Verneuil, Maylis. 2014. "Romani Migration Resulting in Statelessness: The Case of Bosnia and Herzegovina." *Roma Rights: Journal of the European Roma Rights Centre*, 27–33. http://www.errc.org/cms/upload/file/roma-rights-1-2014-going-nowhere-western-balkan-roma-and-eu-visa-liberalisation.pdf?utm_medium=email&utm_campaign=Roma+Rights+1+2014%3A+Going+Nowhere%3F+Western+...&utm_source=YMLP&utm_term=.

Diener, Alexander C., and Joshua Hagen. 2010. "Introduction: Borders, Identity, and Geopolitics." In *Borderlines and Borderlands: Political Oddities at the Edge of the Nation-State*, edited by Alexander C. Diener and Joshua Hagen, 1–14. Lanham, MD: Rowman & Littlefield.

District Detroit. n.d. Homepage. http://www.districtdetroit.com/.

Donahue, Patrick. 2016. "Merkel's Popularity Drops to Four-Year Low after Cologne Attacks." *Bloomburg Business*, January 15, 2016. http://www.bloomberg.com/news/articles/2016-01-15/merkel-s-popularity-drops-to-four-year-low-after-cologne-attacks.

Donnelly, Jack. 2013. *International Human Rights.* 4th ed. New York: Westview Press.

Dreby, Joanna. 2010. *Divided by Borders: Mexican Immigrants and Their Children.* Berkeley: University of California Press.

Dreby, Joanna. 2015. *Everyday Illegal: When Policies Undermine Immigrant Families.* Oakland: University of California Press.

Dupré, Catherine. 2013. "Constructing the Meaning of Human Dignity: Four Questions." In *Understanding Human Dignity*, edited by Christopher McCrudden, 113–121. Proceedings of the British Academy, 192. Oxford: Oxford University Press.

DuVernay, Ava. n.d. "13th." http://www.avaduvernay.com/13th/.

Economist. 2016. "The New Political Divide." July 30, 2016. http://www.economist.com/news/leaders/21702750-farewell-left-versus-right-contest-matters-now-open-against-closed-new.

Edelman, Murray. 1988. *Constructing the Political Spectacle.* Chicago: University of Chicago Press.

Ehrenfreund, Max. 2017. "The Massive Tax Cuts for The Rich Inside the GOP Health-Care Plan." *Washington Post*, March 7, 2017. https://www.washingtonpost.com/news/wonk/wp/2017/03/07/the-massive-tax-cuts-for-the-rich-inside-the-gop-health-care-plan/?utm_term=.9d9c4bc198f8.

Eklund, Monica, Sara Högdin, and Ingegerd Rydin. 2013. "Educational Integration of Asylum-seeking and Refugee Children in Sweden." In *Migrants and Refugees: Equitable Education for Displaced Populations*, edited by Elinor L. Brown and Anna Krasteva, 73–94. Charlotte: Information Age.

Eleftheriou-Smith, Loulla-Mae. 2017. "Standing Rock Protests against Dakota Access Pipeline Erupt Anew as World Focuses on Donald Trump." *Independent*, January 24, 2017. http://www.independent.co.uk/news/world/americas/standing-rock-dakota-access-pipeline-protest-donald-trump-us-presidency-white-house-inauguration-a7542956.html.

Eligon, John. 2015. "A Year after Ferguson, Housing Segregation Defies Tools to Erase It." *New York Times*, August 8, 2015. https://www.nytimes.com/2015/08/09/us/a-year-after-ferguson-housing-segregation-defies-tools-to-erase-it.html?_r=0.

Eligon, John. 2016. "A Question of Environmental Racism in Flint." *New York Times*, January 21, 2016. https://www.nytimes.com/2016/01/22/us/a-question-of-environmental-racism-in-flint.html?_r=1.

Ellinghaus, Katherine. 2017. *Blood Will Tell: Native Americans and Assimilation Policy.* Lincoln: University of Nebraska Press.

Enders, Caty. 2017. "Republicans Move to Sell Off 3.3m Acres of National Land, Sparking Rallies." *Guardian*, January 31, 2017. https://www.theguardian.com/environment/2017/jan/31/public-lands-sell-congress-bureau-management-chaffetz.

Eng'ape E Maa Association and Indigenous Movement for Peace Advancement and Conflict Transformation (IMPACT). 2015. "Segera: A Report of Abuse, Torture and Land Grabbing in Laikipia, Kenya." August 3, 2015. https://www.culturalsurvival.org/sites/default/files/media/laikipia_report_final-1.pdf.

Engel, Else, Lea Fenner, and Martin Lücke. 2016. "Practical Tools for Combining History Learning and Human Rights Education." In *Change: History Learning and Human Rights Education*, edited by Martin Lücke, Felisa Tibbitts, Else Engel, and Lea Fenner, 53–90. Wochenschau Verlag.

Erickson, Kurt. 2017. "Foster Parents Upset by Funding Cuts." *St. Louis Post-Dispatch*, July 14, 2017. http://www.stltoday.com/news/local/govt-and-politics/foster-parents-upset-by-funding-cuts/article_876f2796-eb46-5b91-b778-346867a92d4e.html.

Errico, Stefania. 2011. "The Controversial Issue of Natural Resources: Balancing States' Sovereignty with Indigenous Peoples' Rights." In *Decolonising Indigenous Rights*, edited by Adolfo de Oliveira, 329–366. New York: Routledge.

European Commission. n.d. "EU and Roma." http://ec.europa.eu/justice/discrimination/roma/index_en.htm.

European Network on Statelessness. 2015. *No Child Should Be Stateless.* http://www.statelessness.eu/sites/www.statelessness.eu/files/ENS_NoChildStateless_final.pdf.

European Network on Statelessness. n.d. "Mission Statement." http://www.statelessness.eu/about-us/mission-statement.

European Roma Rights Centre. 2012. "Factsheet: Roma Rights in Jeopardy." February 16, 2012. http://www.errc.org/article/factsheet-roma-rights-in-jeopardy/3828.

European Roma Rights Centre, n.d. "Research and Advocacy." http://www.errc.org/research-and-advocacy.

European Union. 2012. Charter of Fundamental Rights of the European Union. *Official Journal of the European Union*, 2012/C 326/02. http://eur-lex.europa.eu/legal-content/EN/TXT/PDF/?uri=CELEX:12012P/TXT&from=EN.

Fabietti, Ugo. 2006. "Facing Change in Arabia: The Bedouin Community and the Notion of Development." In *Nomadic Societies in the Middle East and North Africa: Entering the 21st Century*, edited by Dawn Chatty, 573–598. Leiden: Brill.

Faist, Thomas, and Christian Ulbricht. 2015. "Constituting National Identity through Transnationality: Categorizations of Inequalities in German Integration Debates." In *Fear, Anxiety, and National Identity: Immigration and Belonging in North America and Western Europe*, edited by Nancy Foner and Patrick Simon, 189–212. New York: Russell Sage Foundation.

Falk, Richard. 2004. "Citizenship and Globalism: Markets, Empire, and Terrorism." In *People Out of Place: Globalization, Human Rights, and the Citizenship Gap*, edited by Alison Brysk and Gershon Shafir, 177–189. New York: Routledge.

Fan, Rebecca C. 2016. "Evolution of Indigenous Peoples' Rights and Indigenous Knowledge Debate." In *Handbook of Indigenous Peoples' Rights*, edited by Corinne Lennox and Damien Short, 237–249. London: Routledge.

Farha, Leilani. 2016. "Palestine's Latest Evictions Are a Human Rights Crisis—World Leaders Must Act." *Guardian*, August 29, 2016. https://www.theguardian.com/commentisfree/2016/aug/29/palestine-evictions-human-rights-susiya-bedouin-un-security-council.

Fassin, Didier. 2012. *Humanitarian Reason: A Moral History of the Present*. Berkeley: University of California Press.

Federal Register. 2015. "Homeless Emergency Assistance and Rapid Transition to Housing: Defining 'Chronically Homeless.'" U.S. Department of Housing and Urban Development 80, no. 233: 75791–75806. https://www.hudexchange.info/resources/documents/Defining-Chronically-Homeless-Final-Rule.pdf.

Fehrenbach, Heide. 2015. "Children and Other Civilians: Photography and the Politics of Humanitarian Image-Making." In *Humanitarian Photography: A History*, edited by Heide Fehrenbach and Davide Rodogno, 165–199. Cambridge: Cambridge University Press.

Fehrenbach, Heide, and Davide Rodogno. 2015. "The Morality of Sight: Humanitarian Photography in History." In *Humanitarian Photography: A History*, edited by Heide Fehrenbach and Davide Rodogno, 1–21. Cambridge: Cambridge University Press.

Fein, Lisa C., and Jeremy B. Straughn. 2014. "How Citizenship Matters: Narratives of Stateless and Citizenship Choice in Estonia." *Citizenship Studies 18*, no. 6–7: 690–706.

Field, Kelly. 2016. "For Native Students, Education's Promise Has Long Been Broken." *Chronicle of Higher Education* 57, no. 42 (August 5): A20–A24.

Finnemore, Martha, and Kathryn Sikkink. 1998. "International Norm Dynamics and Political Change." *International Organization* 52, no. 4: 887–917.

Flaim, Amanda. 2017. "Problems of Evidence, Evidence of Problems: Expanding Citizenship and Reproducing Statelessness among Highlanders in Northern

Thailand." In *Citizenship in Question: Evidentiary Birthright and Statelessness*, edited by Benjamin N. Lawrence and Jacqueline Stevens, 147–164. Durham, NC: Duke University Press.

Follis, Karolina S. 2015. "Responsibility, Emergency, Blame: Reporting on Migrant Deaths on the Mediterranean in the Council of Europe." *Journal of Human Rights* 14, no. 1: 41–62.

Foner, Nancy, and Patrick Simon. 2015. "Introduction." In *Fear, Anxiety, and National Identity: Immigration and Belonging in North America and Western Europe*, edited by Nancy Foner and Patrick Simon, 1–30. New York: Russell Sage Foundation.

Fraser, Nancy. 2003. "Rethinking Recognition: Overcoming Displacement and Reification in Cultural Politics." In *Recognition Struggles and Social Movements: Contested Identities, Agency and Power*, edited by Barbara Hobson, 21–32. Cambridge: Cambridge University Press.

Fresia, Marion, and Andreas Von Känel. 2015. "Beyond Space of Exception? Reflections on the Camp through the Prism of Refugee Schools." *Journal of Refugee Studies*. http://jrs.oxfordjournals.org/content/early/2015/12/02/jrs.fev016.full.

Frontex. n.d. "Western Balkan Route." http://frontex.europa.eu/trends-and-routes/western-balkan-route/.

Gall, Lydia. 2013. "Dispatches: Criminalizing Hungary's Homeless." Human Rights Watch, October 1, 2013. https://www.hrw.org/news/2013/10/01/dispatches-criminalizing-hungarys-homeless.

Gatrell, Peter. 2013. *The Making of the Modern Refugee*. Oxford: Oxford University Press.

Gellner, Ernest. 1983. *Nations and Nationalism*. Ithaca, NY: Cornell University Press.

Gentleman, Amelia. 2017. "Riot Police Stop Refugees Returning to Dunkirk Camp Destroyed by Fire." *Guardian*, April 12, 2017. https://www.theguardian.com/world/2017/apr/12/riot-police-stop-refugees-returning-to-dunkirk-camp-destroyed-by-fire.

Gerber, Paula. 2013. *Understanding Human Rights: Educational Challenges for the Future*. Cheltenham, UK: Edward Elgar.

Gerstle, Gary. 2015. "The Contradictory Character of American Nationality: A Historical Perspective." In *Fear, Anxiety, and National Identity: Immigration and Belonging in North America and Western Europe*, edited by Nancy Foner and Patrick Simon, 33–57. New York: Russell Sage Foundation.

Gettys, Travis. 2016. "New York Firefighter Charged with Setting Fire to Own Home—and Blaming It on Black Lives Matter." *RawStory*, December 8, 2016. https://www.rawstory.com/2016/12/new-york-firefighter-charged-with-setting-fire-to-own-home-and-blaming-it-on-black-lives-matter/.

Ghani, Ashraf, and Clare Lockhart. 2009. *Fixing Failed States: A Framework for Rebuilding a Fractured World*. Oxford: Oxford University Press.

Gibney, Matthew J. 2011. "The Rights of Non-citizens to Membership." In *Statelessness in the European Union: Displaced, Undocumented, Unwanted*, edited by Caroline Sawyer and Brad K. Blitz, 41–68. Cambridge: Cambridge University Press.

Gibney, Matthew. 2013. "Should Citizenship Be Conditional? The Ethics of Denationalization." *Journal of Politics 75*, no. 3: 646–658.

Gibson, Johanna. 2011. "Community Rights to Culture: The UN Declaration on the Rights of Indigenous Peoples." In *Decolonising Indigenous Rights*, edited by Adolfo de Oliveira, 433–453. New York: Routledge.

Gilbert, Jérémie. 2007. "Nomadic Territories: A Human Rights Approach to Nomadic Peoples' Land Rights." *Human Rights Law Review* 7, no. 4: 681–716.

Gilbert, Jérémie. 2014. *Nomadic Peoples and Human Rights*. New York: Routledge.

Gilbert, Jérémie, and Cathal Doyle. 2011. "A New Dawn over the Land: Shedding Light on Collective Ownership and Consent." In *Decolonising Indigenous Rights*, edited by Adolfo de Oliveira, 289–328. New York: Routledge.

Gilbertson, Ashley. 2016. "The Child Migrants of Africa: The Italian Government Has Largely Kept Reporters from Entering Shelters and Interviewing Refugees." *New York Times*, June 10, 2016. http://www.nytimes.com/2016/06/12/opinion/sunday/the-child-migrants-of-africa.html?_r=0.

Gillogly, Kathleen. 2004. "Developing the 'Hill Tribes' of Northern Thailand." In *Civilizing the Margins: Southeast Asian Government Policies for the Development of Minorities*, edited by Christopher R. Duncan, 116–149. Ithaca, NY: Cornell University Press.

Gonzalez, David, and James Estrin. 2016. "Photography Pulitzer for Coverage of Refugee Crisis." *New York Times*, April 18, 2016. http://lens.blogs.nytimes.com/2016/04/18/photography-pulitzer-for-coverage-of-refugee-crisis/.

Gonzales, Roberto G. 2016. *Lives in Limbo: Undocumented and Coming of Age in America*. Oakland: University of California Press.

Gordon, Colin. 2008. *Mapping Decline: St. Louis and the Fate of the American City*. Philadelphia: University of Pennsylvania Press.

Gordon, Colin. 2016. "Making Ferguson: Segregation and Uneven Development in St. Louis and St. Louis County." In *Ferguson's Fault Lines: The Race Quake that Rocked a Nation*, edited by Kimberly Jade Norwood, 75–91. Chicago: American Bar Association.

Gover, Kirsty. 2016. "Indigenous Membership and Human Rights: When Self-Identification Meets Self-Constitution." In *Handbook of Indigenous Peoples' Rights*, edited by Corinne Lennox and Damien Short, 35–48. London: Routledge.

Government of the Netherlands. n.d. "Compulsory Identification." https://www.government.nl/topics/identification-documents/contents/compulsory-identification.

Grahl-Madsen, Atle. 1966. *The Status of Refugees in International Law*. Vol. 1. (Leiden: A.W. Sijthoff).

Gray, Andrew. 2009. "Indigenous Peoples and Their Territories." In *Decolonising Indigenous Rights*, edited by Adolfo de Oliveira, 17–44. New York: Routledge.

Gray, Bryce. 2017. "St. Louis' Largest Homeless Shelter Emptied Following Order from City." *St. Louis Post-Dispatch*, April 2, 2017. http://www.stltoday.com/news/local/govt-and-politics/st-louis-largest-homeless-shelter-emptied-following-order-from-city/article_0027f20a-691c-5125-a902-e1ffe5ff7be7.html.

Gregg, Benjamin. 2016. *The Human Rights State: Justice within and beyond Sovereign Nations*. Philadelphia: University of Pennsylvania Press.

Guardian. 2016. "Operation to Clear Calais Refugee Camp Finishes Ahead of Schedule." October 26, 2016. https://www.theguardian.com/world/2016/oct/26/operation-to-clear-calais-refugee-camp-finishes-ahead-of-schedule.

Guidelli, Matteo. 2016. "Scafisti traditi dal salvagente erano gli unici a bordo ad averlo." *La Sicilia* (Siracusa edition), June 1, 2016: 7.

Gündoğdu, Ayten. 2015. *Rightlessness in an Age of Rights: Hannah Arendt and the Contemporary Struggles of Migrants.* Oxford: Oxford University Press.

Gutmann, Amy. 1994. "Introduction." In *Multiculturalism: Examining the Politics of Recognition,* edited by Amy Gutmann, 3–24. Princeton, NJ: Princeton University Press.

Häkli, Jouni. 2015. "The Border in the Pocket: The Passport as a Boundary Object." In *Borderities and the Politics of Contemporary Mobile Borders,* edited by Anne-Laure Amilhat Szary and Frédéric Giraut, 85–99. London: Palgrave Macmillan.

Hanjian, Clark. 2003. *The Sovrien: An Exploration of the Right to Be Stateless.* Vineyard Haven, MA: Polyspire.

Hanks, Jane Richardson, and Lucien Mason Hanks. 2001. *Tribes of the Northern Thailand Frontier.* New Haven, CT: Yale University Southeast Asia Studies.

Hanson, Gordon H. 2007. "The Economic Logic of Illegal Migration." Council on Foreign Relations, April 2007. http://www.cfr.org/immigration/economic-logic-illegal-immigration/p12969.

Haque, Fahima, and Lela Moore. 2018. "How Some People Avoid Racially Tinged Brushes with the Law." *New York Times,* May 11, 2018. https://www.nytimes.com/2018/05/11/us/racism-america-experiences.html.

Harjo, Suzan Shown. 2014. *Nation to Nation: Treaties between the United States and American Indian Nations.* Washington, DC: Smithsonian Institution.

Harris, LaDonna, Stephen M. Sachs, and Barbara Morris. 2011. *Re-Creating the Circle: The Renewal of American Indian Self-Determination.* Albuquerque: University of New Mexico Press.

Hartigan, John Jr. 1999. *Racial Situations: Class Predicaments of Whiteness in Detroit.* Princeton, NJ: Princeton University Press.

Haygood, Wil. 2010. "Iroquois Nationals lacrosse Team Asks White House to Honor Sovereign Passports." *Washington Post,* July 14, 2010. http://www.washingtonpost.com/wp-dyn/content/article/2010/07/13/AR2010071305993.html.

Hayward, Clarissa Rile. 2013. *How Americans Make Race: Stories, Institutions, Spaces.* Cambridge: Cambridge University Press.

Heater, Derek. 1999. *What Is Citizenship?* Cambridge, MA: Polity Press.

Henley & Partners. 2016. Henley & Partners Visa Restrictions Index. http://visaindex.com/#.

Hibbard, Matthew. 2015. "Metro Campaign Encourages Everyone to 'Don't Be That Guy.'" *Metro St. Louis,* November 19, 2015. https://www.metrostlouis.org/nextstop/metro-campaign-encourages-everyone-to-dont-be-that-guy/.

Hodgson, Dorothy L. 2011. *Being Maasai, Becoming Indigenous: Postcolonial Politics in a Neoliberal World.* Bloomington: Indiana University Press.

Holland, Tracey, and J. Paul Martin. 2017. "Human Rights Education's Role in Peacebuilding: Lessons from the Field." In *Human Rights Education: Theory, Research, Praxis,* edited by Monisha Bajaj, 267–290. Philadelphia: University of Pennsylvania Press.

Holmes, Thalia. 2012. "Rwanda Cancels Exiles' Passports." *Mail & Guardian,* November 30, 2012. http://mg.co.za/article/2012-11-30-00-rwanda-cancels-exiles-passports.

Homewood, Katherine, Patti Kristjanson, and Pippa Chenevix Trench. 2009. "Changing Land Use, Livelihoods and Wildlife Conservation in Maasailand." In *Staying Maasai? Changing Land Use, Conservation and Development in East African Rangelands*, edited by Katherine Homewood, Patti Kristjanson, and Pippa Chenevix Trench, 1–42. New York: Springer.

Hoover, Elizabeth. 2018. "'You Can't Say You're Sovereign If You Can't Feed Yourself': Defining and Enacting Food Sovereignty in American Indian Community Gardening." *American Indian Culture and Research Journal* 41, no 3: 31–70.

Hopgood, Stephen. 2006. *Keepers of the Flame: Understanding Amnesty International.* Ithaca, NY: Cornell University Press.

Housing Authority of St. Louis County. n.d. "Housing: Housing Choice Voucher (Section 8)." http://www.haslc.com/housing/housing-choice-voucher/.

Howard-Hassmann, Rhoda E. 2015. "Introduction: The Human Right to Citizenship." In *The Human Right to Citizenship: A Slippery Concept*, edited by Rhoda E. Howard-Hassmann and Margaret Walton-Roberts, 1–18. Philadelphia: University of Pennsylvania Press.

Huetteman, Emmarie. 2016. "U.S. Placed Immigrant Children with Traffickers, Report Says." *New York Times*, January 28, 2016. http://www.nytimes.com/2016/01/29/us/politics/us-placed-immigrant-children-with-traffickers-report-says.html?_r=0.

Human Rights Education Associates. Homepage. www.hrea.org.

Human Rights Watch. 2007. "Discrimination against Ethnic Nepali Children in Bhutan." September 2007. https://www.hrw.org/news/2007/10/03/discrimination-against-ethnic-nepali-children-bhutan#.

Human Rights Watch. 2013. "Israel: Bedouin Facing Mass Evictions from Their Land: Draft Law Threatens Stepped-Up Demolition of Longstanding Villages." August 30, 2013. https://www.hrw.org/news/2013/08/30/israel-bedouin-facing-mass-evictions-their-land.

Human Rights Watch. 2014. "'You Don't Have Rights Here': US Border Screening and Returns of Central Americans to Risk of Serious Harm." October 16, 2014. https://www.hrw.org/report/2014/10/16/you-dont-have-rights-here/us-border-screening-and-returns-central-americans-risk.

Human Rights Watch. 2015a. "Dominican Republic: Thousands at Risk of Expulsion to Haiti." June 30, 2015. https://www.hrw.org/news/2015/06/30/dominican-republic-thousands-risk-expulsion-haiti.

Human Rights Watch. 2015b. "We Are Dominican: Arbitrary Deprivation in the Dominican Republic." July 1, 2015. https://www.hrw.org/report/2015/07/01/we-are-dominican/arbitrary-deprivation-nationality-dominican-republic.

Human Rights Watch. 2015c. "World Report 2015: Australia, Events of 2014." https://www.hrw.org/world-report/2015/country-chapters/australia.

Human Rights Watch. 2016a. "'Why Are You Keeping Me Here?' Unaccompanied Children Detained in Greece." September 8, 2016. https://www.hrw.org/report/2016/09/08/why-are-you-keeping-me-here/unaccompanied-children-detained-greece.

Human Rights Watch. 2016b. "World Report 2016: Australia, Events of 2015." https://www.hrw.org/world-report/2016/country-chapters/australia.

Human Rights Watch. 2017. "Thailand: Investigate Army Killing of Teenage Activist: Ethnic Lahu Film Producer Shot Dead during Anti-Drug Operation." March 20, 2017. https://www.hrw.org/news/2017/03/20/thailand-investigate-army-killing-teenage-activist.

Hunt, Lynn. 2008. *Inventing Human Rights: A History*. New York: W. W. Norton.

Hyndman, Jennifer. 2000. *Managing Displacement: Refugees and the Politics of Humanitarianism*. Minneapolis: University of Minnesota Press.

Ingleby, David, Sander Kramer, and Michael S. Merry. 2013. "Educational Challenges Raised by Refugee and Asylum-Seeking Children and Other Newcomers: The Dutch Response." In *Migrants and Refugees: Equitable Education for Displaced Populations*, edited by Elinor L. Brown and Anna Krasteva, 29–50. Charlotte: Information Age.

Institute on Statelessness and Inclusion. 2014. *The World's Stateless*. http://www.institutesi.org/worldsstateless.pdf.

Institute on Statelessness and Inclusion. n.d.a. "Our Strategies and Objectives for ful-filling Our Mission Include." http://www.institutesi.org/about/whatwedo.php.

Institute on Statelessness and Inclusion. n.d.b. "What We Do." http://www.institutesi.org/about/whatwedo.php.

International Campaign for Tibet. 2015. "'A Policy Alienating Tibetans': The Denial of Passports to Tibetans as China Intensifies Control." http://www.savetibet.org/policy-alienating-tibetans-denial-passports-tibetans-china-intensifies-control/.

International Labour Organization. n.d.a "C169—Indigenous and Tribal Peoples Convention, 1989 (No. 169)." http://www.ilo.org/dyn/normlex/en/f?p=NORMLEX PUB:12100:0::NO::P12100_ILO_CODE:C169.

International Labour Organization. n.d.b. "Ratifications of C169—Indigenous and Tribal Peoples Convention, 1989 (No. 169)." http://www.ilo.org/dyn/normlex/en/f?p=1000 :11300:0::NO:11300:P11300_INSTRUMENT_ID:312314.

International Organization for Migration. n.d. "Key Migration Terms." http://www.iom.int/key-migration-terms#Irregular-migration.

International Work Group for Indigenous Affairs. n.d. "Who Are the Indigenous Peoples?" http://www.iwgia.org/culture-and-identity/identification-of-indigenous-peoples.

Isin, Engin F. 2002. *Being Political: Genealogies of Citizenship*. Minneapolis: University of Minnesota Press.

Isin, Engin F. 2009. "Citizenship in flux: The Figure of the Activist Citizen." *Subjectivity* 29: 367–388.

Isin, Engin F. 2012. *Citizens without Frontiers*. New York: Bloomsbury.

http://www.iwgia.org/culture-and-identity/identification-of-indigenous-peoples.

Isquith, Elias. 2013. "Obama Laughs Off GOP Critics." *Salon*, September 26, 2013. http://www.salon.com/2013/09/26/obama_laughs_off_gop_critics/.

Izsák, Rita. 2015. "Report of the Special Rapporteur on Minority Issues, Rita Izsák: Comprehensive Study of the Human Rights Situation of Roma Worldwide, with a Particular Focus on the Phenomenon of anti-Gypsyism." United Nations General Assembly, Human Rights Council, May 11, 2015. http://www.ohchr.org/EN/Issues/Minorities/SRMinorities/Pages/GlobalStudyonRomaworldwide.aspx.

Jain, Anil, Arun A. Ross, and Karthik Nandakumar. 2011. *Introduction to Biometrics*. New York: Springer.

Jarvis, Brooke. 2017. "Who Decides Who Counts as Native American?" *New York Times*, January 18, 2017. https://www.nytimes.com/2017/01/18/magazine/who-decides-who-counts-as-native-american.html?_r=0.

Johnson, Heather L. 2014. *Borders, Asylum and Global Non-Citizenship.* Cambridge: Cambridge University Press.

Johnson, Heather L. 2016. "These Fine Lines: Locating Noncitizenship in Political Protest in Europe." *Citizenship Studies* 19, no. 8: 951–965.

Joppke, Christian. 2010. *Citizenship and Immigration.* Cambridge: Polity Press.

Kanstroom, Daniel. 2017. "Afterword." In *Citizenship in Question: Evidentiary Birthright and Statelessness*, edited by Benjamin N. Lawrence and Jacqueline Stevens, 241–246. Durham,NC: Duke University Press.

Karlsen, Elibritt. 2016. "Australia's Offshore Processing of Asylum Seekers in Nauru and PNG: A Quick Guide to Statistics and Resources." Parliament of Australia, June 30, 2016. http://www.aph.gov.au/About_Parliament/Parliamentary_Departments/Parliamentary_Library/pubs/rp/rp1516/Quick_Guides/Offshore.

Kateb, George. 2011. *Human Dignity.* Cambridge. MA: Harvard University Press.

Keck, Margaret, and Kathryn Sikkink. 1998. *Activists beyond Borders: Advocacy Networks in International Politics.* Ithaca, NY: Cornell University Press.

Keeler, Jacqueline. 2016. "Oregon Militia Nuts Hold Paiute History, Artifacts Hostage." *Indian Country Today*, January 19, 2016. https://indiancountrymedianetwork.com/news/native-news/oregon-militia-nuts-hold-paiute-history-artifacts-hostage/.

Kenna, Padraic, and Guillem Fernàndez Evangelista. 2013. "Applying a Human Rights-Based Approach to Homelessness—from Theory to Practice." In *Mean Streets: A Report on the Criminalisation of Homelessness in Europe*, edited by Guillem Fernàndez Evangelista and Samara Jones, 33–51. Housing Rights Watch. http://www.housingrightswatch.org/sites/default/files/4.%20Chapter%201.pdf.

Kennedy, Merrit. 2016. "Native American Tribe Says Oregon Armed Occupiers Are Desecrating Sacred Land." National Public Radio (NPR), January 6, 2016. http://www.npr.org/sections/thetwo-way/2016/01/06/462179325/native-american-tribe-says-oregon-armed-occupiers-are-desecrating-sacred-land.

Kinder, Kimberly. 2016. *DIY Detroit: Making Do in a City without Services.* Minneapolis: University of Minnesota Press.

Kingston, Lindsey N. 2012. "Statelessness and Issue (Non-)Emergence." *Forced Migration Review* 40. http://www.fmreview.org/young-and-out-of-place/kingston.html.

Kingston, Lindsey N. 2013. "'A Forgotten Human Rights Crisis': Statelessness and Issue (Non)Emergence." *Human Rights Review* 14, no. 2: 73–87.

Kingston, Lindsey N. 2014. "Statelessness as a Lack of Functioning Citizenship." *Tilburg Law Review* 19: 127–135.

Kingston, Lindsey N. 2015. "The Destruction of Identity: Cultural Genocide and Indigenous Peoples." *Journal of Human Rights* 14, no. 1: 63–83.

Kingston, Lindsey N. 2017a. "Bringing Rwandan Refugees 'Home': The Cessation Clause, Statelessness, and Forced Repatriation." *Journal of International Refugee Law* 29, no. 3: 417–437.

Kingston, Lindsey N. 2017b. "Worthy of Rights: Statelessness as a Cause and Symptom of Marginalization." In *Understanding Statelessness*, edited by Tendayi Bloom, Katherine Tonkiss, and Philip Cole: 17–34. New York: Routledge.

Kingston, Lindsey N. 2018. "Biometric Identification, Displacement, and Protection Gaps." In *Digital Lifeline? ICTs for Refugees and Displaced Persons*, edited by Carleen Maitland. Cambridge, MA: MIT Press.

Kingston, Lindsey N., and Saheli Datta. 2012. "Strengthening the Norms of Global Responsibility: Structural Violence in Relation to Internal Displacement and Statelessness." *Global Responsibility to Protect* 4: 475–504.

Kingston, Lindsey N., and Kathryn Stam. 2017. "Recovering from Statelessness: Resettled Bhutanese-Nepali and Karen Refugees Reflect on Lack of Legal Nationality." *Journal of Human Rights* 16, no. 4: 389–406.

Kingsley, Patrick. 2016. "Tens of Thousands Migrate through Balkans since Route Declared Shut." *Guardian*, August 30, 2016. https://www.theguardian.com/world/2016/aug/30/tens-of-thousands-migrate-through-balkans-since-route-declared-shut.

Kinney, Rebecca J. 2016. *Beautiful Wasteland: The Rise of Detroit as America's Postindustrial Frontier.* Minneapolis: University of Minnesota Press.

Koch, Bradley. 2015. "Native American/Indian, Asia/Oriental, Latino/Hispanic . . . Who Cares?" In *Getting Real about Race: Hoodies, Mascots, Model Minorities, and Other Conversations*, edited by Stephanie M. McClure and Cherise A. Harris, 259–267. Thousand Oaks, CA: Sage.

Koslowski, Rey. 2011. "Global Mobility Regimes: A Conceptual Framework." In *Global Mobility Regimes*, edited by Rey Koslowski, 1–28. New York: Palgrave Macmillan.

Kotef, Hagar. 2015. *Movement and the Ordering of Freedom: On Liberal Governances of Mobility.* Durham, NC: Duke University Press.

Krasteva, Anna. 2013. "Integrating the Most Vulnerable: Educating Refugee Children in the European Union." In *Migrants and Refugees: Equitable Education for Displaced Populations*, edited by Elinor L. Brown and Anna Krasteva, 3–28. Charlotte: Information Age.

Krause, Monika. 2011. "Stateless People and Undocumented Migrants: An Arendtian Perspective." In *Statelessness in the European Union: Displaced, Undocumented, Unwanted*, edited by Caroline Sawyer and Brad K. Blitz, 22–40. Cambridge: Cambridge University Press.

Krauze, León. 2016. "Is the Mexican Government Finally Fighting Back against Donald Trump? *New Yorker*, February 27, 2016. http://www.newyorker.com/news/news-desk/is-the-mexican-government-finally-fighting-back-against-donald-trump.

Kristof, Nicholas. 2016a. "Do You Care More About a Dog Than a Refugee?" *New York Times*, August 18, 2016. http://nyti.ms/2bpjrA3.

Kristof, Nicholas. 2016b. "Anne Frank Today Is a Syrian Girl." *New York Times*, August 25, 2016. http://nyti.ms/2byDDiG.

Krogstad, Jens Manuel. 2016. "U.S. Border Apprehensions of Families and Unaccompanied Children Jump Dramatically." Pew Research Center, May 4, 2016. http://www.pewresearch.org/fact-tank/2016/05/04/u-s-border-apprehensions-of-families-and-unaccompanied-children-jump-dramatically/.

Krogstad, Jens Manuel, Jeffrey S. Passel, and D'Vera Cohn. 2016. "5 Facts about Illegal Immigration in the U.S." Pew Research Center, November 3, 2016. http://www.pewresearch.org/fact-tank/2016/11/03/5-facts-about-illegal-immigration-in-the-u-s/.

Kukutai, Tahu. 2011. "Building Ethnic Boundaries in New Zealand: Representations of Maori Identity in the Census." In *Indigenous Peoples and Demography: The Complex Relation between Identity and Statistics*, edited by Per Axelsson and Peter Sköld, 33–54. New York: Berghahn Books.

Kymlicka, Will. 1995. *Multicultural Citizenship: A Liberal Theory of Minority Rights*. Oxford: Oxford University Press.

Landolt, Patricia, and Luin Goldring. 2016. "Assembling Noncitizenship through the Work of Conditionality." *Citizenship Studies* 19, no. 8: 853–869.

Larimer, Sarah. 2016. "Some Blamed 'BLM' for a House Fire. Officials Say It Was Started by the Firefighter Who Lived There." *Washington Post*, December 9, 2016. https://www.washingtonpost.com/news/post-nation/wp/2016/12/09/some-blamed-blm-for-a-house-fire-officials-say-it-was-started-by-the-firefighter-who-lived-there/?utm_term=.a4176048eb90.

Law Centres Network. 2015. "Keep Children's Best Interests at Heart of Asylum System—New Report." November 9, 2015. http://www.lawcentres.org.uk/policy/news/news/keep-children-s-best-interests-at-heart-of-asylum-system-new-report.

Lechte, John, and Saul Newman. 2013. *Agamben and the Politics of Human Rights: Statelessness, Images, Violence*. Edinburgh: Edinburgh University Press.

Lederer, Shannon. 2015. "Top 10 Ways Guest Worker Visa Programs Undermine Immigrant Rights." AFL-CIO, September 9, 2015. http://www.aflcio.org/Blog/Political-Action-Legislation/Top-10-Ways-Guest-Worker-Visa-Programs-Undermine-Immigrant-Rights.

Legal Aid Society—Employment Law Center. n.d. "Undocumented Workers: Employment Rights." http://las-elc.org/fact-sheets/undocumented-workers-employment-rights.

Lennox, Corinne, and Damien Short. 2016. "Introduction." In *Handbook of Indigenous Peoples' Rights*, edited by Corinne Lennox and Damien Short, 1–10. London: Routledge.

Leuchter, Noa. 2014. "Creating Other Options: Negotiating the Meanings of Citizenships." *Citizenship Studies 18*, no. 6–7: 776–790.

Levin, Dan. 2017. "Foreign Farmworkers in Canada Fear Deportation if They Complain." *New York Times*, August 13, 2017. https://www.nytimes.com/2017/08/13/world/canada/canada-migrants-temporary-farmworkers-program.html?smprod=nytcore-iphone&smid=nytcore-iphone-share&_r=0.

Lidchi, Henrietta. 2015. "Finding the Right Image: British Development NGOs and the Regulation of Imagery." In *Humanitarian Photography: A History*, edited by Heide Fehrenbach and Davide Rodogno, 275–296. Cambridge: Cambridge University Press.

Lightfoot, Sheryl R. 2016. "Indigenous Mobilization and Activism in the UN System." In *Handbook of Indigenous Peoples' Rights*, edited by Corinne Lennox and Damien Short, 253–267. London: Routledge.

Lipschutz, Ronnie D. 2004. "Constituting Political Community: Globalization, Citizenship, and Human Rights." In *People Out of Place: Globalization, Human Rights, and the Citizenship Gap*, edited by Alison Brysk and Gershon Shafir, 29–51. New York: Routledge.

López, Ian Haney. 2006. *White By Law: The Legal Construction of Race*, 10th Anniversary Edition. New York: New York University Press.

Lohoff, Markus. 2015. "Beyond Mass Media: Representations of War between Art and Journalism." In *Representations of War, Migration, and Refugeehood: Interdisciplinary Perspectives*, edited by Daniel H. Rellstab and Christiane Schlote, 64–89. New York: Routledge.

Long, Katy. 2011. "Permanent Crises? Unlocking the Protracted Displacement of Refugees and Internally Displaced Persons." Refugees Studies Centre, Oxford Department of International Development, University of Oxford. https://www.rsc.ox.ac.uk/publications/permanent-crises-unlocking-the-protracted-displacement-of-refugees-and-internally-displaced-persons.

Lowe, Keith. 2012. *Savage Continent: Europe in the Aftermath of World War II.* New York: Picador, St. Martin's Press.

Lücke, Martin. 2016. "The Change Approach for Combining History Learning and Human Rights Education." In *Change: History Learning and Human Rights Education*, edited by Martin Lücke, Felisa Tibbitts, Else Engel, and Lea Fenner, 39–49. Wochenschau Verlag.

Luna-Firebaugh, Eileen M. 2002. "The Border Crossed Us: Border Crossing Issues of the Indigenous Peoples of the Americas." *Wicazo Sa Review* 17, no. 1: 159–181.

Lusher, Adam. 2016. "Racism Unleashed: True Extent of the 'Explosion of Blatant Hate' that Followed Brexit Result Revealed." *Independent*, July 29, 2016. http://www.independent.co.uk/news/uk/politics/brexit-racism-uk-post-referendum-racism-hate-crime-eu-referendum-racism-unleashed-poland-racist-a7160786.html.

Lynch, Maureen. 2010. "Without Face or Future: Stateless Infants, Children, and Youth." In *Children and Migration: At the Crossroads of Resiliency and Vulnerability*, edited by Marisa O. Ensor and Elżbieta M. Goździak: 117–140. New York: Palgrave Macmillan.

Lynch, Maureen, and Brad K. Blitz. 2011. "Summary and Conclusions." In *Statelessness and Citizenship: A Comparative Study on the Benefits of Nationality*, edited by Brad K. Blitz and Maureen Lynch: 194–208. Cheltenham: Edward Elgar.

MacDonald, Christine. 2016. "Detroit Population Rank Is Lowest since 1850." *Detroit News*, May 20, 2016. http://www.detroitnews.com/story/news/local/detroit-city/2016/05/19/detroit-population-rank-lowest-since/84574198/.

Macklin, Audrey. 2007. "Who Is the Citizen's Other? Considering the Heft of Citizenship." *Theoretical Inquiries in Law 8*, no. 2: 333–366.

Macklin, Audrey. 2015. "Sticky Citizenship." In *The Human Right to Citizenship: A Slippery Concept*, edited by Rhoda E. Howard-Hassmann and Margaret Walton-Roberts, 223–239. Philadelphia: University of Pennsylvania Press.

MacMillan, Fiona. 2015. "Cultural Property and Community Rights to Cultural Heritage." In *Property and Human Rights in a Global Context*, edited by Ting Xu and Jean Allain, 41–62. Oxford: Hart.

Malik, A. Sami. 2016. "Boosting Birth Registration in Pakistan with Mobile Phones." United Nations Children's Fund (UNICEF). http://www.unicef.org/health/pakistan_90880.html.

Malkki, Liisa H. 1996. "Speechless Emissaries: Refugees, Humanitarianism, and Dehistoricization." *Cultural Anthopology* 11, no. 3: 377–404.

Manby, Bronwen. 2009. "Citizenship the Most Important Right of All." *African Arguments*, October 12, 2009. http://africanarguments.org/2009/10/12/citizenship-the-most-important-right-of-all/.

Manjoo, Rashida. 2012. "Continuum of Injustice: Women, Violence, and Housing Rights." In *Indigenous (In)Justice: Human Rights Law and Bedouin Arabs in the Naqab/Negev*, edited by Ahmad Amara, Ismael Abu-Saad, and Oren Yiftachel, 195–226. Cambridge, MA: Human Rights Program at Harvard Law School, Harvard University Press.

Marshall, T. H. 1950. *Citizenship and Social Class and Other Essays.* Cambridge: Cambridge University Press.

Marshall, T. H. 1965. *Class, Citizenship and Social Development: Essays by T. H. Marshall.* New York: Doubleday.

Martínez Cobo, José R. 1987. *Study of the Problem of Discrimination against Indigenous Populations.* Vol. 5: *Conclusions, Proposals and Recommendations.* United Nations publication (Sales No. E.86.XIV.3). New York: United Nations.

Massey, Hugh. 2010. "UNHCR and *De Facto* Statelessness." United Nations High Commissioner for Refugees, Legal and Protection Policy Research Series. http://www.unhcr.org/4bc2ddeb9.pdf.

Mau, Steffen. 2010. "Mobility Citizenship, Inequality, and the Liberal State." *International Political Sociology* 4, no. 4: 339–361.

McAndrew, Mike, and John Mariani. 2010. "Passport Predicament Keeps Iroquois Nationals Team Grounded in New York City." *Post-Standard*, July 13, 2010. http://www.syracuse.com/news/index.ssf/2010/07/passport_predicament_keeps_iro.html.

McAuley, James. 2017. "The Calais 'Jungle' Is Gone, but France's Migrant Crisis Is Far from Over." *Washington Post*, June 10, 2017. https://www.washingtonpost.com/world/europe/the-calais-jungle-is-gone-but-frances-migrant-crisis-is-far-from-over/2017/06/09/45780938-0193-4adf-b318-923c1745abf3_story.html?utm_term=.2ca23886af8c.

McBride, Kelly, and Lindsey N. Kingston. 2014. "Legal Invisibility and the Revolution: Statelessness in Egypt." *Human Rights Review* 15, no. 2: 159–175.

McDougall, Doug. 2008. "'Why Do the Italians Hate Us?'" *Guardian*, August 17, 2008. https://www.theguardian.com/lifeandstyle/2008/aug/17/familyandrelationships.roma.

McNevin, Anne. 2011. *Contesting Citizenship: Irregular Migrants and New Frontiers of the Political.* New York: Columbia University Press.

McPherson, Melinda. 2007. *Refugee Women, Representation and Education: Creating a Discourse of Self-Authorship and Potential.* London: Routledge.

Médecins Sans Frontières. 2016. "Syria: MSF-supported Hospital Hit by Airstrikes." February 9, 2016. http://www.msf.org/article/syria-msf-supported-hospital-hit-airstrikes.

Meer, Nasar, Varun Uberoi, and Tariq Modood. 2015. "Nationhood and Muslims in Britain." In *Fear, Anxiety, and National Identity: Immigration and Belonging in North America and Western Europe*, edited by Nancy Foner and Patrick Simon, 169–188. New York: Russell Sage Foundation.

Mekhennet, Souad. 2011. "A 50-Year Journey for Turkey and Germany." *New York Times*, October 30, 2011. http://www.nytimes.com/2011/10/31/world/europe/turks-recall-german-guest-worker-program.html.

Merkelson, Suzanne. 2010. "Why the Iroquois Lacrosse Team Couldn't Travel Abroad." *Foreign Policy*, July 19, 2010. http://foreignpolicy.com/2010/07/19/why-the-iroquois-lacrosse-team-couldnt-travel-abroad/.

Michigan Gaming Control Board. 2017. "Detroit casinos provide nearly $2 billion in taxes for public education, thousands of jobs since 1997 Michigan Gaming Act signed." July 17, 2017. https://www.michigan.gov/som/0,4669,7-192-29701_74909_74922-426371--,00.html

Migrant Offshore Aid Station. n.d. "Mission: Mediterranean Sea." https://www.moas.eu/central-mediterranean/.

Miller, Bruce Granville. 2008. *Invisible Indigenes: The Politics of Nonrecognition.* Lincoln: University of Nebraska Press.

Miller, Karen R. 2015. *Managing Inequality: Northern Racial Liberalism in Interwar Detroit.* New York: New York University Press.

Mingst, Karen A., and Ivan M. Arreguín-Toft. 2014. *Essentials of International Relations.* 6th ed. New York: W. W. Norton.

Mitchell, Don. 2003. *The Right to the City: Social Justice and the Fight for Public Space.* New York: Guilford Press.

Monmouth University. 2016. "Race Relations Worsen." Monmouth University Polling Institute, July 19, 2016. https://www.monmouth.edu/polling-institute/reports/MonmouthPoll_US_071916/.

Mörkenstam, Ulf. 2015. "Recognition *as if* Sovereigns? A Procedural Understanding of Indigenous Self-Determination." *Citizenship Studies* 19, no. 6-7: 634–648.

Morsink, Johannes. 1999. *The Universal Declaration of Human Rights: Origins, Drafting, and Intent.* Philadelphia: University of Pennsylvania Press.

Morsink, Johannes. 2009. *Inherent Human Rights: Philosophical Roots of the Universal Declaration.* Philadelphia: University of Pennsylvania Press.

Motaparthy, Priyanka. 2017. "Standing Rock's Next Stand: Fight to Protect Indigenous People's Rights in the US Continues." Human Rights Watch, March 9, 2017. https://www.hrw.org/news/2017/03/09/standing-rocks-next-stand.

Motoc, Catrinel. 2017. "'They Are Throwing Us on the Street like Dogs'—Europe Abandons the Roma in Italy." Amnesty International, April 7, 2017. https://www.amnesty.org/en/latest/news/2017/04/they-are-throwing-us-on-the-street-like-dogs-europe-abandons-the-roma-in-italy/.

Mountz, Alison. 2010. *Seeking Asylum: Human Smuggling and Bureaucracy at the Border.* Minneapolis: University of Minnesota Press.

Muntet, Stephen K. 2016. "A Cow Is Life: The Pokot-Turkana Conflict." *Cultural Survival Quarterly* 40, no. 2. https://www.culturalsurvival.org/publications/cultural-survival-quarterly/cow-life-pokot-turkana-conflict.

Narayan, Chandrika. 2016. "Little Boy in Aleppo Is a Vivid Reminder of War's Horror." CNN, August 18, 2016. http://www.cnn.com/2016/08/17/world/syria-little-boy-airstrike-victim/.

National Alliance to End Homelessness. 2016. "The State of Homelessness in America." http://endhomelessness.org/wp-content/uploads/2016/10/2016-soh.pdf.

National Archives. "Declaration of Independence: A Transcript." https://www.archives.gov/founding-docs/declaration-transcript.

National Coalition for the Homeless. 2009. "Why Are People Homeless?" http://www.nationalhomeless.org/factsheets/Why.pdf.

National Economic & Social Rights Initiative. n.d. "What Is the Human Right to Housing?" https://www.nesri.org/programs/what-is-the-human-right-to-housing.

National Public Radio. 2017. "Charlottesville Victim Heather Heyer 'Stood Up' against What She Felt Was Wrong." August 13, 2017. http://www.npr.org/sections/thetwo-way/2017/08/13/543175919/violence-in-charlottesville-claims-3-victims.

Natter, Ari. 2017. "Dakota Access Builder Compares Pipeline Protestors to Terrorists." *Bloomburg*, February 15, 2017. https://www.bloomberg.com/news/articles/2017-02-15/dakota-access-builder-compares-pipeline-protesters-to-terrorists.

Neilson, Susie. 2016. "The Media's Standing Rock Problem Looks a lot like Its Black Lives Matter Problem." *Quartz*, November 22, 2016. https://qz.com/843368/false-balance-in-the-coverage-of-the-police-violence-at-standing-rock-is-undermining-the-nodapl-movement/.

Ngoitiko, Maanda, and Fred Nelson. 2013. "What Africa Can Learn from Tanzania's Remarkable Masai Lands Rights Victory." *Guardian*, October 8, 2013. https://www.theguardian.com/global-development/poverty-matters/2013/oct/08/africa-tanzania-masai-land-rights-victory.

Nicholls, Walter J. 2013. *The DREAMers: How the Undocumented Youth Movement Transformed the Immigrant Rights Debate*. Stanford: Stanford University Press.

Nissinen, Sanna. 2015. "Dilemmas of Ethical Practice in the Production of Contemporary Humanitarian Photography." In *Humanitarian Photography: A History*, edited by Heide Fehrenbach and Davide Rodogno, 297–321. Cambridge: Cambridge University Press.

Nolan, Aoife. 2011. "'Aggravated Violations,' Roma Housing Rights and Forced Expulsions in Italy: Recent Developments under the European Social Charter Collective Complaints System." *Human Rights Law Review* 11, no. 2: 343–361.

Norman, Emma S. 2017. "Standing Up for Inherent Rights: The Role of Indigenous-Led Activism in Protecting Sacred Waters and Ways of Life." *Society & Natural Resources* 30, no. 4: 537–553.

Norman, Jane, and Caitlyn Gribbin. 2017. "Islamic State Fighter Khaled Sharrouf Becomes First to Lose Citizenship under Anti-Terror Laws." ABC News, February 10, 2017. http://www.abc.net.au/news/2017-02-11/islamic-state-fighter-khaled-sharrouf-stripped-of-citizenship/8262268.

Norton, Michael, and Samuel Sommers. 2016. "White People Think Racism Is Getting Worse. against White People." *Washington Post*, July 21, 2016. https://www.washingtonpost.com/posteverything/wp/2016/07/21/white-people-think-racism-is-getting-worse-against-white-people/?utm_term=.8de2b754162c.

Norwood, Kimberly Jade. 2016. "Introduction." In *Ferguson's Fault Lines: The Race Quake that Rocked a Nation*, edited by Kimberly Jade Norwood, xvii–xxii. Chicago: American Bar Association.

Nossiter, Adam. 2016a. "François Hollande Cancels Plan to Strip French Citizenship in Terrorism Cases." *New York Times*, March 30, 2016. http://www.nytimes.com/2016/03/31/world/europe/francois-hollande-france-citizenship-terrorism.html?_r=0.

Nossiter, Adam. 2016b. "What Price to Keep France Safe? Perhaps a Nation's Core Values, Many Fear." *New York Times*, August 5, 2016. http://www.nytimes.com/2016/08/06/world/europe/france-terrorism-security.html?_r=0.

Nussbaum, Martha C. 2011. *Creating Capabilities: The Human Development Approach*. Cambridge, MA: Belknap Press of Harvard University Press.

Nyéléni. 2007. "Declaration of Nyéléni." Sélingué, Mali. February 2, 2007. https://nyeleni.org/spip.php?article290.

Nyers, Peter. 2006. *Rethinking Refugees: Beyond States of Emergency.* New York: Routledge.

O'Connor, Kelly. 2013. "Repatriation: The Politics of (Re)-constructing and Contesting Rwandan Citizenship." Refugees Studies Centre, Working Paper Series No. 92. Oxford Department of International Development, University of Oxford. https://www.rsc.ox.ac.uk/files/publications/working-paper-series/wp92-repatriation-reconstructing-contesting-rwandan-citizenship-2013.pdf.

Odello, Marco. 2016. "The United Nations Declaration on the Rights of Indigenous Peoples." In *Handbook of Indigenous Peoples' Rights*, edited by Corinne Lennox and Damien Short, 51–68. London: Routledge.

Office of the Special Adviser on the Prevention of Genocide. n.d. "The Responsibility to Protect." http://www.un.org/en/preventgenocide/adviser/responsibility.shtml.

Office of the United Nations High Commissioner for Human Rights. 1951. Convention Relating to the Status of Refugees.

Office of US Senator Ted Cruz. 2017. "Sen. Cruz: Americans Who Join ISIS or Other Terrorist Groups Should Have Their Citizenship Revoked." February 14, 2017. https://www.cruz.senate.gov/?p=press_release&id=3005.

http://www.ohchr.org/EN/ProfessionalInterest/Pages/StatusOfRefugees.aspx.

Ó hAodha, Mícheál. 2011. *"Insubordinate Irish": Travellers in the Text.* Manchester: Manchester University Press.

Onondaga Nation n.d.a. "Court Cases." http://www.onondaganation.org/gov/court.html.

Onondaga Nation n.d.b. "Facts." http://www.onondaganation.org/aboutus/facts.html.

Onondaga Nation n.d.c. "The Onondaga Nation Today." http://www.onondaganation.org/aboutus/today.html.

Onondaga Nation n.d.d. "Sovereignty." http://www.onondaganation.org/gov/sovereignty.html.

Ong, Aihwa. 2004. "Latitudes of Citizenship: Membership, Meaning, and Multiculturalism." In *People Out of Place: Globalization, Human Rights, and the Citizenship Gap*, edited by Alison Brysk and Gershon Shafir, 53–70. New York: Routledge.

Ong, Aihwa. 2006. *Neoliberalism as Exception: Mutations in Citizenship and Sovereignty.* Durham, NC: Duke University Press.

Orchard, Phil. 2014. *A Right to Flee: Refugees, States, and the Construction of International Cooperation.* Cambridge: Cambridge University Press.

Osborne, Louise, and Ruby Russell. 2015. "Refugee Crisis Creates 'Stateless Generation' of Children in Limbo." *Guardian*, December 27, 2015. https://www.theguardian.com/world/2015/dec/27/refugee-crisis-creating-stateless-generation-children-experts-warn.

Osburn, Richard. 1999/2000. "Problems and Solutions Regarding Indigenous Peoples Split by International Borders." *American Indian Law Review* 24, no. 2: 471–485.

O'Sullivan, Maria. 2012. "Acting the Part: Can Non-State Entities Provide Protection under International Refugee Law?" *International Journal of Refugee Law* 24, no. 1: 85–110.

Padilla, Lindsay. 2015. "Reframing a Community: College Social Problems Course through a Human Rights Perspective." In *Bringing Human Rights Education to*

US Classrooms: Exemplary Models from Elementary Grades to University, edited by Susan Roberta Katz and Andrea McEvoy Spero, 169–185. New York: Palgrave Macmillan.

Paik, A. Naomi. 2016. *Rightlessness: Testimony and Redress in U.S. Prison Camps since World War II.* Chapel Hill: University of North Carolina Press.

Pasqualucci, Jo M. 2006. "The Evolution of International Indigenous Rights in the Inter-American Human Rights System." *Human Rights Law Review* 6, no. 2: 281–322.

Passport Index. n.d. "Passport Power Rank." http://www.passportindex.org/byRank.php.

Paul, James. 2014. "Faces of Globalization and the Borders of States: From Asylum Seekers to Citizens." *Citizenship Studies* 18, no. 2: 208–223.

Peutz, Nathalie, and Nicholas De Genova. 2010. "Introduction." In *The Deportation Regime: Sovereignty, Space, and the Freedom of Movement*, edited by Nicholas de Genova and Nathalie Peutz, 1–29. Durham, NC : Duke University Press.

Pérez, William. 2012. *Americans by Heart: Undocumented Latino Students and the Promise of Higher Education.* New York: Teachers College Press.

Perkins, Kristin L., and Robert J. Sampson. 2015. "Compound Deprivation in the Transition to Adulthood: The Intersection of Racial and Economic Inequality among Chicagoans, 1995–2013." *Russell Sage Foundation Journal of the Social Sciences* 1, no. 1: 35–54. http://www.rsfjournal.org/doi/full/10.7758/RSF.2015.1.1.03.

Perlez, Jane. 2014. "For Myanmar Muslim Minority, No Escape from Brutality." *New York Times*, March 14, 2014. http://www.nytimes.com/2014/03/15/world/asia/trapped-between-home-and-refuge-burmese-muslims-are-brutalized.html?_r=0.

PEW Charitable Trusts. 2015. "Immigrant Employment by State and Industry." December 2015. https://www.pewtrusts.org/~/media/assets/2015/12/variation_brief.pdf.

Pew Research Center. 2016. "On Views of Race and Inequality, Blacks and Whites Are Worlds Apart." June 27, 2016. http://www.pewsocialtrends.org/2016/06/27/on-views-of-race-and-inequality-blacks-and-whites-are-worlds-apart/.

Phillips, Tom. 2015. "Ai Weiwei Free to Travel Overseas Again after China Returns His Passport." *Guardian*, July 22, 2015. http://www.theguardian.com/artanddesign/2015/jul/22/ai-weiwei-free-to-travel-overseas-again-after-china-returns-his-passport.

Pieper, Kelsey J., Min Tang, and Marc A. Edwards. 2017. "Flint Water Crisis Caused by Interrupted Corrosion Control: Investigating 'Ground Zero' Home." *Environmental Science & Technology* 51, no. 4: 2007–2014. http://pubs.acs.org/doi/pdf/10.1021/acs.est.6b04034.

Piercy, Marge. 2015. *Made in Detroit: Poems.* New York: Alfred A. Knopf.

Pittaway, Eileen, Linda Bartolomei, and Richard Hugman. 2010. "'Stop Stealing Our Stories': The Ethics of Research with Vulnerable Groups." *Journal of Human Rights Practice* 2, no. 2: 229–251.

Plan India. 2009. "Count Every Child: Ensuring Universal Birth Registration in India." https://plan-international.org/files/global/publications/campaigns/count-every-child-india.pdf.

Plan International. 2014. "Birth Registration in Emergencies: A Review of Best Practices in Humanitarian Action." https://plan-international.org/publications/birth-registration-emergencies#download-options.

Plan International. n.d. "Birth Registration." https://plan-international.org/what-we-do/child-participation/birth-registration.

Popescu, Gabriel. 2015. "Controlling Mobility: Embodying Borders." In *Borderities and the Politics of Contemporary Mobile Borders*, edited by Anne-Laure Amilhat Szary and Frédéric Giraut, 100–115. London: Palgrave Macmillan.

Popham, Peter. 2012. "No End in Sight to the Suffering of 'the World's Most Persecuted Minority'—Burma's Rohingya Muslims." *Independent*, October 8, 2012. http://www.independent.co.uk/news/world/asia/no-end-in-sight-to-the-sufferings-of-the-worlds-most-persecuted-minority--burmas-rohingya-muslims-8202784.html.

Powers, Matthew. 2016. "A New Era of Human Rights News? Contrasting Two Paradigms of Human Rights News-Making." *Journal of Human Rights* 15, no. 3: 314–329.

Pralle, Sarah B. 2006. *Branching Out, Digging In: Environmental Advocacy and Agenda Setting* Washington, DC: Georgetown University Press.

Preston, Julia, and Jennifer Medina. 2016. "Immigrants Who Came to U.S. as Children Fear Deportation under Trump." *New York Times*, November 19, 2016. http://www.nytimes.com/2016/11/20/us/immigrants-donald-trump-daca.html.

Price, Polly J. 2017. "Jus Soli and Statelessness: A Comparative Perspective from the Americas." In *Citizenship in Question: Evidentiary Birthright and Statelessness*, edited by Benjamin N. Lawrence and Jacqueline Stevens, 27–42. Durham, NC: Duke University Press.

Price, Richard. 1998. "Reversing the Gun Sights: Transnational Civil Society Targets Land Mines." *International Organization* 52, no. 3: 613–644.

Proctor, Bernadette D., Jessica L. Semega, and Melissa A. Kollar. 2016. "Income and Poverty in the United States: 2015." United States Census Bureau, September 2016. https://www.census.gov/content/dam/Census/library/publications/2016/demo/p60-256.pdf.

Quane, Helen. 2011. "The UN Declaration on the Rights of Indigenous Peoples: New Directions for Self-Determination and Participatory Rights?" In *Reflections on the UN Declaration on the Rights of Indigenous Peoples*, edited by Stephen Allen and Alexandra Xanthaki, 259–287. Oxford: Hart.

Randall, Sara, and Alessandra Giuffrida. 2006. "Forced Migration, Sedentarization and Social Change: Malian Kel Tamasheq." In *Nomadic Societies in the Middle East and North Africa: Entering the 21st Century*, edited by Dawn Chatty, 431–462. Leiden: Koninklijke Brill.

Redclift, Victoria. 2013. *Statelessness and Citizenship: Camps and the Creation of Political Space*. London: Routledge.

Redden, Elizabeth. 2015. "The Syrian Refugee Crisis and Higher Education." *Inside Higher Ed*, September 25, 2015. https://www.insidehighered.com/news/2015/09/25/syrian-refugee-crisis-and-higher-education.

Rellstab, Daniel H. 2015. "Refugees? No Refugees? Categorizations of Migrants in the Wake of the Arab Spring in Swiss Online News and Comments." In *Representations of War, Migration, and Refugeehood: Interdisciplinary Perspectives*, edited by Daniel H. Rellstab and Christiane Schlote, 109–139. New York: Routledge.

Reuters. 2017. "Danish Court Strips Islamic State Fighter of Citizenship." March 31, 2017. http://www.reuters.com/article/us-denmark-islamic-state-idUSKBN1721VF.

Revi, Ben. 2014. "T. H. Marshall and His Critics: Reappraising 'Social Citizenship' in the Twenty-First Century." *Citizenship Studies* 18, no. 3–4: 452–464.

Reynolds, Sarnata, and Daryl Grisgraber. 2015. "Birth Registration in Turkey: Protecting the Future for Syrian Children." Refugees International, Field Report, April 30, 2015. http://www.refworld.org/docid/56272a154.html.

Rickard, Clinton. 1973. *Fighting Tuscarora: The Autobiography of Chief Clinton Rickard.* Syracuse, NY: Syracuse University Press.

Rickert, Levi. 2016. "Tohono O'odham Nation Will Reject Wall on Their Tribal Land that Borders Mexico." *Native News Online*, November 15, 2016. http://nativenewsonline. net/currents/tohono-oodham-nation-will-reject-wall-tribal-land-borders-mexico/.

Rijken, Connie, Laura van Waas, Martin Gramatikov, and Deirdre Brennan. 2015. *The Nexus between Statelessness and Human Trafficking in Thailand.* Oisterwijk: Wolf Legal Publishers. http://www.institutesi.org/Stateless-Trafficking_Thailand.pdf.

Robertson, Craig. 2010. *The Passport in America: The History of a Document.* Oxford: Oxford University Press.

Robertson, Shanthi. 2016. "Contractualization, Depoliticization and the Limits of Solidarity: Noncitizens inContemporary Australia." *Citizenship Studies* 19, no. 8: 936–950.

Robinson, Vaughan. 1998. "Defining and Measuring Successful Refugee Integration." In *Proceedings of ECRE International Conference on Integration of Refugees in Europe.* Brussels: ECRE.

Rosen, Michael. 2012. *Dignity: Its History and Meaning.* Cambridge, MA: Harvard University Press.

Rosenblum, Marc R. 2015. "Unaccompanied Child Migration to the United States: The Tension between Protection and Prevention." Transatlantic Council on Migration, Migration Policy Institute. http://www.migrationpolicy.org/research/unaccompanied-child-migration-united-states-tension-between-protection-and-prevention.

Roseneau, James. 1990. *Turbulence in World Politics: A Theory of Change and Continuity.* Princeton, NJ: Princeton University Press.

Ross, Janell. 2016. "Why Aren't We Calling the Oregon Occupiers 'Terrorists'?" *Washington Post*, January 3, 2016. https://www.washingtonpost.com/news/the-fix/wp/2016/01/03/why-arent-we-calling-the-oregon-militia-terrorists/?utm_term=.ff0e68c31e66.

Rossiter, Marian J., and Tracey M. Derwing. 2012. "Still Far to Go: Programming for Immigrant and Refugee Children and Youth." In *Refugee and Immigrant Students: Achieving Equity in Education*, edited by Florence E. McCarthy and Margaret H. Vickers, 89–106. Charlotte: Information Age.

Rowe, Alan. 2006. "Conservation, Land and Nomadic Pastoralism: Seeking Solutions in the Wadi 'Araba of Jordan." In *Nomadic Societies in the Middle East and North Africa: Entering the 21st Century*, edited by Dawn Chatty, 759–784. Leiden: Brill.

Rozzi, Elena. 2017. "Roma Children and Enduring Educational Exclusions in Italy." In *Realizing Roma Rights*, edited by Jacqueline Bhabha, Andrzej Mirga, and Margareta Matache, 17–38. Philadelphia: University of Pennsylvania Press.

Sadiq, Kamal. 2009. *Paper Citizens: How Illegal Immigrants Acquire Citizenship in Developing Countries.* Oxford: Oxford University Press.

Saliba, Issam. 2016. "Refugee Law and Policy: Jordan." Law Library of Congress, March 2016. https://www.loc.gov/law/help/refugee-law/jordan.php.

Sampson, Anthony. 2000. "Europe's Nomads . . . but not by choice." *Guardian*, April 7, 2000. https://www.theguardian.com/world/2000/apr/08/immigration.uk.

Samuel, Juliet. 2016. "The Calais Jungle Is a Disgrace and Must Never Be Allowed to Rise Again." *Telegraph*, October 26, 2016. http://www.telegraph.co.uk/opinion/2016/10/26/the-calais-jungle-is-a-disgrace-and-must-never-be-allowed-to-ris/.

Sapignoli, Maria. 2016. "Indigenous Mobilization and Activism: The San, the Botswana State and the International Community." In *Handbook of Indigenous Peoples' Rights*, edited by Corinne Lennox and Damien Short, 268–281. London: Routledge.

Sassen, Saskia. 2013. "When Territory Deborders Territoriality." *Territory, Politics, Governance* 1, no. 1: 21–45.

Schattle, Hans. 2008. *The Practices of Global Citizenship*. Lanham, MD: Rowman & Littlefield.

Schattle, Hans. 2012. *Globalization and Citizenship*. Lanham, MD: Rowman & Littlefield.

Schertow, John Ahni. 2013. "US Border Patrol Violates O'odham Rights." *Intercontinental Cry*. July 31, 2013. https://intercontinentalcry.org/us-border-patrol-violates-oodham-rights/.

Schildkraut, Deborah J. 2015. "Does Becoming American Create a Better American? How Identity Attachments and Perceptions of Discrimination Affect Trust and Obligation." In *Fear, Anxiety, and National Identity: Immigration and Belonging in North America and Western Europe*, edited by Nancy Foner and Patrick Simon, 83–114. New York: Russell Sage Foundation.

Schlosberg, David, and David Carruthers. 2010. "Indigenous Struggles, Environmental Justice, and Community Capabilities." *Global Environmental Politics* 10, no. 4: 12–35.

Schwarz, Birgit. 2016. "Nothing to Go Back to—From Kenya Vast Refugee Camp." Human Rights Watch, May 26, 2016. https://www.hrw.org/news/2016/05/26/nothing-go-back-kenyas-vast-refugee-camp.

Scott, James C. 1998. *Seeing Like a State: How Certain Schemes to Improve the Human Condition Have Failed*. New Haven, CT: Yale University Press.

Scott, James. 2009. *The Art of Not Being Governed: An Anarchist History of Upland Southeast Asia*. New Haven, CT: Yale University Press.

Sebastopol Documentary Film Festival, n.d. "Waves of Childhood." 11th Annual: March 22–25, 2018. http://sebastopolfilmfestival.org/films/waves-of-childhood/.

Sehat, Connie Moon. 2017. "Fighting For, Not Fighting Against: Media Coverage and the Dakota Access Pipeline." *News Frames*, March 1, 2017. https://newsframes.globalvoices.org/2017/03/01/fighting-for-not-fighting-against-media-coverage-and-the-dakota-access-pipeline/.

Sengupta, Somini. 2016. "A Mother's Love? Of Course. Her Citizenship? Not So Fast." *New York Times*, August 3, 2016. http://www.nytimes.com/2016/08/04/world/what-in-the-world/mothers-citizenship-laws.html?_r=0.

Shachar, Ayelet. 2009. *The Birthright Lottery: Citizenship and Global Inequality*. Cambridge, MA: Harvard University Press.

Shacknove, Andrew E. 1985. "Who Is a Refugee?" *Ethics* 95, no. 2: 274–284.

Sherwood, Courtney, and Kirk Johnson. 2016. "Bundy Brothers Acquitted in Takeover of Oregon Wildlife Refuge." *New York Times*, October 27, 2016. https://www.nytimes.com/2016/10/28/us/bundy-brothers-acquitted-in-takeover-of-oregon-wildlife-refuge.html?_r=0.

Shmueli, Deborah F., and Rassem Khamaisi. 2015. *Israel's Invisible Negev Bedouin: Issues of Land and Spatial Planning*. New York: Springer.

Sigona, Nando. 2016. "Everyday Statelessness in Italy: Status, Rights, and Camps." *Ethnic and Racial Studies* 39, no. 2: 263–279.

Sissons, Jeffrey. 2005. *First Peoples: Indigenous Cultures and Their Futures*. London: Reaktion Books.

Sliwinski, Sharon. 2011. *Human Rights in Camera*. Chicago: University of Chicago Press.

Slootman, Marieke, and Jan Willem Duyvendak. 2015. "Feeling Dutch: The Culturalization and Emotionalization of Citizenship and Second-Generation Belonging in the Netherlands." In *Fear, Anxiety, and National Identity: Immigration and Belonging in North America and Western Europe*, edited by Nancy Foner and Patrick Simon, 147–168. New York: Russell Sage Foundation.

Smith, Anthony D. 1991. *National Identity*. Reno: University of Nevada Press.

Smith, David M., and Margaret Greenfields. 2013. *Gypsies and Travellers in Housing: The Decline of Nomadism*. Bristol, UK: Policy Press.

Smith, Len, Janet McCalman, Ian Anderson, Sandra Smith, Joanne Evans, Gavan McCarthy, and Jane Beer. 2011. "Fractional Identities: The Political Arithmetic of Aboriginal Victorians." In *Indigenous Peoples and Demography: The Complex Relation between Identity and Statistics*, edited by Per Axelsson and Peter Sköld, 15–31. New York: Berghahn Books.

Smith, Oliver. 2016. "The World's Most Powerful Passports." *Telegraph*, February 29, 2016. http://www.telegraph.co.uk/travel/lists/The-worlds-most-powerful-passports/.

Smith, Paige. 2015. *Tragic Encounters: The People's History of Native Americans*. Berkeley, CA: Counterpoint.

Smith, Tom W. 1992. "Changing Racial Labels: From 'Colored' to 'Negro' to 'Black' to 'African American.'" *Public Opinion Quarterly* 56, no. 4: 496–514.

Snow, David A., and Robert D. Benford. 1988. "Ideology, Frame Resonance, and Participant Mobilization." In *International Social Movement Research* 1, edited by Bert Klandermans, Hanspeter Kries, and Sidney Tarrow, 197–217. Greenwich, CT: Jai Press.

Soguel, Dominique. 2015. "Are Kurds Closer to Realizing Their Dream of an Independent State?" *Christian Science Monitor*, November 3, 2015. http://www.csmonitor.com/World/Middle-East/2015/1103/Are-Kurds-closer-to-realizing-their-dream-of-an-independent-state.

Sokoloff, Constantine, and Richard Lewis. 2005. "Denial of Citizenship: A Challenge to Human Security." European Policy Centre, Issue Paper 28, January 4, 2005. http://www.epc.eu/documents/uploads/724318296_EPC%20Issue%20Paper%2028%20Denial%20of%20Citizenship.pdf.

Somers, Margaret R. 2008. *Genealogies of Citizenship: Markets, Statelessness, and the Right to Have Rights*. Cambridge: Cambridge University Press.

Sontag, Susan. 2003. *Regarding the Pain of Others*. New York: Picador.

Soysal, Yasemin Nuhoğlu. 1994. *Limits of Citizenship: Migrants and Postnational Membership in Europe*. Chicago: University of Chicago Press.

Spanne, Autumn. 2015. "Native American Tribes Tackle Diet and Health Woes with Businesses Built on Traditional Foods." *Guardian*, June 13, 2015. https://www.theguardian.com/sustainable-business/2015/jun/13/native-american-tribes-diet-health-traditional-foods-business-entrepreneur.

Spiro, Peter J. 2004. "Mandated Membership, Diluted Identity: Citizenship, Globalization, and International Law." In *People Out of Place: Globalization, Human Rights, and the Citizenship Gap*, edited by Alison Brysk and Gershon Shafir, 87–105. New York: Routledge.

Spradley, James P. 1970. *You Owe Yourself a Drunk: An Ethnography of Urban Nomads.* Long Grove, IL: Waveland Press.

Spreen, Carol Anne, and Chrissie Monaghan. 2017. "Leveraging Diversity to Become a Global Citizen: Lessons for Human Rights Education." In *Human Rights Education: Theory, Research, Praxis*, edited by Monisha Bajaj, 291–316. Philadelphia: University of Pennsylvania Press.

Stack, Trevor. 2012. "Beyond the State? Civil Sociality and Other Notions of Citizenship." *Citizenship Studies 16*, no. 7: 871–885.

Stam, Kathryn. 2016. "The Information Landscape of Bhutanese-Nepali Refugees in the U.S.: A Case Study of Multicultural Utica, NY." Presentation at the Himalayan Studies Conference, Austin, TX, February 25–28, 2016.

Staples, Kelly. 2012. *Retheorising Statelessness: A Background Theory of Membership in World Politics.* Edinburgh: Edinburgh University Press.

Staples, Kelly. 2017. "Recognition, Nationality, and Statelessness: State-based Challenges for UNHCR's Plan to End Statelessness." In *Understanding Statelessness*, edited by Tendayi Bloom, Katherine Tonkiss, and Phillip Cole, 173–188. London: Routledge.

Stavenhagen, Rodolfo, and Ahmad Amara. 2012. "International Law of Indigenous Peoples and the Naqab Bedouin Arabs." In *Indigenous (In)Justice: Human Rights Law and Bedouin Arabs in the Naqab/Negev*, edited by Ahmad Amara, Ismael Abu-Saad, and Oren Yiftachel, 159–192. Cambridge, MA: Human Rights Program at Harvard Law School, Harvard University Press.

Stephenson, Michèle, and Brian Young. 2017. "A Conversation with Native Americans on Race." *New York Times*, August 15, 2017. https://www.nytimes.com/2017/08/15/opinion/a-conversation-with-native-americans-on-race.html.

Stewart-Harawira, Makere. 2008. "Traditional Peoples and Citizenship in the New Imperial Order." In *Educating for Human Rights and Global Citizenship*, edited by Ali A. Abdi and Lynette Shultz, 159–175. Albany: State University of New York Press.

STL Winter Outreach. n.d. Homepage. https://www.stlwinteroutreach.org/.

Sugrue, Thomas J. 2005. *The Origins of the Urban Crisis: Race and Inequality in Postwar Detroit.* Princeton, NJ: Princeton University Press.

Swider, Katja. 2017. "Why End Statelessness?" In *Understanding Statelessness*, edited by Tendayi Bloom, Katherine Tonkiss, and Phillip Cole, 191–209. London: Routledge.

Talavera, Victor, Guillermina Gina Núñez-Mchiri, and Josiah Heyman. 2010. "Deportation in the U.S.-Mexico Borderlands: Anticipation, Experience, and Memory." In *The Deportation Regime: Sovereignty, Space, and the Freedom of Movement*, edited by Nicholas de Genova and Nathalie Peutz, 166–195. Durham, NC: Duke University Press.

Tambakaki, Paulina. 2016. "Citizenship and Inclusion: Rethinking the Analytical Category of Noncitizenship." *Citizenship Studies 19*, no. 8: 922–935.

Tan, Zhai Yun. 2016. "Bundys Acquitted, Natives Arrested: A Double Standard?" *Christian Science Monitor*, October 28, 2016. https://www.csmonitor.com/USA/2016/1028/Bundys-acquitted-natives-arrested-A-double-standard.

Tarrow, Sidney. 1998. *Power in Movement: Social Movements and Contentious Politics.* 2nd ed. Cambridge: Cambridge University Press.

Taub, Amanda. 2016. "Why Some Wars (Like Syria's) Get More Attention Than Others (Like Yemen's)." *New York Times*, October 1, 2016. https://nyti.ms/2jQH2xg.

Taylor, Becky. 2008. *A Minority and the State: Travellers in Britain in the Twentieth Century.* Manchester, UK: Manchester University Press.

Taylor, Charles. 1994. "The Politics of Recognition." In *Multiculturalism: Examining the Politics of Recognition*, edited by Amy Gutmann, 25–73. Princeton, NJ: Princeton University Press.

Telegraph. 2016. "Syria's Refugees: Girls Use Photography to Document Life in Zaatari Camp." http://www.telegraph.co.uk/news/worldnews/middleeast/syria/11201377/Syrias-refugees-Girls-use-photography-to-document-life-in-the-Zaatari-camp.html.

Thompson, Heather Ann. 2001. *Whose Detroit? Politics, Labor, and Race in a Modern American City.* Ithaca, NY: Cornell University Press.

Tibbitts, Felisa. 2015. "Building a Human Rights Education Movement in the United States." In *Bringing Human Rights Education to US Classrooms: Exemplary Models from Elementary Grades to University*, edited by Susan Roberta Katz and Andrea McEvoy Spero, 3–14. New York: Palgrave MacMillan.

Tomaselli, Alexandra. 2016. "Exploring Indigenous Self-Government and Forms of Autonomy." In *Handbook of Indigenous Peoples' Rights*, edited by Corinne Lennox and Damien Short, 83–100. London: Routledge.

Tonkiss, Katherine. 2017. "Statelessness and the Performance of Citizenship-as-Nationality." In *Understanding Statelessness*, edited by Tendayi Bloom, Katherine Tonkiss, and Phillip Cole, 241–254. New York: Routledge.

Tonkiss, Katherine, and Tendayi Bloom. 2016. "Theorising Noncitizenship: Concepts, Debates and Challenges." *Citizenship Studies* 19, no. 8: 837–852.

Torpey, John. 2000. *The Invention of the Passport: Surveillance, Citizenship and the State.* Cambridge: Cambridge University Press.

Torpey, John. 2001. "The Great War and the Birth of the Modern Passport System." In *Documenting Individual Identity: The Development of State Practices in the Modern World*, edited by Jane Caplan and John Torpey, 256–270. Princeton, NJ: Princeton University Press.

Traub, James. 2016. "The Death of the Most Generous Nation on Earth." *Foreign Policy*, February 10, 2016. http://foreignpolicy.com/2016/02/10/the-death-of-the-most-generous-nation-on-earth-sweden-syria-refugee-europe/.

Tritt, Rachel. 1992. *Struggling for Ethnic Identity: Czechoslavakia's Endangered Gypsies.* Helsinki Watch, Human Rights Watch.

Tucker, Jason, 2014. "Questioning *De Facto* Statelessness." *Tilburg Law Review* 19, no. 1–2: 276–284.

Twomey, Christina. 2015. "Framing Atrocity: Photography and Humanitarianism." In *Humanitarian Photography: A History*, edited by Heide Fehrenbach and Davide Rodogno, 47–63. Cambridge: Cambridge University Press.

Uberti, David. 2014. "The Death of a Great American City: Why Does Anyone Still Live in Detroit?" *Guardian*, April 3, 2014. https://www.theguardian.com/cities/2014/apr/03/the-death-of-a-great-american-city-why-does-anyone-still-live-in-detroit.

UNICEF. 2013. "Every Child's Birth Right: Inequalities and Trends in Birth Registration." http://www.unicef.org/mena/MENA-Birth_Registration_report_low_res-01.pdf.

UNICEF, World Vision, United Nations High Commissioner for Refugees, and Save the Children. 2013. "Syria Crisis: Education Interrupted." http://www.unhcr.org/en-us/publications/operations/52aaebff9/syria-crisis-education-interrupted.html.

United Nations. 1945. Charter of the United Nations. http://www.un.org/en/charter-united-nations/index.html.

United Nations. 2007. United Nations Declaration on the Rights of Indigenous Peoples. http://www.un.org/esa/socdev/unpfii/documents/DRIPS_en.pdf.

United Nations Children's Fund (UNICEF). 2013. "Every Child's Birth Right: Inequities and Trends in Birth Registration." https://www.un.org/ruleoflaw/files/Embargoed_11_Dec_Birth_Registration_report_low_res.pdf.

United Nations General Assembly. 1948. The Universal Declaration of Human Rights. http://www.un.org/Overview/rights.html.

United Nations General Assembly. 2011. United Nations Declaration on Human Rights Education and Training. 66/137. https://documents-dds-ny.un.org/doc/UNDOC/GEN/N11/467/04/PDF/N1146704.pdf?OpenElement.

United Nations High Commissioner for Human Rights. 1966a. International Covenant on Civil and Political Rights. http://www.ohchr.org/en/professionalinterest/pages/ccpr.aspx.

United Nations High Commissioner for Human Rights. 1966b. International Covenant on Economic, Social, and Cultural Rights. http://www.ohchr.org/EN/ProfessionalInterest/Pages/CESCR.aspx.

United Nations High Commissioner for Human Rights. 1989. Convention on the Rights of the Child. http://www.ohchr.org/en/professionalinterest/pages/crc.aspx.

United Nations High Commissioner for Refugees. 1951. Convention Relating to the Status of Refugees. http://www.unhcr.org/3b66c2aa10.html.

United Nations High Commissioner for Refugees. 1954. Convention Relating to the Status of Stateless Persons. http://www.unhcr.org/en-us/protection/statelessness/3bbb25729/convention-relating-status-stateless-persons.html.

United Nations High Commissioner for Refugees. 1961. Convention on the Reduction of Statelessness. http://www.unhcr.org/3bbb286d8.html.

United Nations High Commissioner for Refugees. 1984. "Identity Documents for Refugees." July 20. http://www.unhcr.org/3ae68cce4.html.

United Nations High Commissioner for Refugees. 1992. "Protection of Persons of Concern to UNHCR Who Fall Outside the 1951 Convention: A Discussion Note." EC/1992/SCP/CRP.5, April 2. http://www.unhcr.org/en-us/excom/scip/3ae68cc518/protection-persons-concern-unhcr-fall-outside-1951-convention-discussion.html.

United Nations High Commissioner for Refugees. 2002. "Protecting Refugees: Questions and Answers." February 1. http://www.unhcr.org/en-us/publications/brochures/3b779dfe2/protecting-refugees-questions-answers.html.

United Nations High Commissioner for Refugees. 2003. "Framework for Durable Solutions for Refugees and Persons of Concern." Core Group on Durable Solutions, UNHCR Geneva, May. http://www.unhcr.org/en-us/partners/partners/3f1408764/framework-durable-solutions-refugees-persons-concern.html.

United Nations High Commissioner for Refugees. 2009. "Conclusion on Protracted Refugee Situations No. 109 (LXI)—2009." http://www.unhcr.org/en-us/excom/exconc/4b332bca9/conclusion-protracted-refugee-situations.html.

United Nations High Commissioner for Refugees. 2010. Convention and Protocol Relating to the Status of Refugees. http://www.unhcr.org/en-us/3b66c2aa10.

United Nations High Commissioner for Refugees. 2014a. "Global Action Plan to End Statelessness, 2014-24." http://www.unhcr.org/statelesscampaign2014/Global-Action-Plan-eng.pdf.

United Nations High Commissioner for Refugees. 2014b. "UNHCR Launches 10-Year Global Campaign to End Statelessness." http://www.unhcr.org/545797f06.html.

United Nations High Commissioner for Refugees. 2015a. "Global Trends: Forced Displacement in 2015." https://s3.amazonaws.com/unhcrsharedmedia/2016/2016-06-20-global-trends/2016-06-14-Global-Trends-2015.pdf.

United Nations High Commissioner for Refugees. 2015b. "Higher Education Considerations for Refugees in Countries Affected by the Syria and Iraq Crises." http://www.unhcr.org/en-us/protection/operations/568bc5279/higher-education-considerations-refugees-countries-affected-syria-iraq.html.

United Nations High Commissioner for Refugees. 2016a. "Background Note on Gender Equality, Nationality Laws and Statelessness 2016." http://www.refworld.org/docid/56de83ca4.html.

United Nations High Commissioner for Refugees. 2016b. "First Anniversary of the Abidjan Declaration on the Eradication of Statelessness." February 25. http://www.unhcr.org/print/56ceda796.html.

United Nations High Commissioner for Refugees. 2016c. "Missing Out: Refugee Education in Crisis." http://www.unhcr.org/57d9d01d0.

United Nations High Commissioner for Refugees. n.d.a. "Figures at a Glance." http://www.unhcr.org/en-us/figures-at-a-glance.html.

United Nations High Commissioner for Refugees. n.d.b. "An Introduction to Statelessness." http://www.unhcr.org/pages/49c3646c155.html.

United Nations High Commissioner for Refugees. n.d.c. "Italy Joins Top League of Countries Reducing Statelessness." http://www.unhcr.org/ibelong/italy-joins-top-league-of-countries-reducing-statelessness/.

United Nations High Commissioner for Refugees. n.d.d "Statelessness around the World." http://www.unhcr.org/en-us/statelessness-around-the-world.html.

United Nations Human Rights. 2016. "Flint: 'Not Just about Water, but Human Rights'—UN Experts Remind Ahead of President Obama's Visit." May 3, 2016. https://www.ohchr.org/EN/NewsEvents/Pages/DisplayNews.aspx?NewsID=19917&LangID=E

United Nations Human Rights. n.d. Convention on the Rights of Persons with Disabilities. http://www.ohchr.org/EN/HRBodies/CRPD/Pages/ConventionRightsPersonsWithDisabilities.aspx.

United Nations Human Rights Council. 2014. "Birth Registration and the Right of Everyone to Recognition Everywhere as a Person before the Law." http://www.refworld.org/docid/558ab29a4.html.

United Nations Office for the Coordination of Humanitarian Affairs. 2004. "Guiding Principles on Internal Displacement." https://docs.unocha.org/sites/dms/Documents/ GuidingPrinciplesDispl.pdf.

United Nations Office on Drugs and Crime. 2004. United Nations Convention against Transnational Organized Crime and the Protocols Thereto. https:// www.unodc.org/documents/treaties/UNTOC/Publications/TOC%20Convention/ TOCebook-e.pdf.

United States Department of Justice. 2015. "Justice Department Announces Findings of Two Civil Rights Investigations in Ferguson, Missouri." March 4, 2015. https:// www.justice.gov/opa/pr/justice-department-announces-findings-two-civil-rights-investigations-ferguson-missouri.

United States Holocaust Memorial Museum. n.d. "Sinti & Roma: Victims of the Nazi Era 1933–1945." https://www.ushmm.org/m/pdfs/2000926-Roma-and-Sinti.pdf.

van Waas, Laura. 2011. "Nationality and Rights." In *Statelessness and Citizenship: A Comparative Study on the Benefits of Nationality*, edited by Brad K. Blitz and Maureen Lynch, 23–44. Cheltenham, UK: Edward Elgar.

Vetik, Raivo. 2011. "The Statelessness Issue in Estonia." In *Statelessness in the European Union: Displaced, Undocumented, Unwanted*, edited by Caroline Sawyer and Brad K. Blitz, 230–252. Cambridge: Cambridge University Press.

Victor, Daniel. 2016. "Bill O'Reilly Draws Backlash for Comments on 'Well Fed' Slaves." *New York Times*, July 27, 2016. http://www.nytimes.com/2016/07/28/business/media/bill-oreilly-says-slaves-who-helped-build-white-house-were-well-fed.html?_r=0.

Vidal, John. 2016. "Tanzanian Land Rights Victory Earns Masaai Leader Goldman Prize." *Guardian*, April 17, 2016. https://www.theguardian.com/global-development/2016/apr/18/tanzania-land-rights-victory-earns-masaai-leader-goldman-prize-edward-loure.

Waldron, Jeremy. 2013. "Citizenship and Dignity." In *Understanding Human Dignity*, edited by Christopher McCrudden, 327–343. Proceedings of the British Academy, 192. Oxford: Oxford University Press.

Wagner, David. 1993. *Checkerboard Square: Culture and Resistance in a Homeless Community*. San Francisco: Westview.

Waters, Mary C., and Philip Kasinitz. 2015. "The War on Crime and the War on Immigrants: Racial and Legal Exclusion in the Twenty-First-Century United States." In *Fear, Anxiety, and National Identity: Immigration and Belonging in North America and Western Europe*, edited by Nancy Foner and Patrick Simon, 115–143. New York: Russell Sage Foundation.

Weber-Pillwax, Cora. 2008. "Citizenship and Its Exclusions: The Impact of Legal Definitions on Metis People(s) of Canada." In *Educating for Human Rights and Global Citizenship*, edited by Ali A. Abdi and Lynette Shultz, 193–204. Albany: State University of New York Press.

Weil, Patrick. 2013. *The Sovereign Citizen: Denaturalization and the Origins of the American Republic*. Philadelphia: University of Philadelphia Press.

Weissbrodt, David, and Michael Divine. 2016. "Unequal Access to Human Rights: The Categories of Noncitizenship." *Citizenship Studies* 19, no. 8: 870–891.

Weston, Phoebe. 2015. "Inside Zaatari Refugee Camp: The Fourth Largest City in Jordan." *Telegraph*, August 5, 2015. http://www.telegraph.co.uk/news/worldnews/

middleeast/jordan/11782770/What-is-life-like-inside-the-largest-Syrian-refugee-camp-Zaatari-in-Jordan.html.

White House. 2007. "Immigration's Economic Impact." Council of Economic Advisers. June 20, 2007. http://georgewbush-whitehouse.archives.gov/cea/cea_immigration_062007.html.

Wicker, Hans-Rudolf. 2010. "Deportation and the Limits of 'Tolerance': The Juridical, Institutional, and Social Construction of 'Illegality' in Switzerland." In *The Deportation Regime: Sovereignty, Space, and the Freedom of Movement*, edited by Nicholas de Genova and Nathalie Peutz, 224–244. Durham, NC: Duke University Press.

Wilkinson, Charles. 2005. *Blood Struggle: The Rise of Modern Indian Nations*. New York: W.W. Norton.

Willen, Sarah S. 2010. "Citizens, 'Real' Others, and 'Other' Others: The Biopolitics of Otherness and Deportation of Unauthorized Migrant Workers from Tel Aviv, Israel." In *The Deportation Regime: Sovereignty, Space, and the Freedom of Movement*, edited by Nicholas de Genova and Nathalie Peutz, 262–294. Durham, NC: Duke University Press.

Willsher, Kim. 2017. "Van Driver Dies in Calais Crash Caused by Refugees' Blockade." *Guardian*, June 20, 2017. https://www.theguardian.com/world/2017/jun/20/van-driver-dies-crash-calais-refugees-blockade.

Windle, Joel, and Jennifer Miller. 2013. "Marginal Integration: The Reception of Refugee-Background Students in Australian Schools." In *Refugees, Immigrants, and Education in the Global South: Lives in Motion*, edited by Lesley Bartlett and Ameena Ghaffar-Kucher, 196–210. New York: Routledge.

Woolford, Andrew, Jeff Benvenuto, and Alexander Laban Hinton, eds. 2014. *Colonial Genocide in Indigenous North America*. Durham, NC: Duke University Press.

Xanthaki, Alexandra. 2007. *Indigenous Rights and United Nations Standards: Self-Determination, Culture and Land*. Cambridge: Cambridge University Press.

Yiftachel, Oren. 2012. "Naqab/Negev Bedouins and the (Internal) Colonial Paradigm." In *Indigenous (In)Justice: Human Rights Law and Bedouin Arabs in the Naqab/Negev*, edited by Ahmad Amara, Ismael Abu-Saad, and Oren Yiftachel, 289–318. Cambridge, MA: Human Rights Program at Harvard Law School, Harvard University Press.

Yoshikawa, Hirokazu. 2011. *Immigrants Raising Citizens: Undocumented Parents and Their Young Children*. New York: Russell Sage Foundation.

Young, Iris Marion. 1990. *Justice and the Politics of Difference*. Princeton, NJ: Princeton University Press.

Zambelich, Ariel, and Cassi Alexandra. 2016. "In Their Own Words: The 'Water Protectors' of Standing Rock." National Public Radio (NPR), December 11, 2016. http://www.npr.org/2016/12/11/505147166/in-their-own-words-the-water-protectors-of-standing-rock.

Zotigh, Dennis. 2011. "Will Current Blood Quantum Membership Requirements Make American Indians Extinct?" National Museum of the American Indian, September 15, 2011. http://blog.nmai.si.edu/main/2011/09/will-current-blood-quantum-membership-requirements-make-american-indians-extinct.html.

INDEX